Elderly Client Handbook

Elderly Client Handbook

2nd edition

By Gordon R Ashton LLB, Solicitor and District Judge

with Anne Edis BA, TEP, Solicitor

law society publishing

All rights reserved. No part of this publication may be reproduced in any material form, whether by photocopying, scanning, downloading onto computer or otherwise without the written permission of Law Society Publishing except in accordance with the provisions of the Copyright, Designs and Patents Act 1988.

The material in Appendix 1 is Crown copyright and is reproduced with the permission of The Stationery Office.

© Gordon R Ashton 2000

ISBN 1–85328–467–X

First edition published in 1994

This edition published in 2000 by Law Society Publishing
113 Chancery Lane, London WC2A 1PL

Printed and bound by Biddles Ltd, Guildford and Kings Lynn

Contents

Foreword	xi
Acknowledgements	xiii
Table of Cases	xv
Table of Statutes	xvii
Table of Statutory Instruments and Rules	xxv

PART ONE: ACTING FOR ELDERLY CLIENTS
SECTION A: THE CLIENT

1	**Distinguishing Elderly Clients**	**5**
1.1	Statistics	5
1.2	Distinguishing criteria	6
1.3	Role of the law	9
2	**Capacity**	**10**
2.1	Introduction	10
2.2	Assessment	11
2.3	Decision-making	14

SECTION B: REPRESENTING THE CLIENT

3	**Instructions**	**19**
3.1	Client	19
3.2	Carers	24
3.3	Professionals	25
4	**Information**	**29**
4.1	Sources	29
4.2	Freedom of information	31
5	**Challenging the Authorities**	**35**
5.1	General	35
5.2	Entitlement to services	35
5.3	Ombudsmen	37
5.4	Legal remedies	39
5.5	European courts	45

v

CONTENTS

6	Civil Proceedings	49
6.1	General	49
6.2	Physical disability	51
6.3	Mental disability	54

SECTION C: FINANCIAL MANAGEMENT

7	The Work in Practice	65
7.1	Handling the affairs	65
7.2	Checklist	70
7.3	Powers of delegation compared	72
7.4	Dos and don'ts in the Court of Protection	74

8	Specific Delegations	76
8.1	State benefits	76
8.2	Miscellaneous	77

9	Enduring Powers of Attorney	80
9.1	Powers of attorney	80
9.2	Enduring powers of attorney	80

10	Court of Protection	86
10.1	Status and structure	86
10.2	Powers of the court	89
10.3	Procedure	92
10.4	Receivership	95
10.5	Practical points	99

PART TWO: MANAGING AN ELDERLY CLIENT PRACTICE

11	Professional Matters	105
11.1	Practice rules	105
11.2	Codes of practice	109
11.3	Professional conduct	114

12	Organisation	120
12.1	Office management	120
12.2	Systems	124
12.3	Duties to the client	125
12.4	Charging	128
12.5	Financial services	133

13	Marketing	137
13.1	The market place	137
13.2	Targeting elderly clients	139
13.3	Promoting legal services	144

14	**The Law Society**	**150**
14.1	Practice management standards	150
14.2	Help in promoting the practice	150
14.3	Solicitors Financial Services (SFS)	154
14.4	Publications	154

PART THREE: OVERVIEW OF THE LAW
SECTION A: STATUS

15	**Rights and Obligations**	**161**
15.1	Capacity	161
15.2	Civil status	164
15.3	Civil responsibility	166
15.4	Discrimination	167
16	**Family and Other Relationships**	**170**
16.1	Marriage	170
16.2	Marriage breakdown	171
16.3	Grandchildren	175
16.4	Cohabitation	178
16.5	Abuse and domestic violence	180
16.6	Victims of crime	185
17	**Criminal Responsibility**	**188**
17.1	Safeguards	188
17.2	Prosecution	192
17.3	Sentences	193

SECTION B: FINANCIAL BENEFITS

18	**Social Security Benefits**	**197**
18.1	Social security system	197
18.2	Types of benefits	199
18.3	Procedure	204
18.4	Appeals	207
18.5	National insurance contributions	209
19	**Local Authority Support**	**211**
19.1	Housing benefit	211
19.2	Council tax benefit	214
19.3	Community care funding	214
19.4	Residential care funding	216
20	**Miscellaneous Support**	**225**
20.1	National Health Service	225
20.2	Grants and subsidies	226
20.3	Family and charities	228

SECTION C: COMMUNITY CARE

21 Policies — 233
21.1 Sources — 233
21.2 Role of local authorities — 237
21.3 Role of the private sector — 240

22 Services — 241
22.1 Types of services — 241
22.2 Community care services — 241
22.3 Services for disabled people — 247
22.4 Complaints procedure — 250
22.5 Inadequate provision or failure to act — 251
22.6 Funding — 253

23 Registered Homes — 255
23.1 Legislation — 255
23.2 Types of registered homes — 256
23.3 Regulation — 257
23.4 Codes of practice — 259
23.5 Choosing a home — 260
     Home Life - Guidance — 262

SECTION D: HEALTH CARE

24 Provision of Health Care — 267
24.1 The health service — 267
24.2 Delivery of health care — 269
24.3 Information — 272
24.4 Complaints — 274
24.5 Discharge from hospital — 277

25 Medical Treatment — 279
25.1 Consent to treatment — 279
25.2 Incompetent patients — 280
25.3 Powers of the court — 283
25.4 Living wills — 284

26 Mental Health Legislation — 287
26.1 Legislation — 287
26.2 Admission to hospital — 291
26.3 Community powers — 293
26.4 Review and appeal — 296

SECTION E: EMPLOYMENT, MONEY AND THE HOME

27 Work Activity — 301
27.1 Employment — 301
27.2 Retirement — 306

| 27.3 | Self-employment | 307 |

28 Financial 309
28.1	Investment advice	309
28.2	Pensions	309
28.3	Taxation	312

29 Housing 317
29.1	Owner-occupation	317
29.2	Long residential leases	321
29.3	Tenancies	323
29.4	Licences	335
29.5	Homeless persons	336
29.6	Special arrangements	337
29.7	Special housing	343
29.8	Special situations	346

SECTION F: INHERITANCE AND DEATH

30 Gifts 349
30.1	Validity	349
30.2	Taxation	350
30.3	Charities	352

31 Testamentary Dispositions 354
31.1	Succession	354
31.2	Intestacy	355
31.3	Wills	356
31.4	Statutory wills	359
31.5	Inheritance provision	360
31.6	Family arrangements	362

32 Providing for Infirm or Disabled Beneficiaries 365
32.1	Care provision	366
32.2	Funding	366
32.3	Financial provision	367
32.4	Drafting the trust	369

33 Death 372
33.1	Registration	372
33.2	Coroners and Inquests	374
33.3	Funeral arrangements	376

APPENDICES

SECTION A: FORMS AND PRECEDENTS
| 1 | Enduring Power of Attorney | 383 |

2	Family Wills	392
3	Living Wills	398
4	Letters and Certificates	400

SECTION B: ADDITIONAL INFORMATION

5	Addresses	407
6	Websites	414
7	Further Reading	420

SECTION C: GUIDANCE

8	Law Reform	427
	The Law Commission	427
	The Government response	428
	Specific proposals	430
9	Law Society Guidelines: Enduring Powers of Attorney	432
10	Law Society Guidelines: Gifts of Property: Implications for Future Liability to Pay for Long-Term Care	449
INDEX		**463**

Foreword

In carrying out its task to advise the Government on the funding of long-term care for older people, the Royal Commission on Long Term Care established a set of values to inform its work and recommendations. In its report 'With Respect to Old Age', the Commission stressed that:

> 'In this age of opportunity, while physical capabilities or mental faculties may change, people should not be assumed to be passive recipients of the goodwill of others or inevitably incapacitated, befuddled or redundant. Society should recognise the value inherent in older people, and the value to society in using its ingenuity to help older people to continue to realise their potential more effectively.' (para 1.14)

There is much good advice for solicitors in those words. By making their services more relevant to older people's needs, by using their 'ingenuity' to help older people to protect their interests and solve their legal (sometimes social or health) problems, solicitors can develop a thriving elderly client practice to play a part in recognising and respecting the value of old age. In this book Gordon Ashton provides the means for putting that ingenuity into practice.

I have been privileged to chair the Law Society's Mental Health and Disability Committee during the period that Gordon Ashton has been working on the second edition of the *Elderly Client Handbook* – a period that has seen enormous developments, not only in the many areas of law affecting older clients, but in the way in which legal services are delivered and funded. These changes bring up to date the solid and practical advice given in the first edition, to provide practitioners with the complete range of skills, knowledge and competence required to develop a comprehensive and effective elderly client practice.

Michael Napier

Vice-President, The Law Society

March 2000

Acknowledgements

Just six years ago I completed the first edition of this Handbook with the support of the Law Society's *Mental Health and Disability Committee*. I remain an enthusiastic member of that committee which strives to ensure the provision of better legal services for people who suffer from any form of disability. The purpose of the Handbook was, and remains, to identify older people in society as a discrete client group for whom the legal profession should provide a comprehensive service.

I received help from many lawyers during the writing of the first edition, and the following individuals still deserve specific mention. Denzil Lush (now Master of the Court of Protection) and Lydia Sinclair (who sadly died in May 1998) both then members of the committee, together with Anne Edis, Angela Donen (Bryan & Armstrong), Anthea Grainger (Darlington & Parkinson) and Sarah Hobbs (Tyndallwoods & Millichip) kindly took the trouble to read the text in draft form and made helpful suggestions. Nigel Hodkinson (Hodkinsons), Luke Clements (Thorpes) and Bryan Wordsworth (Eastleys) considered parts of the text and tried to ensure that my material bore a reasonable resemblance to the present state of the law. Penny Letts, secretary of the committee, co-ordinated these and other contributions and supported me from the inception to the conclusion of the work. Evelyn McEwen of Age Concern England, also a member of the committee, showed an interest in the project from its early stages and co-ordinated the support of Age Concern whose practical experience in this field is unrivalled. As always, the then Master of the Court of Protection Mrs A. B. Macfarlane was supportive as regards the material that concerned her role.

I did not then anticipate that the concept of the 'Elderly Client Practice' which I was advocating would become so popular and that so many solicitors would develop expertise in this field. But it is reassuring that this should now be the case. The consequence is that when asked to write a second edition I did not feel competent to do so. It is now approaching eight years since I ceased to practise law and took on a judicial role. But I could not turn my back on the challenge so invited Anne Edis, chairman of *Solicitors for the Elderly*, to cover developments in legal practice and cast an ever watchful eye over my continuing efforts. I am grateful to her for this.

I hope that this second edition will be of assistance to the profession and, above all, to the many elderly clients that we all strive to serve. This must be my final contribution, but if there is a continuing need for a handbook of this nature

ACKNOWLEDGEMENTS

I shall be content for other solicitors to take over the onerous task of writing it. My own energies are increasingly being devoted to encouraging judges to recognise and address the needs of litigants and witnesses who are vulnerable by reason of age or mental and physical disabilities.

Unless the context clearly indicates otherwise, the views expressed in this Handbook do not necessarily represent those of the Law Society and some are my own. I am content if these views provoke discussion in the profession concerning issues of relevance to the older client and not all readers will agree with them. I must accept sole responsibility for the style and content of the Handbook having been given a generous brief by the Law Society, but whilst I have tried to provide a correct summary of the relevant law and procedure I cannot be held liable for any errors. This is merely intended as a Guide and those seeking a definitive statement of the law should refer to more authoritative publications.

Gordon R. Ashton

Grange-over-Sands

March 2000

Table of Cases

Airedale NHS Trust v Bland [1993] AC 789; [1993] 2 WLR 316, HL...282, 283, 284
Associated Provincial Picture Houses Ltd v Wednesbury Corporation
  [1944] 1 KB 223 .... 44, 455

Banks v Goodfellow (1870) 5 QB 549... 357
Barclays Bank plc v Eustice [1995] 1 WLR 1238; [1995] 4 All ER 511, CA 220, 456
Barrett v Enfield London Borough Council [1997] 3 WLR 628;
  [1997] 2 FLR 167, CA 41
Beaney (Deceased), Re [1978] 1 WLR 770; [1978] 2 All ER 595 ....349, 447, 458
Blyth v Blyth (No 2) [1966] AC 643; [1966] 1 All ER 524, HL...................... 249
Bolam v Friern Barnet Hospital Management Committee [1957] 1 WLR 582;
  [1957] 2 All ER 118.. 281

C (A Patient), Re [1991] 3 All ER 866.. 359
C (Adult: Refusal of Medical Treatment), Re [1994] 1 WLR 290;
  [1994] 1 All ER 819..281, 284
Capital and Counties plc v Hampshire County Council [1997] QB 1004;
  (1997) Times, 20 March, CA 41
Clark Boyce v Mouat [1994] 1 AC 428; [1993] 4 All ER 268, PC.............118, 321

D (J), Re [1982] 2 All ER 37... 359
De Court, In re (1997) Times, 27 November... 59, 182
Drew v Nunn [1979] 4 QB 661 162

E G, Re [1914] 1 Ch 927, CA... 433

F v West Berkshire Health Authority [1990] 2 AC 1;
  [1989] 2 All ER 545, HL...281, 283
Freeman v Home Office [1984] QB 524, CA; affirming [1984] 2 WLR 130........ 279

Gillick v West Norfolk and Wisbech Area Health Authority and Anor
  [1986] AC 112; [1986] 1 FLR 224, HL... 280
Grandison (Deceased), Re (1999) Times, 10 July....................................... 376

Hart v O'Connor [1985] AC 1000; [1985] 2 All ER 880, PC 162

K (Enduring Powers of Attorney) Re, F Re [1988] Ch 310;
  [1988] 1 All ER 358.. 85, 433, 446, 447
Kenward v Adams (1975) Times, 29 November... 433

Midland Bank plc v Wyatt [1995] 1 FLR 697... 220

P v P (Contempt of Court: Mental Capacity) [1999] 2 FLR 897;
  (1999) Times, 21 July, CA.. 182
Park, Re [1954] P 112 170

xv

TABLE OF CASES

Practice Direction (Court of Protection) (Authority to Act for Patients or Donors)
9 August 1995 [1995] 2 FLR 1036..23
Practice Note (QBD) (Transfer of Damages to Court of Protection)
7 September 1990 [1991] 1 WLR 2; [1991] 1 All ER 436..........................62

R v Avon County Council, ex p Hazell (unreported, 5 July 1993, QBD)............251
R v Barnet London Borough Council, ex p Shah [1983] 2 AC 309;
[1983] 1 All ER 226, HL..239
R v Birmingham City Council, ex p Taj Mohammed [1999] 1 WLR 33;
(1998) 1 CCL Rep 441..238, 244, 251
R v Bournewood Community and Mental Health NHS Trust, ex p L
[1999] 1 AC 458; (1998) Times, 30 June, HL..291
R v Bristol City Council, ex p Penfold (Alice) (1998) 1 CCL Rep 315..............244
R v Cox (unreported, 18 September 1992)...282
R v East Sussex County Council, ex p Tandy [1998] AC 714;
[1998] 2 All ER 769, HL; reversing [1997] 3 WLR 884, CA........ 244, 245, 251
R v Gloucestershire County Council, ex p Barry [1997] 2 All ER 1, HL;
reversing (1997) 1 CCL Rep 19, CA.................................... 215, 247, 251
R v Islington London Borough Council, ex p Rixon (1998) 1 CCL Rep 119......239
R v North and East Devon Health Authority, ex p Coughlan
(1999) 2 CCL Rep 285, CA..................................224, 236, 244, 253, 461
R v North Yorkshire County Council, ex p Hargreaves (No 2)
[1997] COD 390..246
R v Secretary of State for Social Services, ex p Child Poverty Action Group
[1990] 2 QB 540; [1989] 1 All ER 1047, CA..44
R v Sefton Metropolitan Borough Council, ex p Help the Aged
[1997] 4 All ER 532; (1997) 1 CCL Rep 57, CA 217, 251, 460
Royscott Spa Leasing v Lovett [1995] BCC 502, CA................................220

Sen v Headley [1991] Ch 425; [1991] 2 All ER 636, CA..............................350
Sidaway v Board of Governors of the Bethlem Royal Hospital
[1985] AC 871; [1985] 1 All ER 643, CA 279
Stovin v Wise and Norfolk County Council [1996] AC 923;
[1996] 3 All ER 801, HL..40
Street v Mountford [1985] AC 809; [1985] 2 All ER 289, HL.......................335

T (Consent to Medical Treatment) (Adult Patient), Re [1993] Fam 95;
[1992] 2 FLR 458, CA..280
T v North Yorkshire County Council (1998) Times, 10 September, CA..............42

W v Essex County Council and Goulden [1997] 2 FLR 535;
(1997) Times, 16 July..42
W v L [1974] QB 711; [1973] 3 All ER 884, CA..288
Welton v North Cornwall District Council [1997] 1 WLR 570;
(1996) Times, 19 July, CA..41
Wiltshire County Council v Cornwall County Council (1999) unreported..........239
Wookey v Wookey, Re S (a minor) [1991] Fam. 121;
[1991] 3 All ER 365, CA..59, 60, 182
Wyatt v Hillingdon London Borough Council (1979) 76 LGR 727 40

X v Bedfordshire County Council [1995] 2 AC 633, HL................................41

Yonge v Toynbee [1910] 1 KB 215..56, 61
Yule v South Lanarkshire Council [1999] 1 CCL Rep 546 456

Table of Statutes

Access to Health Records Act 1990 .... 33, 34, 272
    s 3(1) 34
Access to Justice Act 1999 60
Access to Medical Reports Act 1988 .... 32, 272
Access to Personal Files Act 1987 32
Administration of Estates Act 1925 .... 355, 392
    s 55(1)(x) 392
Administration of Justice Act 1982
    s 17 358
Adoption Act 1976 178

Births and Deaths Registration Act 1953 372
Business Names Act 1995 106

Carers (Recognition and Services) Act 1995 .... 24, 25, 234, 236, 238, 249
Children Act 1989 175
    s 1 176
        (3) 175
        (5) 175
    ss 2–4 176
    s 8 176
    ss 31–42 178
Chronically Sick and Disabled Persons Act 1970 .... 227, 235, 249, 252, 345
    s 1 247
    s 2 .... 227, 237, 244, 246, 247, 248, 249, 345
        (1) 249
Civil Evidence Act 1968 s 2 361
Community Care (Direct Payments) Act 1996 234
Community Care (Residential Accommodation) Act 1992 246
Community Care (Residential Accommodation) Act 1998 .... 216, 234, 235
Coroners Act 1988 374
Courts and Legal Services Act 1990 362
    ss 27, 28 53
Crime and Disorder Act 1998 192
Criminal Justice Act 1988 166
Criminal Justice Act 1991 s 4 193
Criminal Procedure (Insanity) Act 1964 192
Criminal Procedure (Insanity and Unfitness to Plead) Act 1991 192

Data Protection Act 1998 32
Defective Premises Act 1972 334
Disability Discrimination Act 1995 .... 49, 53, 166, 167, 234, 249, 301
    Part I (ss 1–3) 168
        s 1 .... 168, 302

TABLE OF STATUTES

Disability Discrimination Act 1995–*cont*
    s 3(3) 168
    Part II (ss 4–18) 168
    Part III (ss 19–28) 168
      s 19 168
      s 20 169
      s 25 169
    Part IV (ss 29–31) 168
    Part V (ss 32–49) 168
    Sched 1 .... 168, 302
    Sched 3, para 7 169
Disabled Persons (Services, Consultation and Representation) Act 1986
    .... 233, 238, 244, 247, 248, 249
    s 3 249
    s 4 .... 235, 248
    s 5 235
    s 6 235
    s 8 .... 24, 248
      (1) 235, 242
    s 9 .... 235, 247
    s 10 235

Employment Relations Act 1999 301
Employment Rights Act 1996 301
    s 1 303
    s 13 302
    s 86 .... 303, 304
    s 92 304
    s 94 304
    s 135 .... 302, 305
    s 155 302
    s 212 302
Enduring Powers of Attorney Act 1985 .... 81, 384, 385, 387, 388,
    .... 390, 391, 435, 444, 446, 448
    s 2(1), (2) 441
    s 2(8) 320
    s 3(3) 85, 320, 438
      (4) 349
      (5) 349, 437
    s 4(5) 445
    s 7 80
    s 8 445
      (2)(e) 349, 437
    s 11(1) 435
    Sched 1 444
      Part I 83
Environmental Protection Act 1990 335
    s 79 334
Equal Pay Act 1970 303

Family Law Act 1996
    Part I (s 1) 172
    Part II (ss 2–25) 172
    Part III (ss 26–29) 172

TABLE OF STATUTES

Part IV (ss 30–63)..182, 184
Financial Services Act 1986..133, 438
    Sched 1
        para 22 134
        para 24 134
Forfeiture Act 1982.. 354

Health and Social Services and Social Security Adjudications Act 1983
    Part VII (ss 17–24)... 233
    s 17 214
        (4) 216
    s 21 ....219, 256
    s 22 ....219, 455
    s 23 219
    s 24 ....219, 455
Health Authorities Act 1995.. 267
Health Services and Public Health Act 1968
    s 45 ....233, 235, 242
Hospital Complaints Procedure Act 1985.. 275
Housing Act 1985 ....323, 333, 345
    Part II (ss 8–57) 324
    Part III (ss 58–78)..234, 336
    Part IV (ss 79–117) 324
    s 83 328
    s 92 331
    s 113 330
    Part V (ss 118–188) 325
    Part VI (ss 189–208) 334
    s 604 334
    Sched 2 328
Housing Act 1988 ....323, 327, 330, 345
    Part I (ss 1–45) 325
    ss 27, 28 330
    Sched 1..325, 329
    Sched 2 329
Housing Act 1996 ....322, 323, 324, 325, 326, 334
    ss 152–157 184
    Part VI (ss 159–174) 327
    Part VII (ss 175–218) 234
Housing and Planning Act 1986... 336
Housing Grants, Construction and Regeneration Act 1996 226
Human Rights Act 1998..47, 48, 49, 232, 245
Human Tissue Act 1961.. 378

Inheritance (Provision for Family and Dependants) Act 1975.........171, 354,
....360, 368, 453
    s 3 360
        (2) 361
Inheritance Tax Act 1984
    s 3A(1), (3) 316, 370
    s 89 ....316, 370, 395
    s 142 362
    s 143 364
    s 144 363

TABLE OF STATUTES

Inheritance Tax Act 1984–*cont*
   s 146 362
Insolvency Act 1986
   ss 339–340 ....220, 456
   s 341 456
   ss 423–425 ....220, 456

Jobseekers Act 1995 197
Juries Act 1974
   s 1 166
   s 9B 166
   Sched 166

Landlord and Tenant Act 1954
   Part I (ss 1–22) 322, 325
Landlord and Tenant Act 1985 ....322, 333
   ss 11–16 333
Landlord and Tenant Act 1987 322
Law of Property Act 1925
   s 30 319
Law of Property (Miscellaneous Provisions) Act 1989 80
   s 1(3) 443
Leasehold Reform Act 1967 ....322, 323
Leasehold Reform, Housing and Urban Development Act 1993 322
   Part I
      Ch I (ss 1–38) 323
      Ch II (ss 39–62) 323
Limitation Act 1980
   s 28(1) 59
   s 33(3)(d) 59
   s 38(2) 59
      (3) 59
Local Authority Social Services Act 1970
   s 2 36
   s 7 239
      (1) 234
   s 7A 239
   s 7B 250
   s 7D 40
Local Government (Access to Information) Act 1985 33
Local Government Act 1970 234
Local Government Act 1972
   ss 100A–100K 33
   s 101(8) 36
   Sched 12A, Part I 33
Local Government Act 1974
   s 27 39
Local Government and Housing Act 1989 ....322, 323, 325

Magistrates' Courts Act 1980
   s 30 193
   s 58(1) 216
Marriage Act 1949
   s 29 170

TABLE OF STATUTES

Marriage Act 1983
    s 1 170
Matrimonial and Family Proceedings Act 1984 171
Matrimonial Causes Act 1973 171
    ss 1–3 173
    s 5 173
    s 10 173
    ss 11–13 172
    ss 21–24 174
    s 25 174
    ss 25A–25D 175
Mental Health Act 1983 .... 11, 13, 27, 54, 59, 164, 166, 172, 191, 193,
              244, 268, 277, 281, 282, 287, 288, 292, 293, 306, 404, 444, 445
    s 1 .... 13, 288
        (2) 55
        (3) 55
    Part II (ss 2–34) 287
    s 2 .... 291, 292, 296
    s 3 .... 224, 243, 291, 292, 296
    s 4 291
    s 5 292
        (2) 288
    s 7 243
    s 8 .... 243, 293
    ss 9, 10 243
    s 16 296
    s 17 288
    s 18 288
    s 20 296
    s 23 296
    s 25 296
    ss 25A–25J 295
    s 26 289
    s 29 296
    Part III (ss 35–55) 287
    s 35 193
    s 36 193
    s 37 .... 193, 224, 243, 292
        (3) 193
    s 38 193
    s 47 .... 243, 292
    s 48 .... 193, 243, 292
    Part IV (ss 56–64) 287, 292, 297
    s 62 292
    Part V (ss 65–79) 287
    s 68 296
    s 72 297
    s 94(2) 95
    s 95 90
        (1)(b), (c) 91
    s 96 .... 90, 359
        (1)(d) 91
    s 97 359
    s 98 90

TABLE OF STATUTES

Mental Health Act 1983–*cont*
- s 99 95
  - (3) 91
- s 102 89
- s 103 89
- s 114 290
- s 115 293
- s 117 .... 215, 224, 233, 243, 249, 295
- s 118(4) 280, 290
- s 124 40
- s 131(1) 291
- s 135 293
- s 136 293
- s 142 78
- s 145(1) 289

Mental Health (Patients in the Community) Act 1995 295
Mobile Homes Act 1983 345

National Assistance Act 1948 .... 235, 239, 278
- Part III (ss 21–35) 233, 241, 336
- s 21 245
  - (1) 235
    - (a) 241
- s 22 216
- s 26 245
  - (1)(A)–(C) 241
- s 26A 222
- s 29 .... 242, 247
  - (1) 235
  - (4)(g) 247
- s 36 40
- s 42 .... 218, 221, 460
- s 43 .... 218, 221, 460
- s 47 .... 242, 278, 293
- s 48 242
- s 56 455

National Assistance (Amendment) Act 1951 242
National Health Service Act 1977
- s 21 .... 233, 242
- s 85 40
- Sched 8 .... 233, 242
  - paras 1, 2 235

National Health Service (Amendment) Act 1995 267
National Health Service and Community Care Act 1990 ..... 237, 241, 252, 259, 267
- s 42(2) 241
- s 43 222
- s 44 237
- s 45 237
- Part III (ss 46–49) 233
- s 46 237
- s 47 .... 237, 239
  - (1) 243, 245
  - (2) 244
  - (3) 244, 245

National Health Service and Community Care Act 1990–*cont*
  (5) 244
  (6) 244
  s 48 237
  s 49 237
  s 50 .... 40, 237, 239
  (1) 250
National Savings Bank Act 1971
  s 8(1)(f) 78, 163

Partnership Act 1890
  s 1 307
  s 14(1) 307
  s 35 307
Pensions Act 1995 234
Powers of Attorney Act 1971 80
  s 3 .... 80, 443
Protection from Eviction Act 1977 330
Protection from Harassment Act 1997 183
Public Health (Control of Diseases) Act 1984
  s 46 377
Public Trustee and Administration of Funds Act 1986 86

Race Relations Act 1976 .... 167, 301
  s 3 .... 167, 302
Registered Homes Act 1984 .... 255, 256
  Part I (ss 1–20) 259
  s 1(1) 256
  s 2 259
  s 3 257
  s 6 257
  s 9 257
  s 17 258
  Part II (ss 21–38) 259
  s 21 256
  s 22 256
  s 23(1) 259
  s 25 257
  Part III (ss 39–45) 259
Registered Homes (Amendment) Act 1991 255
Rent Act 1977 .... 324, 325, 327, 332
  Part I (ss 1–26) 324
  s 2 330
  s 98 328
  Sched 1 330
  Sched 15 328
Road Traffic Act 1988
  ss 87–93 164

Sale of Goods Act 1979
  s 3 162
Sex Discrimination Act 1975 .... 167, 301
  s 82(1) 301
Sexual Offences (Amendment) Act 1976 186

xxiii

TABLE OF STATUTES

Social Security Act 1986..211
Social Security Act 1998..197, 198
Social Security Administration Act 1992..197
Social Security Contributions and Benefits Act 1992..............................197
Social Security (Incapacity for Work) Act 1994.....................................197
Solicitors Act 1974...105, 129
    s 34..109
    s 57..131
    s 70...129, 130
    s 71...129, 130
    s 72...129, 130
    s 85..109
Supply of Goods and Services Act 1982..42
Supreme Court Act 1981
    s 31...43
    s 90...88

Taxation of Chargeable Gains Act 1992
    s 3...316
    s 62(6)–(10)...363
    Sched 1, para 1..316, 370
Taxes Management Act 1970
    s 8...78
Trade Union and Labour Relations (Consolidation) Act 1992......................301
Trustee Act 1925...164
    s 25..85, 320, 438
    s 36(9)..87
    s 54...87
Trustee Delegation Act 1999..85, 320, 438
    s 1(1)..85, 438
    s 2...320
    s 4..320, 438
    s 5...320
    s 7...320
Trusts of Land and Appointment of Trustees Act 1996..............74, 164, 319
    s 11..397

Variation of Trusts Act 1958
    s 1(3)...87

Wages Act 1986...302
Wills Act 1837...444
    s 9...358

Youth Justice and Criminal Evidence Act 1999
    Part II (ss 16–63)...187

Table of Statutory Instruments and Rules

Access to Personal Files (Housing) Regulations 1989 (SI 1989 no 503).............32
Access to Personal Files (Social Services) Regulations 1989 (SI 1989 no 206)....32

Civil Legal Aid (General) Regulations 1989 (SI 1989 no 339)
    reg 16...61
Civil Procedure Rules 1998 (SI 1998 no 3132).........................49, 50, 283, 287
    Part 2, r 2.7...52
    Part 21..54
        r 21.2..54
        r 21.3(2) 56
        r 21.10(2)...58
        r 21.11 62
    Part 27..43
    Part 32..52
    Part 34..52
        rr 34.8–34.12..52
    Part 48, r 48.5 60
        r 48.9(6) 60
    Sched 1..43
Coroners Rules 1984 (SI 1984 no 552) 374, 376
Council Tax Benefit (General) Regulations 1992 (SI 1992 no 1814) 214
County Court Rules 1981 (SI 1981 no 1687) 49
    Ord 1, r 3...54
    Ord 10..54
        r 10...58
    Ord 20, r 13...52
    Ord 49, r 12...287
Court of Protection (Enduring Powers of Attorney) Rules 1986 (SI 1986 no 127).....
    Sched 1...383, 384
Court of Protection (Enduring Powers of Attorney) Rules 1994 (SI 1994 no 3047) 81
Court of Protection Rules 1984 (SI 1984 no 2035)
    r 17..359
    r 18..359
Court of Protection Rules 1994 (SI 1994 no 3046)...........................50, 86, 287
    r 6..88
    r 8(1)..94
    r 9..87, 90
    r 10..92
    r 15..88
    r 16..54
    r 20..88
    r 21(2)..94
    r 26..93
        (2)..93
    r 27..93

TABLE OF STATUTORY INSTRUMENTS AND RULES

Court of Protection Rules 1994–*cont*
    r 39 94
    r 40 94
    r 44 92
    r 48(1) 93
    r 57 94
    r 87(1) 95
    Part XVIII 94
    Appendix 94

Disability Discrimination (Meaning of Disability) Regulations 1996
    (SI 1996 no 1455) 168
Disability Discrimination (Services and Premises) Regulations 1996
    (SI 1996 no 1836) 168
Disability Discrimination (Sub-leases and Sub-tenancies) Regulations 1996
    (SI 1996 no 1333) 168

Enduring Powers of Attorney (Prescribed Form) Regulations 1990
    (SI 1990 no 1376) 81, 383, 384, 441, 443
    reg 2(1) 441

Family Proceedings Rules 1991 (SI 1991 no 1247) 50, 171
    Part I, r 1.3 50
    Part IX, r 9.1 .... 54, 172
        rr 9.2–9.5 172
Family Provision (Intestate Succession) Order 1993 (SI 1993 no 2906) 355

Housing Benefit (General) Regulations 1987 (SI 1987 no 1971) 211

Income Support (General) Regulations 1987 (SI 1987 no 1967) 197
Income Tax (Building Societies) (Dividends and Interest) (Amendment)
    Regulations 1992 (SI 1992 no 11) 78
Income Tax (Deposit-takers) (Interest Payments) (Amendment)
    Regulations 1992 (SI 1992 no 13) 78
Insolvency Rules 1986 (SI 1986 no 1925) 50
    Part 7, Ch 7 54

Local Authority Social Services (Complaints Procedure) Order 1990
    (SI 1990 no 2244) 250

Mental Health Act Commission Regulations 1983 (SI 1983 no 894) 297
Mental Health (After-care under Supervision) Regulations 1996
    (SI 1996 no 294) 287
Mental Health (Hospital, Guardianship and Consent to Treatment)
    (Amendment) Regulations 1996 (SI 1996 no 540) 287
Mental Health (Patients in the Community) (Transfers from Scotland)
    Regulations 1996 (SI 1996 no 295) 287
Mental Health Review Tribunal Rules 1983 (SI 1983 no 942) 287

National Assistance (Assessment of Resources) Regulations 1992
    (SI 1992 no 2977) 216, 219, 461
National Assistance (Charges for Accommodation) Regulations 1992
    (SI 1992 no 563) 216

National Assistance (Sums for Personal Requirements) Regulations 1996
  (SI 1996 no 391) 216
National Health Sevice (General Medical Services) Regulations 1992
  (SI 1992 no 635)
  Sched 2 270
National Savings Bank Regulations 1972 (SI 1972 no 764)
  reg 6 .... 78, 163
  reg 7 .... 78, 163
Nursing Homes and Mental Nursing Homes Regulations 1984
  (SI 1984 no 1578) 255

Parliamentary Elections Rules
  r 35(1) 165
Police (Conduct) Regulations 1999 (SI 1999 no 730) 190

Registered Homes Tribunal Rules 1984 (SI 1984 no 1346) 255, 259
Registration of Births and Deaths Regulations 1987 (SI 1987 no 2088) 372
Removal of Bodies Regulations 1954 375
Residential Accommodation (Relevant Premises, Ordinary Residence
  and Exemptions) Regulations 1993 (SI 1993 no 477) 222, 223
Residential Care Homes (Amendment) (No 2) Regulations 1992
  (SI 1992 no 2241) 256
Residential Care Homes Regulations 1984 (SI 1984 no 1345) 255, 258
  reg 9 258
Rules of the Supreme Court 1965 (SI 1965 no 1776) 49
  Ord 39, r 1 52
  Ord 53 43
  Ord 62 95
  Ord 80 54
    r 1 54
    rr 10, 11 58

Secure Tenancies (Right to Repair Scheme) Regulations 1985
  (SI 1985 no 1493) 331
Social Security (Adjudication) Regulations (SI 1995 no 1689) 197
Social Security (Claims and Payments) Regulations 1979 (SI 1979 no 628) 197
Social Security (Claims and Payments) Regulations 1987 (SI 1987 no 1968) 76, 197
  reg 33 76
  reg 34 77
  reg 35 77
  Sched 9 77
Social Security Contributions (Decisions and Appeals) Regulations 1999
  (SI 1999 no 1027) 197
Social Security (Overlapping Benefits) Regulations 1979 (SI 1979 no 597) 197, 205
Social Security (Payments on Account, Overpayments and Recovery)
  Regulations 1988 (SI 1988 no 664) 197
Social Security (Widow's Benefit and Retirement Pensions) Regulations 1979
  (SI 1979 no 642) 197
Solicitors' Accounts Rules 1998 .... 105, 109
Solicitors' Investment Business Rules 1995 .... 105, 106, 107, 109, 134, 438
Solicitors' (Non-Contentious Business) Remuneration Order 1994
  (SI 1994 no 2616) 128
  art 3 129
  art 4 .... 129, 132

TABLE OF STATUTORY INSTRUMENTS AND RULES

Solicitors' (Non-Contentious Business) Remuneration Order 1994–*cont*
    (1)...130
  art 5..129
  art 6...130, 132
  art 7...130, 131, 132
    (2)(b)..131
  art 8...130, 131, 132
  art 9...130, 132
  art 10...130, 131, 132
  art 11..131
    (1)..130
    (2)..131
  art 12..132
  art 13..132
  art 14...130, 132
  art 15..133
Solicitors' Practice Rules 1990...105
  r 1..105, 115
  r 2..106, 115
  r 3...106, 114, 115
  r 5..106, 115
  r 6..106, 118
  r 7..107
  r 8..107
  r 9..107
  r 10..114, 135
  r 11..107
  r 12..108, 114
  r 13...108, 115, 122
  r 15..108, 126

Working Time Regulations 1998 (SI 1998 no 1833)..............................301

PART ONE
Acting for Elderly Clients

In most respects older people are ordinary clients who seek the same services and present the same problems as younger clients. When applying the law it is inappropriate to identify or classify people by age or the description 'elderly', and we must respect the views and experience of older people and recognise their autonomy and independence. The production of this Handbook does not suggest otherwise, but is an attempt to equip the lawyer with some of the special knowledge and skills that prove to be valuable when dealing with this client group which often has requirements not met by other client groups.

In this Part we identify the needs of the older client and how the solicitor may contribute towards meeting those needs, where appropriate by working with carers and others to represent the client. Dealing with older clients requires an understanding of the problems that they may face and may present to others, in particular the implications of a decline in physical ability or mental capacity. Such decline leads to dependence on others and can result in vulnerability. Solicitors have a role in protecting and empowering their elderly clients.

Throughout the Handbook and where appropriate, the masculine gender includes the feminine and vice versa.

SECTION A
The Client

In this Section we consider:

- the distinguishing features of elderly clients;
- the role of the law in regard to older people;
- the assessment of legal capacity;
- how decisions should be made for those who are incapable of making or communicating their own decisions.

Chapter 1
Distinguishing Elderly Clients

There is no universal definition of 'elderly' but in this Handbook we concentrate on the needs of those over pensionable age, which in England and Wales is presently 65 years for a man and 60 for a woman. This is a different concept from 'normal retirement age' which may be younger or older than this depending upon the particular employment in question. We are thus considering a period of potentially 30 or more years for the client (one-third of a life-span) and the ageing process is slower in some than others.

1.1 STATISTICS

Numbers and proportions

In 1995 there were about 9.25 million people over the age of 65 years in the UK (15.74 per cent of the population) and both the numbers and proportion had steadily increased over the previous 25 years. Roughly 60 per cent were women but there was a trend for the proportion of men to increase. The change in the population structure was more pronounced in those over 85 years of age (1.78 per cent of the population) whose numbers had doubled to about 1.05 million in that period with roughly 75 per cent being women. Government actuaries forecast that by 2011 there would be approaching 10 million people over the age of 65 years in the UK (16.38 per cent of the population) and that 56 per cent of these would be women. The forecast for those over 85 years of age was 1.28 million (2.12 per cent of the population) of whom 70 per cent would be women.

Statistics are also available for those over pensionable age (65 years for men and 60 for women). In 1996 there were 10.5 million of these older people in the UK (8.9 million in England and 0.6 million in Wales) representing 18.14 per cent of the population. Of these 65 per cent were women. A man aged 60 years could then expect to live for another 18.5 years whereas for a woman this was 22.4 years. It is interesting to note that in 1996 there were 6,325 people over the age of 100 years in the UK (5,670 women and 655 men) though a considerable increase in this age group is forecast. Despite the increase in the proportion of older people in our society, the percentage of men and women in the workforce who are within five years of retirement age has decreased markedly.

PART 1: SECTION A The Client

Basic facts

The following information relates to 1996 (or 1995/96 where appropriate):

- 48 per cent of pensioner households depended on state benefits for at least 75 per cent of their income and 14 per cent received all their income from state benefits;
- a substantial proportion of pensioners entitled to benefits did not claim them:
  - up to 40 per cent for income support
  - up to 14 per cent for housing benefit and 34 per cent for council tax benefit
- a higher proportion of the weekly budget was spent on housing, fuel and food where the head of the household was aged 65 or over (and especially for pensioners living alone);
- 21 per cent of men and 39 per cent of women lived alone in the 65–74 age group (31 per cent of men and 58 per cent of women aged 75 and over);
- 53 per cent of carers had dependants aged over 75 years (20 per cent over 85 years);
- (according to estimates) 5 per cent of the population aged 65 and over suffered from dementia (20 per cent aged 80 and over).

Community care

Statistics released by the Department of Health in March 1998 indicate that:

- 24,800 residential care homes offered 347,000 places and 5,800 nursing homes offered 193,900 places (2,109/94,947 being dual registration);
- 88 per cent of all these places were provided by the independent sector (almost 100 per cent in the case of homes for the elderly mentally infirm);
- 13,000 of these residential care homes (246,700 places) were for elderly people (plus 1,200/21,500 for the elderly mentally infirm);
- the number of homes for elderly people had fallen by 1 per cent in the previous year whereas the number of places had increased by 2 per cent.

> In September each year Age Concern produces a fact-card *Older people in the United Kingdom* which contains valuable statistics about the ageing population.

1.2   DISTINGUISHING CRITERIA

In most respects an elderly client may be treated like any other private client and will require the same range of services, whether this be from the conveyancing,

Chapter 1 DISTINGUISHING ELDERLY CLIENTS

matrimonial, criminal, tax, family or trust department of the firm. The attributes which above all else distinguish elderly clients are the possibility of vulnerability and dependence, but the following tendencies may be identified:

Financial

- rely on pensions and savings to live rather than living to create savings:
  - may be dependent upon state benefits or the next generation for support
  - (alternatively) may wish to transfer surplus wealth to the next generation
- concerned at the cost of long-term care yet may not realise that they can still plan for this.

Social

- have more leisure but may live at a slower pace:
  - are more inclined to rely upon acquired attitudes and beliefs than develop new ones, so appear less flexible
- may be or become dependent upon family or others, as distinct from being responsible for family or others:
  - wish to be independent as long as possible and may live alone or in some degree of isolation

Health

- encounter physical limitations and disabilities on an increasing, permanent basis:
  - may become legally incapacitated (see below)
  - the next stage of life to be contemplated becomes preparing for death
- have a longer life span to plan for long-term care.

> These factors influence not only the type of work that a solicitor undertakes for older clients but also the manner in which that work is undertaken – see Chapters 3 and 13.

Needs

When acting for older clients the aim should be to protect those who are vulnerable whilst preserving independence, self-fulfilment and autonomy for as long as possible. This Handbook identifies areas of need for legal services and what is expected of the solicitor.

Financial

The need for financial advice is increasing because older people are living

PART 1: SECTION A The Client

longer, have more money at their disposal (from home ownership, pensions, savings and state benefits) and tend to be cared for in the community rather than in hospitals or institutions.

Personal

People are retiring earlier and the norm for older people is retirement even though this may be involuntary. The need for activity may be satisfied by part-time or voluntary work, but as physical or mental disabilities arise there may be need for a change of life-style or environment, and even support services and personal care. There is a role for the solicitor in these changes.

Legal

All these financial and personal needs have legal implications which should be addressed when necessary, but a key role for solicitors is helping the client prepare for the future and providing assistance with financial affairs when this is needed. This work cannot be done in isolation and financial management must reflect personal needs.

> The solicitor can shield an elderly client from undue influence by relatives and others who may be acting more in their own interests than in the best interests of the vulnerable elderly individual.

Disabilities

Two distinct forms of disability may affect older people:

- physical disability:
    - impaired mobility and dexterity
    - sensory impairment (poor sight or hearing)
    - impaired ability to communicate (implications similar to mental disability)
    - chronic and degenerative conditions
- mental disability:
    - mental illness takes many forms including *neurosis* (a functional derangement, e.g. phobias) and *psychosis* (a severe mental derangement involving the whole personality, e.g. paranoia, schizophrenia)
    - there are ever increasing numbers of elderly senile people who are medically classified as suffering from an *acquired organic brain syndrome* (a neurotic disorder usually due to vascular changes, e.g. dementia, Alzheimer's disease)
    - distinguish learning disability (previously referred to as mental handicap). People *become* mentally ill and some respond to medical treatment but the condition may be untreatable. People *are* learning disabled when they have a brain that will not develop or function normally – there is no cure but educa-

tion and training assists them to become accepted members of society able to fulfil their personal potential

1.3 ROLE OF THE LAW

Not only are the numbers of older people increasing, but policies in regard to their treatment and care are also changing. The emphasis is now upon care in the community which points to an enhanced role for the practising solicitor. Whilst it would be discriminatory to have a separate body of law dealing with older people, many fields of law need to be modified or enhanced to cater for their needs which may become the same as those of other vulnerable groups (e.g. mentally ill and learning disabled people). The elderly client practitioner now needs a working knowledge of both social security law (to advise on entitlement to financial benefits) and public law (to advise fully on community care and the role of the health services).

Objectives

- protect the individual from exploitation and abuse (physical, mental and financial);
- enhance the quality of the individual's life by ensuring the provision of necessary support (financial and through services);
- empower the individual if frail or mentally incapacitated;
- enforce duties owed by society to the individual (and vice versa);
- prevent discrimination on the bases of age and disability.

Guiding principles

- all people are presumed to be competent and to have the same rights and status, except as specifically provided or determined;
- any modification or intervention should be the minimum necessary in that case;
- people should be enabled and encouraged to exercise and develop their own capacity and to participate in decisions to the maximum extent possible.

For further consideration see:
1. the Law Commission consultation papers and Report *Mental Incapacity* (March 1995);
2. the Green Paper *Who Decides? Making Decisions on Behalf of Mentally Incapacitated Adults* (December 1997); and
3. the Government's proposals in *Making Decisions* (October 1999).

These are summarised in Appendix 8.

Chapter 2
Capacity

2.1 INTRODUCTION

If you act for older clients you must be able to recognise and cope with the legal implications of *incapacity* (sometimes referred to as *incompetence*).

Terminology

Terms in this context with distinct meanings are often applied as labels and used in a wrong context. A correct use of the common terms is as follows:

- an individual may suffer from an *illness* or *disorder*;
- this may result in a *disability* which comprises:
  - the limitation imposed upon the individual by reason of his or her physical, mental or sensory impairment, and
  - the *handicap* which this imposes on the individual in his or her environment
- if the disability is of a sufficient degree the individual may be treated as legally *incapacitated* (or *incompetent*):
  - this may be due to *mental incapacity* or *physical inability* or both

Presumptions

There is a presumption that an adult is capable until the contrary is proved, but this may be rebutted by a specific finding of incapacity:

- if a person is proved incapable of entering into contracts generally, the law presumes such condition to continue until it is proved to have ceased, although a lucid interval may still be proved;
- if an act and the manner in which it was carried out are rational, there is a strong presumption that the individual was mentally capable at the time;
- eccentricity of behaviour is not necessarily a sign of incapacity and care should be exercised before any assumption is made.

2.2 ASSESSMENT

It would be convenient if people could be legally categorised as either capable or incapable according to a simple test based upon a general assessment, but this would be inappropriate and discriminatory. Most individuals have some level of capacity and this should be identified and respected, so:

- legal definitions of mental capacity differ for different purposes;
- the severity of the test and means of assessment may depend upon the nature and implications of the particular decision.

In practice assessments tend to be influenced by the perceptions of those applying them, so the method of assessment, whether formal or informal, may be more significant than the legal test to be applied.

> Helpful guidance is given in *Assessment of Mental Capacity: Guidance for Doctors and Lawyers* published jointly by the Law Society and BMA (1995).

Approaches

There are three possible approaches to the question of incapacity:

- *outcome* – determined by the content of the decision (e.g. if it is foolish the maker must be incompetent);
- *status* – judged according to the status of the individual such as age (e.g. over 90 years), a medical diagnosis (e.g. senile dementia) or place of residence (e.g. being in a mental hospital);
- *understanding* – the ability of the individual to understand the nature and effect of the particular decision is assessed.

A test based on understanding is generally appropriate when dealing with elderly people, but in certain circumstances the status test may apply, e.g. if a receiver has been appointed by the Court of Protection the individual ceases to have capacity in regard to financial affairs except to the extent that limited capacity is permitted by the Court (though the individual may retain capacity over personal decisions). Conversely, detention under the Mental Health Act does not automatically deprive the patient of decision-making capacity.

The outcome of a decision may result in such test being applied, e.g.

- an elderly spinster instructs you to sell her substantial house for £900;
- a widow decides to go and live with her 'husband'.

> Being very old, making decisions that others would regard as eccentric or being in a nursing home does not necessarily imply lack of capacity.

Appearances

Whilst the law is concerned with what is going on in the mind, society tends to be concerned with the outward manifestations. Note that:

- you must recognise the difference between ability and capacity as it is not unusual for communication difficulties to disguise mental capacity;
- appearance (perhaps the consequence of physical disabilities) can create an impression of mental incapacity which is not justified;
- conversely, the absence of physical characteristics may disguise an underlying mental disability;
- observance of the conventions of society can disguise lack of capacity when a person is demented, e.g. a learnt behaviour pattern.

Criteria

When making assessments different professions apply different criteria:

- the medical profession is concerned with diagnosis and prognosis, and health authorities are increasingly being relieved of the responsibility to care for those with mental disabilities who will not respond to medical treatment;
- care workers classify people according to their degree of independence which involves consideration of levels of competence in performing skills such as eating, dressing, communication and social skills;
- the lawyer is concerned with legal competence, namely whether the individual is capable of making a reasoned and informed decision (the test of capacity) and able to communicate that decision.

This should be borne in mind when seeking opinions about capacity. A multi-disciplinary approach is usually best when assessing capacity in difficult or disputed cases, and the assessment should not then be left entirely to the doctor.

> Full letters of instruction to fellow professionals will help to set the requisite criteria needed by the lawyer – see Appendix 4.

Legal tests

The problem remains of identifying the definition or test of mental capacity to be applied in any particular circumstances. Relevant tests of capacity, where these have been defined by statute or case law, are mentioned in regard to specific legal transactions throughout this Handbook.

Mental disorder

The Mental Health Act 1983 contains several definitions which are adopted by other statutes – in particular the definition of *mental disorder*.

> **Mental disorder** is defined as: 'mental illness, arrested or incomplete development of mind, psychopathic disorder and any other disorder or disability of mind' (section 1).

This is intentionally wide because it was intended to identify individuals who need protection rather than restriction. Note that it does not involve any assessment of degree of impairment and that a mental illness or disorder does not necessarily result in incapacity: it is a matter of degree. The definition is sometimes used inappropriately in situations where the extent of the mental incapacity (rather than the existence of a mental disorder) is in issue.

Determining capacity

Where doubt is raised as to mental capacity remember that:

- it is necessary to identify and apply the appropriate definition or test;
- capacity depends upon understanding rather than wisdom so the quality of the decision is irrelevant as long as the person understands what he is deciding;
- you should consider whether the client is incapable (rather than capable) because of the presumption of capacity;
- the question is one of fact though the correct legal test must be applied;
- capacity must be judged for each individual in respect of each transaction at that particular moment, as an individual may have a lucid interval;
- in legal proceedings a judge makes his determination not as medical expert but as a lay person influenced by personal observation and on the basis of evidence not only from doctors but also from those who know the individual.

> The question to ask is not 'Is he (or she) capable?' or even 'Is he (or she) incapable?' but rather: **'Is he (or she) incapable of this particular act or decision?'**

Evidence

- Evidence of conduct at other times is admissible, and the general pattern of life of the individual may be of great weight, although it is the state of mind at the time of the act that is material. But be aware that the moment of lucidity may assist on occasions.

- General reputation is not admissible in evidence, but the treatment by friends and family of a person alleged to be suffering from mental disorder may be admissible.
- Medical evidence is admissible and usually important, but it must be considered whether the opinion of a medical witness has been formed on sufficient grounds and on the basis of the correct legal test.
- An order of the Court of Protection based upon a finding of lack of capacity to manage affairs by reason of mental disorder is admissible as prima facie evidence of this fact.

2.3 DECISION-MAKING

Procedures are needed for decision-making on behalf of those who are deemed to be legally incapacitated (i.e. incapable of making or communicating their own decisions).

Types of decision

There are various fields of decision-making:

- management:
    - financial matters (e.g. claiming benefits, managing money)
    - legal matters (e.g. buying property, making a will, court proceedings)
- personal:
    - day-to-day living (e.g. what to eat or wear, to have a haircut)
    - activities involving more risk (e.g. going out alone, holidays)
    - major decisions (e.g. where to live)
    - highly personal decisions (e.g. getting married)
- medical:
    - minor routine treatment (e.g. dentistry, vaccinations)
    - treatment with advantages and disadvantages (e.g. optional minor surgery)
    - controversial treatment (e.g. sterilisation, participation in medical research)
    - refusal of medical treatment (e.g. that would prolong life)

Procedures

Some decisions cannot be delegated, either because they are too personal or the law does not make any provision. The law only makes specific provision for decisions of a management nature (see Chapters 7–10), and medical treatment for certain mental disorders (see Chapter 26).

Chapter 2   CAPACITY

Recently the courts have attempted to enable significant medical decisions to be taken on behalf of mentally incapable people where previously such decisions could not lawfully be made because there was no procedure (see Chapter 25). Other minor personal and medical decisions are taken by carers of necessity without any legal authority or are simply not taken at all. The absence of approved procedures causes problems and uncertainty throughout the whole range of personal decision-making.

Basis of decisions

There are two approaches to making a decision on behalf of an incapacitated person:

- *best interests* – that which the decision-maker considers is in the best interests of the individual;
- *substituted judgment* – that which the individual would have chosen if capable of making the decision.

Both present problems, the former because it denies individuality and poses the risk of the decision-maker imposing his or her view as to what is best, and the latter because in many cases it cannot be conjectured what the individual would have wished. The Law Commission has proposed that a decision-maker should act in the best interests of the incapacitated person, taking into account:

- his or her ascertainable past and present wishes and feelings;
- the need to encourage and permit him or her to participate in any decision-making to the fullest extent to which he or she is capable; and
- the general principle that the course least restrictive of his or her freedom of decision and action is likely to be in his or her best interests.

See the Law Commission consultation papers and Government proposals summarised in Appendix 8.

SECTION B

Representing the Client

In this Section we consider how the solicitor may:

- take instructions from or on behalf of an elderly client whilst being supportive of any carers and dealing with other professionals;
- obtain information relating to the client;
- challenge decisions of the authorities which affect the client; and
- act on the client's behalf in legal proceedings where the client is incapable of dealing with his affairs.

> In all these circumstances the solicitor should ensure that he is acting on the instructions of the client or, if these cannot be obtained because the client lacks capacity to give instructions, that he is acting in the best interests of the client.

Chapter 3

Instructions

3.1 CLIENT

It is of prime importance to:

- identify who the client is (this may not be the person who first approaches you, e.g. a relative or carer);
- take instructions from and advise that client (or confirm the advice and instructions personally with the client if you have initially acted through an intermediary);
- ensure that the client can give instructions freely and is not under the influence of another person (this usually involves seeing the client alone);
- ascertain that the client is mentally capable of giving instructions – see Chapter 2 (if not you must seek to act in the client's best interests);
- identify potential conflicts of interest at an early stage (if appropriate recommend independent legal advice either for the would-be elderly client or for the relatives or carers).

> Act on the instructions of the client or, where the client is incapacitated and instructions are given under lawful authority by someone else, act nevertheless in the best interests of the client.

Communication

A reasoning mind may be locked inside a body that lacks the ability to communicate in a normal manner. In these circumstances:

- the identity of the client does not change merely because of communication difficulties;
- use an interpreter when necessary, and not only when the client talks a foreign language – versions of English can be difficult for some to follow;
- every effort should be made to overcome communication problems:
  - use physical aids where these may assist
  - consider whether a simple response to questions should be accepted, e.g. movement of a finger, a raised eyebrow
  - take care to frame questions so that you do not have control over the outcome

- consider whether the client has received, retained and understood sufficient information on the basis of which to make a reasoned decision
- be aware of potential conflicts of interest – these arise within families as well as having to be faced by lawyers;
- consider whether a medical report (with the client's consent) is appropriate to avoid later allegations of lack of capacity.

> Do not place total reliance upon relatives or carers in identifying the wishes of the client especially where these persons may be affected by the outcome of any decision.

Interviewing techniques

A different technique is required when interviewing clients who are mentally frail or otherwise vulnerable. In general:

- speak slowly, using simple words and sentences;
- avoid 'yes/no' answers and questions suggesting the answer or containing a choice of answers which may not include the correct one;
- do not keep repeating questions as this may suggest that you do not believe the answers and encourages a change. But the same question may be asked at a later stage to check that consistent answers are being given;
- do not move to new topics without explanation (e.g. 'can we now talk about');
- do not ask abstract questions (e.g. 'was it after 9.00 am' – instead ask 'was it after breakfast');
- allow the witness to tell his or her story and do not simply ignore information which does not fit in with your assumptions;
- do not go on too long without a break.

Assessment of capacity

Doubts as to the mental capacity of the client may arise for many reasons:

- the client's circumstances (e.g. in a nursing home);
- what you have been told in advance (e.g. by family, nurses or doctors);
- your own observations (e.g. how the client looks and behaves);
- what the client says (e.g. a widow insists that her husband is still alive);
- the outcome of the client's decisions (e.g. to do impossible things);
- previous knowledge of the client.

Chapter 3 INSTRUCTIONS

Approach

Take the trouble to investigate any of these indications because they could be misleading. Spend enough time with the client to form a considered view. Much of the guidance that follows may be seen as 'best practice' and what can actually be done may be limited by time factors and costs, but once you are involved your professional duty to the client must be an overriding factor in all circumstances. Remember that:

- different tests apply for different purposes so apply the appropriate test;
- capacity is a question of fact and your opinion may be as good as that of others;
- the conclusion should be reached 'on balance of probabilities' – you do not need to be satisfied beyond reasonable doubt;
- there is a presumption of capacity if the client has not previously been found to be incapable;
- carers (lay or professional) may have had more experience than you, so be wary if your conclusions are seriously at variance with theirs;
- be alert to any conflict of interest when others are expressing their view.

Timing

The assessment of capacity must not only be made on the basis of the appropriate test, but also at the correct time. It is not conclusive that the client may have been capable the previous day or on the following day, and a client who is generally incapable may have a lucid interval so an adverse medical report at another date is not always conclusive.

Capacity is (usually) required when a document is signed so when appropriate:

- have a doctor (or trained nurse) witness the document rather than (or in addition to) providing a report a week beforehand;
- consider asking any medical witness to go through the recognised capacity tests set by the BMA if appropriate;
- (if need be) obtain a medical statement at the time of witnessing the document.

Techniques

How and when you see the client may be important. It is suggested that you first chat about matters other than the business that you intend to carry out. It is helpful to know from other sources something of the family background and client's career so that you can verify the client's recollection. Also ask a few questions about current affairs and past events. Then:

- see the client again if there remain doubts as to capacity because first impressions can be misleading (either way) and you may have called at a time when the client could not concentrate for some reason:
  - at a subsequent interview seek to discuss some of the same matters and see if there is consistency in what the client says
  - seek detailed instructions again – if they are materially different there is a good chance that the client is not legally competent
- do not rely upon the views of other persons without question, however well qualified they may seem:
  - they may have applied the wrong legal criteria
  - they may be influenced by a personal interest in the outcome
- involve the client's GP, hospital staff or carers (see para. 3.3);
- if satisfied about capacity confirm instructions in writing and consider asking the client to sign a duplicate letter as confirmation.

> Try to see the client at such time of the day as is best for the client and in the most favourable circumstances. Remember that you are testing the client's understanding of the decision to be made, not whether you agree with this or whether the client could make other decisions.

Previous solicitor

When introduced to a new client who is elderly, ascertain if another solicitor has previously acted and seek the client's permission to enquire of that solicitor whether there is anything that you ought to know. Be cautious if such permission is not forthcoming without an adequate explanation, especially if a member of the family or carer discourages such contact. The former solicitor may have more information than you or may have declined, on grounds of capacity, to take the step that you are now being asked to take and, whilst you are not bound by his view, it is likely to be influential in your own assessment.

> Another solicitor may have known and acted for the client for many years and the family may now be diverting the client to you in order to by-pass advice which is inconvenient to them but in the best interests of the client.

Lawyer's role

The elderly individual is entitled to an independent lawyer prepared to listen to and communicate with the client however much patience this requires. A lawyer may need to act as a 'whistle blower' when neglect or abuse is perceived. Note that:

- instructions will often be given by a son, daughter or carer but conflict of

interest situations do arise and the golden rule is to ask 'Who is my client?':
- the lawyer must act on the instructions of the client or, when these are given on behalf of the client, in the best interests of that client
- a balancing act will often be necessary, but the elderly client's views and wishes must be respected even if they cannot always be followed

- this overriding duty to the client applies even if you are taking instructions from a receiver or attorney:
  - when appropriate you should advise such 'agent' that he may not be acting in the best interests of the 'principal'
  - you should decline to act on the instructions of the 'agent' if you conclude that these are not in the best interests of the 'principal'
  - if necessary you should refer the circumstances to the Court of Protection (because you should not abandon the client at that stage)
  - the duty of care to the intended receiver is replaced by a duty of care to the patient once the First General Order is made – Court of Protection Practice Direction *Authority to Solicitors to act for Patients or Donors* 9 August 1995

Oaths

When administering oaths or declarations you have a duty to ascertain that:

- you are dealing with the correct deponent (enquire as to the name and check the handwriting where possible);
- the deponent knows that he is to be sworn or declared by you to the truth of the statement;
- any exhibits are those referred to;
- the deponent is *competent to depose* to the affidavit or declaration.

> See the *Law Society Guide to Oaths and Affirmations* and also *The Guide to the Professional Conduct of Solicitors 1999* published by Law Society, Principle 18.06.

Termination of retainer

You must not terminate your retainer with an existing client except for good reason and upon reasonable notice. Such retainer terminates by operation of law at the onset of the incapacity of the client, but this is when the client most needs your services so you should consult the relatives and, if appropriate, take steps to ensure that the client's affairs will continue to be dealt with in a proper manner. You may not always be paid for this, but further work will usually result and it is likely that you will act for the receiver (if appointed).

3.2 CARERS

The statutory definition of *carer* found in section 8 of the Disabled Persons (Services, Consultation and Representation) Act 1986, is set out in the box below. In practice the expression does not have so restricted a meaning and includes:

- *informal carers*, e.g. family or friends providing personal care or supervision full time or merely on a casual basis;
- *professional carers*, e.g. care workers, social workers, community nurses.

> 'A person who provides a substantial amount of care on a regular basis for a disabled person living at home.'

Status

Personal carers and family tend to find informal ways of dealing with situations as they arise but may need to ascertain their right to make decisions on behalf of the person cared for:

- family relationship by itself does not confer any legal rights. In practice next of kin will be consulted although this may (wrongly) be in preference to a person who has (or had prior to incapacity) a far closer relationship with the individual (e.g. a cohabitee or partner);
- in so far as the carer has any legal status this can only be based upon agreement with the person cared for, either express or implied. Often the *de facto* relationship is the only evidence of this but the significant point is whether the relationship is recognised by others.

> The role of carers is reinforced by the *Carers (Recognition and Services) Act 1995* and related Policy Guidelines. This applies whether or not the carer is related to the individual.

Consulting carers

It is usually helpful, where the client is (or is becoming) mentally incapable, to develop a dialogue with those responsible for the day-to-day care or supervision of the client. It is also desirable to establish a link with the family or next of kin. Useful information can be obtained in this way, but be careful not to be unduly influenced by their views and to retain your professional independence:

- the views of carers may alert you to problems and limitations, and will be of assistance if you need to consider the extent to which your client is dependent upon others because you will seldom receive a realistic assessment from the client;

- you should still form your own view, taking into account all the available evidence, because carers in particular may be influenced by other factors and cannot be assumed to be acting in the best interests of your client.

> As the client's solicitor you represent one of the safeguards against abuse (see Chapter 16 at para. 16.5).

Caring for carers

Do not assume that informal carers have chosen this role. They are often *involuntary* carers needing encouragement and support because they:

- have a severely restricted lifestyle;
- face substantial costs of caring and loss of personal income;
- feel a mixture of emotions including inadequacy, frustration, resentment, embarrassment and guilt that they are not doing enough;
- need recognition, reassurance and information;
- need practical help in the form of services, financial support and respite care;
- may not always wish to take responsibility for the type of decisions that are often referred to them.

A duty is imposed on the local authority to take into account the ability of the carer to continue to provide care when deciding what services should be provided.

> See *Carers (Recognition and Services) Act 1995* and related Policy Guidelines. For more information on community care see Chapters 21 and 22.

3.3 PROFESSIONALS

When acting for elderly clients you must be prepared to develop relationships with other professionals in the interests of your clients. Often these professionals will already be involved with your client, but on occasions you will take the initiative by seeking their involvement. If possible seek the consent and authority of your client to discuss matters with other professionals – some professionals will refuse to disclose information without such authority.

Medical practitioner

Whilst a doctor does not decide whether a person is legally competent, when there are doubts or the client appears to have medical needs it is valuable to contact the client's own doctor (with the client's permission where appropriate) because that doctor may:

- have significant views and alert you to the possibility that the client may be confused;
- have records of past treatment or symptoms which support a particular view;
- provide a diagnosis of a condition which either produces odd behaviour without there being impairment of reason or affects reason without this being apparent;
- provide a prognosis as to whether any such condition is likely to be temporary or permanent, worsening or improving, changing rapidly or slowly.

Where the client is (or has recently been) in hospital, it will usually be best to refer to the psychogeriatrician or geriatrician who is the client's consultant. Solicitors who fail to look for or disregard the signposts put up by doctors who have treated their clients proceed at their peril!

> See *Assessment of Mental Capacity: Guidance for Doctors and Lawyers* published jointly by the Law Society and BMA (1995).

Reports

Lawyers tend to rely upon the medical profession to express opinions about mental capacity but doctors are not taught the legal definitions and are seldom aware of the legal distinctions between different types of decision-making. In situations where doubt exists as to the capacity of a client to sign a document or take some step it is wise to obtain a medical report. When seeking a report remember that:

- you are not concerned with diagnosing a condition, but judging the effect of the condition upon the individual;
- you must identify why you have asked the question (e.g. can the individual get married or sign a will) and then spell out the appropriate legal test and provide all relevant information;
- it is helpful for the doctor to know whether a finding of incapacity in this instance would take away the freedom of the individual or prevent others from abusing him, as the doctor may be influenced by his perceptions;
- in a contested case much may depend upon the medical evidence, but capacity is a question of fact so a medical opinion is merely part of the evidence and is not conclusive;
- if you witness a signature you should satisfy yourself of the signatory's capacity at the time even if you are relying on a recent medical report.

If the doctor finds it difficult to accept that different legal tests apply for different types of decision a certificate in the form set out below may be offered:

Chapter 3 INSTRUCTIONS

'I ...... of .... hereby certify that ...... of .... who signed .... in my presence fully understood the nature and effect of the document he (she) was signing. In giving this certificate I offer no further opinion with regard to the mental capacity of the said ......'

See *Elderly Clients: A Precedent Manual* by Denzil Lush (Jordans 1996).

Nurses and professional carers

Do not overlook the fact that these are the people who will be in closest day-to-day contact with your client and they may have considerable experience. They can provide valuable information and their views may be relevant although they may not be able to give expert evidence.

Social workers

Social workers are employed by the local authority social services department. They have clients whose welfare and interests they look after by providing support, guidance and advice, and an introduction to services. Note that:

- they also have a statutory role and may need to use their powers to protect the client;
- some social workers have special knowledge, training and responsibilities;
- there are *approved social workers* under the Mental Health Act 1983 with certain statutory powers (see Chapter 26 at para. 26.1).

The social services department now has the key role in the delivery of community care. If your client becomes unable to cope and does not have the necessary support within the family you should take the initiative by contacting the social services department for the area where the client lives and asking for an assessment of welfare and community care services (see Chapter 22). Consent of the client is advisable where possible if you are not the attorney or receiver (or acting on instructions from such person).

Accountants, stockbrokers, etc.

Your client may have used the services of various firms before becoming incapable of instructing them personally and you may now have taken on the role of co-ordinating the management of the client's affairs. It would be inappropriate to disregard these firms unless there were good reason to do so in the client's best interests, not your own:

- it would not be sufficient that you could more conveniently deal with a firm that you usually employ or would receive more commission from such a firm;

PART 1: SECTION B   Representing the Client

- the client's own professional advisers may have considerable knowledge of the client's affairs and preferences, and this represents part of the resources that you can draw upon.

The reality may be that your client has never taken the professional advice that his circumstances require. Whether or not the client is capable, it may be appropriate for you to be involved in the choice of suitable firms to provide services, or provide them yourself if you have resources and expertise to do so:

- work with other professional firms as part of a team acting in the mutual client's best interests:
    - do not see yourself as being in competition with these other firms
    - ensure that you obtain their advice when appropriate
- remember that any action taken may at a later date be challenged by some interested person or by an actual or potential beneficiary after the client's death:
    - keep adequate records and notes of your interviews, telephone attendances and deliberations
    - where advice is given by other professionals which is to be acted upon ensure that it is confirmed by them in writing
- advise your client wherever possible and appropriate to notify members of the family of your involvement and that of other firms:
    - this may be done by a suitable letter retained with the will or enduring power of attorney (EPA)
    - it is usually preferable for the client to inform the family personally
    - if the client is incapable you may wish to ensure that the family knows who is providing advice

> Ensure that any adviser is suitably qualified to give advice appropriate to the needs of the older client and receives all information necessary to do so.

Chapter 4

Information

4.1 SOURCES

Client

Clearly the first source of information is the client from whom instructions are obtained, but be prepared to verify any such information if the client is mentally frail or there is doubt about mental capacity. You will need the client's authority to do this unless the client already lacks capacity in which event it would be wise to explain to those through whom you obtain instructions that corroboration of information may be needed. You may wish to inspect documents when these are significant rather than relying upon the client's interpretation. Where circumstances justify this, a visit to the client's home greatly assists in forming a view about memory and understanding.

Couples

When acting for a couple (now usually referred to as partners) it is essential to see them both at some stage if only to confirm the extent to which one is authorised to give instructions on behalf of both:

- always take care when dealing with elderly couples if you do not know the family background. Ascertain whether they are actually married, it was a recent marriage and either party has previously been married with a family. Be particularly sensitive to long-term cohabitees whether in heterosexual or same sex partnerships;
- be cautious about allowing one partner to obtain the signature of the other on important documents – it is better to see both clients yourself. It may be necessary for each party to be independently advised.

For further information on assessment of capacity see Chapter 2 and on communicating with the client see Chapter 3.

Carers and family

When the client is no longer living an independent life it can be helpful to talk to care workers, nurses, etc., as well as other members of the family, sometimes in the presence of the client. If doubts arise as to the extent that you have implied authority to do this you should clarify your intentions with the client at

29

an early stage. It is desirable to explain the nature of your professional involvement to such persons and give them your name, address and telephone number. Do not omit to check whether anyone else in your practice has acted for the client and whether they have any insights that might help.

Background information and corroboration of essential information can be obtained from these sources; such contact also assists in ascertaining the level of dependence of the client upon other people and services and forming a preliminary view as to the capacity of the client

> For the status and needs of carers see Chapter 3.

Financial bodies

With the authority of the client when capable, or otherwise where possible, useful information or confirmation about the client's financial position can often be obtained from:

- the client's bank, as to balances and documents held in safe custody;
- the Inland Revenue, simply by requesting a copy of the last tax return or repayment claim;
- the client's accountant or tax adviser (if there is one);
- the client's stockbroker or insurance broker (if there is one);
- any trustees making regular payments to the client from some family trust.

Care authorities

Good contacts at a personal level with those involved in the health authority and social services and housing departments for the area where you practise are invaluable:

- in ascertaining any involvement they have previously had with the client;
- if you need to assist in arranging services for the client;
- in avoiding or resolving disputes about service provision or charges;
- in building up your elderly client practice (they increasingly refer clients with resources to independent lawyers).

Although you may not normally deal with these matters, if your client has personal wealth your brief could extend to seeing if you can improve the personal circumstances of the client or reduce the cost to the client. You should become familiar with:

- the range of services and care provision available in the private and public

sectors and the criteria for obtaining those services;
- the authority and department responsible for providing the service and the officials who actually make the decisions.

> For procedures for challenging decisions of the authorities see Chapter 5.

4.2 FREEDOM OF INFORMATION

Code of Practice

A *Code of Practice on Access to Government Information* was introduced in 1994 as part of the *Citizen's Charter* initiative. It covers bodies under the jurisdiction of the Parliamentary Commissioner for Administration (see Chapter 5 at para. 5.3) to whom a complaint may be made if it is not observed, but other recognised government bodies are also expected to comply. This national Code will override any versions produced by individual organisations.

The Code is accompanied by guidance which provides that:

- there is an assumption that information should be released except where disclosure would not be in the public interest;
- reasons should be given for administrative decisions except when there is statutory authority or established convention to the contrary;
- internal procedures, guidance and manuals should be published except where this could prejudice any matter which should be kept confidential (a wide range of internal manuals has since been released by the Benefits Agency).

Requests under the Code referring to it should be made by letter to the source of the information. There is a target response time of 20 days, and although fees can be charged for individual information it may not be reasonable to charge for documents that should be published.

> The *Code of Practice* is available free from Freedom of Information Unit, The Cabinet Office, Room 65d/1, Horse Guards Road, London SW1P 3AL or on the website: **http://www.open.gov.uk/m-of-g/codete.htm**

Legislation

The following statutes already give individuals the personal right to inspect information held about them and a draft Freedom of Information Bill was published on 24 May 1999 for public consultation so more extensive provision is likely.

PART 1: SECTION B   Representing the Client

Data Protection Acts 1984 and 1998

Under the 1984 Act individuals have the right to see most information stored about themselves on a computer. There is a right to have incorrect or misleading information corrected or erased and provision for compensation, but certain types of data are exempt. A *Data Protection Registrar* keeps a Register of computer users who hold personal information, and fees for subject access are set by regulations.

Further provision must be made to comply with the EU Data Protection Directive (95/46/EC) which came into effect in the UK on 24 October 1998. When the 1998 Act is fully brought into force on 1 March 2000 it will replace the 1984 Act and extend the definition of data to information recorded as part of a 'relevant filing system' (as defined). This will include some forms of manual data previously excluded from the data protection regime. More guidance for data controllers is expected from the Registrar.

> See *An Introduction to the Data Protection Act 1998* available from the Data Protection Registrar and also, with other documents, on the website:
> **http://www.open.gov.uk/dpr/dprhome.htm**

Access to Personal Files Act 1987

The extensive information held by local authorities on individuals can contain serious inaccuracies, yet it may be crucial in determining the authority's policy towards an individual. This Act enables ministers to make regulations giving people a right of access to information about themselves on manually held local authority records:

- the *Access to Personal Files (Social Services) Regulations 1989* relate to manually held social services files;

- the *Access to Personal Files (Housing) Regulations 1989* relate to manually held housing files;

- procedures are stipulated in the regulations:
    - the request must be in writing and a fee of up to £10 paid
    - information must be supplied within the specified time and be that held at the time the request is made
    - the individual may require inaccurate information to be rectified or erased, or to have a note placed with it stating that he considers it to be inaccurate
    - some information may be exempt from disclosure
    - there are internal review procedures (with further challenge by judicial review)

Access to Medical Reports Act 1988

People have a right, in respect of a medical report about them prepared after

Chapter 4 INFORMATION

January 1989 for an employer or insurance company, to see the report before it is sent and for six months afterwards and to ask for corrections to be made:

- before applying for a report the employer or insurer must obtain the individual's written consent and inform him of these rights;
- a doctor can withhold information about any third party or which is likely to cause serious harm to the individual.

Access to Health Records Act 1990

People are allowed to see and copy information which has been manually recorded on their health records (as defined) since November 1991. This includes health records in the private sector (e.g. private nursing homes) as well as the NHS. The Act provides that:

- information which in the record holder's opinion is likely to cause serious harm to the physical or mental health of the patient or someone else need not be disclosed;
- a person who believes that part of a record is incorrect, misleading or incomplete can apply for it to be corrected;
- where the patient is incapable of managing his own affairs, any person appointed by a court to manage those affairs may apply;
- there is an internal complaints procedure but if still dissatisfied an application may be made to the court to order compliance.

Local government

A member of the public has the right to attend any meeting of the council or a committee (or sub-committee) unless the council has exercised its power to exclude the public from all or part of the meeting, which it may only do for certain reasons.

Local Government (Access to Information) Act 1985

This Act extends the right of members of the public to information from and about local government:

- see Part VA, sections 100A–100K of the Local Government Act 1972, as inserted by the 1985 Act;
- certain categories of information are exempt from disclosure – see the 1985 Act and Part I of Schedule 12A to the 1972 Act.

> You can inspect the registers of councillors, committees and delegated decision-making powers, and should be able to obtain copies of agendas, minutes, reports discussed at meetings, background papers, etc.

Mentally incapacitated persons

The right to apply for information is given to the individual about whom the information is held, and there is no provision for another person to apply on the individual's behalf. This causes problems when the individual lacks mental capacity, yet it is precisely in that situation that information is likely to exist and be needed by those seeking to make arrangements for care or support. The difficulty lies in identifying those who have a legitimate interest in obtaining the information – the right to confidentiality does not lapse by reason of lack of competence and family or carers might have an ulterior motive for seeking information.

The *Access to Health Records Act 1990* allows access to the medical records of a patient by other persons including 'any person appointed by a court to manage [the] affairs [of the patient]' (section 3(1)). This means a receiver appointed by the Court of Protection (not an attorney under a registered enduring power), yet a receiver will only be appointed where the financial affairs justify this. Accordingly this provision is not adequate to deal with most normal situations.

A solution has yet to be found, and it is probably better to approach this on the basis of when confidential information should be disclosed rather than who has a right to receive it. Carers or next of kin can always ask for information from the health or social services authority and, although there may be no statutory obligation to provide this, the authority may recognise that it is in the best interests of the individual to do so. Policies on disclosure of information should cover this. A climate of mutual co-operation is usually preferable to undue reliance upon legal rights. But there remain situations where information is withheld with no effective remedy in the case of mentally incapacitated persons.

Chapter 5

Challenging the Authorities

5.1 GENERAL

There are many situations in which you may need to help an older client challenge a decision made by the authorities, or even a failure to make a decision. The emphasis in this Chapter is upon the provision of services by the local authority, but the following are examples of other situations in which older clients may seek your assistance:

- appeals against decisions of the Benefits Agency on claims for state benefits – see Chapter 18;
- appeals against decisions of local authorities on claims for housing benefit or council tax rebate – see Chapter 19;
- appeals against decisions of Valuation Officers on council tax banding – see Chapter 15;
- refusals of planning permission – see generally the appeal procedures under the Town and Country Planning Acts;
- compulsory purchase and compensation relating to highway development;
- decisions relating to registration of residential care homes or private nursing homes – see Chapter 23;
- decisions on health care or medical treatment – see Chapters 24, 25 and 26.

For the provision of community care services see Chapter 22.

When acting for a client in dealings with the authorities, do not be too quick to use your letterheading as this can be counter-productive. It may result in a premature reference to the legal department. Assist the client to write a well reasoned letter and then monitor progress. Advising the client in the background is not a sign of weakness and may be effective in clarifying the approach of the authority before seeking to challenge this when necessary.

5.2 ENTITLEMENT TO SERVICES

Assessments and case conferences are part of the procedure for the provision of services. Delay and indecision by the authority may be used to avoid provision when shortage of funds or lack of facilities make it difficult to fulfil a request.

When dissatisfied follow this initial checklist:

- has a decision been made by the relevant authority?
- is it a request which the authority is obliged to consider? The statutory duties of the authority may be general in nature and not enforceable in respect of an individual;
- identify the authority, department and officer responsible for providing the services required and complain to this officer;
- ask for a review of a decision and be prepared to compromise;
- follow any complaints or appeal procedure;
- check the time-limits for taking any other available legal action;
- should the minister be asked to use his default powers?
- is it a case for judicial review?
- is it *maladministration* which can be referred to an Ombudsman?
- reference to the European Court of Human Rights?

Structure of local authorities

There are three tiers of local government:

1 county, metropolitan district and Greater London borough councils – generally responsible for provision of services to elderly persons through their social services departments;

2 district (or borough) councils – responsible for housing and environmental health;

3 parish (or town) councils – responsible for local issues.

The powers of councils are generally delegated: elected councillors are collectively responsible for policy decisions, officers are appointed to carry out policy decisions but have delegated powers, and administration is divided into departments each headed by a senior officer.

Departments

- *Housing* – deals with provision of housing (including homeless persons);
- *Environmental Health* – covers public health and the environment;
- *Social Services* – responsibilities include welfare of the elderly:
  - local authorities must establish a Social Services Committee which appoints a Director of Social Services and employs social workers
  - see Local Authority Social Services Act 1970, s 2, and see Local Government Act 1972, s 101(8)

Chapter 5   CHALLENGING THE AUTHORITIES

Complaints procedures

In many instances internal complaints procedures are available and you should be given information about these on enquiry. Any complaint must be in the appropriate form to the right person, but whether or not there is a formal procedure you may make representations to elected councillors, the chief executive or head of department. Most local authorities now have *service charters* advising of their standards and complaints procedures.

Social Services

Local authorities must establish and publicise the existence of a procedure for considering any representations or complaints with respect to the discharge of their social services functions or the failure to discharge those functions. This must provide:

- a definition of a complaint and identify who can bring a complaint;
- for the role of the *independent person*;
- support for persons who need assistance in bringing a complaint.

> See Chapter 22 at para. 22.4 for further details of social services complaints procedures.

Health Service

For the complaints procedures available in respect of health care see Chapter 24.

Appeal procedures

If not satisfied with a decision always enquire if there is a formal appeal procedure and if so the time-limits for invoking this. The decision-making authority will be under an obligation to tell you if there is a procedure. There is no appeal against financial assessment for community care.

5.3   OMBUDSMEN

Ombudsmen are independent people who investigate and report on complaints by UK residents about treatment by particular public bodies. The complainant must have suffered injustice and the matters complained of must amount to *maladministration* – see box.

Key points

- there is generally a 12-month time-limit:
  - before a complaint can be investigated all existing means of seeking redress

PART 1: SECTION B   Representing the Client

   must first be exhausted
  - matters before the courts cannot be investigated
- the complaint is normally made by the person who claims to have suffered injustice:
  - where he is for any reason unable to act for himself it may usually be made by a member of his family or some body or individual suitable to represent him
  - legal representation is not usually necessary but a solicitor may be able to assist in presenting the complaint
- the procedure is usually private but the resulting report may be published
- findings are not legally enforceable but the report may:
  - result in redress where there is no legal remedy, e.g. compensation or apology
  - discourage similar administrative action in the future

Maladministration includes: delay, incompetence and neglect, discourtesy and harassment, bias and unfair discrimination.

Parliamentary Commissioner for Administration

The Commissioner is someone completely independent of the government who can investigate complaints by members of the public about the way they have been treated by government departments and agencies:

- these include the Departments of Social Security, Transport, Environment and Employment and the Lord Chancellor's Department:
  - also certain non-departmental public bodies such as Inland Revenue, Legal Aid Board, Data Protection Registrar, Commission for Racial Equality – the list was extended in March 1999
  - most complaints relate to the DSS and in particular the Benefits Agency
  - complaints about government policy or the content of legislation are not included but are matters for Parliament
- complaints must be channelled through an MP who will usually seek to sort the matter out with the department concerned first:
  - the Commissioner decides whether to carry out a full investigation
  - he may inspect government files and papers and can summon anyone to give evidence in an investigation

Commissioners for Local Administration

These Local Ombudsmen deal with complaints by anyone who considers that he has suffered injustice because of maladministration by a local authority:

- does not include a parish council or certain other authorities (e.g. police authorities);
- if the complaint passes initial screening it will be taken up in correspondence but there is power to examine the authority's internal papers and to take written and oral evidence from anyone who can provide relevant information.

> See Local Government Act 1974, s 27.

Health Service Commissioner

The Health Service Commissioner is an independent person who investigates certain types of complaint about the NHS which cannot otherwise be resolved:

- he cannot investigate complaints about independent practitioners or matters of clinical judgment;
- the complaint may relate to failure to provide or the provision of a service, or maladministration and may be about attitude as well as actions of staff.

5.4 LEGAL REMEDIES

When negotiation and persuasion, and the use of complaints procedures when available, do not result in the needs of the client being met it becomes necessary to consider the legal remedies that are available. There may be a choice of remedies but equally none may offer the certainty of positive results within an acceptable time-scale. Nevertheless the threat to use one of these remedies or the taking of the initial steps may be sufficient to draw a response and create a further climate for negotiation.

Complaint to the minister

Many statutes vest supervisory powers in government ministers and Codes of Guidance are issued by the government department. Some statutes giving powers to or imposing duties on local authorities authorise the minister to make regulations prescribing how they shall exercise or perform these. A complaint may be made direct to a minister if the authority does not comply with his directions and he may exercise default powers, although these are appropriate to deal with a general breakdown in some service provision rather than individual cases:

- the minister may call the authority to account for failure to exercise its functions, direct the authority to comply and take over the authority's functions, e.g.

- National Assistance Act 1948, s 36
- Mental Health Act 1983, s 124
- National Health Service Act 1977, s 85

- there is a power for the Secretary of State to declare local authorities in default if they fail to comply with their social services duties, to direct compliance within time-limits and to enforce this by judicial review (*mandamus*):
  - Local Authority Social Services Act 1970, s 7D (inserted by National Health Service and Community Care Act 1990, s 50)

Breach of statutory duty

In certain limited situations an action may be brought for breach of statutory duty but it is necessary to ask the following preliminary questions:

- does the statute impose a duty or merely confer a power?
- if the former, is this merely a general duty or is it a specific duty towards the particular individual?

> The trend is against the routine imposition of liability on local authorities where their acts or omissions have caused loss to individuals.

There have been many appeal cases in recent years and it is difficult to discern a consistent approach but the following principles appear to be established:

- policy considerations may make a claim for breach of statutory duty non-justiciable and it is generally necessary to show that the negligence was such that it would give rise to a cause of action at common law apart from the statute;
- the courts will not allow individuals to bring actions for breach of statutory duty unless the legislation expressly or by implication makes this possible:
  - where an authority fails to discharge its general functions the remedy is to ask the Secretary of State to exercise his default powers and an action for breach of statutory duty is not appropriate – see *Wyatt v Hillingdon London Borough Council* 76 LGR 727
  - there must be a public law duty to act (rather than merely a discretion or power) and exceptional circumstances for holding that the policy of the statute requires compensation to be paid to persons who suffer because the power was not exercised – *Stovin v Wise (Norfolk County Council)* [1996] 3 All ER 801, HL (failure by highway authority to modify a dangerous junction where the claimant had an accident)
  - if an authority fails in an irrational manner to carry out its statutory duty (or exercise a power?) a breach of a common law duty of care may possibly arise

Chapter 5 CHALLENGING THE AUTHORITIES

- the careless performance of a statutory duty does not, by itself, result in liability, and it is necessary to show that the circumstances would give rise to a duty of care (at common law):
  - the decision had to extend beyond policy matters and be so unreasonable that it fell outside the ambit of the statutory discretion imposed on the authority – *X v Bedfordshire County Council* [1995] AC 633, HL (no liability for failure to take action to prevent the continuing abuse of children)
  - where there has been an assumption of responsibility by an officer to act carefully but he acts beyond his statutory powers to the detriment of the individual, a claim may arise – *Welton v North Cornwall District Council* (1996) Times, 19 July, CA (environmental health officer imposing expensive and unnecessary requirements under threat of closure; had this merely been a report by the officer with a view to the authority taking action it would probably not have been actionable)
- see also the notes on negligence (below) because failure to exercise a statutory duty at all or in a proper manner may (in limited circumstances as indicated above) amount to a breach of the common law duty of care:
  - it is suggested that where an authority in the exercise of its statutory powers acknowledges that it will make provision and then fails without reasonable excuse to do so to the detriment of an individual, an action for breach of statutory duty may possibly lie at the instance of that individual

> A local authority may also be liable to an elderly client in tort or contract under normal legal principles.

Tort

In the absence of express statutory authority a local authority is liable for torts in the same way as an individual. Damages may be claimed in negligence based upon breach of a common law duty of care although breach of a statutory duty may be pleaded in the alternative (see above):

- even if there is no duty to provide a service (e.g. where there is merely a general duty or a power) there may be a common law duty of care in the manner in which it is carried out:
  - this may possibly extend to administrative or operational failure to provide or in the provision of an agreed service – see *Barrett v Enfield London Borough Council* [1997] 2 FLR 167, CA
  - the negligent manner in which a public authority carried out its statutory duty could give rise to liability where it created the danger which caused the injury – *Capital and Counties Plc v Hampshire County Council* (1997) Times, 20 March, CA (negligence by fire brigade which owed a duty of care when it turned off a sprinkler system)

- there is no public policy reason why an authority may not be vicariously liable for the acts of a social worker who fails to provide significant information to foster parents – *W v Essex County Council and Goulden* (1997) Times, 16 July (they were not told that the foster child was an active sexual abuser and their own children were abused)
  - an authority will not be vicariously liable for an independent act by an employee outside the course of employment – *T v North Yorkshire County Council* (1998) Times, 10 September, CA (sexual abuse by a teacher of a mentally disabled schoolboy in his care)

Breach of contract

If a promise has been made it may be enforceable as such against the authority:

- this may possibly extend to the provision of agreed services for which a payment is made by the recipient;
- consider the Supply of Goods and Services Act 1982.

Small claims procedure

Do not overlook the possibility of assisting the client with a claim in the county court where operational failings by a service provider (including a local authority) have resulted in financial loss to an elderly client or carer. An example is repeated failure to provide agreed transport to a day care centre resulting in expenditure on taxis so that the carer can meet other commitments. Under the above principles there remains some prospect of success, and the threat of a claim or the issue of proceedings may in itself be sufficient to persuade the care provider to be more careful in the future. Repeat claims could be brought if there was a continuing failure.

If the claim is under £5,000 (£1,000 for a personal injury or housing disrepair claim) it may be allocated to the *Small Claims Track* thus providing many advantages to the claimant:

- there is generally no award of legal costs (so no risk of costs) although the court fees and reasonable expenses of attending the hearing may be recovered;
- whilst you may assist with the preparation of the case your client should be able to cope at the hearing itself if funds are limited:
  - the hearing is relatively informal and before a district judge
  - the district judge without 'entering the arena' must seek to make good the deficiencies of an unrepresented party;
  - a lay representative (e.g. a relative or friend) will be permitted
- if legal aid is not available resist any application that the case should not be allocated to the Small Claims Track by arguing that:

Chapter 5 CHALLENGING THE AUTHORITIES

- there is no difficult issue of law or exceptional complexity in the facts
- the client cannot afford legal representation whereas the local authority has the resources of its legal department
- the client could not pursue the claim if faced with an open court trial and the risk of costs

See Civil Procedure Rules 1998, Part 27 and the Practice Direction thereto. For civil proceedings involving infirm or disabled elderly persons see Chapter 6.

Judicial review

The High Court may review the legality of a course of action by a public body and provide one or more of the following remedies in a final order:

- *mandamus* – to require the performance of a specific public law duty;
- *certiorari* – to quash a decision which is invalid;
- *prohibition* – to prohibit the body from acting in an unlawful manner;
- *declaration* – to declare what the law is.

A typical order might be *certiorari* to quash an unlawful decision and *mandamus* to require a new decision according to the law. As an interim measure the Court may grant an injunction (which may be of a mandatory nature).

Relief is available where the decisions of public bodies (and also inferior courts and tribunals) are unlawful, which includes:

- *ultra vires* (i.e. outside the powers of the body making it);
- contrary to the rules of natural justice;
- made in a way that is procedurally incorrect;
- based on a misinterpretation of the law;
- unreasonable or irrational, e.g. a material consideration was not taken into account, or matters have been taken into account which ought not to have been.

The potential for judicial review has increased by reason of the obligation of authorities to assess the needs of individuals for community care services.

Supreme Court Act 1981, s 31;
RSC Ord 53 (in the Civil Procedure Rules 1998, Sched 1).

PART 1: SECTION B   Representing the Client

Procedure

The application must be made promptly and in any event within three months of the grounds arising unless time is extended by the court (e.g. because of the need to get legal aid):

- the applicant must first obtain leave to apply from a High Court judge:
  - this is on a written application made *ex parte* (Form 86A) with an affidavit in support setting out the decision to be challenged, the relief sought and the grounds for doing so
  - there may be a hearing especially if the matter is urgent, and a refused application may be renewed (ultimately to the Court of Appeal)
- if leave is granted:
  - the relevant papers are served on the respondent and other persons affected
  - affidavits are filed in response and these may be relied upon as evidence but oral evidence can be given
  - discovery may not be required and hearings are often short (an expedited hearing may be sought) usually consisting of oral argument on legal matters based on the affidavit evidence

Principles

The remedy is discretionary and rules have developed to define the circumstances in which the court will intervene:

- an applicant must have sufficient interest in the matter (*locus standi*):
  - this may include action groups in appropriate circumstances – see *R. v Secretary of State for Social Services, ex parte CPAG* [1989] 1 All ER 1047
- any alternative remedy should usually have been pursued first:
  - e.g. a complaints procedure though the need for interim relief could be relevant
  - the minister's default powers are not usually an alternative to judicial review
- the courts concern themselves with the decision-making process rather than the merits of the decision:
  - note the Wednesbury principle – *Associated Provincial Picture Houses Ltd v Wednesbury Corporation* [1948] 1 KB 223
- the court will not grant relief if it considers that there is no need or it would be administratively inconvenient or the applicant's conduct does not merit it:
  - lack of resources may prove an effective defence for a local authority in regard to its obligations to provide services (but will not necessarily be so)
- relief may be refused if, by reason of delay, there may be either substantial hardship or prejudice to another person or detriment to good administration.

5.5 EUROPEAN COURTS

Decisions of the European Courts are increasingly shaping our law and it may in extreme cases be necessary to turn to one of them for a remedy, especially in 'test case' situations.

European Court of Justice (ECJ)

This Court is based in Luxembourg and is the ultimate appeal court on matters relating to the *Treaty of the European Community*. Its decisions are binding upon our courts. It has 13 judges and six advocates-general, each appointed for a term of six years and all chosen by member states 'by common accord' based upon qualification for the highest judicial office. An advocate-general provides a written opinion with a recommendation at the end of the oral procedure and this is not binding but assists the judges who hand down a single judgment which may be a compromise because there is no provision for dissenting judgments.

The *Court of First Instance* handles certain cases including those brought against Community institutions by natural or legal persons. It is an inferior court with 12 judges and there is a right of appeal to the full court. There are no advocates-general but one of the judges may adopt this role.

Where an issue of Community law arises before a national court, questions of interpretation or validity can be referred to the ECJ for a preliminary ruling:

- the procedure is available to the national court rather than to the parties;
- it is the court which decides the question to be referred although a party may make the initial request for a reference;
- a legal aid certificate may be extended to cover the reference, but the ECJ may grant legal aid in special circumstances for 'the purpose of facilitating the representation or attendance of a party'.

The European Commission or another member state may bring an action against a member state for failure to fulfil its obligations under the Treaty and national governments are treated as responsible for the acts of local authorities and other public bodies. So instead of bringing a case in the local court an individual whose rights have been infringed by non-implementation of an EC Directive can complain to the Commission which can investigate and bring a case before the ECJ which can award damages to the individual.

European Court of Human Rights (ECHR)

Rights

The following substantive rights guaranteed by the *European Convention on Human Rights* may be of direct relevance to the older citizen, although these are subject to qualifications not mentioned here:

- *Article 2* – 'Everyone's right to life shall be protected by law':
  - this creates a positive obligation to safeguard life and can be relevant to the provision of medical treatment
- *Article 3* – 'No one shall be subjected to ... inhuman or degrading treatment':
  - this may be relevant to standards of care provision
- *Article 5* – 'Everyone has the right to liberty and security of person'. The 'lawful detention of ... persons of unsound mind' is allowed for but everyone who is deprived of his liberty by detention shall be entitled to have the lawfulness tested by a court and to compensation if it was unlawful:
  - this may be relevant in the fields of mental health and other care provision
- *Article 6* – 'In the determination of his civil rights and obligations ... everyone is entitled to a fair and public hearing within a reasonable time by an independent and impartial tribunal established by law':
  - this is relevant to access to justice for people with disabilities
- *Article 8* – 'Everyone has the right to the right to respect for his private and family life, his home and his correspondence':
  - this may prove relevant to standards in residential care and nursing homes as well as sheltered housing, but has far wider potential
- *Article 9* – 'Everyone has the right to freedom of thought, conscience and religion':
  - this right has to date received little scrutiny but may be infringed by procedures to protect an elderly person who is perceived to be vulnerable
- *Article 12* – the right to marry and found a family:
  - only the first part of this right is likely to be relevant to the older person but procedures for assessing capacity for marriage could be questioned
- *Article 1 First Protocol* – 'Every ... person is entitled to the peaceful enjoyment of his possessions':
  - it may be that the absence of accessible legal procedures for decision-making on behalf of those who lack capacity could lead to a breach of this right
- *Article 14* – 'The enjoyment of the rights and freedoms set forth in this Convention shall be secured without discrimination on any grounds such as sex, race ... religion ... property, birth or other status':
  - it has yet to be seen whether this opens the door to the requirement for legislation against age discrimination

Chapter 5 CHALLENGING THE AUTHORITIES

Procedure

An aggrieved person has been able make a direct complaint to the *European Commission of Human Rights* based in Strasbourg which is part of the Council of Europe and acts as the screening and investigative chamber for complaints. The applicant must satisfy the Commission that:

- the complaint relates to a violation of one or more of the Articles of the *European Convention on Human Rights* or the first protocol;
- he is a victim of that violation;
- efforts have been made to resolve the violation using the domestic legal system and all possible domestic remedies (if any) have been exhausted; and
- the complaint to the Commission has been lodged within six months of the exhaustion of the last attempted domestic remedy.

If satisfied that the complaint complies with the admissibility criteria the Commission will investigate the matter and ask the government for its observations:

- at this stage limited legal aid subject to a means test may be available from the Council of Europe;
- the procedure is slow although many cases are settled by the government at a relatively early stage.

If a complaint survives scrutiny it is generally passed to the *European Court of Human Rights* for a final decision. Substantial compensation and legal costs can be awarded to successful complainants under binding judgments, and there are no court fees or costs awards against unsuccessful complainants.

Human Rights Act 1998

The Convention is now to be incorporated into our domestic law, though with some limitation. It is made unlawful for a public authority to act in a way which is incompatible with a Convention right:

- individuals will be able to rely upon the provisions of the Convention in any legal proceedings although claims brought expressly under it will only be permitted in certain courts;
- all legislation must be read so far as is possible to give effect to the Convention in a way that is compatible with the rights that it lays down;
- when a court seeks to determine a question arising in connection with a Convention right it must take into account the case law of the ECHR;
- only a victim of an action by a public authority which is incompatible with a Convention right may complain under the Act and the law cannot be challenged in the abstract;

- there is a one-year time-limit for bringing proceedings under the Act with a discretion to extend this.

If primary legislation proves to be incompatible with the Convention, despite the duty not to so interpret it if possible, all the higher courts can do is make a 'declaration of incompatibility' which may result in the legislation being amended. Courts may, however, within the limit of their general powers, give relief against subordinate legislation. If relief is not granted in our courts it may still be sought in the ECHR.

> The *Human Rights Act 1998* is to be brought into effect on 1 October 2000 thereby largely incorporating the European Convention on Human Rights into British law.

Chapter 6
Civil Proceedings

6.1 GENERAL

An older person may have difficulty coping as a party to proceedings, or as a witness at a hearing, because of some physical or mental impairment. Whilst the court staff should be helpful and judges are being trained so as to become 'disability aware', a litigant is only treated in a different manner by the rules in the case of serious mental disability.

> Advisers should whenever necessary draw to the attention of the court any situation where disabled facilities or special directions are needed.

Discrimination

The civil courts are not exempted from the provisions of the *Disability Discrimination Act 1995* which extend to legal services, and could find themselves in breach of this legislation if they do not take into account the needs of disabled people. There are civil remedies for doing an act made unlawful by the Act, but most non-employment claims will be dealt with as small claims because of the level of damages. To the disabled individual it does not matter whether the problem is physical access to the court, hearing and understanding the proceedings or being heard and understood by the judge – each would be seen as discrimination.

> The Human Rights Act 1998 may also provide some support for disabled litigants when it is in force – see Chapter 5.

Court Rules

There are several sets of rules that apply to different types of proceedings:

- **Civil Procedure Rules 1998** (CPR) for all civil proceedings in the High Court or county courts:
  - replace both the Rules of the Supreme Court 1965 (RSC) and County Court Rules 1981 (CCR), but many of those old rules have been retained in modified form in Schedules to the new rules
  - supplemented by *Practice Directions* that indicate how the rules should be applied. These are made by the new Head of Civil Justice and should always be

referred to when considering a rule. Local practice directions are forbidden
- **Family Proceedings Rules 1991** (FPR) for all family proceedings:
  – the former RSC and CCR (in their final form) fill any gaps (FPR r 1.3)
- **Insolvency Rules 1986** for insolvency proceedings:
  – the CPR will fill any gaps
- **Court of Protection Rules 1994** for matters dealt with by this Court.

Civil Justice Reforms

The rules governing family proceedings were already more interventionist, but the introduction of a new procedural code from 26 April 1999 by the Civil Procedure Rules 1998 represented a change of culture in the civil justice system:

- the problems of the old system were identified as delay, cost and inequality of the parties, and the aim of the reforms was to achieve access to justice for all with procedures that are easier to understand;
- proceedings are henceforth governed by the *overriding objective* of enabling the court to deal with cases justly, which means:
  – ensuring that the parties are on an equal footing
  – saving expense
  – dealing with cases in ways which are proportionate to the money involved, importance of the case, complexity of the issues and financial position of each party
  – ensuring that cases are dealt with expeditiously and fairly
  – allotting to cases an appropriate share of the court's resources
- the court must seek to give effect to the overriding objective and the parties are required to help:
  – instead of leaving the parties to progress litigation, the judge henceforth should act as 'case manager' and adopt an interventionist role
  – this includes encouraging the parties to co-operate, identifying the real issues at an early stage and deciding how they can best be resolved, and fixing timetables
  – a 'cost-benefit' approach is adopted and hearings will be dealt with without the need for the parties to attend at court if possible
  – alternative dispute resolution is encouraged and attempts should be made to settle proceedings at an early stage
- cases are allocated to one of three 'tracks' according to the amount in issue, complexity and other factors:
  – the small claims track for most cases up to £5,000 (£1,000 for personal inju-

Chapter 6 CIVIL PROCEEDINGS

ries or housing disrepair) or by consent
- the 'fast track' for most cases up to £15,000 which can be tried within a day
- the 'multi-track' being a flexible procedure for all other cases

> The Civil Justice Reforms are sometimes referred to as the 'Woolf Reforms' after Lord Woolf, MR, whose Report *Access to Justice* (July 1996) formed the basis for the reforms.

6.2 PHYSICAL DISABILITY

Implications and solutions

Many forms of physical disability (or mental impairment falling short of incapacity) may affect the ability of an older person to participate in litigation, but when the problem is drawn to the attention of the court steps may be taken to cope with the impairment:

- impaired mobility may render it impossible to gain access to the court or cope in a particular courtroom:
  - transfer the case to a court in the area where the disabled party resides or with disabled access
- impaired hearing or vision may make it difficult to follow what is going on:
  - move the hearing to a courtroom or chambers with facilities for the hard of hearing or produce all documents in large print
- communication limitations may prevent others from understanding the individual, or vice versa:
  - arrange for an interpreter to be present and allow a longer time estimate
- limited concentration spans or the need for regular medication may make it impossible to remain in court for more than a limited period:
  - arrange regular adjournments or shorter hearings
- some ailment may make it impossible to attend court at all:
  - arrange for the evidence of the disabled person to be taken away from the court prior to the hearing or for the hearing to take place other than in a courtroom

Evidence

Need to attend court

The court now controls the issues on which it requires evidence and the way that evidence is given:

- it will only be necessary for a party or witness to attend a hearing (other than the trial) to give evidence if cross-examination is required:
  - a statement or pleading verified by a 'statement of truth' may be treated as evidence of the facts stated if it has been duly served on the other parties
- at the trial itself oral evidence is generally required:
  - witness statements will have been served in advance and will generally stand as evidence in chief, being amplified only with the permission of the court
  - the court may take into account the age or infirmity of a potential witness when deciding whether evidence is required from that source

> For evidence see CPR Part 32 and the Practice Direction.
> For the need to attend court see CPR Part 34 and the Practice Direction.

Taking evidence away from court

When an elderly person is too infirm to attend the hearing arrangements may be made for that person's evidence to be taken in advance in a manner that suits the circumstances (the procedure is known as taking *depositions*):

- this could be in a local court before the district judge, or in the individual's own home or a nursing home before an independent solicitor appointed for the purpose;
- the power is discretionary but an order will usually be made (and is often made by consent) where the witness:
  - is too old and decrepit to attend a trial
  - is so ill or infirm that there is no prospect of being able to attend the trial
  - might die before the trial
  - intends to leave the country before the trial

> The procedure for taking *depositions* is to be found in CPR Part 34, rr 34.8–34.12. For family proceedings see RSC Ord 39 r 1; CCR Ord 20 r 13.

Hearings other than in a courtroom

Where the circumstances render it expedient in the interests of justice the court may arrange the trial at or adjourn it to the place where a party or witness is, so as to allow participation in and hear the oral examination at the trial itself:

- this could be the individual's own home or a nursing home;
- see CPR r 2.7 which provides that a court may sit anywhere (family proceedings can be adjourned to such place as the judge thinks fit).

Chapter 6 CIVIL PROCEEDINGS

Interpreters

Regulations under the Disability Discrimination Act 1995 may require the court to take such steps as are reasonable, in all the circumstances, to provide auxiliary aids or services that assist disabled people, and sign language interpreters are specifically mentioned. These may now be provided by the court when required.

An interpreter in court should swear an oath in the following terms which would appear to apply whether the communication difficulty was due to language or some other cause:

> 'I will well and faithfully interpret and true explanation make of all such matters and things as shall be required of me according to the best of my skill and understanding.'

Representation

Rights of audience in court are strictly controlled:

- a party to proceedings has a right of audience in his capacity as such but in general only a barrister, solicitors or Fellows of the Institute of Legal Executives may represent a party:
    - Courts and Legal Services Act 1990, Part II (see sections 27 and 28)
- a person employed or engaged to assist in the conduct of litigation under instructions given by a solicitor may have a right of audience in chambers;
- the judge may refuse to hear a person who would otherwise have a right of audience in a specific instance, but reasons must be given.

'McKenzie friend'

During a hearing in open court (and generally also in chambers) a litigant in person has the right to be accompanied by a 'friend' to take notes, quietly make suggestions and give advice:

- the judge has a discretion to refuse this if the friend is not acting in the best interests of the litigant (e.g. pursuing a personal agenda);
- this is not the same as allowing such person to act as a representative although where a litigant in person is elderly, disabled or inarticulate the judge may seek assistance from any such person present in court who clearly has the confidence of the litigant.

Lay representatives

At a 'small claims' hearing any person (known as a *lay representative*) may speak on behalf of a party on tendering Form EX83. This is a right of audience only and does not extend to the conduct of the litigation generally:

- permission of the court is required if the party is not present:
  - Practice Direction to CPR Part 27, para. 3.2(3)
  - permission is unlikely to be refused in the case of a responsible representative where the party is unable to attend due to infirmity or disability
- the judge may refuse to hear an unsuitable lay representative:
  - the reasons should be stated and then written on form EX83
  - the court is entitled to expect the representative to behave honestly, reasonably and responsibly

6.3 MENTAL DISABILITY

Special procedures apply in respect of proceedings by and against a mentally incapacitated litigant. These ensure that a representative is appointed, compromises and settlements of claims are approved by the court, and there is supervision of any money recovered.

Rules

The procedures are to be found in the following rules:

- Civil Procedure Rules 1998 (CPR), Part 21;
- Family Proceedings Rules 1991 (FPR), Part IX:
  - supplemented by Rules of the Supreme Court 1965 (RSC), Order 80 and County Court Rules 1981 (CCR), Order 10 in their final form
- Insolvency Rules 1986, Part 7, Chapter 7;
- Court of Protection Rules 1994, rule 16.

'Under disability'

The rules (other than CPR) refer to proceedings by and against a *person under disability* which means being under 18 or a *patient* (in CCR *mental patient*):

- both are deemed incapable of conducting proceedings, the latter due to personal factors other than age (old age by itself is not sufficient);

> **Patient** is defined as: 'a person who, by reason of mental disorder within the meaning of the Mental Health Act 1983, is incapable of managing and administering his property and affairs.' – see CPR r 21(2)(b), FPR r 9.1; RSC Ord 80 r 1; CCR Ord 1 r 3.

- this definition is also used to establish the jurisdiction of the Court of Protection to administer the property and affairs of patients – see Chapter 10:

Chapter 6 CIVIL PROCEEDINGS

- there is no reported case on the application of this test, perhaps because lawyers are reluctant to venture into this area and normally rely upon doctors
- the definition in CPR concludes with the words '... his own affairs' but no distinction is intended
- the Insolvency Rules helpfully go further by including a person who is incapable 'due to physical affliction or disability'
- it is the capacity of the patient to manage his own (property and financial) affairs that is relevant rather than capacity to manage the proceedings:
  - the proceedings will comprise part of those affairs
- a three-stage test should be applied:
  - is the party incapable of managing and administering his affairs?
  - does the party suffer from a mental disorder?
  - is the incapacity due to that disorder?

Mental disorder

The use of this term acts as a screening process:

> **Mental disorder** means: 'mental illness, arrested or incomplete development of mind, psychopathic disorder and any other disorder or disability of mind' – Mental Health Act 1983, s 1(2).
>
> Nothing in the definition is to be construed as implying that a person may be dealt with as suffering from mental disorder by reason only of promiscuity, immoral conduct, sexual deviancy or dependence on alcohol or drugs – s 1(3)

- the definition is very wide and comprises any identifiable disorder or disability of mind:
  - being irrational, immoral or eccentric will not by itself be sufficient
  - there is no threshold: the severity of the mental disorder is not assessed and the question is merely whether it exists
- three categories of person come within this definition, namely those with:
  - *a mental illness* – having a mental illness does not necessarily result in lack of capacity
  - *learning disabilities* – sometimes referred to as 'learning difficulties' and previously known as 'mental handicap'
  - *brain damage*
- older people who become mentally impaired (e.g. by senile dementia or Alzheimer's disease) fall within the category of mental illness.

Assessing capacity

The rules assume that you know whether a party is a patient:

- in case of doubt the proceedings should be stayed whilst the court deals with this as a preliminary issue:
  - unlike the Court of Protection, other courts do not have specific facilities to investigate (e.g. to obtain medical evidence)
  - the Official Solicitor may be referred to where assistance is required
  - under CPR (but not FPR) the court can give permission for steps to be taken before the finding has been made and a representative appointed – r 21.3(2)
- if this decision has already been made by the Court of Protection it should be followed and that Court will normally decide who shall conduct proceedings;
- the judge may be prepared to find that a party is incapable of managing his affairs by reason of conduct in or giving rise to the proceedings, and the question is then whether this is by reason of mental disorder:
  - there is no difficulty in the case of a claimant because the proceedings may be stayed until that party submits to a medical examination
  - a defendant who will not submit to a medical examination presents a problem

> For assessment of capacity generally see Chapter 2.

Procedure

Need for a representative

A patient must have a representative to conduct proceedings, whether bringing or defending them:

- in civil proceedings this representative is a *litigation friend*:
  - the patient is referred to as *AB (by CD his litigation friend)*
- in family proceedings it is a *next friend* if bringing the proceedings or a *guardian ad litem* if responding;
- any step which might normally have been taken in the proceedings may be taken by the representative:
  - steps otherwise taken on behalf of a patient may not be effective
  - his solicitor may be personally liable for the costs wasted even though ignorant of the incapacity – see *Yonge v Toynbee* [1910] 1 KB 215

The representative may nominate himself and act as such without a court order or, in default, may be appointed by the court. If a party becomes a patient dur-

Chapter 6 CIVIL PROCEEDINGS

ing the course of proceedings an application must be made for such appointment.

> The procedure for appointing, removing or changing the representative is to be found in the relevant Court Rules.

Who is appointed

A person within the jurisdiction not being under an incapacity and not having an interest adverse to the patient or being connected to an opposing party may be a litigation friend:

- a person authorised by the Court of Protection to conduct proceedings on behalf of a patient (usually the receiver) is entitled to become the representative;
- otherwise it should be a substantial person and a relation of or person connected with the patient, or friend of the family, and not a mere volunteer;
- if no more suitable person can be found the Official Solicitor may be appointed but should first be consulted and give his consent.

The duty of the representative is 'fairly and competently to conduct proceedings on behalf of (the) patient. He must have no interest in the proceedings adverse to that of the ... patient and all steps and decisions he takes in the proceedings must be taken for the benefit of the ... patient' – CPR, PD 21, para. 2.1.

> Unless also a receiver appointed by the Court of Protection or an attorney under a registered enduring power of attorney the representative will have no status in regard to the affairs of the patient outside the proceedings.

Service of proceedings

If a party is a patient proceedings must be served upon:

- initially, the person authorised by the Court of Protection (if any) or 'the person with whom the patient resides or in whose care he is'; and thereafter
- the duly authorised representative of the patient (or solicitor on the record).

The court may make an order for deemed service or dispensing with service in appropriate circumstances.

Compromises and settlements

No compromise or settlement of a claim for a patient is valid without the approval of the court but an action may be brought solely for that purpose:

- this extends to costs and applies even if the representative is the receiver or attorney of the patient;

- the overriding consideration is the interest of the patient, having regard to all the circumstances of the case;
- approval of the Court of Protection will be sought first (if involved);
- it would be an abuse of process to proceed without the court's approval in any subsisting proceedings;
- in view of the cost of obtaining approval small claims are often settled on indemnities being given by the person to whom the money is paid.

> See CPR r 21.10(2) (or for family proceedings RSC Ord 80 rr 10 and 11; CCR Ord 10 r 10).

General matters

Evidence

In civil and family proceedings evidence may only be given by an individual who is considered by the judge to be competent to give evidence:

- unlike criminal proceedings, the oath is not obligatory so there is no requirement of ability to understand the nature and consequences of taking the oath;
- evidence may be admitted as to the capacity of the witness in general terms but not as to the likelihood of being able to give a truthful account.

A different technique is required when examining vulnerable witnesses and the judge should control this where necessary. The aim is to elicit true and accurate information and not to break the already vulnerable witness. In general:

- speak slowly, using simple words and sentences;
- avoid 'yes/no' answers (in particular leading questions) and questions containing a choice of answers which may not include the correct one;
- do not keep repeating questions or move to new topics without explanation;
- do not ask abstract questions (e.g. 'was it after 9.00 am' – instead ask 'was it after breakfast');
- allow the witness to tell his or her story and do not simply ignore information which does not fit in with your assumptions;
- do not go on too long without a break.

Limitation of actions

The limitation periods are 12 years for action on a deed, six years for action on a contract and three years for personal injury claims. Special rules apply if the

Chapter 6 CIVIL PROCEEDINGS

person was under a disability when the right of action accrued:
- the action may be brought within six (or three) years of the date when the disability ceased or the person died;
- it is at the court's discretion whether to grant an extension of time when there is supervening disability;
- a person is treated as under a disability while he is of unsound mind:
  - this means incapable by reason of mental disorder (within the Mental Health Act 1983) of managing and administering his property and affairs
  - it is a question of fact to be decided in each individual case (see Chapter 2 and the earlier part of this chapter)
  - it is conclusively presumed for a person who is liable to be detained or subject to guardianship under the 1983 Act (or receiving in-patient treatment in any hospital within the meaning of that Act immediately thereafter)

> See Limitation Act 1980, ss 28(1), 33(3)(d), 38(2) and 38(3) as amended by Mental Health Act 1983.

Stay of execution

If proceedings are taken to enforce a judgment against a patient a court would stay execution to enable steps to be taken on the patient's behalf, e.g.
- an application to the Court of Protection for the appointment of a receiver;
- registration of enduring power of attorney.

Injunctions

Being a patient is not itself a bar to the granting of an injunction and the question is whether the person understood the particular proceedings and the nature and requirements of the injunction:
- if he intended to do what he did and did it consciously, the necessary *mens rea* existed – *In re de Court* (1997) Times, 27 November;
- an injunction ought not to be granted against a person who is incapable of understanding what he is doing or that it is wrong since he would not be capable of complying with it:
  - any breach would not be subject to effective enforcement since he would have a defence to an application for committal for contempt – *Wookey v Wookey, Re S. (a minor)* [1991] 3 All ER 365;
  - the use of Mental Health Act powers of compulsory admission to hospital might be considered but if the patient's mental state does not justify this no effective remedy is available

- the court could make a hospital order under Contempt of Court Act 1981, s 14(4) where the party was suffering from serious mental incapacity at the time of the contempt proceedings but if that incapacity had existed earlier it would have precluded any contempt – *Wookey v Wookey*.

> For further consideration of domestic violence injunctions see Chapter 16.

Costs

Solicitor and client

Unless the court otherwise directs, the costs payable in any proceedings by a patient to his own solicitor must be assessed by the court and no costs are payable to that solicitor except the amount so allowed:

- CPR r 48.5 which applies also to family proceedings (assessment replaces taxation of costs);
- the rule extends to costs payable to a patient by another party:
  - if those costs can be agreed and the patient's solicitor waives any claim to further costs, the district judge may waive detailed assessment if satisfied with the amount notified – see CPR, PD 48 para. 1.2.

Conditional fees

There is an increasing trend for conditional or contingency fees to be available to cover the costs of the claimant's own solicitor in claims for damages, and a likelihood that legal aid will be withdrawn in all such cases – see Access to Justice Act 1999:

- this may be a 'no win, no fee' arrangement whereby the solicitor receives an enhanced fee if the claim succeeds and no fee at all if it fails:
  - there are restrictions upon the percentage uplift in the fees with a cap on the proportion of the damages that can be taken by the uplift
- the agreement must be concluded before the fees are incurred but where the claimant is a patient no-one has authority to enter into it:
  - the litigation friend's authority is restricted to the conduct of the proceedings and does not extend to advance fee arrangements with the lawyers
  - the rules do not permit a judge to approve a conditional fee arrangement upon issue of proceedings but CPR r 48.9(6) provides some protection

Costs of another party

The representative may be ordered to pay the costs of the proceedings (and will on commencing them have had to give an undertaking to pay any costs which

Chapter 6 CIVIL PROCEEDINGS

the patient may be ordered to pay):

- in the absence of misconduct on his part, the representative is entitled to recover any costs awarded against him from the property of the patient (if any);
- the representative responding to a claim will not be personally liable for costs unless these were occasioned by his personal negligence or misconduct.

Liability of solicitor

A solicitor may be ordered to pay the wasted costs incurred where he brings or continues an action for a claimant, or defends an action for a defendant, who is or has become a patient, without a litigation friend acting for him – *Yonge v Toynbee* [1910] 1 KB 215, CA.

Legal aid

The availability of legal aid or assistance does not depend upon age or mental capacity. It may be sought on behalf of a patient based upon the merits of the case and his or her financial circumstances. The application will be submitted by the person acting (or proposing to act) for the patient but the financial circumstances of this representative will not be taken into account:

- the certificate will not be issued unless that person signs an undertaking to pay to the Board (if required to do so) any sums which an assisted person of full age and capacity may be required to pay;
- the certificate is in the name of the patient but states the name of the person who has applied for it who is treated as an agent.

See generally Civil Legal Aid (General) Regulations 1989, reg. 16.

Disposal of damages

The court must decide how damages awarded to a patient are to be handled. The award itself should allow for the additional cost of administering the damages.

Procedure

Damages awarded to a patient must be paid into court (known as a fund) and not paid out except in accordance with directions which may be specific or general:

- the directions should be sought when the court enters judgment or gives approval to any settlement or compromise;
- funds up to £20,000 can be administered by the court in which recovered, or transferred to the patient's local county court – CPR, PD 21 at para. 11.2:

PART 1: SECTION B   Representing the Client

- – this will not be appropriate where there are other assets and the Court of Protection should be involved
- – an order will be made stating the manner in which the fund is to be invested, though the range of investments is restricted
- – authority can be given for regular interest payments and requests can be made at intervals for other sums to be released for the patient's benefit
- otherwise an order directs the litigation friend to apply to the Court of Protection for the appointment of a receiver and that the fund be then transferred to the credit of the receiver's account:
  - – if a receiver has already been appointed the order will provide for transfer of the fund forthwith
  - – where substantial damages are likely to be recovered consult the Court of Protection at the outset and follow its directions

> See generally: CPR r 21.11 and PD 21 at para. 11.2.
>
> Practice Note (QBD) (Transfer of Damages to Court of Protection), 7 September 1990; [1991] 1 All ER 436).

SECTION C
Financial Management

When elderly people become unable to manage their own financial affairs ways have to be found to do so on their behalf. Informal ways may be adopted which are of doubtful legal validity but unlikely to be questioned and what then matters is whether they work and whom they jeopardise. However, if there is a large amount of money or a dispute arises, formal procedures must be adopted.

The chart overleaf identifies the various procedures available and the following chapter provides a practical overview of the steps to be taken before and after someone becomes incapable of handling their affairs. Checklists are then provided and a comparison is made of the different legal procedures available.

Separate chapters then deal with:

- specific delegations;
- enduring powers of attorney;
- Court of Protection and receivership.

Opportunities also exist for developing areas of practice in the management of financial affairs for people who are legally competent.

PROCEDURES FOR DELEGATION OF FINANCIAL POWERS (ENGLAND)

```
                            ┌─────────────────────────────────────────────────────────────────┐
                            │                                                                 │
                     THIRD PARTY                            INDIVIDUAL
                            │              ┌──────────────────┬──────────────────┐
                            │              │                  │                  │
                         TRUST          AGENCY             STATUTORY          SPECIFIC
                            │              │                  │                  │
                            │              │      ENDURING    │                  │
                       BARE TRUST    POWER OF        POWER OF       COURT OF        DSS APPOINTEE
                       SETTLEMENT    ATTORNEY       ATTORNEY       PROTECTION       LITIGATION FRIEND
                                     THIRD-PARTY                  RECEIVERSHIP      MISCELLANEOUS
                                     MANDATE                      SHORT ORDER
```

Bare Trust / Settlement	Power of Attorney / Third-party Mandate	Enduring Power of Attorney	Court of Protection / Receivership / Short Order	DSS Appointee / Litigation Friend / Miscellaneous
Requires capacity	Requires capacity	Requires capacity	Requires incapacity	Requires incapacity
Survives incapacity	Ceases on incapacity	Survives incapacity	Ceases on capacity	Ceases on capacity
No supervision	No outside control	Power to intervene	Supervision	Some supervision
Trust property only	Any property	Any property	Any property	Specific property

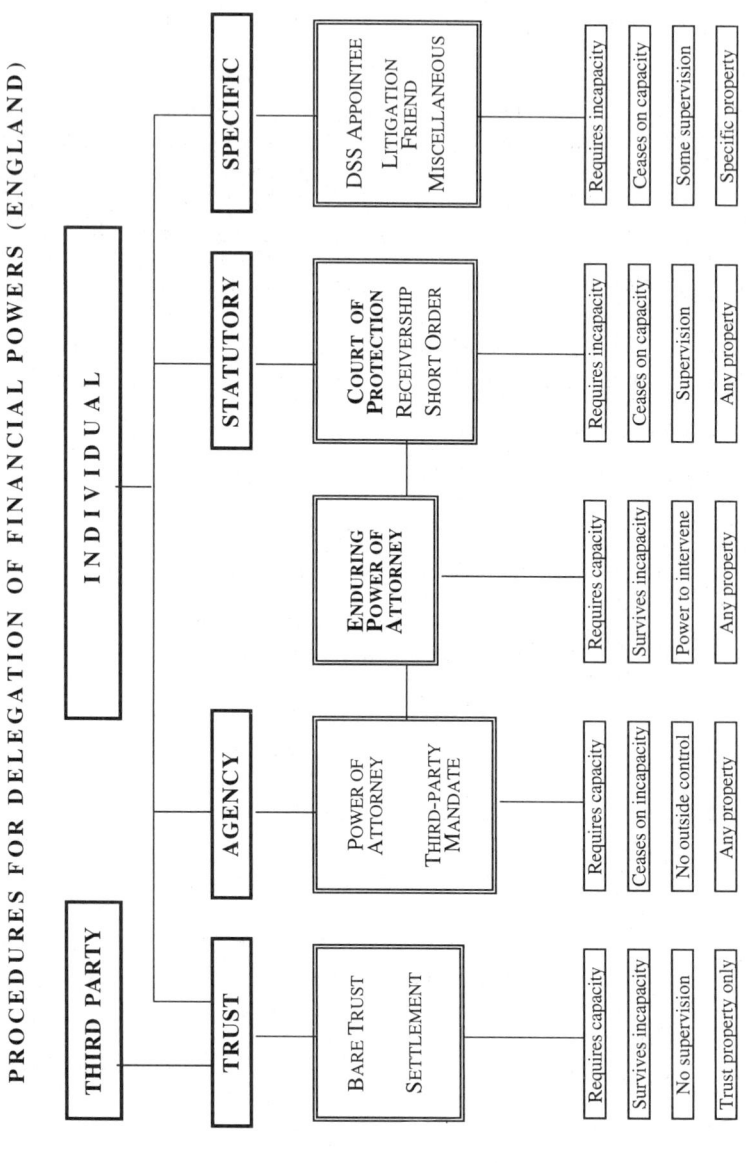

Chapter 7

The Work in Practice

7.1 HANDLING THE AFFAIRS

What do you do when informed that an elderly client is in hospital after a stroke and will never be able to handle a bank account or return home? Do not:

- over-react – how often have you visited someone in hospital and come away convinced that they will never be the same again, only to find later that they have made a full recovery?
- take longer-term decisions, or any serious or irreversible steps, without a medical report – lawyers are not qualified to determine the prognosis and the crystal ball gazing of family (if there is one) can seldom be relied upon.

> Deal with immediate problems, reassure the family and see how things develop whilst knowing what steps to take when the need arises.

Informal steps

Sometimes you can get by without any formal steps if there is little capital and the only real income is from pensions:

- a suitable person (including a relative, carer or solicitor) can become an appointee for claiming state benefits:
  - this will normally comprise the state retirement pension but it may be time to claim other benefits, e.g. attendance allowance (or the care component of disability living allowance if the client is under 65)
- an occupational pension may already be paid into a current bank account on which the bank may allow drawing:
  - if the only need is for a nursing home to be paid and sufficient money is available from these sources the bank may accept a standing order or direct debit for the weekly fees even if the capacity of the client is borderline

Sooner or later a build-up of bills and other commitments may dictate that someone must take overall control of the financial affairs.

PART 1: SECTION C Financial Management

Enduring power of attorney (EPA)

Prevention

Make sure that this situation does not happen to your clients! Offer older clients (or all clients) a package deal of a will plus an enduring power of attorney. Treat the making of a will as an opportunity to offer this extra service by having fact sheets available to show the advantages of having an EPA. Traditionally most solicitors have done wills very cheaply and it is difficult to change especially in a small community when you do many repeats. The package does not involve you in much more time as the same interviews and information are required for both documents, but the clients think they have got much more (as indeed they have) so can be charged accordingly. You may end up with both a will and an EPA in the strong-room and are often personally appointed as an executor and attorney. A few hundred – or thousand – of these tucked away and the long-term future of the practice is secure.

> Prevention is better than cure and we should all prepare for old age and an inability to cope.

Capacity to sign

Is it too late to get an EPA signed if one does not already exist? If you can complete an enduring power at this stage a lot of the problems are solved, but:

- see the donor alone – that is the client, not the person who told you that a power was to be granted in his or her favour. The donor may have different ideas and should be given an opportunity to express them;
- take careful notes at the interview, see the client again if necessary to confirm consistency of instructions and if in doubt get a medical report;
- when asked to see a new elderly client by a member of the family enquire if there is another solicitor who has usually acted for the client, and be wary if there is, because you may have been called in to avoid advice based upon knowledge of the background.

> The test of capacity to execute an EPA is not as high as you may think. It is not the same as ability to handle one's own affairs or testamentary capacity.

Do not forget to suggest to the client that it may be appropriate to tell the family about the existence of the EPA, why it has been signed and where it is.

Who to appoint

Many donors seek to impose conditions as to when the EPA comes into effect or the powers of the attorneys. Any restrictions can be counter-productive and the best advice may be not to appoint any attorney who cannot be entirely

Chapter 7 THE WORK IN PRACTICE

trusted to act in the best interests of the donor. Some strategies are possible:

- two adult children may be appointed jointly so that they can keep an eye on each other, but if either of them dies or becomes incapable the power is rendered ineffectual:
  - it may be preferable to appoint them jointly and severally with an understanding that neither will act without the approval of the other
- if there are more than two children some parents wish to name them all and provide that any two may act jointly, but section 11(1) of the 1985 Act prevents this:
  - a solution may be to appoint them all jointly and severally but include a condition that two of them must act
- a husband and wife may complete separate powers in favour of (i) each other and (ii) the children to act jointly and severally:
  - the incapacity of one may arise following the death of the other
- as the family solicitor you may be appointed either to act alone, or with a partner, or jointly with a relative – many families prefer this course:
  - insert a charging clause to reinforce the professional position of charging for services – this is helpful to your client and good practice (though it may not be strictly necessary)
- beware of 'successor' appointments as these are likely to render the EPA incapable of registration and thereby ineffective:
  - consider a second EPA to operate only if a specified event occurs

Restrictions

The EPA may be limited to certain property or to taking certain steps only, or may be expressed to take effect only in certain circumstances, e.g. when registered (albeit this may be unwise):

- advise the client of the risk of illness or disability which temporarily impairs capacity and means that help is needed to manage financial affairs;
- it is usually best not to impose any restrictions upon the EPA because you can never anticipate the circumstances in which it may be genuinely useful.

> The most important point is to choose attorneys whom the donor can trust with wide discretionary powers and who will prove reliable.

Conflicts of interest

Watch out for conflicts of interest. The money belongs to the donor and should be spent for the benefit of the donor and not accumulated for the family (which may, and often will, include the attorney):

- whenever problems arise they can usually be solved if you ask yourself 'Who is the client?' It is the donor, who is merely acting through the attorney;
- remind the attorney and the donor of the restrictions imposed by the law and also of the duties and liabilities of the attorney (see below).

Will

When you are advising on the creation or exercise of an EPA you should inspect the donor's last will and obtain a copy if you do not hold the original. Another solicitor may be reluctant to reveal its contents at a later stage:

- an express provision in the EPA about inspection may be advisable;
- the attorney probably has power to require it to be produced (a compromise may be for it to be seen only by the solicitor advising the attorney);
- if the EPA is registered the Court of Protection may give a direction.

The reason you must see the will is that the attorney should take into account its terms when deciding what property should be sold and when:

- property which is specifically bequeathed should be sold after property which would fall into residue, though circumstances may dictate otherwise;
- difficult decisions may arise where the attorney is a potential beneficiary under the will;
- if a solicitor is acting as attorney he may be impartial but should still be aware of the effect of any decision upon the donor's testamentary intentions.

Dealing with the affairs

Armed with an enduring power of attorney, registered if appropriate, the house can be sold, investments rearranged and a bank account opened to receive the income and pay fees for a residential care or nursing home. When all this is set up you can probably hand over the administration to the attorney personally, unless that is you.

> The Law Society's *Guidelines on Enduring Powers of Attorney* are reproduced in Part Five of this Handbook.

Receivership

If there is more than a little capital involved and it is too late for an EPA, the proper and only safe course is an application to the Court of Protection under the Mental Health Act 1983, Part VII:

Chapter 7   THE WORK IN PRACTICE

- this will usually be for the appointment of a receiver;
- there is a short procedure for simple cases involving less than £5,000.

> A failed EPA will lead to a receiver being appointed, but if there is an EPA this is generally preferred on the basis that the attorney was chosen by the client.

Contrary to our legal upbringing, the Court of Protection need not be seen as the last resort; it is now more user friendly and there can be advantages in its involvement. Complaints are the size of the fees charged, the legal costs that are incurred and delay caused by the procedures involved, but can this really be avoided if appropriate safeguards are to be provided? The relative instructing you may know just what he wants to do and complain about any obstacles in his way, but do other relatives agree with or trust him? Anyone who has become involved in family disputes regarding an elderly relative will know the sort of problems that can arise and it is then that the procedures of the Court are of great value.

> The work can be well paid if you keep adequate records and work efficiently.

Application

Start by writing to the Public Trust Office for the necessary forms and you will be sent a helpful booklet on receivership which tells you most of what you need to know unless you get involved in a dispute:

- help the proposed receiver to complete the forms:
  - a medical report must be prepared by the doctor presently looking after the mentally incapable person (the patient) who will know his present condition
  - details of the patient's background and property are given on another form
- a bond or insurance guarantee may be required (unless a solicitor from an established firm is to be the receiver);
- a fee is payable which you may need to pay out of office account (it will later be refunded from the patient's estate).

Orders

If all is in order the First General Order will be sent to you in draft form for approval:

- this appoints the receiver and sets out his initial powers so you should check that they cover all that is intended to be done at this stage;
- further orders can be obtained as required following applications in writing and contact with the Court is usually by letter with no great formality.

PART 1: SECTION C   Financial Management

> The patient acts by the receiver so production of the Orders (or office copies) is required as confirmation of authority.

Costs

There are fixed costs for various stages (e.g. First General Order, annual accounts, annual management) but you may submit a bill for taxation if these are not enough:

- costs may be agreed without taxation up to certain limits for work not covered by fixed costs;
- fixed costs are available for conveyancing as an alternative to taxation.

Statutory wills

Whether you are acting for an attorney or a receiver you should inspect the last will (if any) and consider whether it is appropriate to apply to the Court of Protection for a statutory will to be made:

- there may be compelling evidence that the last will no longer represents the wishes of the client (i.e. the donor or patient) especially if it was made many years ago when circumstances were different:
    - it may simply leave everything to a spouse who is now deceased
    - there may be no evidence of a will ever having been made
- the effect of an intestacy must be taken into account:
    - if there are no known relatives the opportunity may be taken to benefit those persons whom the client might have been expected to benefit
    - do not overlook charities which the client has supported – it can be very satisfying to ensure that they receive a share of the estate in this way
- your own activities in dealing with the affairs may themselves affect the balance of any will to the extent that a statutory will should be applied for.

7.2   CHECKLIST

The following checklist may be helpful when a solicitor takes over the affairs of someone who has become incapable of dealing with his or her affairs.

Information

The solicitor, carers and relatives have no legal authority over the affairs and no right to information at this stage so it is necessary to act on the best information available.

- Personal:
  - full name
  - residential address
  - home status (owner-occupier/tenant/licensee)
  - present arrangements for care
  - date of birth
- Family:
  - carers and next of kin
  - spouse (and any previous spouse)
  - children and their families
  - any cohabitee
  - is the present spouse the parent of all the children?
  - is there a former spouse still alive with a financial entitlement?
- Medical:
  - doctor
  - have all necessary medical arrangements been made?
  - have any advance wishes as to treatment been expressed?
  - is there a living will?
- Financial:
  - clarify state benefits being claimed
  - ascertain income and capital (is the estate solvent?)
  - ascertain bills to be paid (now and on regular basis)
  - check details of any nursing home or other care fees
  - check ordinary insurance policies
  - check life insurance policies (including private health and long-term care)
  - check arrangements for making tax returns and claiming allowances
  - are there any trust funds?
  - is there provision for funeral costs?
- Management:
  - is any other solicitor involved?
  - are there any joint accounts or accounts with a second signature?
  - has an EPA been completed?
  - is there an appointee for state benefits?
  - has a short procedure order ever been made by the Court of Protection?
  - is there a will?

Action

The following steps may be necessary and may arise before or after obtaining formal legal authority to handle the affairs according to circumstances.

- Personal:
    - physical security of home and possessions (and pets)
    - notify landlord and deal with rent, re-direct mail, cancel deliveries (milk, etc.)
    - future arrangements for personal care
- Family:
    - notify and consult carers and next of kin
- Medical:
    - contact doctor and obtain report;
    - arrange private treatment/provision?
- Financial:
    - intercept state benefits and other income
    - security of passbooks, share certificates, deeds, etc.
    - notify bank and any trustees, confirm insurances and deal with tax affairs
- Management:
    - arrange appointee for state benefits or complete and/or register an EPA or obtain and complete Court of Protection forms;
    - apply for a statutory will?

7.3 POWERS OF DELEGATION COMPARED

Attorney

Advantages

- Can be a third party to avoid family conflicts.
- Can relate to all money and property of donor and is suitable for small sums.
- Very flexible with self-imposed restrictions upon financial powers.
- Cheap and easy to set up (minimum formality, no delay) and operate (no annual fees or accounts).
- Enables donor to choose who to appoint as attorney.
- Continues (if an enduring power) once incapacity arises.

Disadvantages

- Only available where there is sufficient understanding (but note the legal test).
- Ceases to be available if the attorney dies or becomes incapable (unless another attorney is appointed jointly and severally).
- No effective supervision and no obligation to consult or visit the donor.
- Attorney's authority may be challenged.

Receiver

Advantages

- Available in all cases where there is no capacity.
- Relates to all money and property held by individual.
- Supervision by the court and change of receiver is possible.
- Authority of receiver cannot be questioned.

Disadvantages

- Not suitable for small amounts (though special procedures are available).
- Expensive to set up and operate (annual accounts must be produced).
- Limited discretion (frequent reference to court required).
- No obligation to consult or visit the individual.
- Individual has little choice as to who is appointed as receiver.

Trust

Advantages

- Trustees may be given wide discretionary powers.
- Self-perpetuating trustees.
- No annual fees payable to the court or need to produce annual accounts.
- (For the trustees) their financial authority cannot be questioned.
- May avoid means-testing for welfare and other benefits.

Disadvantages

- Only relates to money placed in trust.

PART 1: SECTION C   Financial Management

- Inadequate supervision (little control over charges of professional trustees).
- No obligation to consult or visit the individual.
- (For the beneficiary) the trustees' financial authority cannot be questioned.
- Note the effect of the Trusts of Land and Appointment of Trustees Act 1996.
- Administration costs.
- Problems of unspent income and tax repayments.
- Can affect means testing if wrong trust instrument is used.

7.4   DOS AND DON'TS IN THE COURT OF PROTECTION

Applications under Mental Health Act 1983 Part VII

DO

- Give as the applicant your client, not your firm.
- Complete as many as possible of the paragraphs of CP5.
- Insert a figure for the patient's approximate net annual income.
- Make sure the doctor giving the CP3 has seen the patient within the last six months.
- Get the doctor to give reasons for his or her diagnosis.
- Enclose all the documents you say you are enclosing.
- Quote the Public Trust Office's case reference.
- Give your firm's own reference.
- Ask for any urgent directions you need.
- Remember to enclose the commencement fee.
- Follow the procedure notes for sales and purchases or statutory wills, and follow the recommended precedents set out in the procedure note.
- Arrange service at least 10 days before the hearing of first applications.
- Consider seeking directions by letter prior to any order being made.

DON'T

- Send in the CP1 or CP5 unsigned.
- Staple or sew documents into the CP5.
- Bind up exhibits with affidavits.

Chapter 7 THE WORK IN PRACTICE

- Use your own forms instead of the printed forms.

Enduring powers of attorney

DO

- Enclose the original EPA with any application.
- Notify the donor and the required relatives before applying for registration.
- Apply for registration within three days from the notification of the last person required to be notified.
- Send medical evidence in support of any application to dispense with notification.
- Insert on form EP2 the dates on which the people concerned were notified and the date of your application.
- Send the fee with the application.
- Remember class rules for notification.

DON'T

- Use a form of EPA other than the current one when preparing the EPA.
- Omit any of the marginal notes or explanatory information.

Chapter 8

Specific Delegations

8.1 STATE BENEFITS

Benefits may be paid to another person when the claimant is unable to claim personally – see Social Security (Claims and Payments) Regulations 1987.

Agency

A claimant may nominate someone to collect benefit by signing the form of authority on the allowance order slip:

- an *agency card* may be obtained where this is to be done long term;
- residents in local authority accommodation can nominate an official of the authority to act as *signing agent* and collect payments.

It is not wise to appoint a residential care or nursing home owner who would be subject to special Benefits Agency requirements.

> This procedure should not be used if the claimant is incapable of handling his affairs because it relies upon an express delegation.

Appointee

If the claimant is 'unable for the time being to act' and a receiver has not been appointed the Secretary of State can appoint someone to claim any benefits on his behalf – reg. 33. The appointee can collect, and must deal with and spend, the money for the benefit of the claimant but his powers do not extend beyond handling the social security benefit:

- application is in writing and staff at the Benefits Agency satisfy themselves as to the claimant's inability to manage his affairs and the suitability of the appointee:
  - a close relative who lives with or someone else who cares for the claimant is usually the most suitable person to be the appointee
  - the proprietor of a residential care home should only be appointed as a last resort (some local authorities frown on it)
- the appointee is under a duty to disclose relevant information to the Benefits Agency when claiming benefits (and may be personally liable in the event of non-disclosure).

Chapter 8 SPECIFIC DELEGATIONS

> The appointment may be revoked if the appointee is not acting properly or in the best interests of the claimant.

Other powers

- The Secretary of State may direct that benefit be paid to another person acting on behalf of the claimant if this appears necessary for protecting the interests of the claimant or a dependant – reg. 34.
- Costs of housing, accommodation and fuel and water services may be deducted from certain benefits and paid direct to third parties on behalf of the claimant in accordance with detailed procedures – reg. 35 and Sched. 9.

8.2 MISCELLANEOUS

> The special procedures for the administration of damages awarded by a court to a person who lacks mental capacity are dealt with in Chapter 6.

Bank or building society accounts

There are five possibilities in respect of accounts for elderly individuals:

- a *third party mandate* can be completed allowing another person to conduct the account:
  - this arrangement may be convenient in cases of physical disability
  - the mandate would be revoked by the subsequent mental incapacity of the account-holder
- the account can for convenience be held in the *joint names* of the individual and another person on the basis of either to sign:
  - such authority may be revoked if either account-holder loses mental capacity (that is not the view of some solicitors but is the view of the clearing banks)
  - it should be recorded (when appropriate) that this is not intended to be a joint account that passes to the survivor on death but that the money belongs to the elderly individual
- the account can be in the name of another as express *nominee* for the elderly individual;
- the account can simply be in the name of another although it belongs to the elderly individual:
  - this can result in tax problems
  - it is vulnerable to misappropriation so not suitable for larger sums
- in some situations deposits and withdrawals may be allowed on a National

77

Savings Bank account in the name of a person who lacks mental capacity:
- National Savings Bank Act 1971, s 8(1)(f)
- National Savings Bank Regulations 1972, regs. 6 and 7

Government payments

Any pay, pensions or other periodical payments due from the government to a person who is, by reason of mental disorder, unable to manage his affairs may be paid to the person having care of the patient for his benefit – Mental Health Act 1983, s 142. Similar arrangements apply to local authority pensions.

Income tax

Tax returns must generally be signed by the taxpayer in person but under section 8 of the Taxes Management Act 1970 may be signed by:

- a receiver appointed by the Court of Protection;
- an attorney in cases of physical inability to sign;
- an attorney under a registered EPA in cases of mental incapacity.

Tax repayments may be claimed by the next of kin of a mentally incapacitated person in the absence of a receiver up to certain financial limits (a trustee will only have authority to sign tax returns relating to the particular trust).

Deduction of tax

A parent, guardian, spouse, son or daughter of a person suffering from mental disorder may register on the person's behalf for interest to be paid without deduction of tax on bank and building society accounts:

- Income Tax (Deposit-takers) (Interest Payments) (Amendment) Regulations 1992; Income Tax (Building Societies) (Dividends and Interest) (Amendment) Regulations 1992.

Trusts

Where it is desired to make testamentary provision for a person who may be or become incapable of dealing with his own affairs, the problem may be avoided by appointing trustees and leaving property to them on suitably worded trusts:

- the trustees may hold and manage the trust property with power to use and expend it for the benefit of the beneficiary;
- the financial powers of the beneficiary need not then be delegated in regard to the trust property.

Informal trusts

Money may be held in the name of another person who acknowledges (formally or informally) the true ownership. In some family situations a trust is not even created, but money or assets are simply given to children or other relatives in the expectation that it will be made available in case of need:

- this is only suitable for relatively small sums because tax and other complications can arise;
- it may work in practice but can cause serious problems if the understanding goes wrong.

> The powers of the trustees will not extend to property of the beneficiary.

Hospitals

A hospital does not provide for all personal needs and some spending money in the hands of the patient is desirable. If relatives are attending to the patient's financial affairs they may hand over regular sums in cash when they visit, but if these visits are not regular or the patient cannot cope with cash the following procedures apply:

- monies are held in the hospital bank:
  - an initial sum may be deposited by the patient
  - relatives may also deposit money
  - further money will come from continuing state benefits
- where there is no-one available to handle the patient's money a welfare officer will assist:
  - with benefit claims
  - in making money available for the patient's benefit
- where the patient is able to cope with small sums of cash, a form can be obtained and taken either by the patient or a member of staff to the hospital bank or cash office to effect withdrawals;
- the hospital must keep an account of all money held for a patient and produce this to the patient on request;
- upon leaving hospital any balance must be accounted for to the patient or to the patient's representative or estate.

> The money belongs to the patient and not to the hospital which is merely providing a facility for it to be looked after.

Chapter 9
Enduring Powers of Attorney

9.1 POWERS OF ATTORNEY

A power of attorney is a document whereby a person (the *donor*) gives another person (an *attorney*) power to act on his behalf in his name in regard to his financial affairs. Note that the power:

- must be executed as a deed:
  - see Law of Property (Miscellaneous Provisions) Act 1989 as to execution
- may be in general terms or limited to specific acts or circumstances:
  - consider the simple form of general power under Powers of Attorney Act 1971
- can only be granted by a competent person, so an attorney under an ordinary power can no longer act if the donor becomes mentally incapable:
  - but see 'Enduring powers of attorney', para. 9.2 below

Production of powers

A photocopy which bears a certificate signed by a solicitor at the end (of each page) that it is a true and complete copy of the original must be accepted as proof of the contents of the original:

- a certified copy of a certified copy must be accepted if satisfying these requirements (this also applies to enduring powers of attorney):
  - see Powers of Attorney Act 1971, s 3
- an office copy of an enduring power of attorney is evidence of the contents:
  - see Enduring Powers of Attorney Act 1985, s 7 and below

9.2 ENDURING POWERS OF ATTORNEY

Legislation in 1985 created the enduring power of attorney ('EPA') which remains valid notwithstanding the donor's subsequent incapacity to manage his own affairs. They are of general application and should not be thought of merely as a way of coping with a loss of mental capacity.

Legislation

- Powers of Attorney Act 1971

- Enduring Powers of Attorney Act 1985
  - Enduring Powers of Attorney (Prescribed Form) Regulations 1990
- Court of Protection (Enduring Powers of Attorney) Rules 1994

Requirements

An EPA must be executed in the manner and form prescribed in regulations:

- printed forms are available and these should be used because the information and marginal notes thereon are part of the form;
- there are alternatives with space for additional wording so the form may be adapted to the wishes of the donor;
- explanatory information tells the donor the effect of executing the power and must be read by or to the donor *and* understood by the donor.

> The form prescribed by the 1990 Regulations must be used. The forms prescribed by the previous 1986 and 1987 Regulations applied to EPAs executed whilst current.

The form must be signed by the donor and also by the attorney(s) to signify acceptance and acknowledge the duty to register in certain circumstances:

- the signatures of donor and attorney(s) should be witnessed by an independent person or persons:
  - they cannot witness each other's signatures
  - a spouse should not be asked to witness
  - they do not all need to sign at the same time but the donor should sign first and the attorneys must have signed before the donor loses mental capacity
- a donor unable to sign may make a mark and the attestation clause should be amended to explain this:
  - an authorised person may sign on behalf of a donor or attorney in certain circumstances but two witnesses are then needed and that person should not witness any other signature
- deletions or additions need not be initialled as they are presumed to have been made before execution.

> An individual may complete more than one EPA and a new EPA will not revoke an earlier one unless express provision is made.

Restrictions

An EPA may be general in its terms or for specific purposes only, and the

PART 1: SECTION C Financial Management

donor may place restrictions or conditions on the power including:

- only for dealing with specific property;
- only exercisable if the donor ceases to have mental capacity (otherwise the EPA will be effective as a general power immediately) – but this can impose limitations in case of physical incapacity

There are statutory restrictions on what an attorney under an EPA can do including:

- not benefit himself or persons other than the donor except to the extent that the donor might have been expected to provide for his or their needs;
- not make gifts except for presents of reasonable value at Christmas, birthdays, weddings and such like to persons related to or connected with the donor or charitable gifts which the donor might have been expected to make.

Professional attorneys

Those who are professional attorneys should be reminded of their personal liability for actions taken whilst acting for the donor of the EPA. It is recommended that protocols are adopted within the practice over the conduct of clients' affairs when a member of the firm is acting under an EPA – see generally Part II.

It is good practice where a solicitor, accountant or other professional is appointed as attorney to include a charging clause in the EPA so that it is clear to the donor (and others) that professional costs will be incurred. This should avoid any later queries (save as to the amount of the charges).

Registration

Registration provides safeguards because certain relatives must be given notice, and although the Court does have supervisory powers it is only where problems are brought to its attention that they are likely to be used. Note that:

- an attorney is under a duty to apply to the Court of Protection for registration of the EPA as soon as practicable after he has reason to believe that the donor is or *is becoming* mentally incapable;
- this means 'incapable by reason of mental disorder of managing and administering his property and affairs';
- once this situation arises the EPA is suspended (save for essential action) until submission of an application for registration whereupon certain limited authority is automatically restored.

Chapter 9   ENDURING POWERS OF ATTORNEY

Notice

Notice must first be given to the donor and to the donor's closest relatives in the prescribed form (EP1), which states that the attorney proposes to apply for registration of the EPA and that the recipient may object to this within four weeks on any ground therein specified. Note that:

- notice must be handed to the donor personally but relatives may be served by first class post;
- the specified relatives must be taken in order of priority from the statutory list, class by class:
  - at least three relatives must be served but if anyone from a class has to be served then all of that class must be served
  - see 1985 Act, Sched. 1, Part 1
- notice need not be given to anyone who:
  - has not attained 18 years
  - is mentally incapable
  - cannot be traced
- if there are less than three living relatives only they need be given notice.

> Application can be made to dispense with giving notice to a person for special reasons (Form EP3).

Objections

The persons to whom notice is given may object to registration on the following grounds and there are procedures for dealing with objections:

- the power was not validly created or no longer subsists;
- the application is premature;
- fraud or undue pressure was used to induce the donor to create the power;
- having regard to all the circumstances and in particular the attorney's relationship to or connection with the donor he is unsuitable to be the donor's attorney.

Application

The attorney(s) must send the application in Form EP2 together with the original EPA and registration fee to the Public Trust Office within three [*ten*] days of service of the last relevant notice. If no objections are received after 35 days the power is registered and the original is returned to the attorney(s) duly stamped and sealed.

83

PART 1: SECTION C   Financial Management

Implications of registration

Once an EPA is registered the attorney(s) can again operate under its authority, but registration does not amount to certification that it is valid. Note that:

- once the EPA has been registered it cannot be revoked by the donor without the confirmation of the Court;
- the Court can cancel registration on certain grounds;
- the Court can also impose a receivership instead if it thinks fit.

> The Register is open to the public. Applications to inspect are on Form EP4 on payment of a fee.

The attorney

Anyone over 18 and not bankrupt or mentally incapable may be appointed as an attorney, and two or more people may be appointed to act jointly or jointly and severally. Statutory protection is available for attorneys in specific circumstances.

Duties

An attorney is expected to manage the donor's affairs in accordance with the EPA, but may seek the guidance of the Court which only has supervisory powers in the case of a registered power and may not exercise or enlarge the attorney's powers except as provided in the Act (e.g. by authorising gifts). Note that an attorney:

- must use such skill as he possesses and show such care as he would in conducting his own affairs;
- if being paid must exercise the care, skill and diligence of a reasonable person, and if acting in the course of a profession must exercise proper professional competence;
- may not appoint a substitute or otherwise delegate his general authority, but may employ persons to do specific tasks;
- has no power over the donor so cannot dictate where he shall live (but may have influence over such matters);
- should keep accounts but only need produce these to the Court if so directed.

Capacity of donor

An EPA is valid if the donor understood its nature and effect notwithstanding that he was at the time of its execution incapable by reason of mental disorder

Chapter 9 ENDURING POWERS OF ATTORNEY

of managing his property and affairs. Thus in some cases a valid power may be executed even though it must be immediately registered.

> See judgment of Hoffmann J. in *Re K., Re F.* [1988] 1 All ER 358.

Solicitor's duty

Though instructions to prepare an EPA may come from the intended attorney a solicitor is acting for the donor so should see him personally and alone so that independent advice may be given and confirmation of instructions obtained.

When acting on the instructions of an attorney (whether or not the EPA is registered) a solicitor should remember that his client is the donor whose best interests should be safeguarded even if this results in conflict with the attorney.

Trustees

The Trustee Delegation Act 1999 makes changes to the use of enduring powers by trustees with effect from 1 January 2000:

- section 3(3) of the Enduring Powers of Attorney Act 1985 (which allowed this) has been repealed:
  - detailed transitional provisions affect existing EPAs, both registered and unregistered
- the general rule is that any trustee functions delegated to an attorney (whether under an ordinary power or an enduring power) must comply with the provisions of the Trustee Act 1925, s 25 (as amended by the 1999 Act);
- section 1(1) of the 1999 Act provides an exception to this general rule:
  - an attorney can exercise a trustee function of the donor if it relates to land, or the capital proceeds or income from land, in which the donor has a beneficial interest
  - this is subject to any provision to the contrary contained in the trust instrument or the power of attorney itself

Pitfalls

1. The marginal notes are part of the prescribed form and must not be omitted.
2. The donor cannot appoint 'any two of' several named attorneys (but several attorneys can be appointed jointly and severally with a condition that at least two must act).

Chapter 10

Court of Protection

10.1 STATUS AND STRUCTURE

The Court of Protection is an office of the Supreme Court which exercises judicial functions over the property and affairs of persons who are incapable, by reason of mental disorder, of managing and administering their property and affairs. Such people are known as *patients* and their financial affairs are managed on a day-to-day basis by a *receiver*. The Court is financed by those who use it.

Legislation

- Mental Health Act 1983, Part VII
- Public Trustee and Administration of Funds Act 1986
- Court of Protection Rules 1994

Information

- An *Information Pack* available free from the Public Trust Office contains details of forms and procedures used by the Court and the following booklets:
  - Handbook for Receivers
  - Enduring Powers of Attorney
- *Procedure Notes* and *Fact Sheets* have been issued on specific topics;
- *Notes for the Guidance of Solicitors on Costs in Court of Protection Matters* may be obtained from Supreme Court Taxing Office (Court of Protection Branch);
- The Supreme Court Practice (*White Book*), Volume II, Part 9 contains information on the Court and its jurisdiction and sets out the relevant statutes and rules.

Jurisdiction

It is necessary to apply to the Court of Protection when an elderly person who has money or property is incapable by reason of mental disorder of managing his financial affairs and is also unable to execute a valid enduring power of attorney:

Chapter 10 COURT OF PROTECTION

- the procedure can be helpful and provide a degree of supervision not available under other forms of delegation, but disincentives are the formality, delay and cost involved;
- jurisdiction is limited to the property and financial affairs of the patient and does not extend to the management or care of the person, i.e. there is no authority to direct where the patient shall live or authorise medical treatment.

> It is easy to overstate the disadvantages of applying to the Court of Protection. There are advantages which may outweigh the disadvantages, not least being that someone is clothed with authority which others are not inclined to question.

The Court's officers

The staff consists of only eight people:

- the Master who deals with:
    - all originating applications for the appointment of a receiver where the patient's net income exceeds £15,000 a year and all subsequent applications and directions in such matters
    - the appointment of interim receivers
    - the making of orders where the patient is resident outside England and Wales
    - contentious applications for the appointment of a receiver or the registration of an enduring power of attorney
    - applications for settlements or gifts of a patient's property
    - applications for the execution of a statutory will for a patient
    - applications under section 1(3) of the Variation of Trusts Act 1958
- two Assistant Masters who:
    - adjudicate in contentious cases and pronounce orders in matters where the patient's annual net income does not exceed £15,000 a year
    - split the Protection Division cases between themselves alphabetically (one deals with Receivership Division cases and the other EPAs)
- two nominated officers who process all originating applications for:
    - appointment of a receiver where the patient's net annual income does not exceed £15,000
    - the making of short orders pursuant to the Court of Protection Rules 1994, rule 9 where the property of the patient does not exceed £5000 in value
    - orders under sections 36(9) and 54 of the Trustee Act 1925
- the Registrar and his two assistants who are responsible for:

87

PART 1: SECTION C   Financial Management

- processing all applications for gifts or settlements of a patient's property
- applications for orders authorising the execution of a statutory will
- appeals and references to the nominated judge

The Public Trust Office

The Public Trustee has since 2 January 1987 been responsibility for the management (as distinct from judicial) functions of the Court of Protection and the functions of the Official Solicitor as receiver of last resort and operates from the Public Trust Office. The functions of the Public Trustee under Part VII of the Mental Health Act 1983 are found in Court of Protection Rules 1994, rule 6.

The Public Trust Office consists of four divisions:

- *Receivership Division* – the Public Trustee acts as the receiver;
- *Protection Division* – deals with external receivers;
- *Trust Division* – the Public Trustee is an executor or trustee;
- *Court Funds Office* – provides a banking and investment service for funds deposited in court.

The Public Trust Office employs 555 staff, has a gross budget of £19.75 million and is responsible for the management of approximately £3.75 billion of the private assets of individuals. It may be contacted at:

Customer Services Unit,	Tel 020 7 664 7000
Public Trust Office,	Fax 020 7 404 1725
Stewart House, 24 Kingsway,	
LONDON WC2B 6JX	DX 37965 Kingsway

On 1 July 1994 the Public Trust Office became an executive agency within the Lord Chancellor's Department.

The Official Solicitor

The Official Solicitor is a confidential adviser and assistant to the Supreme Court whose principal function is to ensure, by intervention in proceedings or otherwise, that the legal rights and duties of persons under a disability are recognised and enforced – see Supreme Court Act 1981, s 90.

Although the Public Trustee has assumed the role of 'receiver of last resort' where nobody else is willing, able or suitable to act, the Official Solicitor is still invited to intervene in proceedings where the Court of Protection considers that the interests of a patient are not adequately represented – Court of Protection Rules 1994, rule 15.

The Lord Chancellor's Visitors

Visitors are appointed by the Lord Chancellor to visit people who are, or are alleged to be, patients and to report to the Court of Protection (they may also visit the donor of an enduring power of attorney). For their terms and conditions of appointment and functions see Mental Health Act 1983, ss 102 and 103.

Medical Visitors

There are currently six registered medical practitioners with special knowledge and experience of mental disorder and each covers a particular Circuit. They visit patients for the purpose of assessing their mental capacity and may also report on any other relevant matters (e.g. suitability of care).

General Visitors

There are currently six General Visitors for Protection Division patients who are not required to possess either a medical or a legal qualification. They report on whether a patient's property and affairs are being handled in his best interests and are regarded as 'the eyes and ears of the Court of Protection and the voice of the patient'.

Legal Visitor

The Legal Visitor is a barrister or solicitor of not less than 10 years' standing whose main function is to advise Medical and General Visitors on questions of law, evidence and procedure arising out of their visits to patients.

10.2 POWERS OF THE COURT

General

The Court may with respect to property and affairs of a patient do or secure the doing of all such things as appear necessary or expedient:

- for the maintenance or other benefit of the patient;
- for the maintenance or other benefit of members of the patient's family;
- for making provision for other persons or purposes for whom or which the patient might be expected to provide if he were not mentally disordered; or
- otherwise for administering the patient's affairs.

The Court has power to make such orders and give such directions and authorities as it thinks fit for these purposes, and there is a non-exhaustive list of specific powers.

Exercise

The Court must have regard first to the requirements of the patient, but shall also take into account:

- the interests of creditors;
- the desirability of making provisions for obligations of the patient even if these are not legally enforceable.

Although having exclusive powers to control and manage the patient's property the Court usually exercises these powers through a receiver.

> Mental Health Act 1983, ss 95 and 96.

Urgency

Once the Court has received a medical report indicating that it has jurisdiction it may give directions by an order or certificate before the first hearing and appointment of a receiver.

Emergency

Under section 98 of the Mental Health Act 1983 the Court can give directions or appoint an interim receiver with limited powers before medical evidence is available, provided the Master:

- has been given reason to believe the person concerned may be incapable; and
- is of the opinion that it is *necessary* to make immediate provision.

Orders

Short orders (and directions of the Public Trustee)

If the patient's estate is simple and straightforward, or is less than about £5,000, the Court can issue an order (or the Public Trustee can issue a direction) authorising the patient's assets to be used in a specified way for his benefit rather than appointing a receiver:

- appropriate where something needs authorising on a 'one-off' basis (e.g. signing a tenancy agreement or residential care home contract, disposing of money accumulated whilst in hospital);
- application is as for appointment of a receiver but include a letter explaining the circumstances and what is proposed (fees are less than for receivership).

> Court of Protection Rules 1994, rule 9.

Chapter 10 COURT OF PROTECTION

First General Order

If the Court is satisfied that this step is necessary, the first order is for the appointment of a receiver who takes over control of the financial affairs of the patient subject to the directions and supervision of the Court. The powers of the receiver are stated including any special powers needed.

Subsequent orders

Orders containing further directions and powers will be made as and when needed, usually following an application. These may include authority to sell a house, make a gift, change investments or become involved in proceedings.

Gifts and settlements

A gift of a patient's money or property must be authorised by either the Public Trustee or the Court but there is power to order the creation of a settlement of any property of the patient – see section 96(1)(d):

- the persons entitled to apply are listed in the Court of Protection Rules 1994, rule 20;
- a formal application must be made, the Official Solicitor may be asked to represent the patient and an attended hearing may be required.

A proposed gift cannot be considered unless it is – see sections 95(1)(b) and (c):

- 'for the maintenance or other benefit of members of the patient's family'; or
- 'for making provision for other persons or purposes for whom or which the patient might be expected to provide if he were not mentally disordered':
    - inheritance tax mitigation is acceptable
    - any gift the prime purpose of which is to avoid the payment of means-tested maintenance charges is unlikely to be approved

Statutory wills

For the powers of the Court to authorise the execution of a will on behalf of a patient see Chapter 31 at para. 31.4.

> Procedure Note PN9 *Applications for the execution of statutory wills and codicils and for gifts, settlements and other similar dealings.*

Order Determining Proceedings

Where the patient's mental capacity has improved sufficiently for him to be restored to the management of his own affairs an application should be made for this order – section 99(3).

PART 1: SECTION C   Financial Management

10.3   PROCEDURE

The appropriate forms are sent out by the Customer Services Unit at the Public Trust Office (PTO) in response to an initial enquiry, and many applications thereafter can be made by letter. The most frequently used forms available from the Court are:

CP1 First application for the appointment of a receiver

CP3 Medical certificate

CP5 Certificate of family and property

CP6 Notification to patient of first application

CP7 Certificate of service of notification to patient

CP9 General form of application

First application

The initial application will usually be for appointment of a receiver, but the Court may make other types of order. The applicant is usually a relative, friend or solicitor but anyone can apply.

Documents submitted

The appropriate forms (CP1 in duplicate, CP3 and CP5) are completed and submitted together with:

- a copy of the patient's will and any other testamentary document;
- a cheque for the Commencement Fee, currently £100 made payable to 'Public Trust Office'.

Medical evidence is required because jurisdiction only arises if the Court is satisfied after considering such evidence that the person is not only suffering from a mental disorder but also incapable of managing his financial affairs by reason of that mental disorder.

> **Urgent cases:** If immediate action is needed (e.g. payment of home fees) give an explanation in Form CP5 and a covering letter. The Court will then issue an interim order, certificate or directions as appropriate – see rule 44.

Hearing

One copy of Form CP1 is then returned by the PTO marked with the date and time when the Court will consider the application. Unless the solicitors are otherwise notified, no attendance is necessary – see rule 10.

Notice to relatives and others

Before applying, the applicant must give notice of his intention to all the patient's relatives of a degree of relationship equal to or nearer than the applicant or proposed receiver – see rule 27:

- where a solicitor is seeking to be appointed as receiver notice is only given to the patient's closest relatives rather than the entire family;
- the Court may specify other persons who appear to be interested and should be given notice (e.g. cohabitees or partners).

Notice to the patient

The PTO also sends the applicant's solicitors a letter addressed to the patient notifying the date on which the application will be considered and explaining how representations and observations can be made (Form CP6) – see rule 26:

- this letter is to be personally served on the patient:
    - the person who serves it must complete a certificate of service (Form CP7)
    - the letter must be delivered to the patient at least 10 clear days before the date when the application will be considered by the Court – rule 48(1)
- the Court has power under rule 26(2) to dispense with such notification, but:
    - is reluctant to do so because the patient may wish to object to the appointment of a particular person or may have useful information to contribute
    - is only likely to do so if satisfied, after considering medical evidence, that the patient is incapable of understanding the letter, or that such notification would be injurious to his health

References and security

A reference is usually required as to the suitability of the proposed receiver who may be required to give security for the due performance of his duties. A questionnaire (Form CP8) is sent by the PTO to the referee named by the applicant in Form CP5.

First General Order

When everything is in order the First General Order will be issued:

- all dealings with the patient's capital must be authorised in this order or by subsequent orders or directions;
- an office copy should be registered with all banks and building societies with which the patient has accounts and all companies in which he holds shares.

The First General Order sets out the receiver's powers and duties.

PART 1: SECTION C   Financial Management

Subsequent applications

These are made on Form CP9 or by letter if straightforward – see rule 8(1). They are usually made by the receiver who does not need to give notice to any other person (unless the Court so directs):

- if not made by the receiver he should be notified – rule 21(2);
- special provisions relate to applications for a new or replacement receiver and for statutory wills, settlements and gifts.

Hearings

All applications are heard in chambers (rule 39) and the Court determines who attends the hearings (rule 40). In many cases an attendance will not be necessary.

Complaints, reviews and appeals

There is an internal complaints procedure – see the PTO's Charter Statements.

Where a decision is made by the Public Trustee or by the Court other than on a hearing the applicant may apply within eight days for review of the matter at a hearing. There is no review of a decision about fee remission, postponement or exemption.

A person dissatisfied with a decision made on a hearing may appeal within 14 days to a nominated judge – rule 57.

Fees

Fees are payable out of the patient's estate at various stages to cover the cost of applications to the Court and administration by the PTO. They comprise a commencement fee, administration fees and transaction fees. A request may be made to postpone or waive the fees in case of hardship. The fees:

- are on a scale and do not relate to the complexity of the patient's affairs;
- are calculated on *clear annual income* – the income available to be paid to or for the benefit of the patient (certain types of income are exempt, e.g. non-taxable social security benefits).

> For fees see Part XVIII of and the Appendix to the Rules.

Costs

Costs are normally ordered to be paid from the patient's estate (legal aid is not available) and the methods for claiming are:

Chapter 10 COURT OF PROTECTION

- *fixed costs* – annually reviewed amounts for different classes of work which the solicitor can claim by letter, plus VAT and disbursements;
- *agreed costs* – where costs (excluding VAT and disbursements) do not exceed a specified sum and there is no provision for fixed costs – see Practice Direction dated 17 March 1992:
  - the sum was £1,000 as at January 1998 and is reviewed at intervals
  - submit a narrative bill summarising the work done, hours spent and level of fee-earner together with counsel's fee notes and vouchers for disbursements
- *taxation* – where fixed or agreed costs are not sufficient obtain authority and then lodge a bill for taxation which may be a *summary bill* or an *itemised bill* depending on the complexity of the matter. Costs are then assessed on the indemnity basis and RSC Order 62 (in its final form) still applies.

Prior costs

A summary bill may be submitted for work not connected with the receivership for a period before appointment with a request that it be taxed as 'prior costs'.

Conveyancing

A category of fixed costs has been introduced for conveyancing work comprising a fixed sum plus a value element (generally one-half per cent of consideration).

An estate agent's bill is not treated as a disbursement but is shown as an expense in the completion statement lodged with the Court. Approval should be obtained before payment unless the amount is within the limit set in the order authorising sale – see Practice Direction dated 9 April 1992. Charges not exceeding 2.5 per cent of the sale price (to include commission, expenses, etc.) are normally considered reasonable, but the receiver has a duty to act in the best interests of the patient so should negotiate any lower level of charges that applies in the locality.

> All costs incurred in relation to proceedings under the Court of Protection Rules 1994 are in the discretion of the Court or the Public Trustee – rule 87(1).

10.4 RECEIVERSHIP

The Court will generally appoint a receiver for a person when, after considering medical evidence, it is satisfied that the person in question is incapable, by reason of mental disorder, of managing and administering his property and affairs – see Mental Health Act 1983, ss 94(2) and 99:

- usually unnecessary if the incapacitated person has created a valid enduring power of attorney – see Chapter 9;

- may not be necessary if his only assets consist of:
  - social security benefits or other government payments – see Chapter 8
  - entitlement under a discretionary trust
  - property which does not exceed £5,000 in value: a short order or direction can then be made

> A receiver is an individual appointed by the Court of Protection to deal with the financial affairs of a patient, subject to supervision.

Appointment

The duties of the receiver commence with the order of appointment and normally end only when:

- the Court is satisfied that the patient has become capable of handling his own affairs;
- the patient dies (automatic discharge); or
- all assets become exhausted.

A new receiver may be appointed on death or retirement, and a receiver may be replaced if:

- he has failed to carry out the directions of the Court; or
- the Court decides that it would be in the best interests of the patient for someone else to be appointed.

Identity

The receiver will usually be a relative or friend of the patient, but a referee as to fitness and an adequate fidelity guarantee bond or other security to safeguard the patient's assets may be required:

- joint receivers or persons residing out of the jurisdiction are discouraged;
- no one may be appointed without their consent;
- a solicitor, accountant or representative of a local authority may be appointed (and the bond is not always required for a practising solicitor).

> The Public Trustee will be appointed as receiver of last resort.

Status

When the Court makes a receivership order the patient ceases to have any powers over his financial affairs and these are transferred to the Court which dele-

Chapter 10 COURT OF PROTECTION

gates certain powers to the receiver (and may allow the patient to retain some limited powers).

Powers

The receiver's powers are clearly defined in the order of appointment and cannot extend to deciding where or with whom the patient shall live, consenting to medical treatment or other personal decisions (though in practice personal and financial decisions are often linked). The receiver:

- may be given general power to spend income (subject to annual accounting) but must seek specific authority from the Court to spend or re-invest capital;
- is not entitled to any remuneration save that:
  - a solicitor may be entitled to costs (see below)
  - other professional receivers (accountants, bank managers, local authority) may be allowed remuneration as specified in the First General Order
  - reasonable out-of-pocket expenses are reimbursed and fees for professional advice will be covered (though approval must be obtained in advance)

Duties

A receiver is generally responsible for collecting the patient's income, paying the bills and administering the patient's affairs in his best interests. He should endeavour to be aware of the patient's wishes and use the patient's money for his benefit during his lifetime. He must:

- comply with all orders and directions issued by the Court and act within the powers and authorities given to him;
  - promptly notify the Court of certain matters concerning the patient in case further directions should be given (e.g. marriage, death, change of address)
  - submit annual accounts to the Public Trust Office in regard to the patient's estate on forms provided for the purpose
- take control of investments and professional advice as to suitability, and seek authority for any changes:
  - be responsible for documents relating to investments and deposit these with the bank or solicitor
- be aware of his responsibilities and liabilities in applying for state benefits.

> The receiver's powers are limited to dealing with the patient's financial affairs.

Sale of the patient's property

Where the patient is the sole owner of a residential property, is already living in

PART 1: SECTION C   Financial Management

alternative accommodation and there is no prospect of his returning to live in his own home, an order or direction for sale will be issued if the sale has not already been authorised in the First General Order:

- if the property has been specifically bequeathed in his will, the net proceeds of sale will be held in a designated account to preserve the funds for the intended beneficiary:
    - this does not prevent these funds being used if needed for the patient's maintenance or other requirements but a statutory will may then be appropriate
- where the patient is a co-owner of the property it may be necessary to apply for an order appointing a new trustee in place of the patient:
    - there is a procedure note on making such an application (PN9)

> A procedure note on the sale and purchase of property generally (PN4) is available from the Public Trust Office.

Investment management

An investment policy is set for each patient, usually when the First General Order is made. The Court first considers the patient's age and prospects of life:

- if the patient is unlikely to live for five years a short-term (ST) policy is set;
- if the patient is expected to live for more than five years, a long-term (LT) policy is set.

There is a choice between investing the monies in Court in the name of the Accountant General, or authorising the receiver to handle investments subject to all necessary authorities being obtained from the Court.

Funds in Court

When funds are held in Court the receiver is insulated from investment problems but a choice of funds is available:

- *Common Investment Funds* – only available to courts but suitable in all but the larger cases. There are three unit trusts with different objectives:
    - *Capital Fund* – for capital growth
    - *High Yield Fund* – for income with growth
    - *Gross Income Fund* – tax-free income for non-taxpayers
- *Special Account* – a deposit account which pays a competitive rate of interest twice a year without deduction of tax although the interest is taxable. No notice of withdrawal is required and interest accrues on a day-to-day basis.

The Court is not restricted to using the Common Investment Funds and may

98

invest directly on the stock market by instructing a panel stockbroker.

Funds out of Court

There are three forms of investment management which the Court may authorise the receiver to undertake in larger cases, with the Court overseeing the investment policy:

- *general powers authority* – stockbrokers manage the investments and deal directly with the receiver;
- *investment powers authority* – stockbrokers hold investments in their nominee company and distribute income quarterly;
- *investment management agreement* – management delegated to the trust branch of a bank.

Stockbrokers

The patient's own stockbroker will normally be consulted or any preference of the receiver or solicitors taken into account, but failing this the Court consults one of a panel of firms normally used by the Protection Division. A stockbroker should be notified of:

- the investment policy fixed by the Court and any changes;
- the patient's estimated income from all sources and anticipated expenditure on an annual basis;
- the patient's capital assets (with acquisition details for capital gains tax purposes);
- the patient's age, state of health and life expectancy.

The stockbroker's recommendations should be sent to the Court with the receiver's observations and a formal authority is then issued in respect of the release of cash for specific investment.

10.5 PRACTICAL POINTS

It is the solicitor's duty to advise the Court on behalf of the patient and in co-operation with a receiver to bring all relevant information to the notice of the Court.

Orders

- In urgent cases telephone the Court to confirm that an emergency application is appropriate and then include with the application a letter asking for interim directions and setting out what is required and the reasons for urgency.

PART 1: SECTION C   Financial Management

- Use the short procedure where formal authority is required for a person to take a specific step (e.g. enter into a tenancy) and receivership is not otherwise necessary.
- When a draft order is submitted by the Court for approval, any questions should be dealt with and any necessary amendments sought.
- Draw attention to any additional powers of the receiver that are needed:
  - power to resort to capital to the extent that income will not be sufficient for maintenance (e.g. to pay nursing home fees)
  - authority to hand an appropriate sum to the patient periodically for expenditure of choice and for the patient to operate a personal bank or building society account (in suitable cases)
- When appropriate seek authority to make gifts or settlements for the benefit of members of the patient's family, other persons and charities for whom the patient might be expected to provide.
- Ensure that the First General Order includes adequate provision for costs:
  - a receiver may not, without prior authority, employ a professional person at the expense of the estate to do any work not usually requiring professional assistance

> Delay in referring an incapacitated client's affairs to the Court of Protection (once it becomes clear that this step is necessary) can result in those affairs becoming unnecessarily complicated. It is generally better to make the application sooner rather than later.

Administration

- Retain all original orders but obtain office copies and produce these to third parties as required:
  - notify persons dealing with the patient (e.g. the staff at a residential care home) of the receiver's appointment so that they do not inadvertently seek to enter into transactions with the patient directly
  - a new bank account should be opened in the receiver's name as receiver for the purpose of receiving all income due to the patient, discharging liabilities and providing such funding as the patient requires
  - the receiver should sign any authorised document in his own name adding: 'as receiver of *(patient)*'. Wider authority may be given, e.g. to execute deeds or statutory wills
- Remember that the money is there to be used for the patient's benefit rather than preserved for those who would inherit on the patient's death:
  - financial arrangements should reflect the needs of the patient and be structured

Chapter 10 COURT OF PROTECTION

   so as to be as supportive and provide as much freedom as circumstances permit
 - whenever guidance is needed consult the patient's doctor and the social services department for the area in which the patient resides, as appropriate
 - continuity of care is desirable so elderly patients should not be moved to a private nursing home where the costs would be likely to exhaust resources during their lifetime unless financial assistance from some other source is assured
 - the receiver should be aware of his duty to disclose assets to the Benefits Agency and social services department where means assessment applies
- Submit a full bill for taxation where fixed or agreed costs would be inadequate.

Do not treat receivership work as being of low priority or importance. This can create the very problems of which some solicitors complain.

PART TWO

Managing an Elderly Client Practice

This second part considers how a practice (or department) dealing with elderly clients should be managed. Relevant professional rules and codes of conduct are identified along with the services available from the Law Society, and suggestions are made as to organisation and delegation. Guidance is given as to how your firm may target elderly clients and provide an all round and quality service for older clients.

It should be emphasised that what a solicitor is obliged by rules of professional practice to do, and what he may choose to do, over and above this, in order to develop a practice and gain a good reputation will often be the way forward to delivering a quality service. Many suggestions are made, some would say these are counsels of perfection, and accordingly they should not be treated as indicating the standard of conduct necessarily expected of a solicitor.

In setting up and managing an elderly client practice the use and onward development of a specific business plan is crucial in promoting the strength and growth of a department.

Chapter 11

Professional Matters

All solicitors in whatever area of practice are subject to the general law, the Solicitors Act 1974 (as amended), the Solicitors' Practice Rules, Solicitors' Accounts Rules, Solicitors' Investment Business Rules, various Codes of Practice and the other requirements in *The Guide to the Professional Conduct of Solicitors 1999,* published by the Law Society. Reference may also be made to the following publications by the Law Society and further enquiry should be to the guidance officers at Redditch, Professional Ethics Division (address in Appendix 5):

- The Solicitors Guide to Good Management
- Office Procedures Manual
- Solicitors Accounts Manual
- Setting up and Managing a Small Practice

Elderly clients are in many respects indistinguishable from other clients, but it is possible to identify such clients and their needs. Practitioners who wish to develop an elderly client practice will not only wish but will increasingly need to be conversant with these matters.

11.1 PRACTICE RULES

Only those rules of significance to an elderly client practice are set out or referred to in this Handbook, and all references to practice outside England and Wales have been omitted.

Solicitors' Practice Rules 1990

(with consolidated amendments)

Rule 1 (Basic principles)

A solicitor shall not do anything in the course of practising as a solicitor, or permit another person to do anything on his or her behalf, which compromises or impairs or is likely to compromise or impair any of the following:

a) the solicitor's independence or integrity;

b) a person's freedom to instruct a solicitor of his or her choice;

PART 2: Managing an Elderly Client Practice

c) the solicitor's duty to act in the best interests of the client;

d) the good repute of the solicitor or of the solicitors' profession;

e) the solicitor's proper standard of work;

f) the solicitor's duty to the Court.

> All references to the Guide below are to *The Guide to the Professional Conduct of Solicitors 1999*.
>
> For additional guidance on the implications of Rule 1 see Chapter 1 at p 2 of the Guide.

Rule 2 (Publicity)

Solicitors may at their discretion publicise their practices, or permit other persons to do so, or publicise the businesses or activities of other persons, provided there is no breach of these rules and provided there is compliance with a Solicitors' Publicity Code promulgated from time to time by the Council of the Law Society with the concurrence of the Master of the Rolls.

> Solicitors' Publicity Code 1990
> Business Names Act 1985
> Solicitors' Investment Business Rules 1995
> The Law Society Code for Advocacy

Rule 3 (Introductions and referrals)

Solicitors may accept introductions and referrals of business from other persons and may make introductions and refer business to other persons, provided there is no breach of these rules and provided there is compliance with a Solicitors' Introduction and Referral Code promulgated from time to time by the Council of the Law Society with the concurrence of the Master of the Rolls.

Rule 5 (Offering services other than as a solicitor)

Solicitors must comply with the Solicitors' Separate Business Code in controlling, actively participating in or operating (in each case alone, or by or with others) a business which:

1. provides any service which may properly be provided by a solicitors' practice, and
2. is not itself a solicitors' practice or a multi-national partnership.

Rule 6 (Avoidance of conflicts of interest in conveyancing, property selling and mortgage related services)

See the Guide at pp 10–22 and 455.

Chapter 11 PROFESSIONAL MATTERS

Rule 7 (Fee sharing)

A solicitor shall not share or agree to share his or her professional fees with any person except:

a) a practising solicitor ...;

b) a practising foreign lawyer (other than a foreign lawyer whose registration in the register of foreign lawyers is suspended or whose name has been struck off the register);

c) the solicitor's *bona fide* employee, which provision shall not permit under the cloak of employment a partnership prohibited by paragraph 6 of this rule [a partnership with a non-solicitor]; or

d) a retired partner or predecessor of the solicitor or the dependants or personal representatives of a deceased partner or predecessor ....

Rule 8 (Contingency fees)

Rule 9 (Claims assessors)

Rule 10 (Receipt of commissions from third parties)

1. Solicitors shall account to their clients for any commission received of more than £20 unless, having disclosed to the client in writing the amount or basis of calculation of the commission or (if the precise amount or basis cannot be ascertained) an approximation thereof, they have the client's agreement to retain it.

2. Where the commission actually received is materially in excess of the amount or basis or approximation disclosed to the client the solicitor shall account to the client for the excess.

3. This rule does not apply where a member of the public deposits money with a solicitor who is acting as agent of a building society or other financial institution and the solicitor has not advised that person as a client as to the disposition of the money.

> For further guidance see the Guide at p 308 and the Solicitors' Investment Business Rules 1995.

Rule 11 (Names used by a firm)

1. A firm may not use a name which:
    a) is misleading; or
    b) brings the profession into disrepute.
2. A firm name appearing on any letterhead (or fax heading or heading used for

bills), if the same does not itself include the word solicitor(s), must be accompanied by either:

a) the word 'solicitor(s)'; or

b) the words 'regulated by the Law Society'.

> For further guidance see the Guide at pp 24, 25.

Rule 12 (Investment business)

1. Without prejudice to the generality of the principles embodied in Rule 1 of these Rules, solicitors shall not in connection with investment business:
   a) be appointed representatives; or
   b) have any arrangements with other persons under which the solicitors could be constrained to recommend to clients or effect for them (or refrain from doing so) transactions in some investments but not others, with some persons but not others, or through the agency of some persons but not others; or to introduce or refer clients or other persons with whom the solicitors deal to some persons but not others.
2. Solicitors shall not alone or by or with others control, actively participate in or operate a separate business which is an appointed representative, unless it is the appointed representative of an independent financial adviser.
3. Where a solicitor, authorised to conduct investment business, is required by the rules of the relevant regulatory body to use a particular terms of business letter, the solicitor shall use a terms of business letter in a form which has been approved by the Council of the Law Society.
4. This rule shall have effect in relation to the conduct of investment business within or into any part of the United Kingdom.
5. In this rule 'appointed representative', 'investment' and 'investment business' have the meanings assigned to them by the Financial Services Act 1986.

> For more guidance see the Guide, Chapter 27.

Rule 13 (Supervision and management of an office)

See the Guide at Chapter 12, 'Branch offices'.

Rule 15 (Costs information and client care)

Solicitors shall:

a) give information about costs and other matters, and

b) operate a complaints handling procedure

Chapter 11 PROFESSIONAL MATTERS

in accordance with a Solicitors' Costs Information and Client Care Code made from time to time by the Council of the Law Society with the concurrence of the Master of the Rolls but subject to the notes.

See more particularly the Guide at Chapter 13.

Solicitors' Accounts Rules

These Rules regulate the keeping of accounts – see the Guide at pp 677–781.

28A	Solicitors Act 1974, ss 34, 85
28B	Solicitors' Accounts Rules 1998
28C	Guidance – transitional arrangements
28D	Tax on bank and building society accounts – practice information
28E	Treatment of VAT on counsel's fees

Solicitors' Investment Business Rules 1995

For a full explanation and detailed discussion of investment business the reader is referred to the Guide at pp 522–676.

11.2 CODES OF PRACTICE

Solicitors' Publicity Code 1990

(as amended)

'It is the responsibility of solicitors to ensure that all their publicity, and all publicity for their services which is conducted by other persons, complies with the provisions of this code. The responsibility cannot be delegated. Where solicitors become aware of any impropriety in any publicity appearing on their behalf, they must use their best endeavours to have the publicity rectified or withdrawn as appropriate.' – *para. 1(f)*.

' "advertisement" and "advertising", except where the context otherwise requires, refer to any form of advertisement and include *inter alia* brochures, directory entries, stationery, and press releases promoting a solicitor's practice; but exclude press releases prepared on behalf of a client.' – *para. 16(ii)*.

109

General principles – para. 1

- Comply with all other professional obligations.
- Avoid publicity that is misleading, inaccurate or in bad taste.
- Comply with all statutory requirements and the general law.
- Do not breach any advertising codes of practice.

Contents – para. 2

- Your name or firm must be identified on all publicity.
- Do not claim that you are an expert or a specialist unless this can be justified.
- Do not refer to a success rate.
- Do not make comparisons with or criticisms of any other firms.
- You may use the legal aid logo but not the Law Society's coat of arms.
- Do not mention any part-time judicial appointment.

Unsolicited contacts – para. 3

Do not make unsolicited visits or telephone calls except:

- phone calls to current or former clients;
- to other solicitors or existing or potential professional connections;
- in connection with properties for sale or to let.

Naming clients – para. 4

You may in publicity material name or identify clients if:

- the client consents (usually in writing); and
- it is not likely to prejudice the client's interests.

Statements as to charges – para. 5

- Publicity as to charges must be clear:
  - state what services will be provided or the basis of charging
  - indicate circumstances in which charges may be increased or the basis changed
  - clarify whether disbursements and VAT are included
- Do not quote a fee as being from or upwards of a figure.
- Any service stated as being free must not be conditional upon other instruc-

tions, or on receipt of commission or other benefit.

- Do not quote a composite fee unless you are willing to:
  - quote separate fees for the individual services (not more in total) and
  - carry out only one of those services
- Do not quote net fees (ie. reduced by assumed commissions) though you may quote gross fees and indicate that commission may reduce the cost.

Designation of your practice – para. 6

If, in addition to the firm name, you use a designation of the practice this must:

- include the word 'solicitor(s)';
- not be misleading;
- not involve an improper claim to expertise or specialisation (see *Contents* above).

Naming partners and staff – para. 7

Clearly state the status of any person named who is not a practising solicitor:

- 'legal executive' and 'trainee solicitor' should only be used for those so qualified;
- the list of partners should be clearly distinguished from non-partners;
- the terms 'associate', 'assistant' and 'consultant' relate to practising solicitors unless the contrary is made clear;
- the terms 'executive', 'clerk', 'manager' and 'secretary' indicate that the individual is not a practising solicitor unless the contrary is made clear.

Directory headings – para. 8

You may have an entry or advertisement in a directory or listing under any appropriate heading provided that the word 'solicitor' appears either:

- in the heading of the directory; or
- in a designation of the practice in the entry or advertisement.

Subsidiary practising style – para. 9

This may be used (either for the firm or part of the firm) in conjunction with the name of the firm, provided that the word 'solicitor(s)' is also used.

Flag advertising – para. 10

This means advertising by or on your behalf of your firm under the logo of or in the name of a group or association including solicitors but not naming the firms. Note that:

- the word 'solicitor(s)' and an address at which the names of all the firms involved are available must be quoted;
- any notepaper used on legal professional business must include the name of the firm concerned.

Professional stationery – para. 12

Professional stationery must include your practising address, not merely a box number:

- the frontsheet of any fax that you send should contain your address if this is not on the following pages;
- special rules apply to use of stationery of a client, employer or recognised body.

Professional announcement, advertisement for staff, etc – para. 13

Institutional publicity – para. 15

Unless individual firms are referred to, this Code does not apply to publicity by:

- the Law Society concerning the services of solicitors in general or any class or group of solicitors;
- a local law society concerning the services of solicitors in general.

Solicitors' Introduction and Referral Code 1990

(as amended)

This code states the principles to be observed in relation to the introduction of clients by third parties to solicitors or by solicitors to third parties:

- it does not apply to introductions and referrals between solicitors, between solicitors and barristers or between solicitors and lawyers of other jurisdictions;
- it does not affect the need for you to communicate directly with the client to obtain or confirm instructions;
- non-compliance, evasion or disregard of the code could represent breach of practice rules, and conduct unbefitting a solicitor;
- those wishing to advertise the services of solicitors to whom they refer work should publicise their adherence to the code by a notice on the lines set out in the box below.

Chapter 11 PROFESSIONAL MATTERS

> 'We comply with the Solicitors' Introduction and Referral Code published by the Law Society, and any solicitor to whom we may refer you is an independent professional from whom you will receive impartial and confidential advice. You are free to choose another solicitor.'

Section 1: Basic principles

You must:

- always retain your professional independence and ability to advise clients fearlessly and objectively;
- never permit the requirements of an introducer to undermine this independence;
- in making or accepting introductions or referrals, do nothing which would be likely to compromise or impair any of the principles set out in Practice Rule 1.

Section 2: Introduction or referral of business to solicitors

- You must:
  - not reward introducers by the payment of commission or otherwise (this does not prevent normal hospitality)
  - ensure that you alone are responsible for any decisions taken in relation to the nature, style or extent of your practice
- You may:
  - discuss and make known to potential introducers the basis upon which you may be prepared to accept instructions and the fees that you would charge to clients referred
- You should:
  - draw the attention of potential introducers to this code and the relevant provisions of the Solicitors' Publicity Code
  - not allow yourself to become so reliant on a limited number of sources of referrals that the interests of an introducer affect advice given by you to clients
  - be conscious of the need to advise impartially and independently clients referred by introducers, and ensure that the wish to avoid offending the introducer does not colour the advice given
  - have regard to the suitability of the policy where a tied agent refers to you a client who is proposing to take out a company life policy
  - keep a record of agreements for the introduction of work
- You should conduct a review at six-monthly intervals to check:
  - that the provisions of this code have been complied with

- that referred clients have received impartial advice which has not been tainted by the relationship between your firm and the introducer and
- the income arising from each agreement for the introduction of business

- Where more than 20 per cent of your firm's income arises from a single source, consider whether steps should be taken to reduce this taking into account:
  - the percentage of income deriving from that source
  - the number of clients introduced by that source
  - the nature of the clients and the work
  - whether the introducer could be affected by the advice that you give

> See Practice Rule 12 re *Introductions and referrals in the field of investment business.*

Section 3: Agreeing to be paid by a third party to do work for the third party's customers other than conveyancing work

Section 3A: Contractual referrals for conveyancing

Section 4: Referral of clients by solicitors

- If you recommend that a client use a particular firm, agency or business, you must do so in good faith, judging what is in the client's best interest.
- You should not enter into any agreement or association which would restrict your freedom to recommend any particular firm, agency or business.
- Referral to a tied agent of a client requiring life insurance does not discharge your duty to give independent advice so any referral must be to an independent intermediary.
- If the best interests of the client require it, you may refer a client requiring a mortgage to a tied agent provided that the client is informed that the agent offers products from only one company.

> Note also Practice Rule 3, and see Practice Rule 10 re *Commissions for the introduction of clients to third parties.*

11.3 PROFESSIONAL CONDUCT

Reference should be made to *The Guide to the Professional Conduct of Solicitors 1999* published by the Law Society. Further guidance is available from the Professional Ethics Division. Those Principles of particular interest to practitioners dealing with elderly clients are set out below.

Requirements of practice

Partners and certain others must hold a current practising certificate. Clients must be notified of a material change in the composition of the firm. A solicitor is responsible for exercising proper supervision over both admitted and unadmitted staff (3.07):

- see Chapter 3 of the Guide;
- Practice Rule 13 sets minimum standards;
- a partner is responsible for the acts or omissions of his firm including staff.

Relationship with the client

Obtaining instructions

Practice Rules 1, 2 and 3 deal with instructions, but note that:

- you must be free to give impartial and frank advice to your client;
- there must be no improper influence upon the client to come to you;
- you must not allow yourself to be placed in a position where your own interests or those of a third party to whom you owe a duty conflict with those of the client;
- the normal solicitor–client relationship exists even if your costs are to be paid by another (e.g. an association which has introduced the client).

> See Rule 5 (3.20) for restrictions on the activities that you can carry out other than as part of your practice.

Communications with the client

Written professional standards concerning communications with the client have been laid down by Council. The material in para. 12.3 of this Handbook under the heading *Duties to the Client* is based upon these standards.

It is for you to decide whether in a particular case a given standard is inapplicable, but you will have to justify your decision if the client makes a complaint and you must set up a proper complaints procedure (see pp 265–266 and 270–271 of the Guide). A material breach of the standards could lead to a finding that you have provided inadequate professional services or, in a serious or persistent case, of professional misconduct. Unreasonable failure properly to advise the client on some matters (e.g. availability of legal aid) may also amount to negligence.

Retainer

You are generally free to decide whether to accept instructions from a client but

PART 2: Managing an Elderly Client Practice

any refusal to act must not amount to race or sex discrimination. You must not act, or continue to act, if:

- your instructions would involve you in a breach of the law or the principles of professional conduct;
- you cannot represent the client with competence or diligence;
- you believe the client gives instructions under duress or undue influence;
- there is a conflict of interests (see below).

Where you receive instructions through a third party purporting to represent the client:

- obtain written instructions from the client that you are to act;
- take appropriate steps to confirm instructions, especially that they are those of the client, and see the client personally in any case of doubt (e.g. if capacity to give instructions may be questioned);
- advise the client without regard to the interests of the third party, except to the extent that those interests coincide with those of the client (e.g. individuals who seek to give instructions on behalf of an elderly relative).

You should refuse to take action which you believe is motivated solely by malice or vindictiveness.

Do not accept instructions to act in a matter where another solicitor is acting for the client in the same matter, until either the first retainer has been determined by the client, or the first solicitor has consented:

- if the first retainer has already been determined you do not need to inform the first solicitor of your involvement (but in the case of an elderly client this may be wise);
- you may give a second opinion without the first solicitor's knowledge but should not seek to influence the client to leave the first solicitor.

Having accepted instructions you must:

- carry them out with diligence and exercise reasonable care and skill;
- keep your client's business and affairs confidential;
- not take advantage of the age, inexperience, want of education or business experience, or ill health of the client;
- keep your client properly informed and comply with his requests for information concerning his affairs (though in exceptional circumstances you may be justified in withholding information);
- not terminate the retainer except for good reason and on reasonable notice:
    - the client can terminate the retainer at any time for any reason

Chapter 11 PROFESSIONAL MATTERS

- the retainer may terminate by operation of law if the client becomes legally incompetent, but you should then consult with relatives and (if appropriate) contact the Court of Protection or the Official Solicitor

On termination deliver to the client all papers and property to which the client is entitled or hold them to his order, and account for all funds held by you although you may have a lien for your unpaid costs.

Fees

Written professional standards about information on costs have been laid down by the Council of the Law Society. The material in para. 12.3 of this Handbook under the heading *Costs* is based upon these standards but the following Principles justify special mention:

- on taking instructions give the client the best information you can about the likely costs of the matter, discuss how charges and disbursements are to be met and consider whether the client is eligible for legal aid;

- record in writing whether a fee has been agreed and what it covers; if no fee has been agreed or estimate given, tell the client how the fee will be calculated and what other payments may be anticipated;

- confirm estimates in writing and keep to them unless changed circumstances have been confirmed in writing. If the client is bearing the costs tell him that he may set a limit which will not be exceeded without reference to him;

- tell the client at least every six months the approximate costs to date and render an interim bill if appropriate – you may at the outset require the client to make payments on account;

- for contentious cases and legal aid see para. 12.3 of this Handbook;

- in all matters consider with the client whether the likely outcome will justify the expense or risk involved;

- you must not share your costs with a non-solicitor or arrange a contingency fee – see the Guide at p 278 for more guidance;

- render your bill within a reasonable time containing sufficient information to identify the matter and period to which it relates;

- there are steps that you must take before you can sue on your bill but you may be able to charge interest;

- unless you agree to the contrary, you are personally responsible for paying anyone you instruct on behalf of a client even if the client does not pay you.

> For information on fees generally see Chapter 14 of the Guide.

Conflict of interests

You must not act, or continue to act, if there is a conflict of interests between yourself (or the firm) and the client, or between two clients, past or present, or a serious risk of such conflict. Disclosure of the conflict does not permit you to act even if the client consents:

- if you have acquired relevant knowledge concerning a former client whilst acting for him you may not subsequently act against him:
  - as to acting for both parties in conveyancing transactions see Practice Rule 6
  - you may act as mediator in a domestic dispute but if this fails you may not act for either party to the dispute
- if a client contemplates a claim against your firm, or you consider that a claim may be justified, inform that client that he should take independent advice;
- neither you nor any member of your family may make a secret profit out of your relationship with the client:
  - see Practice Rule 10 as regards commission
  - if you are attorney for a client you must not take a benefit which you would not allow to an independent third party if acting as professional adviser
  - if your client wishes to make a gift to you, your partner or staff (or family of any such persons) *inter vivos* or by will, and it is of a significant amount either in itself or in relation to the client's estate, you must advise the client to be independently advised and refuse to act

> There is no general rule of law that a solicitor should never act for both parties in a transaction where their interests might conflict, but in such situation the solicitor should get the informed consent of both parties – see *Clark Boyce v Mouat* [1993] 4 All ER 268, PC).

Confidentiality

You must keep the affairs of your clients confidential to your firm and ensure that the staff do the same:

- this applies irrespective of the source of the information and until the client permits disclosure and it may extend to the client's address;
- the duty can be overridden in certain exceptional circumstances (e.g. the duty to report to the Legal Aid Board; the bankruptcy of the client).

It is suggested by the writer, but has not been confirmed by the Council of the Law Society, that if the client becomes legally incompetent (see Chapter 2) the solicitor may disclose information when he considers this to be in the best interests of the client even though he has no express authority to do so and the retainer will have terminated (note the Law Commission recommendations and Government proposals summarised in Appendix 8).

The following are also dealt with in *The Guide to the Professional Conduct of Solicitors 1999*:

Particular areas of practice

- Litigation and advocacy – Chapter 21
- Insolvency practice – Chapter 23
- Conveyancing – Chapter 25
- Property selling – Chapter 26
- Investment business – Chapter 27

Financial regulation

- Accounts – Chapter 28
- Professional indemnity – Chapter 29
- Compensation Fund – Chapter 30

Disciplinary process

- Office for the Supervision of Solicitors – Chapter 30
- Solicitors' Indemnity Fund – Chapter 29

Your relations with others are dealt with in the Principles:

- With third parties – Chapter 17
- With other solicitors – Chapter 19
- With the Bar and professional agents – Chapter 20
- Professional undertakings – Chapter 18

Chapter 12

Organisation

12.1 OFFICE MANAGEMENT

Ensure that the office has the relevant knowledge and expertise to handle the many problems that arise and have efficient office systems to cope with the administration. Clients or those assisting with their affairs will soon become dissatisfied if there is delay and uncertainty or they are not kept advised. Encourage personal links between the client and an individual solicitor or suitable member of staff according to the needs of the client, bearing in mind that continuity and availability are the things that elderly clients appreciate most.

Staff

From the outset make clear to staff the basic standards of good practice which they are expected to follow. Value their contribution and recognise the particular stresses working with the elderly client can cause. Ensure that:

- fee earners and support staff receive proper training and are continually updated on changes in the law, rules and regulations;

- all staff can recognise particular problems which may arise in working with older clients, e.g. questions of capacity, inter-generational conflicts, long-term care issues;

- there are opportunities for obtaining specialist qualifications (e.g. Society of Estate and Trust Practitioners) or to join specialist groups (e.g. the Probate Practitioners Section, Solicitors for the Elderly).

Delegation

Individual case work can be delegated to staff, leaving a supervising partner or senior solicitor to cope with problems and develop a relationship with the client. But ensure that the client is made aware of this and of the status of the person doing the work. Adequate, regular and continuing supervision of staff with the use of clear office protocols and guidance is essential because:

- there is scope for financial mismanagement so the introduction of independent audit of passbooks, cheque books, pensions, etc. handled by staff acting as attorneys, etc. is good practice;

- there may be neglect of vulnerable clients who place their total trust in your firm (or you personally):

- set up regular file audits and client reviews
- help attorneys to understand their role and offer support to lay attorneys
- remember the overall common law duty of care to clients

Consider whether you wish to restrict unqualified staff in their contracts of employment from being appointed as attorney or executor for clients:

- it may not be in the best interests of clients to have a blanket restriction so other controls may be appropriate, e.g:
  - a joint and several appointment, or a second signature
  - quarterly accounts or regular audit (which could be by your firm)
- remember that an unqualified person is not subject to any of the professional duties or controls that apply to a solicitor, and effective supervision would cease if the member of staff left your employment:
  - have arrangements to replace attorneys or cover by partner plus non-partner appointment (i.e. joint and several appointments)
- set up regular client reviews and training in case management.
- Have clear-cut protocols for managing elderly clients' affairs and ensure all staff looking after those clients receive proper induction and training from the outset of their appointment:
  - ensure that any gifts from clients are disclosed and recorded
  - make clear to staff any professional implications of their role

Recognise that:
- the client may not realise if matters are not properly dealt with
- the client may not be capable of complaining
- you are responsible for the acts and omissions of your staff

Departments

It may be appropriate to set up a department dealing with older clients or a small dedicated section within a larger department. If your firm has various specialised departments it may be desirable to arrange for a partner or fee-earner to co-ordinate the affairs of each elderly client as a personal adviser rather than expecting the client to move around the office as different problems arise, because:

- unlike the corporate client, elderly people usually want an individual rather than a firm to look after them; they want continuity and stability of service;
- a relationship with the client coupled with access to specific expertise is generally more valuable than expertise in a particular field of law but no knowledge of the client;

- many areas of law relevant to elderly clients do not belong to any of the traditional departments so it may be worth setting up a separate department;
- moving into a care home may involve conveyancing, wills, advice on residential care contracts, financial services, tax planning and welfare benefits in addition to co-ordination by the personal adviser.

Links between departments

Links between departments are essential, for example:

- when dealing with the financial affairs of a client it will be important to keep up-to-date with social security benefits (these comprise not only means-tested or welfare benefits but also disability benefits). Make it a rule when seeing older clients to do an automatic benefits check:
  - many clients assume all benefits are means tested
  - disability benefits are often passports to other concessions, e.g. orange badge parking, concessionary travel (this is 'added' value)
- the tax department may then identify the need to provide investment advice;
- a link between probate and tax departments enables a recently widowed client's tax affairs to continue to be dealt with.

> The role of the practice is as much in giving support to the client as in giving legal advice and this needs to be conveyed to colleagues.

Branch offices

Every office where your firm practises must conform with Rule 13 of the Solicitors' Practice Rules 1990 and be (and reasonably be seen to be) properly supervised in accordance with certain minimum standards:

- it must be attended on each day when open to the public by a solicitor who holds a practising certificate and has been admitted for at least three years:
  - that solicitor must spend sufficient time at the office to ensure adequate control of the staff employed there and afford requisite facilities for consultation with clients
  - that solicitor may be a principal, employee or consultant of your firm
- it must be managed by a practising solicitor or suitably qualified legal executive (or licensed conveyancer if solely dealing with conveyancing):
  - that person must normally be in attendance at that office during all the hours when it is open to the public (including for telephone calls)
- in cases of absence due to illness, accident, etc. for a prolonged period, suitable alternative arrangements should be made.

Monitoring

Clients will not always know when they need further legal assistance and it may be beneficial for you to keep a watching brief. Consider for example offering older clients a regular fixed fee legal audit every three years – this will maintain contact. If the client is incapacitated and acting through a receiver or attorney (and if you are acting) you must do this in any event. For example:

- do not overlook the need for a will to be updated or a statutory will considered (a statutory will can deal with changed circumstances);
- is any enduring power of attorney still operable or should it be registered? Is it properly executed?
- are all current state benefits being claimed (the qualifying conditions or the needs of the client may have changed)?
- are the client's financial affairs still being handled properly and have they been reviewed in light of the current situation?
  - is it time for a change of investment policy?
  - is the client living on capital and if so how long will this last – can/should changes be made?
  - should the client consider some tax planning measures?
  - should assistance be offered to cope with self-assessment?
  - is there any reason to suspect that the client is vulnerable to financial exploitation or any other form of abuse?
- do the present housing arrangements still meet the client's needs?
- should the client be advised on community care services and how to obtain best delivery of services?
  - is assistance needed in negotiating any contract with social services or a residential care or nursing home?

Addressing the client

Establish a policy throughout the firm as to the manner in which clients are addressed, in particular in letters. Do not assume that a first name approach should be encouraged:

- elderly clients tend to prefer a more formal approach;
- would the client wish to address you in the same manner (and would you wish the client to do so)?
- although partners and senior staff may wish to be on first name terms with clients, would you wish employees also to be and to address them in that manner in letters?

PART 2: Managing an Elderly Client Practice

- today's client may be at odds with your firm tomorrow, and how will that over-friendly letter look then?

Have you a policy as to who signs letters on the firm notepaper, and in what style (firm name, writer's name/first name)? Is there any check on outgoing post?

> Is the client to be addressed as:
> - Dear Madam
> - Dear Mrs Smith
> - Dear Ethel

12.2 SYSTEMS

Systems introduced in the office make monitoring clients' affairs and safe custody of papers and documents more effective. The use of computerised systems will ease:

- access to current files:
    - archiving of old files
- storage of documents:
    - deeds
    - wills
    - ordinary and enduring powers of attorney
    - securities
    - birth, death or marriage certificates
- maintenance of accounting records:
    - clients' account
    - trust accounts
    - accounts in the name of individual clients
- upkeep of diaries of reminders of significant dates;
- effective use of client database to target or review for new work.

There are many ways in which computers can help to provide a more effective and efficient service, for example:

- word processing can be used for:
    - standard form letters
    - precedents of regularly used documents
    - storage of client's previous will for easy amendment
    - documents to be tailormade e.g. larger fonts, heavier type

- databases:
  - of clients with whom regular contact should be maintained
  - of current and old files
  - of deeds and documents in safe custody
  - of clients falling into specific work areas/age groups
- spreadsheets:
  - schedules of investments
  - tax returns and interest schedules for reproducing annually (but ensure these comply with current revenue practice. Some IT packages do not comply and may lead to tax penalties following under self-assessment)
- accounting software:
  - clients' accounts and trust accounts
  - facility to calculate interest
- diaries:
  - appointments
  - reminders of action to take

Client database

You may have a database containing information about individual clients from which all other storage records are derived. All relevant information can then be seen in respect of a client at a glance, whilst lists of deeds, wills, securities, etc. can still be produced (according to categories of client, date, name or otherwise as desired).

> Advice about suitable systems can be obtained from The Business Improvements Manager at the Law Society's Legal Practice Directorate (address in Appendix 5).

12.3 DUTIES TO THE CLIENT

The first duty is always to identify the client – this is not always as obvious as it may appear (see Chapter 3). Professional duties are, throughout, owed to the client and not, where the client lacks legal competence, to the person through whom instructions are given although all communications may well be with that person:

- do not be too easily persuaded by third parties as to the client's best interests, because however well intentioned these people seem, they may have a personal interest (e.g. the interest of the younger generation is not that of their parents);

PART 2: Managing an Elderly Client Practice

- be alert to the potential for financial abuse with enduring powers of attorney.

Client care

The principal aim to be communicated to the client should be to:

- reply to correspondence within three working days;
- keep the client informed of progress:
  - advise of any delays and explain the reasons
  - send copies of significant letters
- explain the effect of any important documents;
- explain promptly to the client any changes:
  - to the costs forecast or basis of assessment
  - of staff affecting the client or of law affecting the matter

At the outset you should confirm to the client in writing:

- the person responsible for day-to-day conduct of the matter and their status or qualification, and also the partner responsible for overall supervision;
- the instructions that you have received and any advice you have given;
- what action you will be taking and what action you need the client to take;
- any further information you need from the client;
- the approximate time the matter will take and when the client is next likely to hear from you;
- about costs (see below);
- the likely effect of their actions – give any relevant warnings;
- the complaints procedures for use if the client is not satisfied.

> This can be done effectively in the Rule 15 letter supplemented by information leaflets relevant to the area of work.

At the end of the matter you should:

- confirm to the client, in writing, how the matter has been concluded;
- explain any continuing consequences and risks from their action;
- render your bill as promptly as possible and account to the client for all money due;
- consider with the client whether any papers and property are to be handed

over or retained by your firm.

> You may wish to include a simple questionnaire on the service rendered.

Costs

Advise clients and potential clients in advance what costs and expenses they may expect. Consider with the client whether the likely outcome will justify the expense or risk involved. The following should be covered:

- basis of charging including hourly rates and mark-up:
  - prospects of a free initial interview or fixed fee interviews or work
  - best estimate of the likely costs involved and placing a limit on total costs
  - choice and cost of fee earners
  - interim estimates of costs incurred and any options on billing e.g. quarterly, monthly, etc.
  - implications of VAT
- means of payment and when costs may be deducted:
  - eligibility for legal aid (and the effect of the statutory charge)
  - whether a payment in advance is required and why
  - nature and frequency of interim bills and treatment of disbursements
  - charges for interest on unpaid bills and any credit facilities available
- prospect of recovering all or any part of the cost:
  - from the Legal Aid fund (have relevant leaflets from the Legal Aid Board)
  - from the other party
  - from insurance or some other source
- procedure if the client is not satisfied about the level of costs:
  - right to an itemised bill, remuneration certificate or assessment by the Court
  - complaints to the firm
  - reference to the local Law Society, the Office for the Supervision of Solicitors or the Legal Services Ombudsman

> Have a statement of *Terms and Conditions of Business* sent to the client at the outset and consider sending a duplicate to sign confirming agreement.

Contentious cases

Inform the client at the outset and at appropriate stages of the matter:

- that he will be personally responsible for payment of your bill unless entitled to legal aid regardless of any order for costs made against his opponent;

- that if he loses he will probably have to pay his opponent's costs as well as his own;
- that even if he wins his opponent may not be ordered to pay the full amount of his costs and may not be capable of paying what he is ordered to pay;
- that if his opponent is legally aided he may not recover costs even if successful;
- if the firm operates a 'no win/no fee' scheme or uses contingency fee agreements.

Legal aid

If the client is legally aided in civil proceedings he should be informed:

- of his obligation to pay any contribution assessed, the consequences of any failure to do so and the effect of the statutory charge;
- that if he loses he may still be ordered to contribute to his opponent's costs even though his own costs are covered by legal aid;
- that even if he wins his opponent may not be ordered to pay the full amount of his costs and may not be capable of paying what he is ordered to pay.

12.4 CHARGING

For fees generally see *The Guide to the Professional Conduct of Solicitors 1999*, Chapter 14. For guidance on charging refer to the following Law Society publications:

Solicitors' Accounts Manual
> Includes the new accounts rules and all the information solicitors' accounts staff need to ensure compliance.

Solicitors' Charges: Understanding Your Solicitor's Bill
> Practice advice.

Conditional Fees: A Survival Guide
> Offers a step-by-step guide to making conditional fees pay.

Litigation Funding
> A journal published five times a year. For a sample copy call 020 7316 5599.

Solicitors' (Non-Contentious Business) Remuneration Order 1994

[Note: all references to 'taxation' in the following articles should now be read as being to 'assessment'].

Article 3

A solicitor's costs shall be such sum as may be fair and reasonable to both solicitor and entitled person having regard to all the circumstances of the case and in particular to:

a) the complexity of the matter or the difficulty or novelty of the questions raised;

b) the skill, labour, specialised knowledge and responsibility involved;

c) the time spent on the business;

d) the number and importance of the documents prepared or perused without regard to length;

e) the place where and the circumstances in which the business or any part thereof is transacted;

f) the amount or value of any property involved;

g) whether any land is registered land;

h) the importance of the matter to the client; and

i) the approval (express or implied) of the entitled person or the express approval of the testator to:

(i) the solicitor undertaking all or any part of the work giving rise to the costs or

(ii) the amount of the costs

Article 4

1. Without prejudice to the provisions of sections 70, 71 and 72 of the Solicitors Act 1974 (which relate to taxation of costs), an entitled person may, subject to the provisions of this Order, require a solicitor to obtain a remuneration certificate from the Council in respect of a bill which has been delivered where the costs are not more than £50,000.

2. The remuneration certificate must state what sum, in the opinion of the Council, would be a fair and reasonable charge for the business covered by the bill (whether it be the sum charged or a lesser sum). In the absence of taxation the sum payable in respect of such costs is the sum stated in the remuneration certificate.

Article 5

1. If on a taxation the taxing officer allows less than one half of the costs, he must bring the facts of the case to the attention of the Council.

2. The provisions of this Order are without prejudice to the general powers of the Council under the Solicitors Act 1974.

PART 2: Managing an Elderly Client Practice

Article 6

Before a solicitor brings proceedings to recover costs against a client on a bill for non-contentious business he must inform the client of the matters specified article 8, except where the bill has been taxed.

Article 7

1. If a solicitor deducts his costs from monies held for or on behalf of a client or of an estate in satisfaction of a bill and an entitled person objects in writing to the amount of the bill within the prescribed time, the solicitor must immediately inform the entitled person in writing of the matters specified in article 8, unless he has already done so.
2. In this article and in article 10 'the prescribed time' means:
    a) in respect of a client, three months after the delivery of the relevant bill, or a lesser time (which may not be less than one month) specified in writing to the client at the time of delivery of the bill; or
    b) in respect of the entitled third party, three months after delivery of notification to the entitled third party of the amount of the costs, or a lesser time (which may not be less than one month) specified in writing to the entitled third party at the time of such notification.

Article 8

When required by articles 6 or 7, a solicitor shall inform an entitled person in writing of the following matters:

1. where article 4(1) applies:
    a) that the entitled person may, within one month of receiving from the solicitor the information specified in this article or (if later) of delivery of the bill or notification of the amount of the costs, require the solicitor to obtain a remuneration certificate and
    b) that (unless the solicitor has agreed to do so) the Council may waive the requirements of article 11(1), if satisfied from the client's written application that exceptional circumstances exist to justify granting a waiver.
2. that sections 70, 71 and 72 of the Solicitors Act 1974 set out the entitled person's rights to taxation;
3. that (where the whole of the bill has not been paid, by deduction or otherwise) the solicitor may charge interest on the outstanding amount of the bill in accordance with article 14.

Article 9

A client may not require a solicitor to obtain a remuneration certificate:

a) after a bill has been delivered and paid by the client, other than by deduction;

b) where a bill has been delivered, after the expiry of one month from the date on which the client was informed in writing of the matters specified in article 8 or from delivery of the bill if later;

c) after the solicitor and client have entered into a non-contentious business agreement in accordance with the provisions of section 57 of the Solicitors Act 1974;

d) after a court has ordered the bill to be taxed (assessed);

e) if article 11(2) applies.

Article 10

An entitled third party may not require a solicitor to obtain a remuneration certificate:

a) after the prescribed time (within the meaning of article 7(2)(b)) has elapsed without any objection being received to the amount of the costs;

b) after the expiry of one month from the date on which the entitled third party was (in compliance with article 7) informed in writing of the matters specified in article 8 or from notification of the costs if later;

c) after a court has ordered the bill to be taxed.

Article 11

1. On requiring a solicitor to obtain a remuneration certificate a client must pay to the solicitor the paid disbursements and value added tax comprised in the bill together with 50 per cent of the costs unless:
   a) the client has already paid the amount required under this article, by deduction from monies held or otherwise; or
   b) the solicitor or (if the solicitor refuses) the Council has agreed in writing, to waive all or part of this requirement.

2. The Council shall be under no obligation to provide a remuneration certificate, and the solicitor may take steps to obtain payment of his bill if the client, having been informed of his right to seek a waiver of the requirements of paragraph (1), has not:
   a) within one month of receipt of the information specified in article 8, either paid in accordance with paragraph (1) or applied to the Council in writing for a waiver of the requirements of paragraph (1); or
   b) made payments in accordance with the requirements of paragraph (1) within one month of written notification that he has been refused a waiver of these requirements by the Council.

Article 12

1. After an application has been made by a solicitor for a remuneration certificate the client may pay the bill in full without invalidating the application.

2. A solicitor and entitled person may agree in writing to waive the provisions of sub-paragraphs a) or b) of articles 9 or 10.

3. A solicitor may take from his client security for the payment of any costs, including the amount of any interest to which the solicitor may become entitled under article 14.

Article 13

1. If a solicitor has received payment of all or part of his costs and a remuneration certificate is issued for less than the sum already paid, the solicitor must immediately pay to the entitled person any refund which may be due (after taking into account any other sums which may properly be payable to the solicitor whether for costs, paid disbursements, value added tax or otherwise) unless the solicitor has applied for an order for taxation within one month of receipt by him of the remuneration certificate.

2. Where a solicitor applies for taxation, his liability to pay any refund under paragraph (1) shall be suspended for so long as the taxation is still pending.

3. The obligation of the solicitor to repay costs under paragraph (1) is without prejudice to any liability of the solicitor to pay interest on the repayment by virtue of any enactment, rule of law or professional rule.

Article 14

1. After the information specified in article 8 has been given to an entitled person in compliance with articles 6 or 7, a solicitor may charge interest on the unpaid amount of his costs plus any paid disbursements and value added tax, subject to paragraphs (2) and (3) below.

2. Where an entitlement to interest arises under paragraph (1), and subject to any agreement made between a solicitor and client, the period for which interest may be charged may run for one month after the date of delivery of a bill, unless the solicitor fails to lodge an application within one month of receipt of a request for a remuneration certificate under article 4, in which case no interest is payable in respect of the period between one month after receiving the request and the actual date on which the application is lodged.

3. Subject to any agreement made between a solicitor and client, the rate of interest must not exceed the rate for the time being payable on judgment debts.

4. Interest charged under this article must be calculated, where applicable, by reference to the following:

a) if a solicitor is required to obtain a remuneration certificate, the total amount of the costs certified by the Council to be fair and reasonable plus paid disbursements and value added tax;

b) if an application is made for the bill to be taxed, the amount ascertained on taxation;

c) if an application is made for the bill to be taxed or a solicitor is required to obtain a remuneration certificate and for any reason the taxation or application for a remuneration certificate does not proceed, the unpaid amount of the costs shown in the bill or such lesser sum as may be agreed between the solicitor and the client, plus paid disbursements and value added tax.

Article 15

(1) A solicitor, when making an application for a remuneration certificate in accordance with the provisions of this Order, must deliver to the Council the complete relevant file and working papers, and any other information or documentation which the Council may require for the purpose of providing a remuneration certificate.

12.5 FINANCIAL SERVICES

Financial services should be seen as an integral part of general legal services and is only dealt with under a separate heading for convenience.

The Financial Services Act 1986

This Act (FSA 86), currently regulates the financial services industry.

The Securities and Investment Board (SIB), now the Financial Services Authority (FSA), is a designated agency responsible for authorisation and rule making:

- if you carry on investment business in the UK you must be an authorised or exempted person;

- as a recognised professional body (RPB), the Law Society is able to authorise solicitors, multi-national partnerships and recognised bodies to conduct *investment* business, by issuing firms with either a category 1 investment business certificate, or a category 2 certificate;

- under the FSA 86, the Law Society must have rules governing the conduct of investment business which provide adequate investor protection.

> The Financial Services and Markets Bill, which is expected to come into force in late 2000, should reduce the need for authorisation for many firms of solicitors. However, the position will not be clear until the legislation is finalised.

Regulation

The Solicitors' Investment Business Rules 1995

These are explained in *The Guide to the Professional Conduct of Solicitors 1999*. This further regulation is imposed upon the legal profession despite the fact that it is already heavily regulated. Experience shows that if you are acting for elderly clients you will inevitably carry on investment business activities and to that extent that you must be authorised. For most solicitors authorisation means holding a certificate issued by the Law Society as an RPB.

Investment business

If you are practising as a solicitor you are carrying on a business. Investments include stocks and shares, debentures, government and public securities, unit trusts, endowment and pension policies and annuities but not bank/building society accounts, land and tangible assets. Activities which will require authorisation include:

- dealing or arranging deals in investments;
- managing investments and investment advice;
- custody of investments.

> Further guidance on the definition of investment business may be found in Chapter 27 of *The Guide to the Professional Conduct of Solicitors 1999*.

Certain activities are excluded under FSA 86, for example:

- trustees and personal representatives who buy and sell investments in their own name, but this does not extend to activities of your firm where you are the trustee (FSA 86, Sched. 1, para. 22);
- advice given and arrangements made in the course of carrying on a profession, but only where this is 'necessary', provided that there is no separate remuneration for those services (FSA 86, Sched. 1, para. 24).

It will be difficult to avoid the need for authorisation when acting for elderly clients, but further guidance is available from Professional Ethics at the Law Society.

Certification

If you seek authorisation through certification from the Law Society you must:

- make application on form RF2;
- submit an annual renewal form RF1 or RF2 and pay the current annual fee;
- comply with the regulations in conducting investment business.

The Council of the Law Society has power to suspend, withdraw or impose conditions on any certificate that it issues and there are appeal procedures.

Your firm's approach

You will need to decide whether to apply for:

- a category 1 investment business certificate, which will allow you to do non-discrete investment business; or
- a category 2 investment business certificate, which will allow you to conduct discrete investment business.

Discrete investment business (DIB)

This may be defined as essentially mainstream business where you advise clients directly on investments and make arrangements for them directly based on your own expertise or knowledge. In order to obtain a category 2 certificate, you will need to have in post a 'qualified person', who is approved by the Law Society to conduct one or more of three types of DIB. Further details may be found at Principle 27.07 of *The Guide to the Professional Conduct of Solicitors 1999*. If you conduct DIB, then the detailed rules set out in Chapter 6 of the Solicitors' Investment Business Rules 1995 will apply.

Most firms, on the other hand, will obtain a category 1 certificate and will have to avoid DIB. There are limited rules set out in Chapter 5 of the Solicitors' Investment Business Rules 1995. The two main exceptions to DIB are (a) where the services of a 'permitted third party' such as a stockbroker or other independent financial adviser are used, and (b) the 'incidental' exception: see Principle 27.13 of the Guide.

If yours is one of the 2.5 per cent of firms already involved in giving investment advice to clients through an in-house specialist, you will be involved in DIB. You should be conversant and complying with the Solicitors' Investment Business Rules 1995 which control your activities and it is likely that the Society's Monitoring and Investigation Unit will have visited your firm to ensure full compliance. Guidance on the Rules is available in confidence from the Professional Ethics division.

Commission

If you receive commission, then you will need to comply with Rule 10 of the Solicitors' Practice Rules 1990 and either pay or credit commission to the client or obtain the client's agreement to retaining the commission. The options are to hand the commission over and charge for your time or with the client's agreement, retain a share of the commission but without charging. In either event, there must be full disclosure to the client. Most clients will be impressed with this arrangement, which is to mutual benefit.

PART 2: Managing an Elderly Client Practice

The marketplace

Research and the experience of many practitioners indicates that elderly people are very receptive to the idea of seeking financial advice through their solicitor. Having encountered (as we all do) the constant marketing of financial services and products through advertisements and mail-shots, a client believes that he will not be sold something or indeed rushed into anything against his interests by his solicitor. It is far safer to introduce your elderly client to an independent financial adviser that you know and trust than to leave the client to the mercies of the financial services market. If you ignore the client's financial requirements all your good work in other areas could be rendered ineffective by someone selling the client an inappropriate or unwise investment.

General advice

You should not be deterred from providing any financial advice to your client simply by reason of the Financial Services Act, because much of the advice that a typical elderly client needs will not come within the scope of that legislation. The client's affairs may be neglected and simply need to be tidied up and simplified. You should consider whether:

- money is best placed. The client may have:
  - large sums of cash in the house which should be banked or a large balance on current account could be put on deposit
  - a number of small building society accounts which could be amalgamated or on which a better rate of interest obtained in a different class of account (but beware of flotations as the client could lose out)
  - long matured savings certificates which should be encashed (that type of investment is in any event inappropriate if the client needs more income)
- income is being paid net of tax if the client would benefit from gross income, and recoverable tax deducted is being recovered;
- any increase or decrease in income would affect social security benefits;
- capital could be preserved by purchasing an annuity or even whether to purchase long-term care assurance or an impaired life annuity to fund residential or nursing care, thus enabling the client to be self funding with the consequent beneficial effects on state benefits and in preserving assets.

These examples may not include 'investments' but do refer to the list in Principle 27.02 of the Guide. An annuity can be an investment and long-term care assurance may become an investment in the future.

Chapter 13

Marketing

Marketing is promoting your practice or particular specialist services which you can offer to potential clients, but it also involves making existing clients aware of the services you provide. Advertising is only one aspect and may not appeal to you; other possibilities can and should be considered. You may employ the services of marketing consultants but there is much that you can do yourself. In this Handbook we seek to identify matters of particular significance to elderly clients which you should consider in developing your practice.

See *Marketing for Lawyers* (Law Society Publishing, 1994).

13.1 THE MARKET PLACE

Solicitors do not have a monopoly in providing for the legally related needs of elderly people, but there are many areas of this work that the profession should seek to retain and develop in the face of growing competition from others in the market place. The solicitor in general practice is uniquely qualified to respond to the legal needs of older members of the local community, and the consequence of doing so may be a wide range of new work and an introduction to new clients (not only elderly ones, as many satisfied clients will have families, friends, etc.). Note that:

- financial (and other) problems of older people are increasing because they:
  - are living longer
  - tend to be cared for in the community rather than in hospitals or institutions
  - have more money (from home ownership, pensions and state benefits)
  - now have to cover long-term care costs
- the need for delegation arises more often in the case of women because:
  - men generally die younger
  - men are more reluctant to give up management of their affairs
  - many widows have been wholly dependent on their husbands for managing financial matters

Areas of work

An elderly client practice is recommended to develop, and may wish to market,

PART 2: Managing an Elderly Client Practice

expertise in the following areas of work (references are to this Handbook):

Financial

- state benefits (means tested / non means tested) – para. 8.1 and Chapter 18;
- local authority benefits – paras 19.1 and 19.2;
- investments and pensions – paras 28.1 and 28.2;
- tax and tax planning – paras 28.3 and 30.2;
- providing for infirm or disabled relatives – Chapter 32;
- wills and gifts – Chapters 30 and 31;
- loans to relatives and guarantees for their liabilities – paras 3.1 and 29.6;
- best use of resources – an overview is needed;
- long-term care planning – paras 19.3 and 19.4, Chapter 22, paras 23.5 and 29.6.

Management

- coping with mental and/or physical frailty – Chapter 3;
- issues as to capacity – Chapter 2 and para. 15.1;
- handling financial affairs and dealing with problems – Chapter 7 and para. 8.2;
- enduring powers of attorney – Chapter 9;
- Court of Protection applications and receivership – Chapter 10;
- negotiating service delivery for domiciliary, residential or nursing care – Chapters 22 and 24.

Personal

- continuing employment or involvement in business – Chapter 27;
- involvement with the police – Chapter 17;
- issues of civil status – para. 15.2;
- planning for the future (e.g. residential care, funeral) – paras 23.5 and 33.3;
- community care provision and funding and advocacy services for service delivery – Chapters 5 and 22;
- accidents (e.g. tripping on pavement) – Chapter 6;
- environmental problems (e.g. neighbouring development);
- consumer problems – para. 15.1.

Relationships

- supporting carers and dealing with professionals – paras 3.2 and 3.3;
- marriage and cohabitation difficulties (of self or children) – Chapter 16;
- problems with family (e.g. contact with grandchildren) – para. 16.3;
- abuse and domestic violence – para. 16.5;
- disputes with others (e.g. neighbours, social workers) – Chapter 5 and para. 16.5.

Housing

- moving house (e.g. to a smaller home) – Chapter 29;
- sharing the home or moving in with relatives – para. 29.6;
- exercising the 'right to buy' council accommodation – para. 29.3;
- disabled facilities and grants – para. 20.2;
- home income plans – para. 29.6;
- sheltered housing schemes – para. 29.7;
- moving into residential care – Chapter 23.

Health

- coping with the NHS (e.g. complaints procedures) – para. 20.1 and Chapter 24;
- private medical schemes – para. 24.2;
- medical negligence claims – see para. 24.4;
- implications of mental incapacity – Chapter 25;
- implications of mental illness – Chapter 26;
- living wills (and other forms of advance directives) – para. 25.4;
- arrangements immediately following death – Chapter 33.

13.2 TARGETING ELDERLY CLIENTS

To expand this area of work you may need to make changes to and within your office and change attitudes to clients. The ideas that follow are of general application but some relate specifically to the elderly client. However, do appreciate that you cannot offer or change everything instantly but can continue to update and improve.

PART 2: Managing an Elderly Client Practice

A user-friendly office

Examine the facilities your firm has and the services that are offered from the point of view of the elderly client. Use the following checklist to help:

Access

- to your office:
  - public transport, parking, crossing the road, etc.
  - provision of a map or written instructions
- into and within your office:
  - signs, steps, staircases, stair rails, ramps, door widths, etc.
  - obstructions, clear signs to reception area, well lit
- offer of home visits where the client is unable to visit your office:
  - make clear if this will add to costs

Facilities (where available)

- room to leave bags, shopping trolleys, umbrellas, etc.;
- suitable waiting area:
  - warm and draught free
  - choice of seating (e.g. higher/upright chairs with arms)
  - accessible toilet facilities (a disabled toilet may not be feasible)
- suitable interview room:
  - on ground floor
  - choice of seating (e.g. higher/upright chairs with arms)
  - private (especially if having to speak loudly)
  - consider hearing loop
- aids for those with disabilities – contact:
  - the Royal National Institute for the Deaf
  - the Royal National Institute for the Blind
- if suitable facilities are not available consider home visit.

Impressions

- impressions of the office:
  - premises appear well cared for
  - furniture, carpets, decorations in good condition (with pictures and flowers)
- atmosphere within the office:

Chapter 13 MARKETING

- clean and tidy
- staff cheerful
* helpful and efficient staff:
  - train all staff in their roles
  - provide special training for support staff in working with older clients

Communication:

* clear and friendly receptionist and telephonist;
* provision of information:
  - legal services available
  - people in the office
  - costs
  - leaflets about common issues (wills, long term care, EPAs, etc.)
* clients kept informed about progress and the reasons for any delays;
* suitable methods of communication:
  - large print used in letters and documents
  - plain English used in letters, documents and speech (avoid legal jargon)
  - loop hearing systems available or minicom facilities

Convenience:

* appointments offered that suit the client;
* appointments adhered to and clients not kept waiting;
* staff offer to ring for a taxi or escort clients across the road, etc.;
* clinics or surgeries available.

> Consider problems caused by limited mobility, use of wheelchairs, visual and hearing impairments and communication difficulties.

Relationship with elderly clients

Dealing with older people is often based upon a one-to-one relationship working at the client's pace and level of understanding:

* do not seek to be competitive as when dealing with other solicitors or commercial clients;
* ensure that the client knows who you are and that you are dealing personally with his or her matter:
  - explain how you may be contacted when the need arises

PART 2: Managing an Elderly Client Practice

- introduce an alternative contact for occasions when you are not available
- make sure the client has the option of private discussion with you and thus is alerted to any potential problems or conflicts which may arise:
    - if the client wishes to bring a friend to interviews do not discourage this, because that friend will discuss the matter with the client when you are not there
    - be aware of undue influence but do not see this as a spectre in every situation
- avoid being patronising and do not assume that older people are less legally competent merely because they are mentally or physically infirm.

> Treat the client wholly professionally but at the same time as you would wish your elderly parent (or grandparent) to be treated in this situation.

How does the client view you?

Do you:

- appear too busy to discuss the client's problem or not easily available?
- talk down to the client?
- explain matters clearly to the client and appear to enjoy doing so?
- offer the client alternatives or impose your own viewpoint?
- give the client time to decide and consider matters with a follow-up letter?
- greet the client in reception or expect him or her to find your room and enter whilst you are working?
- take care how you address the client and invite the client to address you?

How can the client help you (and indirectly himself)?

Ask the client in a brochure or by a personally circulated questionnaire to:

- prepare for the meeting by drawing up a statement of facts and questions;
- give you clear instructions:
    - explain if there are any important time constraints
    - make sure that you have understood each other
    - ask if not sure or worried about anything
- keep in regular touch with you:
    - deal promptly with any important questions that arise
    - ask for a progress report if has not heard from you when expecting to do so
- help you plan your working day by:
    - writing rather than telephoning unless it is urgent

- making an appointment if wanting to see you
- avoiding unnecessary calls (which may increase the cost)

How can you help older clients?

Consider whether as a matter of policy you:

- have information packs to send in advance of an appointment to help prepare for any meeting relating to (for example):
  - wills (and tax planning where appropriate)
  - enduring powers of attorney (and living wills?)
  - long-term care
- routinely visit elderly clients at their homes:
  - if it is difficult for them to get out
  - if your office premises are not suitable for visits by them and cannot be adapted
  - just for a chat when they have not asked to see you and you have no specific business but feel concerned about their welfare
- tell clients in advance that you are willing to visit them (without adding substantially to the bill):
  - make appointments at a time that suits them or in a residential care home or hospital at a convenient time (check with the nurse in charge)
  - keep these appointments (and conduct them in a cheerful manner)

Office brochures

Each firm will have its own style and the use of a 'logo' may create continuity between documents and give the firm an identity. Different brochures may be produced for different purposes, and it may be relevant to ask clients what their needs are. The following general brochures may be helpful to the older client:

An Introduction to the Firm

A marketing brochure or leaflet to inform potential clients about your firm and create the appropriate image. This may provide information (with photographs) about the firm's:

- name, address and telephone numbers;
- history – formation, growth, previous partners, names and locations;
- premises – history, location, access and facilities;
- partners – qualifications, expertise, interests and backgrounds;
- staff – number, nature and any special experience;

PART 2: Managing an Elderly Client Practice

- availability during and outside normal office hours;
- areas of work, particular expertise and philosophy;

and other relevant information used in marketing.

A Guide for Clients

Separate client brochures to provide a range of information to persons who are or become clients of the firm. These may include:

- basic information relating to the firm:
    - name, addresses, telephone numbers, fax numbers and e-mail address
    - list of partners and relevant department managers or fee-earners
    - office hours (and days when the office will be closed)
    - emergency telephone numbers
- details (added to the printed brochure) of persons with whom the client may become involved:
    - the person dealing with the client's matter
    - another person in the event that this person is unavailable
    - the supervising partner
- guidance to the client on dealing effectively with the firm:
    - standards that the firm seeks to maintain
    - basis of charging
    - complaints procedures
- an overview of legal services provided by the firm:
    - general range of work undertaken
    - specialist services which are unique to the firm
    - any newsletters promoting different services and issues

13.3 PROMOTING LEGAL SERVICES

Getting known

Some firms will already have a sound reputation for specialising in elderly client work built up over several generations, but positive steps can be taken either to ensure that the firm is known locally as being willing and able to undertake this area of work, or to maintain the reputation. Remember existing clients will bring most work. Suggestions are:

- join specialist legal groups, e.g. Society for Trust and Estate Practitioners, Probate Practitioner Section, Solicitors for the Elderly;

Chapter 13 MARKETING

- offer of free diagnostic initial interviews for retired people;
- support for suitable organisations, e.g.:
  - staff associations
  - pensioners' groups
  - charities working with the elderly
- provision of guidance about legal matters concerning elderly people:
  - through articles in local newspapers
  - using local radio and television
- sponsorship of:
  - suitable events (local dramatics or music, but not boxing or racing!)
  - activities of voluntary services and organisations
- advertisements targeted at older people and their needs, e.g.:
  - in magazines for older people
  - in nursing home guides
  - in local papers (especially special supplements)
- distribution of information leaflets of interest to the client group, e.g.:
  - through CABs, health centres, day centres
  - as inserts in local magazines, newspapers, etc.
- mailshots to:
  - existing clients (to advise on the extent of your services)
  - potential new clients about particular services

But beware the scattergun approach. This is less effective than specially focused campaigns to become known. It is also worth assessing, prior to launching a campaign, whether the firm has the relevant expertise and can service the work. Marketing without the necessary back-up is a waste of skills and energies. Bringing in work and not being able to service it is a pointless exercise.

> Ensure that your firm complies with the Solicitors' Publicity Code 1990 and other relevant professional guidance.
>
> For an overview see Chapter 11 and for support see Chapter 14. If in doubt contact the Law Society.

Contacts

Developing personal contacts in the community reaps its own rewards, and willingness to offer your services without charge on occasions can be valuable:

- give talks to local groups/societies e.g. Rotary, pensioners, Age Concern:

PART 2: Managing an Elderly Client Practice

- keep talks in stock on subjects such as EPAs, wills, state benefits, community care and the role of a solicitor and tie these in with information packs
- attend national conferences and seminars on issues relevant to older people:
  - these may involve other professionals working with the elderly, e.g. specialist financial advisers, local and health authority, accountants and charities
- organise your firm's local seminars on matters of concern to older people:
  - consider whether by invitation only or publicly advertised, free or for a fee
  - open them to *all* clients and the public
  - publicise these at the office and in the local press
  - invite organisations and professionals involved with older people

---

Suitable topics for seminars

1. providing for long-term care

2. financial management for those who become incapable

3. employment issues for residential care and nursing homes

- work for local societies, e.g. Age Concern, Help the Aged:
  - join committees and accept unpaid positions
  - do voluntary work for organisations providing services to elderly people
- cultivate contacts with:
  - retirement and nursing homes and sheltered housing complexes (make it known that you are prepared to visit residents)
  - officers of the health authority and local authority (they need to know who specialises so ask if they keep a register of solicitors for their clients – not all will be without assets)

Image

The current use of advertising and publicity by solicitors is something which many older clients do not associate with the professions. However, it is part of modern practice and is significant in this particular marketplace when so many people are competing for other clients' business. Thus, although the more formal approach may be appropriate, in today's competitive marketplace this needs to be linked with the use of information technology and systems as well as well trained, informed staff. So consider:

- adopting a conservative approach to marketing legal services to the elderly;
- getting known not only as having expertise in working with and for older clients but also:
  - being able to understand and communicate with them

- being flexible and allowing them to develop their own wishes
- not promoting a level of expertise which your firm does not have!
• providing information on services and why using a solicitor is preferable, i.e.:
  - independence
  - all round advice
  - professional standards
  - professional indemnity

> By their very nature older clients will in general be resistant to an over aggressive commercial approach.

Quality of service

However much trouble you take to get known and develop the right image, it will be wasted if your firm does not have the knowledge and expertise to do the work and the staff and facilities to do it efficiently. Expectations must be fulfilled so concentrate on:

- developing relationships with older clients (see Part 1);
- acquiring knowledge of relevant areas of law (see Part 3);
- ascertaining necessary procedures (see Part 1);
- ensuring that all staff are suitably qualified to deal with older clients:
  - train fee-earners in new skills (see Part 2)
  - train support staff to meet the needs of older clients
  - offer support and recognition to staff who may often work in stressful and distressing circumstances, e.g. with the terminally ill
- establishing an office which is as user friendly as possible (see para. 13.2).

Providing information

Clients need information as well as advice and it is time consuming to provide this, so:

- keep a supply of leaflets on relevant topics for handing to clients:
  - free Inland Revenue leaflets – see Chapter 28
  - free Benefits Agency leaflets – see Chapter 18
  - Court of Protection booklets – see Chapter 10
- make available in-house information packs:

PART 2: Managing an Elderly Client Practice

- print your own elderly client newsletter or booklets on particular topics
- provide an introduction to the services that you offer
- inexpensive books can be purchased and provided for clients:
  - see Age Concern Books in Appendix 7, some of which can be customised for your firm

Packages of services

Simple packages may be appropriate in providing your services to older clients:

- offer an *enduring power of attorney* when you make a will, but advise as to the dangers as well as the potential advantages (see Chapter 9);
- discuss a *living will* when making an ordinary will, but be tactful as many people have no wish to address this aspect (see para. 25.4);
- provide a stockbroker's valuation with recommendations when completing annual tax returns or repayment claims.

You may wish to market special packages in conjunction with other professionals for older clients, such as:

- an annual 'wealth check' – investment review *plus* tax planning assessment *plus* state benefit survey;
- a 'plan ahead' programme – consideration of appropriate options for housing and care based upon client's wealth and needs;
- a 're-housing' package – support and legal services on finding and moving to a more suitable home;
- a 'balance the family' package – advice and preparation of wills and EPAs for cohabitees/second marriages;
- a 'family support' programme – support for children looking after parents;
- a 'residential care' package – legal assistance in respect of a move into residential care and disposal of the home;
- a 'financial management' package – legal services in respect of the registration of an EPA or application for receivership followed by first year support for the attorney or receiver.

Specialist or expert?

The Solicitors' Publicity Code 1990, para. 2(b) merely provides that any claims to be a specialist or expert must be justified but the following guidance published in an earlier edition of *The Guide to the Professional Conduct of Solicitors* may be worth noting:

Chapter 13 MARKETING

'A claim to specialisation or expertise in a particular field will imply that the solicitor making the claim has skills, knowledge or expertise in that field over and above that of other solicitors who could not make such a claim. The onus of deciding whether a particular claim can be justified is on the solicitor or the firm making the claim. The Professional Ethics Division can only give guidance as to the factors you may wish to consider before making that decision. Ultimately, it would be for the Adjudication Committee or the Solicitors' Disciplinary Tribunal to determine whether a particular claim was justified, should a complaint reach that stage. There are not yet any committee or tribunal decisions to use as indicators.'

'It is likely that a complaint by a client that a solicitor or firm had wrongly claimed to be a specialist or an expert could be coupled with an allegation of inadequate professional services and it may be that the adequacy of the service provided will be measured against any claims made. Further, there are dicta in some cases which suggest that if a solicitor holds himself or herself out as a specialist or expert in a particular field, the client can expect a higher standard than that of a reasonably competent solicitor. You should therefore carefully consider whether, if you choose to describe yourself as an expert or a specialist in a particular field, this could lead to complaints that the claim is unjustified and whether, if a complaint should be made, you would be able to justify your claim on the basis of the factors set out above or on any other basis which you feel entitles you to make such a claim.'

Chapter 14

The Law Society

14.1 PRACTICE MANAGEMENT STANDARDS

The Law Society developed these standards as a management tool to address the particular business needs of legal practices. They have gained wide acceptance as an aid to effective practice management and client care. The standards cover:

- management structure;
- services and forward planning;
- financial management;
- managing people;
- office administration;
- case management.

Lexcel

This is the new quality mark available to law firms and legal departments which meet the Law Society's Practice Management Standards. The mark will confer a marketing advantage in that it is evidence of a well-managed practice, and assessment is by independent bodies.

> A brochure is available from Practice Advice on 0870-606-2522.

14.2 HELP IN PROMOTING THE PRACTICE

How can I stimulate client awareness?

Keeping clients abreast of legal issues by a series of newsletters produced to promote awareness of specific new issues on which they need legal advice is important and the Law Society has such newsletters available on disk or in folio format, for reproduction to the firm's own design, e.g.

- *Your Business and the Law*
- *You and the Law*

> For subscriptions enquiries contact Gazette Newsletters: 020-7320-5830.

How can I offer financial services to clients?

Support and guidance to practitioners to enable them to develop this growing area of activity is available from *Solicitors Financial Services*:

- Tel: 020-7320-5698

Promoting will making

A wide range of publications to help promote your practice are available. For further information contact *Law Society Publications*:

- Tel: 020-7316-5599
- Fax: 020-7404-1124

Practical advice

'Where can I get practical advice on running a sound and profitable business? What is the most effective way to run my practice?'

The Law Management Section is fast becoming an indispensable resource for practice managers. For more information:

- Tel: 020-7316-5736
- visit the website www.lms.lawsociety.org.uk

The Gazette has regular pages on practice management and information technology and there is a wide range of publications to help in running practices which includes:

The Solicitors' Guide to Good Management

Profitability and Financial Management

Cashflow and Improved Financial Management

Office Procedures Manual

Solicitors Accounts Manual

Probate Practitioner's Handbook

Setting Up and Managing a Small Practice

Marketing for Lawyers

Survival Guide for Law Clerks

An Approach to Non-Contentious Costs

For further information contact Marston Book Services on 01235-465656 (Mail-order Line).

PART 2: Managing an Elderly Client Practice

How do I explain costs to my clients?

Practical Advice is an information service for solicitors covering all aspects of legal practice including costs:

- Tel: 020-7320-5708/5709 or
- Fax: 020-7320-5918 or
- E-mail: Lib_PAS@lawsociety.org.uk

Information technology?

Your first point of contact is the *Practical Advice* service, which will be able to point you in the right direction, explain the help that is available and tell you how to get it. Contact:

- Tel: 0870-606-2522 or
- Fax: 020-7316-5541 or
- www.it.lawsociety.org.uk

There is also the Software Solutions guide, which lists five suppliers who meet the Law Society's criteria – in particular, on features, functionality and track record with customers. Contact *Practical Advice* for further information.

Law Society information on the Internet

The Law Society website is undergoing continual change and improvement to achieve its core aim: Serving Solicitors, Serving Society. The main sections are:

- The Gazette (including recruitment and up-to-the minute news stories);
- Membership Services (with briefings for solicitors and essential legal services);
- Recruitment;
- The OSS;
- Choosing a Solicitor;
- Publishing.

On-line versions of *The Guide to the Professional Conduct of Solicitors 1999* and *The Law Society's Directory of Solicitors and Barristers* are soon to go live.

Visit the Law Society web site at: www.lawsociety.org.uk

Chapter 14   THE LAW SOCIETY

Where do I go for recruitment advice?

The *Recruitment Service* helps employers recruiting paralegals, trainees, newly-qualified, fully-qualified and locum staff. Contact:

- Tel: 020-7320-5940
- Fax: 020-7583-5561
- E-mail: Lib-recruitment@lawsociety.org.uk.

Benefits for your clients and your practice

Discounts

The Law Society has negotiated special pricing on a range of products including computer/car finance, practice finance, health care plans, hotels, household insurance for solicitors' clients, income replacement insurance, judicial delay insurance, motor/household insurance, office insurance, personal accident insurance, personal loans, short-term income replacement insurance, travel insurance (multi-trip), unoccupied property insurance, defective title insurance and the Law Society Visa card which may assist. Contact:

- Tel: 020-7320-5698

Library services

The Library answers enquiries on UK and EU law and parliamentary affairs. Other services include photocopying and computer resources. Opening hours: Monday to Friday 9.00 am to 5.00 pm.

- For Library enquiries contact:
  - Tel: 0870-606-2511
  - E-mail: lib-enq@lawsociety.org.uk
- For photocopying services contact:
  - Tel: 020-7320-5929
  - Fax: 020-7831-1687

Probate Section

This is a specialist section run by its members and open to all those holding a current practising certificate, who pay an annual fee. It provides:

- a service for solicitors who work in the areas of:
  - wills and trusts
  - tax planning
  - financial planning

PART 2: Managing an Elderly Client Practice

- Court of Protection
- care planning
- estate management

- practical help to solicitors, with member benefits including a regular newsletter, low-cost seminars, information on marketing and a web site:
    - www.probatesection.org.uk

> All enquiries to Sonia Purser at the Probate Section, The Law Society, 113 Chancery Lane, London WC2A 1PL – DX 56 London/Chancery Lane.

14.3 SOLICITORS FINANCIAL SERVICES (SFS)

SFS has acquired substantial experience in showing practices how to profit from investment business by using the permitted third party route while not becoming involved in discrete investment business themselves. SFS has much to offer a practice in return for a very reasonable outlay:

- excellent advice on how to get started with investment business;
- first class marketing materials and good back-up;
- a formal link to a nationwide network of major independent financial advisers with whom the Law Society has a contractual agreement;
- will act as permitted third parties on generous commission sharing terms.

Elderly clients may welcome the offer of financial advice by their solicitors. They may not seek it because it may not occur to them but they can be assured that by using a solicitor who is associated with SFS they will receive top quality, independent financial advice and will not be sold or rushed into anything against their interests.

> A practice support section operating within the Society's Legal Practice Directorate, its role is to:
> - encourage the profession to provide clients with independent financial advice;
> - give help and guidance as to how this can be achieved in a cost effective and protected manner.

14.4 PUBLICATIONS

The Law Society has published a number of handbooks dealing with specialist areas of practice as well as a number of publications dealing with practice management and practice management standards:

- for a list of these refer to Appendix 7;

- a full Catalogue can be obtained from:
    Law Society Publishing
    113 Chancery Lane
    London   WC2A 1PL

The following booklets and leaflets can be obtained in packs of 25 or more for distribution to clients:

- Your Will: Client Questionnaire
- Personal Assets Log
- *Making a Will Won't Kill You* booklet
- Questionnaire for Personal Representative Clients

PART THREE
Overview of the Law

This third part identifies the areas of law commonly encountered when representing elderly clients and their families and carers. It provides merely an outline with references to relevant legislation and other material. It is divided into six sections, each dealing with a general topic, namely:

- Status
- Financial Benefits
- Community Care
- Health Care
- Work, Money and the Home
- Inheritance and Death

SECTION A
Status

The rights and responsibilities of the older client are considered separately in the context of the individual as a member of society, family relationships and involvement with the criminal justice system.

Elderly people have the same rights, duties and legal responsibilities as younger members of society but these may be modified or supplemented to cope with their needs and circumstances (in some instances in common with younger people with similar disabilities).

Chapter 15

Rights and Obligations

15.1 CAPACITY

Overview

In order to exercise legal rights and powers a person must have the necessary mental capacity to do so. No one is legally incapable in the total sense but capacity may be taken away by law (e.g. minors, Court of Protection patients). Capacity is a question of fact, though the correct legal test must be applied:

- the test varies according to the circumstances and is determined by statute or common law:
  - capacity depends upon understanding rather than wisdom
  - it is the state of mind at the time that is material but do not ignore windows of opportunity
  - evidence of conduct at other times is admissible, e.g. general pattern of life
  - inability to communicate does not necessarily mean lack of capacity
- there is a presumption of capacity:
  - the presumption may be rebutted by evidence to the contrary
  - medical evidence is admitted but the court must decide whether any opinion is based on sufficient grounds and the application of the correct legal test in the particular circumstances
  - unusual or eccentric behaviour does not give rise to a presumption of incapacity but may cause capacity to be questioned

For assessment of mental capacity see Chapter 2.

It is also necessary to consider in the case of agreements whether there was an intention to create legal relations, and for social and domestic arrangements it is presumed that there is no such intention:

- this may also be the case in regard to financial arrangements within the family so it may be advisable for these to be put on a legal footing;
- the presumption may be rebutted by evidence to the contrary.

General contracts

A contract may be set aside at the option of a party if it can be shown that he did not understand its nature due to mental disorder and that the other party knew (or should have been aware) of this:

- the fact that the contract is unfair will not by itself be sufficient;
- see *Hart v O'Connor* [1985] 2 All ER 880.

The individual must understand the nature and effect of what he is doing and be capable of agreeing to it:

- the extent of that understanding depends upon the implications of the contract (in the case of an elderly person it may need to extend to the effect upon state benefits and local authority support);
- capacity is judged in respect of each transaction at that moment and a lucid interval is sufficient.

> A person must have the necessary capacity to enter into a contract.

Necessaries

A person who lacks capacity to contract may be required to pay a reasonable price for the purchase of items that are deemed to be necessary in everyday living:

- this means goods suitable to his condition in life at the time, e.g. ordinary food, drink, clothing (a status test);
- query whether under common law principles a person may be required to pay a reasonable price for services (as distinct from goods).

> Sale of Goods Act 1979, s 3.

Specific contracts

Bank accounts

In regard to bank and building society accounts (and perhaps credit or charge cards):

- the duty and authority to pay a customer's cheque is determined by notice of mental disorder of a sufficient degree to prevent an understanding of the transaction:
    - the size and nature of the cheque or payment is relevant
    - see *Drew v Nunn* [1979] 4 QB 661

Chapter 15 RIGHTS AND OBLIGATIONS

- by custom a bank is entitled to charge simple interest at a reasonable rate upon overdrafts but a loan is a matter for specific agreement;
- a guarantor may not be liable if the fact of mental incapacity on the part of the debtor was known to all parties but a separate contract of indemnity could be enforced;
- National Savings Bank accounts may be opened on behalf and in the name of persons of unsound mind:
  - National Savings Bank Act 1971, s 8(1)(f)
  - National Savings Bank Regulations 1972, regs. 6 and 7
- accounts may be opened by a receiver or registered attorney for a person without capacity.

> In practice banks tend to look for the ability to provide a consistent signature rather than applying more sophisticated tests.

Insurance policies

Any relevant disability must be disclosed on the proposal form and also on renewal, and a policy may be void for non-disclosure. An express declaration as to medical condition or disability may be required.

If the proposer is incapable when money is payable the insurers may insist upon appointment of a receiver before paying out:

- to avoid this it may be appropriate to appoint trustees of a policy and give them power to expend the monies for the beneficiary;
- it may also be advisable to write policies into trust when an elderly person will inherit on death to protect that individual.

Agency

The authority of an agent depends upon the mental capacity of the principal at the time of appointment and terminates if there is a subsequent loss of capacity:

- a power of attorney is an agency appointment;
- an enduring power of attorney overcomes the latter problem – see Chapter 9;
- a form of agency may be used to draw state benefits but this ceases on subsequent incapacity of either party – see Chapter 18.

> Partnership and directorships are considered in Chapter 27.

PART 3: SECTION A Status

Trustees

Under the Trustee Act 1925 there is no upper age limit for a trustee but:

- persons with power to appoint new trustees have power to do so in place of a trustee who is 'incapable of acting' but if the trustee is entitled to a beneficial interest in possession leave of the Court of Protection is required;
- the court has power to appoint a substitute for a trustee incapable of acting by reason of mental disorder and may vest trust property in trustees on various occasions including where a person entitled is under disability.

> Note the new powers of beneficiaries to replace trustees under the Trusts of Land and Appointment of Trustees Act 1996.

15.2 CIVIL STATUS

Driving licences

It is an offence to drive a motor vehicle on a road unless the driver holds a licence authorising him to drive a vehicle of the class being driven. An applicant for a licence must state whether he is suffering from a 'relevant disability':

- this means either a disability prescribed by the Secretary of State or any other disability which is or may become likely to cause the driving of a vehicle by the applicant to be a source of danger to the public (being under a guardianship order under the Mental Health Act 1983 is a prescribed disability);
- the holder of a licence must also report any subsequent disability that arises unless it is not expected to last for more than three months.

The Driver and Vehicle Licensing Agency (DVLA), Swansea SA6 7JL (tel: 01792-772151) may revoke the licence of a person who suffers from such a disability:

- doctors are required to inform DVLA if they consider that there is any question about a patient's ability to drive;
- DVLA medical officers tend to adhere to rigid guidelines so it is difficult to persuade DVLA to reverse a decision;
- a right of appeal against a refusal to grant or revocation of a driving licence lies to the magistrates' court for the petty sessional area in which the aggrieved person resides and few applications are successful:
    - DVLA usually instruct lawyers and call medical evidence
    - costs may be awarded against the appellant

> Road Traffic Act 1988, ss 87–93.

Chapter 15 RIGHTS AND OBLIGATIONS

Passports

Where a person is unable to sign a passport application form through mental disability a declaration signed by a person responsible for the applicant's welfare may be accepted:

- this could be a son or daughter, doctor, social worker or officer-in-charge of a residential care home, or a receiver or attorney;
- the signatory should explain in the 'Other Information' section of the form, or in a separate letter if preferred, that the applicant is incapacitated and that the signatory (in whatever relevant capacity) has signed on his behalf.

Privileges

Certain privileges or concessions may be available to older people:

- parking schemes (the 'orange badge scheme' allows parking concessions to be made to assist people with mobility problems);
- disabled persons' rail travel may apply to older people and enables an escort to travel with them at a discounted rate;
- for concessionary payments see Chapter 20, *Subsidies*.

Voting

There is no upper age bar to voting but legal capacity to vote is unclear:

- the presiding officer may challenge a person who requests a ballot paper if lack of mental capacity is suspected and the test is then ability to answer statutory questions in an intelligible manner (Parliamentary Election Rules, r 35(1));
- the Code of Practice for Electoral Registration Officers, Practice Note no.5: *Voting Rights and Electoral Registration of People with a Mental Illness or Learning Disability* accompanying Home Office Circular RPA 379, dated 27 August 1993 may be relevant to an elderly person who is confused or mentally unstable.

> There are procedures for postal and proxy voting and no test of capacity may then apply in practice.

Jury service

An individual is eligible for jury service up to the age of 70 years. The individual must also be registered as a parliamentary or local government elector and have been ordinarily resident in the United Kingdom (or the Isle of Man or the Channel Islands) for at least five years since the age of 13 years:

PART 3: SECTION A Status

- various categories of person are ineligible, disqualified or excused, including:
  - anyone in a hospital or similar institution, or regularly attending for treatment by a medical practitioner, due to mental illness
  - a person in guardianship or under the jurisdiction of the Court of Protection
- a judge may discharge a juror who is considered unable to understand the nature of the oath or the evidence:
  - if a person called for jury service is not thought fit to sit the jury officer or court clerk should be informed and the summons may be withdrawn

When a person with a disability is called for jury service it is for the judge to determine whether or not that person should act as a juror:

- the presumption is that they should unless the judge is of the opinion that the person will not, on account of disability, be capable of acting effectively
- there have been many cases in which blind persons have served on juries;
- no evidence has ever been presented that a deaf juror is less able to assess the demeanour of a witness but the need for a communicator in the jury room would be a fundamental obstacle;
- the Disability Discrimination Act 1995 does not apply because jury service is not deemed to be a 'service to the public'.

> Juries Act 1974, ss 1 and 9B and Schedule (as amended by Mental Health Act 1983 and Criminal Justice Act 1988).

15.3 CIVIL RESPONSIBILITY

Council tax

This is a property tax with a personal element charged on an adult resident in a dwelling which is his sole or main residence. Joint and several liability can arise but not every individual will be liable. The tax assumes that two people live in a dwelling and assesses properties in valuation bands:

- there is a 25 per cent discount for a sole resident and this also applies where a person in a disregarded category is living in the house with a person who is liable for the tax:
  - disregarded categories include people who are 'severely mentally impaired', some carers and those living in residential care or nursing homes
  - the maximum discount when all residents are disregarded is 50 per cent
- special band reductions apply to houses adapted for people with disabilities;
- appeals are to a tribunal, e.g. in respect of the band in which a property is

Chapter 15 RIGHTS AND OBLIGATIONS

placed (the time-limit for appeals against initial assessments has passed).

> Local Government Finance Act 1992.
> See Age Concern Fact Sheet 21 *The council tax and older people*.
> *Council tax benefit* helps those on low incomes (see Chapter 19 para. 19.2.)

National insurance contributions

Contributions are not payable by those over pensionable age but an adequate contributions record of the individual (or spouse) is required if the normal state retirement pension is to be paid:

- a contributions record may be checked by completing form BR 19 and sending this to Benefits Agency, RPFA Unit (Correspondence), Room 37D, DSS Longbenton, Benton Park Road, Newcastle-upon-Tyne NE98 1YX. In response a comprehensive pensions forecast is received;
- the record may also be made up by:
  - credits, e.g. whilst unemployed and signing on or off work sick
  - *home responsibilities protection* for periods when unable to work whilst caring for a child or an elderly or disabled person (since 1978 only)
- voluntary or late contributions can in some circumstances be made to protect a pension record.

> A series of leaflets is available from the Benefits Agency about contributions. For pensions generally see Chapter 28 para. 28.2.

Income and capital taxes

> For income and capital taxes see Chapter 28 para. 28.3.

15.4 DISCRIMINATION

There is no law to prevent discrimination on grounds of age but other forms of discrimination may be relevant to an older persons. Everyone has a right not to be discriminated against on the grounds of sex, race or disability. At present anti-discrimination legislation comprises:

- Sex Discrimination Act 1975;
- Race Relations Act 1976 – 'race' covers colour, race, ethnic or national origins and nationality (s 3);
- Disability Discrimination Act 1995.

Disability discrimination

The Disability Discrimination Act 1995 is likely to prove of most significance to older people although parts will not be brought into force until 2004 (e.g. the duty to make physical alterations to premises). The Act is divided into several distinct parts:

- *Part I* provides a definition of 'disability' and for guidance to be issued;
- *Part II* deals with discrimination by employers;
- *Part III* deals with discrimination in relation to goods, facilities and services and also in relation to premises;
- *Part IV* deals with education (including further and higher education);
- *Part V* deals with public transport.

> A National Disability Council was set up under the Act.

Regulations and guidance

There has been a proliferation of secondary legislation and other sources of guidance including:

- Disability Discrimination (Meaning of Disability) Regulations 1996;
- Disability Discrimination (Services and Premises) Regulations 1996;
- Disability Discrimination (Sub-leases and Sub-tenancies) Regulations 1996;
- Code of Practice: *Rights of Access: Goods, facilities, services and premises.*

Definitions

A person has a 'disability' if he has 'a physical or mental impairment which has a substantial and long-term adverse effect on his ability to carry out normal day-to-day activities':

- the concepts of 'impairment', 'long-term effects', 'normal day-to-day activities' and 'substantial adverse effects' are interpreted in Schedule 1 to the Act;
- the Secretary of State issues guidance about such matters, and the courts must take this into account – see s 3(3).

> 'Disabled person means a person who has a disability' – s 1.

Goods, facilities and services (s 19)

It is unlawful for a provider of services to discriminate against a disabled person:

- in refusing to provide, or deliberately not providing, to the disabled person any service which he provides, or is prepared to provide, to members of the

Chapter 15 RIGHTS AND OBLIGATIONS

public;

- in the standard of service which he provides to the disabled person or the manner in which he provides it to him; or
- in the terms on which he provides a service to the disabled person.

The provision of services includes the provision of any goods or facilities. A person is 'a provider of services' if he is concerned with the provision of services to the public or to a section of the public; it is irrelevant whether a service is provided on payment or without payment.

> Discrimination in employment is covered in Chapter 27.

Meaning of 'discrimination' (s 20)

A provider of services discriminates against a disabled person if:

- for a reason which relates to the disabled person's disability, he treats him less favourably than he treats or would treat others to whom that reason does not or would not apply; and
- he cannot show that the treatment in question is justified.

Enforcement, remedies and procedure (s 25)

A claim by any person that another person has discriminated against him in a way which is unlawful may be made the subject of civil proceedings in the same way as any other claim in tort:

- proceedings must be in the county court and brought within six months;
- damages may include compensation for injury to feelings whether or not they include compensation under any other head (this may be limited to a prescribed sum – Schedule 3 para. 7);
- the remedies are those which are available in the High Court so include the granting of a declaration that there has been discrimination.

Disability Rights Commission

This has recently been set up under the Disability Rights Commission Act 1999. In addition to promoting equal opportunities and encouraging good practice the Commission will provide information and advice and may provide legal help to disabled people.

Chapter 16

Family and Other Relationships

16.1 MARRIAGE

Competence

Marriage is 'a simple contract which it does not require a high degree of intelligence to understand'. The parties must understand the nature of marriage and the duties and responsibilities it creates, and must truly consent to the particular marriage but lack of consent only makes a marriage *voidable* and not *void* – see *Re Park* [1954] P 112.

Formalities

A *caveat* can be entered at the relevant register office, church or place registered for the celebration of marriage if it is believed that a party to a proposed marriage does not have the necessary capacity:

- this puts the registrar or clergyman on notice and creates a requirement to investigate the matter – see Marriage Act 1949, s 29;
- the reading of banns in church may give an opportunity to concerned persons to record an objection to a proposed marriage, in which event an enquiry is made as to the capacity of the parties to enter into the ceremony.

It is now possible for a marriage ceremony to take place in a mental hospital for a detained patient – see Marriage Act 1983, s 1.

There may be an objection to a marriage.

Implications

Despite the relative ease with which a person can marry, there is a change of status with long-term financial implications and no warning is given to the parties of this:

- assets/chattels owned and used jointly need to be clearly defined and proper transfer on death ensured (this avoids potential litigation and post death claims);
- assets may be redistributed in the event of a divorce;

- entitlement to state benefits and community care services may be affected:
  - a widow's pension may be lost
  - a joint means test may apply
- remarriage may lead to loss of a surviving spouse pension under an occupational pensions scheme;
- marriage revokes an existing will unless made in contemplation of the marriage:
  - this can cause problems because of the low capacity threshold for marriage and the high threshold for testamentary capacity
  - consider a statutory will – see Chapter 31 at para. 31.4
- claims can arise under the Inheritance (Provision for Family and Dependants) Act 1975 – see Chapter 31 at para. 31.5.

Cohabitation (or sharing a home) may be an alternative to marriage and does not have all the above implications (but may have some of them). Proper legal and financial advice is still needed – see generally para. 16.4.

> Marriage changes the status of the parties.

Ante-nuptial agreements

These are particularly appropriate for second, or subsequent, marriages usually between an older couple, when either or both have children and wish to keep their own property separate in order to protect the children's inheritance.

> See the Law Society Family Law Committee's Memorandum: *Maintenance and Capital Provision on Divorce* (May 1991). Law reform is likely in this area.

16.2 MARRIAGE BREAKDOWN

For the law relating to the breakdown of marriage see the *Matrimonial Causes Act 1973* (MCA) as amended by the Matrimonial and Family Proceedings Act 1984.

For the procedures adopted by the court see the Family Proceedings Rules 1991:

- most proceedings are now brought in a county court with divorce jurisdiction;
- proceedings are generally commenced by a 'petition' and a defence is known as an 'answer';
- the 'petitioner' brings the proceedings and the 'respondent' responds to them;

PART 3: SECTION A Status

- refer to Part IX, rr 9.1–9.5 when a party to proceedings is incapable by reason of mental disorder of managing and administering his property and affairs (i.e. a 'patient') – see generally Chapter 6.

> The Family Law Act 1996, Parts I, II and III (if ever brought into force) will change the whole basis of divorce law and procedure.

Nullity

Marriages may be void or voidable (MCA, ss 11–13). Check whether the marriage was before or after 31 July 1971 because the Nullity of Marriage Act 1971 changed the common law from that date (previously the grounds were restricted but may have made the marriage void):

- a marriage is now **void** if *inter alia*:
  - certain of the necessary formalities have not been complied with
  - the parties are within the prohibited degrees of relationship
- a marriage is now **voidable** at the instance of one party (*inter alia*) on proof:
  - of incapacity by either party to consummate the marriage
  - of wilful refusal by the respondent to consummate the marriage
  - that either party did not validly consent to the marriage (this may be due to duress, mistake, unsoundness of mind or otherwise)
  - that at the time of the marriage either party, though capable of consenting, was suffering from mental disorder within the meaning of the Mental Health Act 1983, of such a kind or to such an extent as to be unfitted for marriage
  - that at the time of the marriage the respondent was suffering from VD or pregnant by another
- bars to the granting of a decree in respect of a voidable marriage now include:
  - (for lack of consent) proceedings were not commenced within three years
  - the petitioner, knowing that the marriage could be avoided, so conducted *him*self in relation to the respondent as to lead *her* reasonably to believe that *he* would not seek to do so, and it would be unjust to grant a decree (this may be relevant to a marriage for companionship only)

> Marriages may be void or voidable.

Divorce

Divorce is based on irretrievable breakdown of the marriage but no petition may be presented before the expiration of one year from the marriage, and one of five

Chapter 16 FAMILY AND OTHER RELATIONSHIPS

facts must also be established (MCA, ss 1–3):

1. respondent has committed adultery and petitioner finds it intolerable to live with respondent;
2. respondent has behaved in such a way that petitioner cannot reasonably be expected to live with respondent;
3. respondent has deserted petitioner for a continuous period of at least two years immediately preceding the presentation of the petition;
4. parties to the marriage have lived apart for a continuous period of at least two years immediately preceding the presentation of the petition and respondent consents to a decree being granted;
5. parties to the marriage have lived apart for a continuous period of at least five years immediately preceding the presentation of the petition.

The respondent may oppose dissolution on grounds of hardship when the petition is based upon 'living apart' – see MCA, ss 5 and 10. This will usually mean financial hardship though loss of pension rights may be relevant.

Orders may be made in the divorce proceedings dealing with:

- arrangements for any relevant children;
- molestation and occupation of the home;
- temporary maintenance;
- a final financial settlement.

Judicial separation

A decree of judicial separation is obtained on the same basis as a divorce and orders relating to financial matters and children may be made but:

- a petition may be presented in the first year;
- the parties are not free to remarry;
- pension and inheritance rights should not be affected.

Financial provision

Orders made

The court can make all or any of the following *ancillary relief orders* for the benefit of a spouse:

- on or after filing of the petition:
    - maintenance pending suit

PART 3: SECTION A Status

- on or after granting a decree (but with effect in the case of divorce or nullity from decree absolute):
  - periodical payments (including secured periodical payments)
  - lump sum
  - property adjustment (transfer/settlement of property, variation of settlement)
  - pension adjustment
  - avoidance of disposition
  - release of future inheritance claims against the estate of the other spouse
- variation of periodical payments orders following a change of circumstances.

Most cases are resolved by *consent orders* but these must be approved by the district judge after full disclosure of the financial position of each party.

> For orders that may be made see MCA, ss 21–24.

Matters taken into account

When making financial orders the court must 'have regard to all the circumstances of the case', first consideration being given to the welfare of any relevant minor child. The court (which generally means the district judge) will in particular have regard to the following matters:

- the income, earning capacity, property and other financial resources which each of the parties to the marriage has or is likely to have in the foreseeable future, including in the case of earning capacity any increase in that capacity which it would in the opinion of the court be reasonable to expect a party to the marriage to take steps to acquire;
- the financial needs, obligations and responsibilities which each of the parties to the marriage has or is likely to have in the foreseeable future;
- the standard of living enjoyed by the family before the breakdown of the marriage;
- the age of each party to the marriage and the duration of the marriage;
- any physical or mental disability of either of the parties to the marriage;
- contributions made by each of the parties to the welfare of the family, including any contribution made by looking after the home or caring for family;
- the conduct of each of the parties, if that conduct is such that it would in the opinion of the court be inequitable to disregard it.

> For the basis of financial provision see MCA, s 25.

Chapter 16 FAMILY AND OTHER RELATIONSHIPS

Outcome

The court seeks to achieve a *clean break* wherever possible, i.e. no continuing financial provision between the parties (see MCA, s 25A):

- this may not be possible following a long marriage where pension rights are involved and there is little further employment potential unless:
  - there is adequate capital to provide for the security of both parties; or
  - both parties are likely to depend on state benefits
- the court now has powers to make provision involving pension schemes (see MCA, ss 25B, 25C and 25D);
- ownership and continued occupation of the former matrimonial home is usually of paramount importance and this may be:
  - ordered to be sold and the net proceeds divided in specified proportions with a view to each party making their own provision
  - transferred to one party outright or with a deferred charge to the other for a fixed sum or share of the value

16.3 GRANDCHILDREN

Grandparents may become involved in disputes relating to their grandchildren following the breakdown of the marriage of the parents. They may find themselves looking after these grandchildren on a full-time basis or wish to seek regular contact with them when this is denied.

Children Act 1989

This statute governs:

- *private law* disputes (involving the family) about the upbringing of children;
- *public law* applications (involving local authorities) relating to their welfare.

Key principles

The emphasis is on *parental responsibility* and agreement being reached as to the future upbringing of children. The court will not make an order unless it considers that doing so is better for the child than making no order at all (s 1(5)). The welfare of the child is the paramount consideration and when considering whether to make most orders, the court must have particular regard to the matters stated in s 1(3):

- the ascertainable wishes and feelings of the child;
- the physical, emotional and educational needs of the child;
- the likely effect on the child of a change of circumstances;

- the age, sex, background and any characteristics of the child which the court considers relevant;
- any harm which the child has suffered or is at risk of suffering;
- how capable each of the child's parents (and any other person) is of meeting the child's needs;
- the range of powers available to the court.

Although the wishes and feelings of the child, if of sufficient age and maturity, are ascertained and taken into account, a child should not be expected to choose.

> For key principles in regard to welfare of a child see Children Act 1989, s 1.

Parental responsibility

This means the authority, along with others similarly entitled, to make normal decisions relating to education, medical treatment and other such matters normally dealt with by parents. Married parents automatically each have parental responsibility as do single mothers, but unmarried fathers may acquire it by registered agreement or court order. A residence order confers parental responsibility but the court may also award it in appropriate circumstances. There is a proposal that an unmarried father who is named on the birth certificate should automatically have parental responsibility.

> For parental responsibility in respect of a child see Children Act 1989, ss 2–4.

Private law applications

A wide range of orders can be made (known as *section 8 orders*):

- **contact** – requires the person with whom a child lives, or is to live, to allow the child to visit or stay with the person named in the order, or provides for that person and the child otherwise to have contact with each other;
- **prohibited steps** – an order that no step which could be taken by a parent in meeting his parental responsibility for a child, and which is of a kind specified in the order, shall be taken by any person without the consent of the court;
- **residence** – settles the arrangements as to the person with whom a child is to live;
- **specific issue** – gives directions for the purpose of determining a specific question which has arisen, or which may arise, in connection with any aspect of parental responsibility for a child.

Interim orders can be made (e.g. to deal with an emergency) and the court has power to make a desired order even if no application has been made. No order is ever final although the court may be reluctant to disturb the *status quo* unless there are compelling reasons to do so.

The emphasis is now on the responsibility of the parents rather than their rights in regard to the child, hence the change of terminology from 'custody' and 'access' to 'residence' and 'contact'. The courts tend to concentrate upon the needs of the child but, all things being equal, it is thought best that the child should grow up knowing both parents (and both their families).

Role of grandparents

Grandparents may initiate or become involved in applications to the court for orders governing their relationship with grandchildren:

- when appropriate in the best interests of the child a grandparent may be joined as a party in proceedings between the parents:
  - it should be shown that there is a need for such intervention and usually the grandparent will co-operate with and support the case of a parent
  - this may be appropriate when the grandparent is at odds with both parents
- a grandparent can apply, with leave of the court (which must be justified), for a residence or contact order in respect of a grandchild:
  - such application will not be appropriate when the same result can be achieved through a parent (e.g. contact may take place when that parent has contact)
  - an order may be made requiring the person with whom a child lives, or is to live, to allow the child to visit or stay with a grandparent, or for that grandparent and the child otherwise to have contact with each other
  - although it is generally in the best interests of a child to remain with the parents or one of them, a grandmother supported by a grandfather may be able to make out a stronger case especially if the parents are not stable
  - where a child is living with grandparents with the agreement of parents, it may be necessary to apply for a residence order to achieve stability

If grandparents are able to see both sides of the problem and avoid taking sides, they can be particularly helpful in facilitating contact in the best interests of the child or children when the relationship between the parents is hostile.

Public law applications

When a child is suffering, or likely to suffer, significant harm and this is attributable to inadequate care by the parent(s) the local authority in whose area the child is ordinarily resident may apply for a *care order* or a *supervision order*:

- grandparents may apply for leave to be made parties and to be heard;
- an order for reasonable contact may be made in favour of grandparents;

PART 3: SECTION A Status

- where a *care order* is made in favour of the local authority, the child may be accommodated with grandparents:
  - the court cannot order this but failure by the authority to carry out its care plan might justify subsequent revocation of the care order on an application by the grandparents for a residence order
  - they may be paid an allowance if the child is placed with them by the authority but may not receive financial support under a residence order unless the parents are able to provide this or the authority makes payments under its discretionary powers

> For local authority applications see Children Act 1989, Part IV, ss 31–42.

Adoption

Grandparents are unlikely to be permitted to adopt a grandchild because of their age and the confusion of roles that would result. An adoption order will only be made if it is in the best interests of the child but if a grandchild is placed for adoption all legal ties with the grandparents are severed:

- the grandparents may apply for leave to intervene and oppose this step;
- there can be post-adoption contact with parents or grandparents but this is unusual and likely to be restricted in its nature;
- adoption is a last resort so grandparents may wish to consider an application for a residence order.

> See the Adoption Act 1976 and the current review of adoption law.

16.4 COHABITATION

An elderly couple may contemplate living together and it may be convenient, economical and mutually supportive for them to do so. In that event a formal agreement may be prepared.

Implications

Legal and practical implications which should be discussed in advance include:

- where they are to live:
  - who is to own the home or hold the tenancy?
  - is the non-owning party to make a capital contribution and on what basis?
  - if the home is to be owned jointly, on what basis will it be held beneficially?
- the shares and manner in which they are to meet household expenses:

Chapter 16 FAMILY AND OTHER RELATIONSHIPS

- will there be a pooling of expenses?
- is a joint bank account appropriate?
- is one party to be merely a lodger at home and if so on what terms?
- the basis on which they are to live together:
  - is an intimate relationship intended or merely companionship?
  - will they take holidays together and share leisure activities?
  - what will be the attitude of their respective families?
- the effect on any benefit claims or services provided:
  - will they be 'living together as man and wife' for benefits purposes?
  - will any services be withdrawn or restricted?
  - will increased charges be made for services?
- whether the relationship is intended to be mutually supportive for life:
  - does this mean financially or on a caring basis, or both?
  - what will be the effect upon any pension entitlement of the parties?
  - should any home and furnishings be owned jointly?
  - should enduring powers of attorney be completed?
- if financially supportive, is this until the first death or the second death?
  - if until death of survivor, what steps are to be taken to secure the intention?
  - should the home be held as joint tenants or on a tenancy in common?
  - are new wills required to ensure that the needs of the survivor are protected and dependency claims avoided?

Marriage?

Advice may be sought as to whether it is in their best interests to marry, but if there is a possible conflict of interest each party should be separately advised:

- consider the effect on any benefits claims or liabilities, e.g. funding for community care services (what happens if one of them goes into a residential care home?)
- consider the implications for income tax and capital taxes.

Testamentary provision would be affected by marriage so each party should make a new will immediately following (or in contemplation of) the marriage especially if they have their own families.

> Cohabitation precedents are now available.

179

16.5 ABUSE AND DOMESTIC VIOLENCE

Nature of abuse

Abuse of older people is more prevalent than previously recognised and may:

- take place in a family or domestic environment, in the community, or in a residential care or nursing home;
- be by a relative, a friend or neighbour (or even a stranger), or be by an informal carer or a professional carer or trustee;
- take the form of (a) physical assault or threatening behaviour, (b) sexual abuse, (c) verbal or emotional pressure, (d) neglect, abandonment or isolation, or (e) misuse of money or property;
- amount to (a) a criminal offence, (b) the tort of trespass to the person (assault, battery or false imprisonment), (c) the tort of negligence, or (d) a theft.

The abused individual may not be in a position to complain or to seek a remedy so lawyers must be vigilant. Failure to recognise the personal and civil rights of an elderly person is a form of abuse, and this includes:

- undue influence and denial of access to independent legal advice;
- medical paternalism whereby the doctor administers treatment on the basis that he knows best without troubling to obtain the informed consent of the patient or ascertain what the patient would have wished.

Lawyers should not make the same mistake by advising relatives or carers without seeking to communicate with their elderly client.

> For more information contact: *Action on Elder Abuse*, Astral House, 1268 London Road, London SW16 4ER.

The right to intervene

Unless the abuse amounts to a serious criminal offence the victim is expected to initiate his own remedies or at least complain. We can counsel and advise, but cannot initiate action without the consent of the individual involved if he is competent. Older people are entitled to put themselves at risk and no-one can legally interfere in their lives simply because it is considered that they are vulnerable to abuse. Any form of intervention against their wishes can only be justified when they lack the mental capacity to take the particular decision involved. It will then be lawful if it is in the best interests of the incapacitated person, but any intervention should be the least restrictive possible.

> Seeking remedies without consulting the victim may amount to further abuse.

Remedies

Recourse to the law, whether civil or criminal, may not be the only way of achieving a remedy. Unless the abuse is particularly serious the victim will not be seeking compensation or retribution but merely wish to ensure that the abuse does not continue or is not repeated. Remedies that may be available include:

- civil court proceedings (the standard of proof is the balance of probabilities):
  - a claim may be made for damages or an injunction (see below)
  - for the ability to initiate proceedings when the individual is mentally incapacitated see Chapter 6
- criminal proceedings (the standard of proof is beyond reasonable doubt):
  - the police may prosecute on information given by a third party
  - a compensation order may be made (if the offender can pay)
  - a claim may be made to the Criminal Injuries Compensation Authority under the statutory scheme
- non-legal remedies:
  - the victim may be moved away from the abusive situation
  - the abuser may be a carer who simply cannot cope without additional help – see Chapter 22 for community care services
  - a professional carer may be dismissed
- use of complaints procedures:
  - if the abuse is by a care professional this may be appropriate and sufficient
  - for the regulation of residential care or nursing homes see Chapter 23
- report the situation to the appropriate authority:
  - the social services department of the local authority should investigate all alleged incidents of abuse where a vulnerable older person is involved
- put financial affairs on a proper footing:
  - see Chapters 7 to 10 for the legal procedures

> Failure to intervene may allow abuse to continue, but too much intervention may be a greater abuse than that which it is intended to prevent.

Injunctions

Enhanced protection for people who suffer from violence or harassment is now available through the courts. The victim may be given protection under one of the three recent statutes mentioned below in addition (or as an alternative) to bringing an action in tort.

> Local courts provide effective remedies in a wide range of abusive situations.

Effect of mental disorder

An elderly person may become an abuser. Where persistent inappropriate behaviour is due to mental disorder an injunction may not be available to control this:

- an injunction ought not to be granted against a person who is incapable of understanding what he is doing and that it is wrong, because a breach could not then be the subject of effective enforcement proceedings – *Wookey v Wookey* [1991] 3 All ER 365, CA:
  - it is possible for an injunction to be granted against a person who is or may be a patient because the tests of capacity are different
  - see *In re de Court* (1997) Times, 27 November clarified in *P v P (Contempt of court: Mental capacity)* (1999) Times, 21 July, CA
- there may be a 'gap' with an elderly mentally disordered individual causing disruption to the lives of others which is not restrained by the health or social services authorities yet cannot be controlled by the courts.

Family Law Act 1996, Part IV

Proceedings may be brought against an abuser in the magistrates' or county court by an *associated person* which includes:

- existing and former spouses and cohabitants;
- those who live or have lived in the same household, other than merely by reason of one of them being the other's employee, tenant, lodger or boarder;
- 'relatives' as widely defined;
- persons who have agreed to marry one another.

Various orders may be made or provisions included in the order. Urgent relief can even be obtained without giving notice to the other party (know as an *ex parte* order) although notice is then given of a later hearing when the need for continuing orders will be considered:

- *non-molestation order* – the respondent is forbidden to use or threaten violence against the applicant or to intimidate, harass or pester the applicant:
  - the respondent may also be ordered not to instruct, encourage or in any way suggest that any other person should do these things
  - the court must have regard to all the circumstances including the need to secure the health, safety and well-being of the applicant
- *occupation order – see below* (this controls occupation of the home);
- *undertaking* – instead of an injunction the respondent may undertake (i.e. promise the court) not to behave in a particular way in future:
  - the alleged behaviour is not admitted and the court makes no findings but a contested hearing is avoided and there is usually no costs order

- breach is contempt of court so committal proceedings can be brought, but a power of arrest cannot be attached to the undertaking so the court should not accept it if this protection is needed

There are enhanced enforcement provisions in this new legislation:

- *power of arrest* – attached to the order if violence has been used or threatened against the applicant unless the applicant will be adequately protected without it:
  - a constable may then arrest without warrant a person whom he has reasonable cause for suspecting to be in breach
  - an arrested person must be brought before a court within 24 hours but the court can remand the arrested person in custody or on bail pending a hearing
  - the court has power to remand to enable a medical report to be obtained
- *warrant for arrest* – where breach of an injunction is alleged (and there is no power of arrest) an application may be made for the issue of a warrant;
- *committal proceedings* – application can still be made on notice for a committal order under the 'show cause' procedure.

> A power to make rules providing for a representative to act on behalf of another person in applying for or enforcing an occupation order or a non-molestation order has not yet been implemented. Such power could be used to assist a vulnerable elderly person.

Protection from Harassment Act 1997

The wording of this Act is broad enough to encompass a wide range of activities which may include 'elder abuse'. A person must not pursue a course of conduct (i.e. conduct on at least two occasions) which amounts to *harassment* of another and which he knows or ought to know amounts to harassment of the other:

- references to harassing a person include alarming the person or causing the person distress, and 'conduct' includes speech;
- if a reasonable person would know that the course of conduct would amount to harassment then the person whose conduct is in question ought to know (there is an exception if in the circumstances the course of conduct was 'reasonable').

Harassment is made a criminal offence as well as a tort, and breach of a civil injunction is a specific offence in addition to civil enforcement procedures:

- civil proceedings are brought in a county court (or the High Court);
- criminal proceedings are dealt with in the magistrates' court or (for the more serious offences) the Crown Court.

An actual or apprehended breach may be the subject of a claim in civil proceedings by the victim of the course of conduct:

- the court may grant an injunction to restrain such conduct and damages may be awarded for any anxiety caused or financial loss resulting from the harassment;
- if the claimant thereafter considers that the defendant has done anything which is prohibited by the injunction he may apply to the court *ex parte* (i.e. without notice to the other party) for a warrant of arrest against the defendant;
- if after considering all the evidence the defendant is found to have been in breach of the injunction he may be fined or committed to prison for contempt.

> This legislation was hastily enacted to control 'stalking' but is not restricted to this and may assist in a wide range of other situations.

Housing Act 1996, Part V, ss 152–157

Local authorities (and to some extent public sector landlords) are given enhanced powers to control anti-social behaviour on housing estates. They may evict tenants who are responsible for the suffering of other tenants and may also apply for free-standing injunctions to prohibit anyone, whether or not a tenant from:

- engaging in or threatening to engage in conduct causing or likely to cause a nuisance or annoyance to anyone residing in, visiting or otherwise engaging in lawful activity in residential premises or in the locality of such premises;
- using or threatening to use residential premises for immoral or illegal purposes;
- entering residential premises or being found in the locality of such premises.

> More effective control of anti-social behaviour on housing estates may assist vulnerable elderly residents.

Occupation of the home

Under the *Family Law Act 1996, Part IV* (see under 'Injunctions' above) a wide range of orders can also be made to regulate the occupation of a dwellinghouse as between spouses and cohabitants. The terms and duration of the order depend upon whether or not the applicant has an estate or interest in the home:

- this could include matrimonial home rights, i.e. the right by virtue of a subsisting marriage to live in the home of the spouse;

- where the parties are not existing or former spouses or cohabitants but are within some other category of 'associated person' (see above) the applicant must have some pre-existing right to occupy before an order can be made.

Where a party is to be excluded from the home a 'balance of harm' test is applied. 'Harm' means ill-treatment or impairment of health, and 'ill-treatment' includes non-physical forms. The court must have regard to all relevant circumstances including:

- the housing needs and resources of the parties;
- the financial resources of the parties;
- the nature and length of their relationship (and otherwise);
- their conduct in relation to each other;
- the effect of an order upon the health, safety or well-being of the parties or a child.

These orders relate to 'dwellinghouses' but this includes a part of a building occupied as a dwellinghouse, a caravan, houseboat or structure occupied as a dwellinghouse, and any yard, garden, garage or outhouse occupied with the dwellinghouse. Mortgagees or landlords are given a chance to make representations, but an order may include provision that in respect of the home or a part of the home:

- the applicant is entitled to occupy it and the respondent shall allow this;
- the respondent shall not obstruct, harass or interfere with peaceful occupation;
- the respondent shall not occupy it at all or between specified times or dates;
- the respondent shall leave it by a specified time and not return to, enter or attempt to enter it or go within a specified distance of it;
- a party maintain and repair the home or furnishings and contents, and pay the rent or mortgage.

> Where drunken grandson or drug using granddaughter is abusing infirm grandmother in her own home whilst posing as a carer, it may be more effective to exclude this person from the home and arrange alternative support (if required) rather than to move grandmother to a residential care home.

16.6 VICTIMS OF CRIME

Procedure

When it is alleged that an offence has been committed there must be an early decision about involving the police. Any serious offence should be reported promptly. If the victim wishes to press charges or the police decide to proceed anyway, an investigation begins:

- in cases of physical or sexual abuse immediate police involvement is important to enable them to examine the victim and collect corroborative forensic evidence;
- the victim may be asked to take part in identification of suspects either informally or by means of a formal identification parade, and to identify photographs.

> The victim may go to the police direct or with help from a third party, but should be consulted and where possible consent to a referral to the police.

Prosecution

There is a discretion whether to prosecute. The victim will not be involved in this but the effect of a prosecution on the victim's physical/mental health is taken into consideration. There may be no prosecution in the case of a victim who would make a poor witness because of lack of reliable evidence or corroboration.

> The *Code for Crown Prosecutors* states that there should only be a prosecution if there is a 'realistic prospect of conviction'.

Information

Policy varies as to how much information is given to victims. The general practice is to tell victims of an arrest, a decision to prosecute or not and the outcome of a trial. Victims may feel excluded from the process and require advice and support to clarify their role as a prosecution witness and not as a party to proceedings:

- legal aid is not available for a vulnerable witness in connection with a prosecution because the person is not a party to the proceedings;
- reports of the offence in the press can cause distress and the victim may suffer media attention during or after the trial:
    - vulnerable victims may request the police to withhold their name and address
    - rape victims must not be identified – Sexual Offences (Amendment) Act 1976

> Many police forces have 'vulnerable persons officers' experienced in interviewing mentally vulnerable victims and investigating reports of crimes involving them.

Evidence

The victim's capacity to give clear evidence and cope with cross-examination and the trauma of a public appearance in the witness box may be crucial to the trial:

- screens to prevent eye-contact with a defendant will only be used in exceptional circumstances and age or infirmity by themselves will not be sufficient;
- the judge decides if a potential witness has the necessary understanding of the concepts of truth and duty:
  - the burden of proving this rests with the party calling the witness
  - if not satisfied beyond reasonable doubt the person will not be allowed to give evidence
- once the decision has been made to admit the evidence it is for the jury to decide what weight to attach to it:
  - the prosecution cannot call medical evidence to support the reliability of one of its witnesses unless this is to rebut a challenge by the defence

Speaking up for Justice (1998)

This Report made many proposals designed to encourage and support vulnerable or intimidated witnesses to give their best evidence in criminal cases in both the Crown Court and the magistrates' courts:

- some of these are implemented in the Youth Justice and Criminal Evidence Act 1999, Part II;
- measures of interest to vulnerable elderly witnesses include:
  - guidance for practitioners including a memorandum of good practice for adult vulnerable witnesses
  - the use of screens and provision of more video and television equipment

Chapter 17

Criminal Responsibility

Special consideration has to be given to people suffering from mental disorder who become caught up in the criminal justice system, and this may include confused elderly people more often than is generally realised. It is important to identify any mental disorder at an early stage so that:

- the safeguards of the PACE Codes of Practice are observed by the police in conducting their interrogation;
- prosecution may be avoided;
- issues such as fitness to plead and the insanity defence are addressed;
- Mental Health Act disposals and other sentencing options are considered;
- where appropriate treatment is provided rather than punishment.

The legal representative should advise the client and the court on these matters where relevant and obtain expert medical and social reports as soon as possible. For the definition of 'mental disorder' see Chapter 2 at para. 2.2.

> Persons with mental health problems who are accused of crimes should be prosecuted only if this is in the public interest and those convicted of crimes should be cared for in the hospital system whenever this is appropriate.

17.1 SAFEGUARDS

Police investigation

Guidance as to treatment and questioning of any detainee and interviewee is provided in the *Codes of Practice* to the Police and Criminal Evidence Act 1984 (PACE) and the Notes for Guidance. A breach in circumstances regarded as unreasonable would raise questions about the validity of police evidence, particularly statements by vulnerable people in the absence of an appropriate adult.

Key points

The general rights of people in police custody and being questioned are:

- to be given information about and notice of their rights;
- to have someone informed of their arrest;

Chapter 17 CRIMINAL RESPONSIBILITY

- to be told that free independent legal advice is available;
- to consult privately with a solicitor;
- to consult the Code of Practice (and any other codes).

Appearance of disability

If the person in detention:

- appears to be suffering from physical illness or mental disorder;
- fails to respond normally to questions or conversation; or
- otherwise appears to need medical attention

then the custody officer must immediately call the police surgeon or send the person to hospital. The person does not need to request medical attention and this should not delay a mental health assessment.

Appropriate adult

If an officer has any suspicion, or is told in good faith, that the person may be mentally disordered or mentally incapable of understanding the significance of questions put to him or his replies then:

- an *appropriate adult* must be brought in to safeguard the rights of the person by being present at interviews and having other functions. This will be:
  - a relative, guardian or other person responsible for his care or custody; or
  - a responsible adult, preferably with experience of mental disorder (a social worker but not a solicitor or police officer or person employed by the police)
- the appropriate adult will be present with the detained person when he is cautioned or questioned:
  - he should act as observer and assist with communication
  - he may make representations on the need for detention

> A solicitor should not take instructions from the detained person in the presence of the appropriate adult because privilege will not apply.

Complaints about the police

Any member of the public can make a complaint (not just the victim) but the complaint should be made as soon as possible after the incident. The complaint can be made orally but it is advisable to do this in writing. It should be addressed to the Chief Constable (or the Commissioner of Police in London) as these chief officers have a duty to record all complaints. There are three ways of dealing with complaints about the police:

- informal resolution, for less serious complaints;
- formal investigation, for more serious allegations;
- supervised formal investigation, for the most serious cases such as death, assault and serious injury.

There are new procedures for dealing with complaints against the police:

- the *Police (Conduct) Regulations 1999* apply from April 1999 (with transitional provisions);
- the new regulations contain a Code of Conduct which provides for 'honesty and integrity', 'fairness and impartiality', 'politeness and tolerance';
- disciplinary offences no longer have to be substantiated 'beyond reasonable doubt' but hearings are not in public;
- a complainant may attend the hearing while witnesses are being examined (but not before giving evidence) and request that questions are put to the officer, and may be permitted to be accompanied by a relative or friend;
- a complainant should be notified of the outcome as soon as possible and of any sanction imposed.

The Police Complaints Authority (PCA) supervises investigation of serious cases and supervises the bringing or consideration of disciplinary or criminal charges in cases where these are not informally resolved.

Police discipline code

If a complaint is upheld about the conduct of an officer the police may take disciplinary proceedings. Complaints can be made about two categories of police conduct: (i) poor performance, and (ii) misconduct.

Civil action

A complainant may also have a right to sue in the civil courts for compensation for damage caused by police action. Documents which have formed part of a complaint investigation can be disclosed for the purpose of the civil action but some documents may be privileged and attract public interest immunity. These may include the investigating officer's reports and documents identifying informants.

The decision to prosecute

The police investigate crime and the Crown Prosecution Service (CPS) prosecutes crime:

- the police decide whether to charge the individual and this will depend on whether it is in the public interest:

Chapter 17 CRIMINAL RESPONSIBILITY

- the police may consider that it is not in the public interest or in the interests of the accused person to charge someone who is suffering from a mental disorder or who is elderly and/or frail
 - see Home Office circular 12/95 para 12
- once the police have charged the individual the file is passed to the CPS for a decision about prosecution. The tests used are contained in the *Code for Crown Prosecutors*:
 - the evidence is assessed to see if there is a realistic prospect of conviction
 - if so, the CPS then considers whether a prosecution is in the public interest
 - factors to be considered include the existence of a mental disorder and the effect of prosecution on the person's mental health and these matters must be balanced against the needs of society
 - representations can be considered about the mental or physical state of the accused

In the case of an older accused person consideration should be given to alternatives such as cautioning, or hospital or social service care and support, but the individual may wish to be given the opportunity to answer any charges in court.

Alternatives to prosecution

Mentally disordered people should be diverted from the criminal justice system and receive care and treatment from the health and social services, if necessary under Mental Health Act powers:

- Home Office guidance states good practice and gives information about alternatives to the criminal justice system for police, the courts and statutory services:
 - Circular 66/90: *Provision for Mentally Disordered Offenders* supplemented by Circular 12/95: *Mentally Disordered Offenders: Inter-Agency Working* with accompanying booklet
 - Circular 29/1993: *Community Care Reforms and the Criminal Justice System*
 - there is emphasis on collaborative working between health, social services, probation, prisons, courts and lawyers
 - diversion schemes have been established to provide a referral and assessment service locally
- cautioning is now used more frequently as an alternative to prosecution:
 - special considerations apply to older people and other vulnerable groups
 - see Circular 59/90: *Cautioning of Offenders*, Home Office

PART 3: SECTION A Status

17.2   PROSECUTION

The Narey scheme

As a result of the *Narey Report* (which addressed ways of expediting the criminal justice process) and the Crime and Disorder Act 1998, changes have taken place in which may affect vulnerable older people:

- CPS staff are to be available at all times to advise the police on charge decisions and assist in preparing and reviewing files;
- there may be an 'early first hearing' in the magistrates' court for a guilty plea and sentence (an adjournment for reports might be appropriate);
- the alternative is an 'early administrative hearing' in the magistrates' court when eligibility for legal aid will be considered;
- representation at these hearings may be by a 'duty solicitor' or solicitor of choice usually under the legal aid scheme.

There is thus less opportunity for discussions with a defence lawyer and for that lawyer to make representations about the prosecution, and older people may find that the matter has been disposed of with serious consequences to their future state of mind before they really understand what has been going on.

Pleas and defences

Several special pleas and defences are available in particular circumstances where some degree of mental disorder is involved:

- in the Crown Court where an accused is *unfit to plead* the accused is treated as under a disability in relation to the trial:
  - there will be a trial of the facts to allow the jury to decide, beyond all reasonable doubt, that he did the act or made the omission charged
  - if the accused is not acquitted following a finding of unfitness to plead the court has a wide range of sentencing options including a hospital or guardianship order, a supervision and treatment order or an absolute discharge
  - see Criminal Procedure (Insanity) Act 1964 amended by Criminal Procedure (Insanity and Unfitness to Plead) Act 1991
  - see Circular 93/91: *The Criminal Procedure (Insanity and Unfitness to Plead) Act 1991*
- a jury may return a *special verdict* that the defendant is not guilty by reason of insanity:
  - the court has a range of disposal options in addition to detention in a hospital
  - see the Criminal Procedure (Insanity and Unfitness to Plead) Act 1991

Chapter 17 CRIMINAL RESPONSIBILITY

- the defence of *non-insane automatism* is available when it is proved that a defendant acted unconsciously in doing the act for which he is charged.

Remand

An accused person can be remanded in custody or on bail and an application for bail may be made with a condition of residence or treatment:

- if the person requires hospital treatment this may be appropriate but the hospital will have no authority to prevent the person on bail leaving the ward;
- there are special powers under the Mental Health Act in the case of imprisonable offences to remand to hospital for periods of up to 28 days and a total period not exceeding 12 weeks:
  - for reports (s 35)
  - for treatment (s 36)
- a person remanded to prison may be transferred to hospital (s 48);
- a magistrates' court may remand a defendant who has consented to summary trial in custody or on bail for medical examination (Magistrates' Courts Act 1980, s 30).

17.3 SENTENCES

A wider range of options is now available to the courts following conviction (see Home Office Circular 66/90):

- if the court thinks the offender is suffering from a mental disorder a psychiatric report must be obtained before sentencing:
  - when contemplating a custodial sentence the court must consider the effect this will have on the mental condition of the offender and his need for treatment (Criminal Justice Act 1991, s 4)
- a hospital or guardianship order may be made under Mental Health Act 1983, s 37 or an interim order under s 38:
  - for the magistrates' court see s 37(3)

SECTION B
Financial Benefits

The weekly funding of an elderly person may come from:

- full-time, part-time or casual earnings;
- pensions;
- income from savings;
- income from trust provision;
- state benefits;
- local authority benefits;
- family support on a voluntary basis;
- use of capital (including capital 'unlocking' schemes);
- charities.

Provision of services and subsidised facilities may be as significant as cash benefits but these sources of support interact and charges may be made for services and facilities on a means-tested basis.

It is usually desired that any voluntary support supplements that otherwise available from the state or local authority.

Chapter 18
Social Security Benefits

18.1 SOCIAL SECURITY SYSTEM

Sources of law

The relevant enabling statutory provisions are:

- Social Security Administration Act 1992
- Social Security Contributions and Benefits Act 1992
- Social Security (Incapacity for Work) Act 1994
- Jobseekers Act 1995
- Social Security Act 1998

Regulations

Regulations are made under powers granted by the legislation and:

- provide detailed law as to entitlement to particular benefits, e.g:
  - Social Security (Widow's Benefit and Retirement Pensions) Regulations 1979
  - Income Support (General) Regulations 1987
- specify procedure, in particular:
  - Social Security (Claims and Payments) Regulations 1979 and 1987
  - Social Security (Adjudication) Regulations 1995
  - Social Security (Payments on Account, Overpayments and Recovery) Regulations 1988
  - Social Security (Decisions and Appeal) Regulations 1999

Commissioners' decisions

Decisions of the Commissioners on appeals from tribunals are sources of law:

- significant decisons are published;
- the reference indicates the type of benefit, number of decision and year:
  - *R(IS)1/98* is the first reported income support decision of 1998
  - an unreported income support decision might be referred to as *CIS 13/98*

Further *appeals* to the courts may be found in the law reports.

Administration

In 1991 the *Benefits Agency* took over the administration of most benefits from the DSS and the *Contributions Agency* took over NI contributions:

- some benefits are dealt with at local offices but others in a single location (e.g. disability living allowance in Blackpool). Income support is handled by local offices but attendance allowance by regional centres;
- in 1994 the *War Pensions Agency* took over the assessment of war pensions and the welfare service for war pensioners.

A *Customer Charter* sets out the standards of service which all customers can reasonably expect from the Benefits Agency, how customers can help the Agency to help them and what they can do if things go wrong.

Significant changes in the decision-making and appeals process were made by the Social Security Act 1998 and regulations under the Act. Decisions on benefit claims are now made by the Secretary of State acting through authorised officers rather than by independent adjudication officers.

> *Appeals* are to special tribunals (see below).

Different countries

The same social security system covers Great Britain with some variations. A claimant living elsewhere in the European Union may qualify for benefit under the basic rules about going abroad or under EU rules.

Information

Practical information about benefits and claims is readily available:

- an invaluable series of free leaflets can be collected from Benefits Agency offices (and most post offices):
  - GL23 *Social security benefit rates* and MG1 *A guide to benefits* are a good starting point;
  - RM1 *Retirement* and SD1 *Sick or disabled* are particularly relevant
  - leaflets can also be obtained in other languages, Braille and large print
- a catalogue of leaflets, posters and information is available and solicitors should be able to add their firms to the *Benefits Agency Publicity Register* and receive updating information at intervals;
- for general benefit advice enquire of the local Benefits Agency office:
  - in local telephone directory (Business Section) under Benefits Agency
  - free Benefit Enquiry Line (BEL) for people with disabilities: 0800 88 22 00

Chapter 18 SOCIAL SECURITY BENEFITS

- there are now a number of informative internet sites (with links to other sites) – see Appendix 6.

> Rights membership of Child Poverty Action Group brings an annual selection of invaluable books and material – address in Appendix 5.

- reference may be made to the books mentioned in Appendix 7:
  - Benefits Information Guide HMSO (revised annually)
  - *Your Rights: A guide to money benefits for older people* published annually by Age Concern (this is inexpensive and could be handed to clients)
  - Age Concern *Fact Sheets* deal with particular benefits
- in the event of an appeal the relevant statutes, regulations and Commissioners' decisions should be referred to:
  - the leaflets may have misled the client or matters of interpretation may arise
  - up-to-date annotated statutory material is available at a moderate price – see Appendix 7

> When a dispute arises the leaflets issued by the Benefits Agency should not be treated as authoritative and reference should be made to the original statutory material and court or Commissioners' decisions.

18.2 TYPES OF BENEFITS

Weekly benefits

Weekly cash benefits are paid to meet different needs, but rates change yearly and the qualifying criteria are constantly amended. A claimant may not receive two overlapping benefits and it is important to claim the one that pays the highest rate.

> GL23 *Social security benefit rates* and MG1 *A guide to benefits*.
> Age Concern Fact Sheet 18 *A brief guide to money benefits*.
> Help the Aged leaflets on *Pensions* and *Benefits – disability*.

Contributory benefits

These depend upon NI contributions paid during normal working life but people resident in Great Britain are entitled regardless of personal means. Most are taxable and all are taken into account when claiming means-tested benefits. Those claimable by an older person are:

- *incapacity benefit* (ICB – formerly sickness benefit and invalidity benefit) is payable if working and up to age 70 for men and 65 for women;

PART 3: SECTION B Financial Benefits

> See leaflet SD1 *Sick or disabled* and IB202 *Incapacity benefit.*

- *jobseekers allowance* (JSA – formerly unemployment benefit) is payable for the first 26 weeks of unemployment only and disqualification may arise if a job has been left 'without just cause';

- *retirement pension,* over 80s pension and *widow's benefits* (see Chapter 28 at para. 28.2).

> RM1 *Retirement;* NP46 *A guide to retirement pensions;* PM8 *Making the most of your personal pension;* NP45 *A guide to widow's benefits.*
> Age Concern Fact Sheet 19 *Your state pension and carrying on working.*
> Help the Aged - *Pensions.*

Non-contributory benefits

There is no need to have paid NI contributions to qualify for non-contributory benefits and people resident in Great Britain are entitled regardless of personal means. There may be additions for dependants, but some benefits cannot overlap. Some are non-taxable and/or not taken into account for means-tested benefits. Many benefits awarded on disability are passports to other benefits and concessions.

> See leaflet HB5 *A guide to non-contributory benefits for disabled people* and HB6 *A practical guide for disabled people.*

Claimable by an older person are:

- *attendance allowance* (AA) is available where disability begins at or after 65, and special rules and rates may apply for those terminally ill:
  - two rates (higher rate for those needing supervision day and night)
  - tax free and non-contributory

> Obtain claim pack DS702 *Attendance allowance.*

- *disability living allowance* (DLA) is available where disability begins before 65 but must be claimed before the 66th birthday and special rules may apply for those terminally ill:
  - *care component* at three levels
  - *mobility component* at two levels

> See leaflet DS704 *Disability living allowance* and claim packs DLA1, DLA2.

- *severe disablement allowance* (SDA) is payable up to age 65 only and for those who do not satisfy contribution conditions for incapacity benefit;

Chapter 18 SOCIAL SECURITY BENEFITS

> See leaflet SD1 *Sick or disabled*.

- *invalid care allowance* (ICA) is paid to a carer in receipt of AA or DLA care component (upper rates) up to age 65 only and earning less than a specified sum (note the qualifying hours to obtain this benefit):
  - taxable but provides class I NI contributions credits

> See leaflet SD4 *Caring for someone*.

- *industrial disablement benefit* is paid to those who became ill or disabled as a result of work for an employer

> See leaflets GL27 *Compensation and social security benefits* and SD5 *Ill or disabled because of work?*

In appropriate circumstances the following may also be claimable:

- *disability working allowance*;
- *guardians allowance* (where a minor child is cared for).

Means-tested benefits

These are weekly income supplements to which GB residents may be entitled whether or not they have paid NI contributions. They are assessed on the needs of a family living in the same household which includes the claimant and any partner with whom he or she is living 'as man and wife'. Either partner may claim and they may be non-taxable:

- *income support* brings the income up to a minimum level (see below);
- *family credit* is only claimable by an older person if there is a dependent child. An award is made for a six-month period and the assessment rules are complex so not dealt with here.

> Age Concern Fact Sheet 16 *Income related benefits: income and capital*.

Christmas bonus

A non-taxable bonus is paid to those receiving one or more qualifying benefits but each claimant is only entitled to one such bonus.

Income support

Income support is claimable by an elderly person or couple to whom the obligation to be available for and seeking work does not apply and it operates as a passport to some other benefits:

PART 3: SECTION B Financial Benefits

- it brings income up to an *applicable amount* representing needs based on:
  - a *personal allowance* depending on age, marital status and children
  - *premiums* for family, age and disability
  - an allowance for *housing costs*, e.g. mortgage interest (assistance with rent will be provided by housing benefit – see Chapter 19 at para. 19.1)
  - a *residential allowance* paid to those in residential care or nursing homes (see Chapter 19 at para. 19.4)
- there is no entitlement if capital resources (as assessed) exceed a *capital cut-off limit*: this is presently £8,000 but capital resources over £3,000 are assessed on the basis of a tariff income (£1 per week for every £250 or part) and these limits are increased to £16,000 and £10,000 if in a residential care or nursing home:
  - almost all capital is included (cash, savings, property, assets abroad) but personal possessions and surrender value of life policies are not counted (personal injury settlements may not be taken into account)
  - rules for *notional capital* may include capital of which claimant has deprived himself (e.g. failed to obtain or given away) in order to get benefit
  - a home that is occupied by the claimant is not taken into account and this may include occupation by a partner or a relative who is aged 60 or incapacitated (a period may be allowed for a home to be sold when not occupied)
- almost all income of the claimant and partner is taken into account but there are rules for *notional income* (see notional capital above):
  - regular voluntary payments (e.g. from relatives or charities) are included but irregular payments may count as capital
  - some income is disregarded including the first £5 (or £15) of income from employment, specified weekly amounts paid by sub-tenants or boarders, certain weekly social security benefits based on disability (e.g. DLA, war disablement pensions), actual interest on savings (the capital may be assessed) and payments by others for items not covered by income support (e.g. by a relative for a telephone)
- married couples and unmarried persons 'living together as husband and wife' are assessed together:
  - there are limitations: if in doubt discuss with the Benefits Agency or seek advice from a welfare rights agency with specialised knowledge
  - spouses will be assessed separately when separated for a period or under a court order or where one spouse is in a residential care or nursing home

---

IS20 *A guide to income support.*
Age Concern Fact Sheet 25 *Income support and the social fund.*
Help the Aged publications.

The Social Fund

Lump sums are available to meet needs 'in accordance with directions given or guidance issued by the Secretary of State' (refer to the *Social Fund Manual* for the policy). Regard must be had to a statutory list of factors and directions must be followed but the guidance is persuasive:

- means-testing is on the income support basis;
- payments are rationed on the basis of annual allocations for each office divided between loans and grants;
- review is by *Social Fund Inspectors* but there is no appeal to a tribunal.

> GL18 *Help from the Social*; SB16 *A Guide to the Social Fund.*
> Age Concern Fact Sheet 25 *Income Support and the Social Fund.*

Community care grants

Non-repayable grants are available to help people stay in the community rather than residential care and also to help people move out of institutional care into the community or to meet certain travel expenses:

- targeted at priority situations, groups and items but there is a discretion
- any capital over £1,000 will reduce the amount (£500 if under the age of 60)

Loans

Budgeting loans assist in meeting important intermittent expenses for which it is difficult for those receiving income support to budget:

- there are maximum and minimum amounts:
    - the maximum takes into account any outstanding balance of previous loans
    - any capital over £1,000 will reduce the amount (£500 if under the age of 60)
    - may not exceed £1,000 or the amount which the applicant can afford to repay
- there is a list of items divided into high, medium and low priority.

Crisis loans assist a person in an emergency or following a disaster but may need to be the only means by which serious damage or risk to the health or safety of the claimant or a family member may be prevented:

- various types of claimant are excluded, e.g.:
    - people in 'Part III accommodation' (see Chapter 22 para. 22.2)
    - people in a nursing home or hospital
- any available resources will be taken into account including credit facilities.

> *Funeral payments* are also available from the Social Fund – see Chapter 33.

PART 3: SECTION B Financial Benefits

Loans are interest free but recovery is normally by deduction from subsequent income support or other benefits of the applicant or a partner.

Cold weather payments

Payments are sent automatically to those on income support who are getting a pensioner or disability premium during periods of cold weather (as defined) and unlike the other grants and loans these are not discretionary.

18.3 PROCEDURE

Claims

A properly completed form (obtained from the local Benefits Agency office) must reach the appropriate Benefits Agency office in order for a claim to be validly made:

- the claim may be amended or withdrawn before a decision is made but further information may be required in support of the claim;
- the claim may be treated as having been made on the date of receipt of a letter asking about the benefit if the form sent out in response is returned within a month:
  - if the form is sent back because it is not properly completed but returned duly completed within a month, the claim is treated as made when first submitted

> Professional persons who claim benefits on behalf of elderly persons should make clear to the Benefits Agency the capacity in which they act and the limit of their experience.

Backdating

Most benefits are paid from the date of claim and there are strict time-limits on backdating:

- the maximum period for which any benefit can be backdated is three months:
  - some benefits (e.g. retirement pension) can be automatically backdated for three months
  - others (e.g. income support) can only be backdated in prescribed circumstances (e.g. the claimant was caring for an invalid and could not obtain assistance from another person to make the claim)
- it may be possible to get round this but the rules have been tightened up;
- special rules may apply (e.g. disability benefit claims for the terminally ill).

> For **agents** and **appointees** generally see Chapter 8 at para. 8.1.

Decisions

The claim is now decided by the Secretary of State (in practice by his authorised representative). Payments of benefit are also controlled in certain ways:

- a claimant may not receive two *overlapping* benefits but receives the higher:
  - Social Security (Overlapping Benefits) Regulations 1979
  - benefits providing for different purposes can be claimed simultaneously
- changes in circumstances that may affect entitlement must be reported:
  - a list will be found in the order book
  - for those whose benefit is credited direct to an account, the list is sent yearly
- a claimant may have benefits reduced or withdrawn whilst in hospital.

> See leaflet GL12 *Going into hospital?*

Revision and supersession

The Secretary of State may revise a decision of his own initiative or on an application within one month of notification.

A decision (whether or not on appeal) may be superseded by the Secretary of State of his own initiative or on an application outside the one-month period. In some circumstances this may be backdated to the original decision if this is advantageous to the claimant.

Suspension

The Secretary of State may suspend payment of benefit in certain circumstances (e.g. for failure to provide information or if an appeal is pending against a decision in a 'lead case').

Payment

Benefits have traditionally been paid weekly by order book or girocheque and cashed at a post office, some in arrears and others in advance. Payment of some benefits may now be by direct credit to a bank or building society account either four-weekly or quarterly in arrears, and practitioners should recommend this to all going into residential care if appropriate.

Payment may be direct into the account of the spouse or other person acting on behalf of the claimant, and this may be helpful to older people.

Delegation

There are procedures for authorising others to collect benefit:

- an *agent* may be nominated by the claimant using the form of authority printed on the allowance order slip – the agent accounts to the claimant;
- an *appointee* may be appointed when the claimant is unable to act through mental disability – the agent collects and spends the benefit for the claimant.

> Those acting as appointees should be advised of the personal liability that can attach to this role – see generally Chapter 8.

Overpayments

An *overpayment* of benefit may be recovered where any person whether fraudulently or otherwise misrepresents, or fails to disclose, any material fact and this results in the overpayment:

- the original decision (either to pay benefit or determining the amount of benefit) must first be *revised*;
- a *misrepresentation* can be wholly innocent and a *failure to disclose* may be the result of forgetfulness but knowledge of the material fact by the person who fails to disclose it must be established:
    - disclosure need not be in writing but must be made in such a manner that it is likely to be brought to the attention of the office handling the claim and if it appears that it has not been further disclosure may be required
    - the claimant is expected to have read the information in the back of the order book or in any leaflets forwarded with payment, and these may indicate the changes of circumstances which affect the benefit and should be disclosed
- overpayment calculations tend to be complicated because of the need to take into account the claimant's position as it would have been if the overpayment had not been made – the '*diminishing capital* rule'.

> Overpayments may be recovered from the claimant (or the appointee) or the estate of a deceased claimant in cases of *misrepresentation* or *failure to disclose*.

Underpayments

Claimants are entitled to compensation if they are *underpaid* benefit of £50 or more resulting from clear and unambiguous error by the Benefits Agency and the delay in payment was more than 12 months:

- there is no leaflet or claim form, but the DSS Administrative Code instructs local offices to consider *ex gratia* payments in such cases (the onus is on the claimant to raise the issue with the office dealing with the claim);
- the benefit itself may also be backdated.

18.4 APPEALS

Appeals against a refusal of benefit or the amount awarded are dealt with by independent local tribunals with further appeal to the Social Security Commissioners on a point of law. Legal aid is not available but assistance and advice under Claim 10 may be available (previously 'Green Form'). Considering the amount of money that may be in issue it is surprising that solicitors are so seldom instructed in appeals. Many claimants deal with their own appeals and most representatives come from CABs or are welfare benefits advisers. A word of caution – advocacy is not enough and advisers need a detailed knowledge of the regulations and procedures as well as current Commissioners' decisions. All this is available from the books listed in Appendix 7 but membership of Child Poverty Action Group helps to keep one up to date.

> See leaflet NI246 *How to appeal* and NI260 *A guide to reviews and appeals*.

Tribunals

Most readers will have been aware of the *Independent Tribunal Service* (ITS) and its range of tribunals including the Social Security Appeal Tribunal (SSAT), Disability Appeal Tribunal (DAT), Medical Appeal Tribunal (MAT), Vaccine Damage Tribunal (VDT) and Child Support Appeal Tribunal (CSAT). These have been replaced with effect from April 2000 by The Appeals Service (TAS) which is headed by a President and The Appeals Service, an agency headed by a Chief Executive accountable to the Secretary of State.

The new unified Appeals Service is organised (as previously) in regions under a regional chairman. District chairmen and panel members (some of whom including all full-time chairmen are legally qualified – LQPM) are appointed by the Lord Chancellor. There are a number of differently constituted tribunals but each includes a LQPM and is attended by a full-time clerk. Some tribunals comprise only the LQPM rather than a chairman and two lay members. Many hearings are dealt with 'on paper' without the attendance of the appellant.

Procedure

An appeal is made to the Benefits Agency office within one month of notification of the decision, but if this does not include a statement of reasons one may be requested within one month and the time limit is then six weeks. The time-limit may be extended up to one year. The procedure is then quite strict:

- the appeal must be in writing, signed by the appellant or an authorised representative, and state the grounds on which it is made;
- submissions will be sent out by the Benefits Agency with a form directing the appellant to opt for an oral or paper hearing:
  - if the form is not returned within 14 days a clerk may strike out the appeal (it

PART 3: SECTION B Financial Benefits

  can be reinstated on request within one month if there are reasonable grounds)
- withdrawal of an appeal no longer requires leave or consent and there is power to strike out an appeal where it has no chance of success

> Appeals should be lodged in time if possible.

The hearing

If the appellant requests an oral hearing this takes place before a tribunal in the area in which the appellant resides:

- 14 days notice must be given to the appellant or representative (not both) and the tribunal can proceed in the absence of the appellant;
- hearings are informal and should be attended by the appellant if possible:
  - procedure is in the chairman's discretion but the rules of natural justice apply
  - expenses may be paid for attending (but not for legal representatives)
- the chairman must make a record of an oral hearing.

> Appellants should request an oral hearing and attend, especially where there is a dispute as to the facts.

The decision

This may be unanimous or by majority and a summary written decision is usually handed out at the end of the hearing:

- a full statement may be requested within one month of receiving the summary decision;
- the decision may be set aside:
  - at the discretion of a chairman if a relevant document was not received or a party or representative was not present
  - if the chairman or both parties consider that it is wrong (rather than have a hearing before the Commissioners)
- an application for leave to appeal to a Commissioner must be made within one month of receipt of a full statement:
  - there is a discretion to extend this period to 13 months

Social Security Commissioners

Commissioners hear appeals from tribunals on points of law only, but this includes cases where the decision was based on a mistaken interpretation of the law, inadequate reasons and/or findings of fact were recorded so that it is unclear how or why the decision was arrived at, the decision is not supported by any or any sufficient evidence and is therefore perverse, or there was a breach of the rules of natural justice.

The process normally takes many months and most appeals are dealt with on written representations. The appellant can ask for an oral hearing. This is not always granted but a written decision is ultimately sent to the parties. The Commissioners may make the final decision (if the tribunal determined all the material facts) or send the case back to a tribunal with directions as to how it should be dealt with.

Courts

There is a further right of appeal to the Court of Appeal and this will be on a question of law. Leave to appeal must be obtained from the Commissioner within three months or, if refused, from the Court of Appeal. After the House of Lords the ultimate right of appeal is to the European Court of Human Rights and issues may be referred there at an earlier stage.

> Legal aid is available for the first time at this stage, subject to means.

Judicial review

An application may be made to the High Court for judicial review but this will be refused if another remedy is available (e.g. the normal appeal process). Excessive delay by the DSS in carrying out its statutory duties may justify application. Some benefit decisions are taken by the Secretary of State without a right of appeal so there is scope for judicial review if he exercises his powers improperly.

European Court of Justice

Any issue of European Community law arising before a national court concerning questions of interpretation or validity can be referred to this court for a preliminary ruling (Article 177 of the Treaty of Rome). In social security matters, a reference can be made by an SSAT, a Commissioner or the courts.

18.5 NATIONAL INSURANCE CONTRIBUTIONS

National insurance contributions are intended to be paid during a normal working life so are not payable by those over pensionable age.

Types

There are different classes of contribution depending on the status of the individual and a series of leaflets dealing with contributions is available from the Benefits Agency:

PART 3: SECTION B Financial Benefits

- *Class 1* earnings-related contributions are paid by both employers and employees in respect of anyone in employment;
- flat-rate *Class 3* contributions can be paid voluntarily by those wishing to improve an incomplete record (within time limits);
- self-employed people pay flat-rate *Class 2* contributions together with profit-related *Class 4* contributions if their profits exceed a certain sum up to a defined maximum.

> NI contributions are not paid beyond the age of 65 for a man and 60 for a woman.

Contributions record

Entitlement to certain benefits (including retirement pension) depends upon an adequate contributions record. This can be made up by credits rather than by actual payment of contributions. Either the claimant or spouse must have an adequate record but a man can only rely upon his wife's record if widowed or divorced. Those with an inadequate record should consider paying additional contributions before retirement.

Credits and protection

Credits are earned whilst a person is unemployed and registering for employment, off work sick or entitled to certain benefits paid during a working life e.g. severe disablement allowance.

Since 1978 *Home Responsibilities Protection* provides some assistance with contribution conditions for periods when a person is unable to work because he or she is caring for someone. This might be a child or an elderly or disabled person:

- if receiving child benefit or income support the necessary credits will be automatically recorded each year;
- otherwise Form CF411 should be requested from the local DSS office at the end of each year to ensure that credits are given.

Pension forecasts

A comprehensive retirement pension forecast is available for those who have not yet drawn their pension and this indicates the effect of postponing the pension. Voluntary or late contributions can in some circumstances be paid in order to top up a pension contributions record:

- apply on form BR19 to the Benefits Agency, RPFA Unit (Correspondence), Room 37D, DSS Longbenton, Benton Park Road, Newcastle-upon-Tyne NE98 1YX.

Chapter 19

Local Authority Support

19.1 HOUSING BENEFIT

Sources of law

- Social Security Act 1986
- Housing Benefit (General) Regulations 1987

> See leaflet RR2 *A guide to housing benefit and council tax benefit*.
> Age Concern Fact Sheet 17 *Housing benefit and council tax benefit*.
> Also refer to the books mentioned in Appendix 7.

Purpose

This benefit helps people on low incomes to pay rent in respect of a dwelling which they normally occupy:

- includes hotels, hostels or lodgings and residential accommodation in Great Britain whether furnished or unfurnished in the public or private sector;
- does not usually include residential care or nursing homes.

> Housing benefit provides help with the cost of providing (but not owning) a home for those on low incomes.

Entitlement

Benefit may be claimed by people who are in full-time work or self-employed as well as those who are unemployed, sick or retired. The claimant must be the person who is legally liable to pay the rent (or treated as such):

- in order to prevent abuse certain claimants are treated as not liable, e.g. someone living with the person to whom the rent is paid where that person is a close relative or the agreement is not on a commercial basis.

Amount

The amount depends upon the amount of rent paid, the claimant's income (including that of a spouse or partner), the number of people in the family and

PART 3: SECTION B Financial Benefits

the age or disability of the claimant, partner or child. It is tax free, not dependent on NI contributions and paid in addition to other benefits:

- up to 100 per cent of the eligible rent can be allowed;
- claimants on income support receive maximum benefit and others a proportion according to their income.

Assessment

This is complicated. Income is compared with the statutory sum needed to live on (the applicable amount) calculated as for income support and the maximum benefit is reduced by any excess income:

- a deduction may be made for non-dependants living with the claimant:
    - non-dependants are people who are not tenants and are over the age of 18 years
    - if a claimant is registered blind or receives attendance allowance or the highest or middle rate care component of disability living allowance then no non-dependant deductions will be made
- a claimant may have up to £16,000 in capital:
    - defined as for income support and certain income and capital is disregarded
    - the first £3,000 is disregarded and any amount above that figure is deemed to generate £1 per week for every £250 or part thereof
    - notional income and capital rules apply as for income support

Eligible rent

There are restrictions upon the amount and nature of the rent that can be claimed and eligible rent cannot exceed any registered rent:

- rent may include a non-eligible element:
    - *eligible* charges include wardens and caretakers, removal of refuse, lifts, portering, gardening and general management charges
    - *non-eligible* charges include water and sewerage charges, meals, fuel, laundry, leisure items, cleaning of personal rooms, transport, medical expenses, nursing or personal care, and other services not connected with the provision of accommodation
    - non-eligible services must be identified and the cost deducted from the charges made so as to identify the true rent
- the local authority may reduce the rent in certain circumstances by such amount as it considers appropriate having regard in particular to the cost of suitable alternative accommodation elsewhere:
    - no deduction may be made if claimant or a member of the family is over 60 unless suitable cheaper alternative accommodation is available and it is rea-

sonable to expect claimant to move
- the rent may be referred to the Rent Officer for consideration but a claimant can request that a determination of rent be made prior to his entering into a tenancy agreement
- certain claimants are protected for a period and claimants already receiving benefit prior to 1996 may not be affected unless they move home
- there is some discretion to allow an increase in the maximum eligible rent when *exceptional hardship* can be established

> Rules for entitlement change at intervals and are being made progressively more stringent so up-to-date material should be relied upon.

Procedure

A claim form is submitted to the district council (or other housing authority). Couples make a single claim but either partner may claim. There are time-limits:

- the claim may be made up to 13 weeks in advance but may only be back-dated for a maximum of 52 weeks if there is good cause for a late claim;
- those away from home for a long period can still claim if they are intending to (and do) return within 52 weeks;
- claimants should be supplied with a written statement of their claim calculation within six weeks of a request.

> Those in receipt of income support have a passported claim.

Payment

Private tenants receive benefit by cheque or credit to a bank or building society account, but for council tenants the benefit simply reduces the rent. Benefit is paid to the landlord in certain circumstances where there are arrears:

- *overpayments* may be recovered from the claimant (or the landlord) in certain circumstances.

Review and appeal

There may on request within 28 days be an administrative review of the decision followed by an appeal to a Housing Benefit Review Board set up by the authority. There is no further right of appeal (apart from judicial review).

PART 3: SECTION B Financial Benefits

19.2   COUNCIL TAX BENEFIT

Sources of law

- Council Tax Benefit (General) Regulations 1992

> See leaflet RR2 *A guide to housing benefit and council tax benefit.*
> Age Concern Fact Sheet 17 *Housing benefit and council tax benefit.*
> Also refer to the books mentioned in Appendix 7.

Nature

This benefit helps people on low incomes to pay council tax (see Chapter 15, para. 15.3) whether they rent or own their home. Entitlement does not depend on NI contributions and benefit is tax free and allowed in addition to other benefits. It is paid by the local authority to whom claims must be made and can be claimed on the same form as housing benefit. A *review* can be requested followed by a reference to a Review Board.

Amount

Financial eligibility is broadly similar to that for housing benefit. A householder on income support automatically has a 100 per cent rebate unless there are non-dependant deductions.

Second adult rebate is available where another adult on a low income also lives in the home which can provide a rebate of up to 25 per cent for claimants even if they do not qualify for help based on their income and savings.

> Council tax benefit provides help with council tax for those on low incomes.

19.3   COMMUNITY CARE FUNDING

Sources of law

- Health and Social Services and Social Security Adjudications Act 1983 (HASSASSAA), s 17
- DoH Circular LAC(94)1 and Social Services Inspectorate Advice Note: *Discretionary Charges for Adult Social Services.*

Services

Local authorities are responsible for funding services needed by elderly people but may make whatever charges they think reasonable for non-residential services:

- for details of the types of services involved see Chapter 22 (e.g. home help, meals on wheels, day care);
- local authorities are expected to make charges for these services but only the person receiving the services may be charged (i.e. not the carers);
- assessment for the service is a separate process from the assessment of means to pay contributions. Failure to pay does not mean that the service can be withdrawn and the remedy for the local authority is an action in court to recover the debt.

> Local authorities may charge for the provision of community care services.

Charges

There is no national scheme and charges vary between authorities. The maximum charge is the portion of the total cost of the service that is attributable to the particular service user:

- it is not policy to charge for social work support, occupational therapy, advice and assessments of need;
- there is no power to charge for services provided pursuant to section 117 of the Mental Health Act 1983 (aftercare services);
- authorities cannot charge more than it is reasonably practicable for the client to pay, so if the recipient states that he or she is unable to meet the charges the authority must consider this and reduce or waive them if appropriate:
  - if the service user does not provide information as to personal means the full charge may be imposed for services
  - most authorities have hardship or exemption policies
- many authorities take state benefits (e.g. attendance allowance) into account when considering ability to pay:
  - any allowance for mobility cannot be assessed
  - it may be inappropriate to assess means-tested benefits (e.g. income support) although some authorities are doing so
- resources available to the local authority may now be taken into account although charges should not be used as a way of avoiding the obligation to provide (*R v Gloucestershire CC ex p Barry* (HL)).

> Charges for services should be means-tested.

PART 3: SECTION B Financial Benefits

Enforcement

Any charge levied 'may, without prejudice to any other method of recovery, be recovered summarily as a civil debt' – HASSASSAA 1983, s 17(4):

- this means through the magistrates' courts (cf council tax and see the Magistrates' Courts Act 1980, s 58(1)) although a far more appropriate course would be the use of the small claims system in the county courts;
- disputes as to charges should be dealt with under the social services complaints procedure and there is no separate appeal procedure (see Chapter 22 at para. 22.4).

19.4 RESIDENTIAL CARE FUNDING

Sources of law

- National Assistance Act 1948, s 22
- Community Care (Residential Accommodation) Act 1998
- National Assistance (Assessment of Resources) Regulations 1992 (as amended)
- National Assistance (Charges for Accommodation) Regulations 1992
- National Assistance (Sums for Personal Requirements) Regulations 1996
- *Charging for Residential Accommodation Guide* (CRAG) (comprising LAC(95)7, LAC(95)21, LAC(96)6 and LAC(96)9 and later amendments)

> See Age Concern Fact Sheet 10 *Local authority charging procedures for residential and nursing home care.*

Charges

Individuals who can afford to pay for a place in a residential care or nursing home may arrange this independently, though it is advisable to seek a 'needs' assessment prior to entering residential or nursing care in order to achieve continuity if local authority funding may be needed in future:

- if met with a refusal to assess in advance, point out that the assessment of need for care provision does not depend upon the need for funding;
- it may also be wise to ensure that the particular home is willing to accommodate residents on local authority funding;
- in regard to assessment of the need for residential care see Chapter 22 at para. 22.2.

Chapter 19 LOCAL AUTHORITY SUPPORT

Local authority

Those who enter such a home through an arrangement made by the local authority must pay or contribute to the cost, whether the authority provides or buys in the accommodation:

- each authority must fix a standard weekly charge for its own homes which should represent the true economic cost of providing the accommodation – many have a standard scale of fees geared to their eligibility criteria;
- where the authority purchases a place from an independent home the weekly charge to the resident should represent the cost of the place to the authority;
- residents must generally contribute in accordance with their resources up to the appropriate charge, but no one will be required to pay more;
- the authority either:
  - pays the full fee to the home and collects the resident's contribution; or
  - pays its share whilst the resident and any third party pay the balance
- a contract with the authority or the home should state what is included in the charge and what are extras – see Chapter 23.

Health authority

Where a health authority arranges a place in a nursing home under a contractual arrangement the individual remains an NHS patient and no charge is made but social security benefits may be withdrawn or reduced – see Chapters 20 and 24.

> It is important to ascertain whether a move from hospital to a private nursing home also involves a transfer of responsibility from the health authority to social services.

Means-testing

When the resident cannot afford the full charge an assessment is made of ability to pay and this is reviewed annually but a resident should ask for re-assessment at any time if this would be beneficial:

- the assessment relates to both income and capital:
  - since April 1993 assessment has been brought largely into line with that for income support, though local authorities retain some discretion
  - the capital cut-off point is £16,000 but capital above £10,000 will result in a tariff income (an attempt to apply a lower financial threshold before acknowledging need failed in *R v Sefton Metropolitan Borough Council, ex p Help the Aged* (1997), CA)
  - *notional capital* and *notional income* rules apply as for income support – see Chapter 18 at para. 18.2

PART 3: SECTION B Financial Benefits

- assessment relates only to the means of the resident (unlike for income support where spouses and partners are generally assessed together):
  - there is no power to oblige a spouse/partner to take part *but* spouses are liable to maintain each other (National Assistance Act 1948, s 42) and court action may be taken against a liable relative (s 43)
  - jointly owned property may be deemed to be owned in equal shares (but query whether it has a value if a home is occupied by the joint owner)
  - since 1996 one-half of occupational and private pensions of the resident are re-routed back to the non-resident spouse
- the value of the resident's home is disregarded during a temporary stay or:
  - if occupied by a spouse/partner, or a relative who is aged 60 or over or incapacitated
  - if occupied by someone else and the local authority exercises its discretion
- there is a minimum charge payable by all residents and the assessment determines what should be paid above this, but all residents retain a personal expenses allowance (revised annually):
  - to be used by the resident for expenditure of personal choice such as stationery, personal toiletries, treats (e.g. sweets, drinks, cigarettes) and presents
  - the authority has a discretion to increase the amount, but it should not be used for top-up to provide more expensive accommodation
- authorities should carry out a benefits check because they have an incentive to ensure that people in homes are receiving maximum state benefits:
  - this should only be with the informed consent of the resident
  - income support will include a *residential allowance* (not for local authority homes)

> Means-testing (similar to that for income support) also applies to the provision or funding by local authorities of residential care, but provision by the health authority is free.

Enforcement

The local authority is expressly empowered to recover sums due from the resident as a civil debt through the magistrates' court (National Assistance Act 1948, s 56). This is 'without prejudice to any other enforcement procedures' so does not preclude a debt claim in the county court or bankruptcy proceedings.

First avoidance provision

Where a resident disposed of assets by way of gift or at an undervalue within six months before (or during) admission to residential accommodation knowingly

Chapter 19 LOCAL AUTHORITY SUPPORT

and with the intention of avoiding charges for the accommodation then sums due may be recovered (Health and Social Services and Social Security Adjudications Act 1983, ss 21–24):

- the period can be longer in some circumstances;
- liability may be imposed on a third party to whom assets have been transferred, though only for any shortfall in the amount received from the resident and to the extent of the benefit accruing to that party;
- a legal charge can be imposed on a property of the resident (to the level of the resident's share) to secure arrears, with interest chargeable from the day after death – enforcement of the accruing debt is thus left to a later stage.

Second avoidance provision

Under the *notional capital* rules (see above), the resident may be treated as possessing an asset which has been given away (or not obtained) for the purpose of avoiding assessment (National Assistance (Assessment of Resources) Regulations 1992):

- if the authority can establish that the purpose of a gift was to avoid means-testing the asset may be treated as notional capital in the hands of the resident and a contribution assessed on it:
  - avoiding the charge need not be the main purpose but must have been a significant one
  - any gift made immediately before (or after) admission to the home is vulnerable even if a further purpose can be established
- there is no time-limit but the longer it is since a gift was made the more difficult it will be to establish that the purpose was to avoid financial assessment;
- this capital is deemed to diminish over a period of time so that ultimately the resident will re-qualify for care costs (the *diminishing capital rule*).

> There are two distinct procedures for taking into account the value of gifts and the six month time-limit so often relied upon only applies to one of these.

Recovery

The local authority is obliged to meet the continuing cost of residential or nursing home care even if any assessed financial contribution is not paid. How can a contribution be enforced against an individual who no longer has assets, but has made a gift (e.g. of the home) more than six months before admission?

- recovery may be possible through three sets of proceedings but timing is difficult:

- judgment is obtain for the unpaid contributions
- the individual is made bankrupt
- application is made to set aside the gift (Insolvency Act 1986, ss 339–340)

- other provisions enable transactions at an undervalue to be set aside without time-limit and without bankruptcy by a single application to the court if there was an intention to defraud creditors at the time of the transaction even if the transferor was then solvent. The court may then make orders to restore the position to what it would have been had the transaction not taken place (Insolvency Act 1986, ss 423–425):
  - it is sufficient if the purpose was to put the asset beyond the reach of a person who might at some time make a claim or otherwise prejudice the interests of such a person (*Midland Bank v Wyatt* [1995] 1 FLR 697)
  - it may be sufficient for this to be a substantial rather than a dominant purpose (a finding of purpose sufficient for the gift to be treated as notional capital would also appear to justify the subsequent setting aside procedure)

> A gift may be disregarded and set aside by a single application to the court.

Establishing the purpose

How is the authority to establish the purpose of a gift? If the family cannot point to another purpose the judge may conclude that it must have been made to avoid future care costs as gifts for this reason have become so prevalent. Can the elderly resident or donee really give evidence and face cross-examination? In the case of gifts of the home:

- it will have been prudent for the solicitor to advise in writing that the gift may be vulnerable, so discovery of the file relating to the transfer may reveal the true or dominant purpose:
  - the file will normally be covered by legal professional privilege, but the court may order discovery if there is *prima facie* proof of fraud and also for public policy considerations (see *Royscott Spa Leasing v Lovett* [1995] BCC 502, CA; *Barclays Bank Plc v Eustice* [1995] 4 All ER 511)
  - if the court considers that the purpose of the transaction may have been to avoid means-testing, disclosure of the solicitor's file may be required to ascertain whether this really was the case
- if one of the marketed schemes has been used an inspection of the documents may reveal the source and thereby the motivation behind the transfer.

> The solicitor's file may be examined to establish the true purpose of the gift or this may be apparent from the documentation used.

Chapter 19 LOCAL AUTHORITY SUPPORT

Liable relatives

Other provisions allow the local authority to recover the cost of residential care from a person 'liable to maintain' the resident (National Assistance Act 1948, ss 42 and 43). This includes a spouse but not unmarried couples. Liable relatives should not be asked to pay more than they can reasonably afford:

- there is no power to require the spouse to provide details of personal assets and income;
- the authority will seek to agree a reasonable amount taking into account all that spouse's circumstances so as not to cause hardship;
- the remedy available to the local authority is a complaint to the magistrates' court and the spouse may be ordered to pay such weekly or other sum as the court thinks appropriate.

> A spouse may be liable but not a cohabitee.

Choice of home

Within resource constraints residents are to be provided with their choice of home (*preferred accommodation*). The local authority should provide information about homes in its area but the choice is not restricted to these and homes in other areas may be chosen though fees will only be met to the local level:

- the chosen home must appear to the authority to be suitable for the assessed needs and the cost should not exceed what it would normally expect to pay for these needs;
- where no place is available at the price the local authority would usually expect to pay, it must pay a higher price if necessary;
- top-up of fees by non-liable relatives or others should be permitted thereby enabling more expensive accommodation to be provided.

> National Assistance Act 1948 (Choice of Accommodation) Directions 1992 and Circulars LAC(92)27 and LAC(93)18.

Temporary stays

Admission to a residential care or nursing home may be for respite care or convalescence:

- for stays of up to eight weeks the authority need not carry out a means-test but may charge what is reasonable for the resident to pay and income support may include both the residential allowance and housing costs;

PART 3: SECTION B Financial Benefits

- for longer stays there must be a means-test (as above) but the resident's home is disregarded if there is an intention to return and income support or housing benefit for housing costs is ignored.

Income support (preserved rights)

Until April 1993 higher rates of income support were available for people needing support from public funds to pay for care in private or charitable homes:

- the following people have *preserved rights* to these higher rates:
    - those living in such registered homes on 31 March 1993 (whether currently claiming benefit or not)
    - those living in small homes that fulfilled certain stringent staffing requirements (or continued to qualify under transitional provisions) if actually in receipt of higher rates on 31 March 1993
    - those who would qualify but are temporarily away
- moving from one registered home to another will not cause this right to be lost, but the right is lost if the resident moves out of such a home for a period of 13 weeks (up to 52 weeks for a hospital stay);
- local authorities are prohibited from making residential accommodation arrangements for those on preserved rights to income support:
    - National Assistance Act 1948, s 26A inserted by National Health Service and Community Care Act 1990, s 43
    - for complex exceptions see Residential Accommodation (Relevant Premises, Ordinary Residence and Exemptions) Regulations 1993 and guidance in LAC (93)6

> It may be possible to retain income support funding in residential care.

Amount

These higher rates were and remain subject to nationally defined limits dependent on type of home and nature of disability, but top-up by third parties to cover any shortfall of fees is still allowed:

- fees of up to 80 per cent can be paid during temporary absences of one to four weeks (if in hospital full fees for six weeks and 80 per cent for 46 weeks);
- attendance allowance and the care (not mobility) component of disability living allowance are taken into account in the means assessment for those claiming these higher rates of income support, but not otherwise;
- couples are normally assessed together but not if one is permanently in a

Chapter 19 LOCAL AUTHORITY SUPPORT

home, though spouses may be expected to maintain one another (see above);

- the net value of the resident's own home (or an equal share if owned jointly) will be assessed except:
  - for six months (or longer) whilst it is being sold
  - if occupied by a spouse/partner or certain relatives if over 60 or incapacitated
  - the *notional capital* rules deal with deprivation of assets

Sources of law and guidance

- Residential Accommodation (Relevant Premises, Ordinary Residence and Exemptions) Regulations 1993
- Circular LAC93(6): *Local authorities' powers to make arrangements for people who are in independent sector residential care and nursing homes on March 31, 1993*
- SSCC1 *Care in the community: Changes in income support and other social security benefits from 1 April 1993*

IS50 *Income support: help if you live in a residential care or nursing home.* Age Concern Fact Sheet 11 *Preserved entitlement to income support for residential and nursing home care.*

Entitlement to other benefits

Housing benefit

This cannot be claimed by those moving into registered residential care or nursing homes, but those in such homes before April 1993 and already claiming may continue to do so as long as they stay in the same home. If the home is not registered it may be claimable.

Income support

If the resident entered a residential care or nursing home in the private sector after April 1993 and is in receipt of income support this will include a *residential allowance*. This is not available for those in local authority homes, thus providing an incentive to authorities to look to the private sector for provision.

Attendance allowance

Attendance allowance, or the care component of disability living allowance, may continue whilst the resident is privately funding residential care but will cease after four weeks of receiving local authority financial support. It is taken into account in the means test for those receiving income support with preserved rights.

PART 3: SECTION B Financial Benefits

Practitioner's problems

When considering means-testing for services provided by local authorities and in particular admission to a residential care or nursing home, problem areas include:

- transfer of assets - see Chapter 29 at para. 29.6;
- liable relatives and means-testing of spouses;
- limited availability of occupational or personal pensions;
- choice of residential accommodation and shortfall in fees;
- run-down in resources and refusal of the local authority to assess in advance;
- presence of a non-relative or carer in a home belonging to the individual which is being assessed (the authority but not DSS has a discretion in this situation);
- local authority's available resources (there have been several appeal decisions concerning the implications of this).

Power to charge?

In two main situations no charges may be made for the care of an individual:

- where, following discharge from detention under one of the longer treatment sections of the Mental Health Act 1983 (usually s.3 or s.37), he or she requires residential or nursing home care as a result of mental disorder:
  - no charge may be made for care as this is deemed 'aftercare' service provision under Mental Health Act 1983, s.117
  - that section places a joint duty on the health and local authorities to provide the services required free of charge, unless it is decided by both that the person is no longer in need of these by virtue of their mental disorder
- (only applicable to placements in nursing homes) where his or her need is primarily a health care need:
  - the health authority must fund the entire cost of the placement and the local authority has no power to purchase such care and pass the costs to the client
  - the only exception is where the nursing care is 'merely ancillary or incidental to the provision of the accommodation' in a nursing home. This will depend on the level and type of care. Most nursing homes placements will be the responsibility of the NHS because a client will not be placed there unless their primary need is for nursing care, i.e. health care

See *R v North and East Devon Health Authority ex p Coughlan* (1999) 2 CCL Rep 285; *R v London Borough of Richmond ex p Watson* (1992) 2 CCL Rep 402.

Chapter 20

Miscellaneous Support

20.1 NATIONAL HEALTH SERVICE

Support for an individual who is ill, infirm or otherwise in need of medical or nursing services is available through health authorities and the provision of these services is considered in Chapter 24.

Charges

Prescriptions

Free prescriptions are available for those over state retirement age or with certain illnesses under that age. Other people on low incomes get help with the cost of prescriptions, dental check-ups and treatment, sight tests and vouchers for glasses:

- those on income support or family credit get help automatically;
- others on low incomes may apply on form AG1 (or AG2 for sight tests).

Hospital services

No charge is made for NHS hospital services, whether or not as an in-patient, but social security benefits are affected whilst in hospital. This depends on the benefit and the length of stay:

- usually there is no change for the first four weeks, but then invalid care allowance ceases and after six weeks severe disablement allowance and certain other benefits are reduced:
  - a carer loses invalid care allowance after being in hospital for 12 weeks and sometimes earlier
  - the mobility component of disability living allowance is the only benefit that survives a lengthy period in hospital
  - means-tested benefits will be re-assessed
- benefits are reinstated during temporary absences but there are linking provisions for successive hospital stays;
- after one year in hospital the benefit paid to a patient is reduced to a weekly sum fixed annually:
  - further benefits may be paid to any dependants

PART 3: SECTION B Financial Benefits

- – a personal expenses allowance is retained and when the patient is mentally incapacitated this may be collected by the hospital authorities and held in a special account
- it is not always easy to determine whether a claimant is in hospital. The question is 'is the individual receiving free in-patient treatment in a hospital or similar institution?';
- assistance may be provided for the cost of travel to hospital and a companion's travelling expenses where this is medically necessary.

> No charges are made for health care and prescriptions to those over state retirement age but state benefits may be reduced for those in hospital.

Information

A series of leaflets is available free from Benefits Agency offices, and some family doctors:

P11 NHS prescriptions;	AB11 Help with NHS costs;
D11 NHS dental treatment;	G11 NHS sight tests and vouchers for glasses;
NI9 Going into hospital?	H11 NHS hospital travel costs

20.2 GRANTS AND SUBSIDIES

Housing grants

Almost all housing grants are now payable at the discretion of the local authority, including renovation grants, and grants for works to common parts of a building and houses in multiple occupation. 'Home repairs assistance' can be provided to someone in receipt of income support or housing benefit but this may include older people.

A grant is only likely to be mandatory when it is for defined works to make the dwelling suitable for a disabled occupier. For example, an application might be made to meet part or all of the cost of works needed to facilitate access to the dwelling, but the authority must be satisfied that the works are:

- necessary and appropriate to meet the need; and
- reasonable and practicable having regard to the age and condition of the dwelling.

> Housing Grants, Construction and Regeneration Act 1996.

Chapter 20 MISCELLANEOUS BENEFITS

Home Energy Efficiency Scheme

Grants are available to those aged 60 or over for insulation, draught-proofing and energy advice and those in receipt of most means-tested benefits are eligible. Contact:

- Energy Action Grants Agency, Freepost, PO Box 130, Newcastle-upon-Tyne NE99 2RP (tel: 0800-181667)

Subsidies

Travel concessions, etc.

Concession schemes exist for public transport (e.g. senior railcards) and local authorities have power to set up schemes.

Help may be available to obtain a suitable vehicle and a free road tax disc is available in certain circumstances (see leaflet V188 *Exemption from vehicle excise duty for disabled people*). There is no VAT on certain vehicles extensively modified to carry a person in a wheelchair, and a car or powered wheelchair may be available under the *Motability* scheme (contact MAVIS for advice on adapting a car – addresses in Appendix 7).

> See generally Age Concern Fact Sheet 26 *Travel information for older people.*

Gas and electricity

Suppliers have codes of practice which should be referred to if problems arise and payment schemes include prepayment, monthly budget and flexible payments. Consumers receiving income support may arrange direct payments.

Protection against disconnection is given to customers – customers of pensionable age will not be disconnected between 1 October and 31 March if they cannot pay. Licence conditions 12A (British Gas) and 19 (Public Electricity Companies) set out procedures to be followed.

> See generally Age Concern Fact Sheet 1 *Help with heating.*

Telephone

Help may be available from:

- the social services department of the local authority under the Chronically Sick and Disabled Persons Act 1970 – see Chapter 22, para. 22.3;
- the Social Fund with a budgeting loan – see Chapter 18, para. 18.2;
- DHSS Circular HSS(OS5A)5/78 *Telephones for the handicapped and elderly.*

227

British Telecom operate rebate schemes and a protected service scheme:

- see *The BT guide for people who are disabled or elderly* and the information pack available;
- contact DIEL (The Advisory Committee on Telecommunications for Disabled and Elderly People), Export House, 50 Ludgate Hill, London EC4M 7JJ.

> See Age Concern Fact Sheet 28 *Help with telephones*.

Television licence

Concessions are available to retired people of pensionable age who live in certain types of accommodation (residential care homes and some sheltered accommodation):

- Wireless Telegraphy (Television Licence Fees) Regulations 1997;
- Concessionary Licensing Centre, TV Licensing, Barton House, Bond Street, Bristol BS19 1TL (tel: 01272-230130).

> See Age Concern Fact Sheet 3 *Television licence concessions*.

Water

Protection is afforded against disconnection in certain circumstances and it is unlawful to arrange automatic disconnection on non-payment.

> Note in general that many concessions for the elderly are little more than marketing techniques.

20.3 FAMILY AND CHARITIES

Family

Financial support may also be given to an older person by members of the family, normally on an informal basis without any legal commitment:

- care should be taken to ensure that support does not result in the reduction or loss of means-tested funding or increased charges for local authority services;
- informal carers should not neglect to claim all financial benefits that are available as of right either in respect of the person cared for or for themselves as carers.

> In case means-testing applies it may be better to buy useful items and give these rather than to make gifts of money.

Chapter 20 MISCELLANEOUS BENEFITS

Charities

Many charities, national and local, exist for the purpose of giving support to elderly or disabled people and this may include help with long-term care costs. Contact *Charity Search* (see Appendix 5) and check with charities assisting the professions or the elderly.

Independent Living Fund

This Fund was set up to make payments to severely disabled people who needed to pay for care in order to continue living at home. In April 1993 it was replaced by:

- *Independent Living (Extension) Fund* which continues to make payments to those supported by the original Fund;
- *Independent Living (1993) Fund* which deals with new applications but on a more restricted basis and only for those aged under 66 years.

SECTION C
Community Care

'Community care' is not a new concept but has existed for older people in the form of care in the community for generations. The phrase is now commonly, if inaccurately, used to identify policy changes which took effect in April 1993. Descriptions of 'community care' include:

- the provision of care for individuals in such a way as to enable them to lead as normal an existence as possible given their particular disabilities and to minimise disruption of life within their community – *Social Services Committee*;

- providing clients with a full range of services, and a wide range of options; bringing services to people, rather than people to services; the adjustment of services to meet the needs of people, rather than the adjustment of people to meet the needs of services – *Audit Commission*;

- providing the services and support which people who are affected by problems of ageing, mental illness, mental handicap or physical or sensory disability need to be able to live as independently as possible in their own homes, or in homely settings in the community – *Government White Paper*.

An older person may rely upon a variety of services and resources from various sources, some of which cover special needs. Services may also support carers who have legal status to seek help. While the social services department of the local authority may have statutory power, and in some cases a duty, to provide or secure appropriate support, individual social services can seldom be obtained by the client as a legal right. The services potentially available are set out in statute, government circulars, guidance and codes of practice.

Community care is the sum of many areas of social policy. It involves health, housing, transport and utilities as well as social services. Access to services is largely defined by policy and practice but may in some circumstances be by specific entitlements in law. There is much variation in provision and standards between authorities, shortfall in funding, and frequently too little co-operation between the various agencies involved (i.e. joint planning and sharing of resources). This will change with the setting up of Primary Care Groups, with more emphasis being placed on joint service planning and provision by health authorities and social services.

Legislation may relate to older people, or to disabled people of all ages (to include both physical and mental disabilities). Strictly speaking, residential care is not a form of community care but many of the provisions apply also to those in residential homes so it is included in this Section.

This is a fast developing, complex area of the law and only a general guide can be provided in this Handbook. Practitioners should be alive to the potential areas of work in this field for their existing and potential clients. They will need to be familiar with what happens in their own area and liaison with local social services and their legal advisers will be valuable. Increasingly they will also need to become aware of the Human Rights Act 1998 (which comes into force in October 2000) and its relevance in this field.

Chapter 21
Policies

21.1 SOURCES

Reports

The formal policy of community care grew out of a series of reports, in particular:

- Making a Reality of Community Care – Audit Commission Report 1986;
- Social Services Committee of the House of Commons – Reports 1989–90;
- Community Care: Agenda for Action – Report to the Secretary of State for Social Services by Sir Roy Griffiths, 1988;
- Caring for People: Community Care in the Next Decade and Beyond – White Paper (HMSO 1989).

New policies will be implemented as a result of White Papers on modernising social services, mental health services and the provision of long-term care for the elderly.

Legislation

The White Paper proposals were fully implemented from April 1993 by the:

- National Health Service and Community Care Act 1990 (Part III)

This Act devotes a mere nine sections to the topic in England but relies upon the following earlier statutes:

- National Assistance Act 1948 (Part III)
- Health Services and Public Health Act 1968 (s 45)
- Chronically Sick and Disabled Persons Act 1970 (s 2)
- National Health Service Act 1977 (s 21 and Schedule 8)
- Mental Health Act 1983 (s 117)
- Health and Social Services and Social Security Adjudications Act 1983 (Part VII)
- Disabled Persons (Services, Consultation and Representation) Act 1986

PART 3: SECTION C Community Care

- Carers (Recognition and Services) Act 1995
- Community Care (Direct Payments) Act 1996
- Housing Act 1996 (Part VII) (replacing Housing Act 1985 (Part III))
- Community Care (Residential Accommodation) Act 1998

The following statutes should also be considered:

- Local Government Act 1970
- Pensions Act 1995
- Disability Discrimination Act 1995

The 1990 Act does not create new rights to new services, although local authorities have a new duty to assess anyone who appears to them to need a community care service which they may provide and anyone who may request an assessment. It is supplemented by regulations, government guidance, circulars and policy documents.

Directions and guidance

Many aspects of an authority's powers and duties are subject to *directions* issued by a Secretary of State and *guidance* issued by departments, and good policies are also identified by other sources. Some are issued jointly as health and local authority circulars with alternative references, and earlier ones may have been issued by the former DHSS. They are constantly being updated (i.e. cancelled or superseded) but old guidance may remain relevant as to what could be expected at the time. Note that:

- *directions* are mandatory and are usually published separately but may appear as appendices to local authority circulars;
- *guidance* can take many forms:
  - 'LAC (93)7' would be the seventh local authority circular issued by the Department of Health in 1993
  - *policy guidance* may be issued by the Secretary of State (if under s 7(1) of the Local Authority Social Services Act 1970 it is generally mandatory and should only be departed from for good reason)
  - *practice guidance* is advice which an authority should have regard to when reaching a decision but need not follow

Examples of special significance are mentioned in the following list but this should not be assumed to be up to date and can be little more than an illustration of the extent to which policy and procedure is covered by the range of directions, circulars and general guidance from government departments or officials.

Chapter 21 POLICIES

Directions

- National Assistance Act 1948 (Choice of Accommodation) Directions 1992:
  - with DoH Circular LAC (92)27
- Directions by the Secretary of State as to the Conditions Governing Payments by Health Authorities to Local Authorities and Other Bodies:
  - with DoH Circular LAC (92)17
- Secretary of State's Approvals and Directions under:
  - section 21(1) of the National Assistance Act 1948
  - section 29(1) of the National Assistance Act 1948
  - paragraphs 1 and 2 of Schedule 8 to the National Health Service Act 1977
  - DoH Circular LAC (93)10 relates to the above Directions
- Complaints Procedure Directions 1990;
- Community Care Plans Directions 1991 (with LAC(91)6);
- Directions by the Secretary of State as to the Establishment of Primary Care Groups by Health Authorities.

Circulars

- DHSS Circular 12/70: *The Chronically Sick and Disabled Persons Act 1970*;
- DHSS Circular 19/71: *Welfare of the elderly: Implementation of section 45 of the Health Services and Public Health Act 1968*;
- DHSS Circular LAC(87)6: *Disabled Persons (Services Consultation and Representation) Act 1986: Implementation of sections 4, 8(1), 9 and 10*;
- DHSS Circular LAC(88)2: *Disabled Persons (Services Consultation and Representation) Act 1986: Implementation of sections 5 and 6*;
- DoH Circular LAC(89)7: *Discharge of patients from hospital*;
- DoH Circular LAC(90)12: *Community care: policy guidance*;
- DoH Circular LAC(92)17: *Health authority payments in respect of social services functions* [also issued as HSG(92)43];
- DoH Circular LAC(92)27: *National Assistance Act 1948 (Choice of Accommodation) Directions 1992*;
- DoH Circular LAC(93)6: *Local authorities' powers to make arrangements for people who are in independent sector residential care and nursing homes on March 31, 1993*;
- DoH Circular LAC (98)19: *Community Care (Residential Accommodation) Act 1998*;

235

PART 3: SECTION C Community Care

- DoH Circular LAC(98)21: *Developing primary care groups*;
- DoH Circular LAC (98)167: *Health improvement programmes; Planning for better health and better health care*;
- DoH Circular LAC (99)30: *Continuing health care: Follow up to the Court of Appeal judgment in the case of R v North East Devon Health Authority, ex parte Coughlan*;
- Circular CI (92)34: Social Services Inspectorate *Implementing caring for people: assessment*(from the Chief Inspector dated 14 December 1992 and known as 'the Laming letter' and later clarification);
- NHS Executive Circular HSC 1998/048: *Transfer of frail older NHS patients to other long stay settings*;
- DoH Circular HSC 1998/220: *Standards of NHS hospital care for older people*;
- DoH Circular HSG (95)8: *NHS responsibilities for meeting continuing health care needs*;
- DoH Circular HSG (95)39: *Discharge from NHS inpatient care of people with continuing health or social care needs: arrangements for reviewing decisions on eligibility for NHS continuing inpatient care*;
- *Charges for residential accommodation guidelines (CRAG)* with Circulars at intervals (e.g. LAC(94)1 and LAC(98)8).

At intervals lists of current circulars are published by the Department of Health e.g. LASSL(98)14.

General guidance

- Community Care in the Next Decade and Beyond: Policy Guidance (HMSO 1990);
- Care Management and Assessment: Managers' Guide (HMSO 1991);
- Care Management and Assessment: Practitioners' Guide (HMSO 1991);
- Care Management and Assessment: Summary of Practice Guidance (HMSO 1991);
- Getting the Message Across: a Guide to Developing and Communicating Policies, Principles and Procedures on Assessment (HMSO 1991);
- Carers (Recognition and Services) Act 1995 Policy Guidance HMSO 1995.

Codes of practice

- *Community Life: a Code of Practice for Community Care* (1990) – from Centre for Policy on Ageing 25-31 Ironmonger Row, London EC1V 3QP.

Chapter 21 POLICIES

Overview

- The Community Care Handbook (Age Concern).

Further reference should be made to the books mentioned in Appendix 7.

21.2 ROLE OF LOCAL AUTHORITIES

Responsibilities

One intention of the reforms was to clarify responsibilities and secure better results by making those involved spell out what they are doing and why. The following responsibilities are allocated to local authorities by the 1990 Act and guidance:

- assess the needs of people who:
  - appear to need care services, and then decide what services (if any) may be provided (s 47)
  - must be provided with services if need is identified under the Chronically Sick and Disabled Persons Act 1970, s 2
  - request an assessment
- adopt an enabling role and stimulate the provision of services by the private and not-for-profit sectors (a 'mixed economy of care');
- charge for residential accommodation on a basis that is more in line with that for income support (ss 44 and 45);
- consult with health and housing authorities and voluntary organisations and publish annual *Community Care Plans* which are reviewed regularly (s 46);
- provide access to information and also a complaints procedure (s 50);
- inspect certain premises used for community care services (s 48);
- take over staff from health authorities as hospitals close and patients are moved into the community (s 49);
- work jointly with health and Primary Care Groups.

Social Services Department (SSD)

The lead role in the arrangements is given to the SSD which should:

- disseminate information about statutory and voluntary services in their areas which would be of assistance to carers and their dependants;
- assess the needs of the person cared for and see how these may best be met – there is a statutory duty to take into account the needs of the carer:

237

- Carers (Recognition and Services) Act 1995
- Disabled Persons (Services, Consultation and Representation) Act 1986

- make a decision about what – if any – services to provide for these needs (most older people needing support will remain in the community);
- appoint a case manager to keep under review the provision (if appropriate):
  - regularly review need and service provision for each service user
- ensure that resources are managed efficiently (as this area has developed overall resources available to SSD can be taken into account although recent case law throws doubt on this – see *R v Birmingham CC ex p Taj Mohammed* (1998) 1 CCLR 441);
- have an enhanced inspection role of residential care homes which operates independently of the authority's own residential provision;
- respond to requests for assistance from carers (they may not impose services on a carer without agreement).

Other authorities

Neither the local authority nor its social services department can oblige the health authority (which includes fund-holding GPs) or the housing authority to provide any services to an individual and this effectively limits the SSD's control over community care provision to that which it can itself provide. For many people the failure in community care may relate to health or housing provision and with evolution of policies, agreed discharge procedures have had to be formulated with health authorities. Increasingly health, housing and social services departments are expected to work together. However, the new unitary authorities must work not as separate departments but as one authority.

> Disputes arise as to which authority is responsible for a particular type of care provision.

Powers and duties

Although it may appear that a local authority is obliged to provide a service this may not be enforceable in law by an individual. A distinction must be drawn between a power to provide a service and a duty to do so, and between a general duty to provide services and a duty to a particular individual:

- where an authority is not under a duty to an individual action may only be taken if:
  - there is discrimination on grounds of sex, race or disability; or
  - the authority blindly follows a particular policy without considering individual circumstances; or

- the authority makes an unreasonable decision (the *Wednesbury* principle)
- where an authority has a discretion it must exercise this:
  - each case must be dealt with on its merits
  - an authority cannot fetter its discretion by imposing a blanket policy

> If the assessment of an individual (under the 1990 Act, s 47) states that a particular service is needed then the obligation of the local authority to provide this is greater but the service may not necessarily have to be provided.

Guidance and directions

An authority is only obliged to take account of advice contained in circulars but is under a positive duty to comply if the circular is issued under the Local Authority Social Services Act 1970, s 7:

- *R v Islington LBC ex p Rixon* (1998) 1 CCLR 119;
- guidance is likely to be quoted in court proceedings and could form the basis for a legal challenge of an authority's action or inaction;
- the policy documents of a local authority (including its community care plan) should take account of any directions and guidance in circulars.

Where an appeal to the Secretary of State is provided for it may be expected that he will follow his own advice, and he may issue directions which must be observed by local authorities in carrying out their social services functions, the sanction being the use of default powers – s 7A (added by 1990 Act, s 50).

Ordinary residence

The duties of a local authority apply in respect of an individual who is ordinarily resident in its area. In determining ordinary residence it must have been voluntarily adopted and there must have been a degree of settled purpose in relation to that decision:

- *R v Barnet LBC ex p Shah* [1983] 1 All ER 226;
- 'ordinarily resident' should be given its ordinary and natural meaning, subject to any interpretation in the courts (consider the National Assistance Act 1948 in this respect):
  - see DoH Circular LAC (93)7: *Ordinary Residence*
  - *Wiltshire County Council v Cornwall County Council* (1999) unreported

> Disputes as to which authority is responsible for a particular individual must be resolved on the basis of 'ordinary residence' but service provision if identified must continue notwithstanding the dispute as to which authority pays.

21.3 ROLE OF THE PRIVATE SECTOR

The private and voluntary sectors (whether commercial, not-for-profit or charitable) have an enhanced role in the delivery of services:

- local authorities are given a financial incentive to buy residential care rather than provide it and have been required to spend a certain proportion of new money for the reformed system on independent sector services;

- the government has encouraged a division between the purchaser and provider roles, this market approach being intended to keep costs down and improve quality.

> 'It will be the responsibility of social services departments to make maximum possible use of private and voluntary providers and so increase the available range of options and widen consumer choice . . .' – Circular LAC (93)10.

Chapter 22

Services

22.1 TYPES OF SERVICES

Care services may be for the benefit of a disabled or ill person or to assist a carer to provide care. There are three broad categories:

- *domiciliary* services provided in the home comprising domestic help (cleaning, shopping, cooking, laundry, etc.) and personal care (bathing, washing, dressing, eating, etc.);
- *day* services provided outside the home;
- *residential* services (short or long term including both residential care and nursing homes).

There may also be assistance for the physically disabled with:

- aids and appliances (incontinence pads, walking aids, wheelchairs, etc.);
- the home (adaptations or provision of a suitable home).

It was suggested that a distinction could be drawn between community care services (as defined in the National Health Service and Community Care Act 1990) which were based (with certain exceptions) on general duties and powers, and some specific services provided to disabled people under earlier legislation which involve specific duties. This has proved not to be the case.

22.2 COMMUNITY CARE SERVICES

Statutory basis

These are services provided under the following statutes:

National Assistance Act 1948, Part III

Local authorities are under a duty 'to provide residential accommodation for persons who, by reason of age, [illness, disability] or any other circumstances are in need of care and attention which is not otherwise available to them' – section 21(1)(a) (Part III accommodation). They:

- can now place and fund people in private nursing homes – s 26(1)(A)–(C) [inserted by 1990 Act, s 42(2)];

- may (and where so directed by the minister must) make arrangements for promoting the welfare of certain classes of disabled persons – s 29;
- have a duty to take reasonable steps to prevent or mitigate loss or damage to the movable property of a person admitted as a patient to hospital, or to Part III accommodation or removed to suitable premises – s 48.

> For the provision that must be made and that which is authorised see Circular LAC(93)10.

A magistrates' court may in certain circumstances authorise removal of persons to suitable premises for the purpose of securing necessary care and attention if they are (a) suffering from grave chronic disease, or being aged, infirm or physically incapacitated, living in insanitary conditions, and (b) unable to devote themselves, and not receiving from other persons, proper care and attention – s 47:

- there is an *ex parte* emergency procedure under the National Assistance (Amendment) Act 1951 but *inter partes* applications are to be preferred;
- this remedy is generally only available in extreme cases.

Health Services and Public Health Act 1968, s 45

A local authority may, with the approval of the Secretary of State, and to such an extent as he may direct shall, make arrangements for promotion of the welfare of old people:

- the purpose is to secure services to those still managing to cope in order to prevent or postpone deterioration and dependence;
- possible services are described in Circular 19/71 and include provision of:
    - meals and recreation
    - facilities or assistance in travelling to services
    - visiting and advisory services and social work support
    - practical assistance in the home
    - wardens or warden services

> No direction has yet been made, so this remains a power and not a duty.

National Health Service Act 1977, s 21 and Schedule 8

Social services departments may make provision for the prevention of illness and for the care and after-care of persons suffering from illness, including mental illness:

- in deciding what provision to make for a person living at home and receiv-

ing substantial care from another person, they must have regard to the ability of that other person to continue to provide care – added by Disabled Persons (Services, Consultation and Representation) Act 1986, s 8(1);
- types of provision include day centres, meals and social work support.

They must provide (or arrange) on a scale adequate for the needs of the area home helps for households where help is required owing to the presence of a person who is aged.

> For the provision that must be made and that which is authorised see Circular LAC(93)10.

Mental Health Act 1983, s 117

A duty is imposed on social services departments and district health authorities to assess for and provide after-care to those who leave hospital after ceasing to be detained (this applies only to those admitted under sections 3, 37, 47 and 48):
- services provided under this section (including residential care) may not at present be charged for.

Guardianship

Statutory guardianship under sections 7–10 of the Mental Health Act 1983 should not be overlooked when considering the powers of the local authority, because a social worker will be involved. The purpose is to enable an adult to receive community care where this cannot be provided without the use of compulsory powers, but where it is used it must be part of the overall care and treatment plan.

> See Chapter 26 at para. 26.3 (and also 'place of safety' orders) and the Mental Health Act *Code of Practice* at para. 13.

Assessment

Duty to assess

Authorities have a statutory duty to assess the needs of a person who requests an assessment and for whom they may provide and who appears to them to need community care services (as defined in the above four statutes) – 1990 Act, s 47(1):
- whilst the individual or a carer may request an assessment there is no need for this as the duty arises when the authority finds an appearance of need:
  - no authority can refuse assessment even if no service need is identified but a person cannot be required to co-operate

- if whilst carrying out this assessment it appears to the authority that the person being assessed is a disabled person it must proceed to assess the need for services under the Disabled Persons (Services, Consultation and Representation) Act 1986 without being asked, and inform the person of his rights in that respect – s 47(2)
  - the authority must consider whether the person being assessed should also be assessed under section 2 of the Chronically Sick and Disabled Persons Act 1970, and/or the Mental Health Act 1983
- where services are required as a matter of urgency they may be temporarily provided prior to an assessment (s 47(5)) but as soon as possible thereafter an assessment of need must be made (s 47(6));
- it must be established that the person is one for whom the authority may provide and this is based on ordinary residence (see Chapter 21 at para. 21.2) though the requirement can be dispensed with in regard to certain services;
- assessments should normally be multi-disciplinary involving housing and health authorities (where appropriate):
  - *R v North and East Devon Health Authority ex p Coughlan* (1999) 2 CCLR 285
- the duty to assess is independent of provision, so exists even if the authority does not provide or have the resources to provide the services likely to be needed, and is a continuing duty so extends to a regular review of the assessment when changes of circumstances must be taken into account. See:
  - *R v East Sussex CC ex p Tandy* [1998] 2 All ER 769
  - *R v Birmingham CC ex p Taj Mohammed* (1998) 1 CCLR 441

> The district health authority or local housing authority shall be invited to assist in the assessment, where appropriate – see s 47(3).

Form of assessment

The Secretary of State may give directions as to the manner in which an assessment is to be carried out or the form that it shall take (but had not done so as at January 2000). There are no nationally agreed standards and these vary from one area to another:

- the authority must make public their criteria of eligibility for assessment (i.e. definition of need) and provide information about the process:
  - ask 'what is needed' rather than 'which of our existing services would assist' – see Care Management and Assessment: Practitioners' Guide (HMSO 1991)
  - the assessment must be carried out reasonably: *R v Bristol CC ex p Penfold (Alice)* (1998) 1 CCLR 315

Chapter 22 SERVICES

- the person should be informed of any assessment and of his statutory rights, which include the right to choose and to have a copy of the assessment.

> Assessment is an ongoing and continuous procedure and should be multi-disciplinary. Re-assessment should be regularly undertaken in order to make proper service provision to meet current need.

Provision

Following assessment of an individual the local authority 'having regard to the results of that assessment, shall then decide whether his needs call for the provision' by the authority of particular services – 1990 Act, s 47(1):

- it follows that there is no absolute duty to provide or arrange all the services that are assessed as being needed:
  - in *R v Gloucestershire CC ex p Barry* [1997] 2 All ER 1, the House of Lords held that the authority must take the assessment into account but may also take into account what it can afford, is available or may be provided by other authorities. It has since been held in *R v East Sussex CC ex p Tandy* [1997] 3 WLR 884 that when a duty to provide exists resources are not to be taken into account
  - lack of resources does not justify delaying assessment where there is clearly a need, or making no provision at all, but priority may be given to those with the greatest need
  - the district health authority (DHA) or local housing authority shall be invited to assist in the provision of services, where appropriate (s 47(3)) and the DHA must be involved where a place in a nursing home is sought
- any provision that is to be made must be made within a reasonable time. A waiting list is permissible but an excessive delay could be open to challenge unless due to factors outside the control of the local authority (this may be challenged under the Human Rights Act 1998).

> All clients and carers should be provided with a copy of the assessment and the agreed care plan stating services to be provided. Best practice is to show who will provide services, when they are available and the cost. A person is not obliged to accept the services that are offered following an assessment.

Who provides

The authority must not seek to provide all services itself, but make use of the voluntary and commercial sectors. Care services may be provided by health authorities, charities and private agencies as well as other local authorities (1948 Act, ss 21 and 26), and may revolve round the care already being provided by family, friends and neighbours:

- placements may be made with voluntary organisations and the private sector in registered homes, and there is also power to place residents in residential accommodation that does not need to be registered – Community Care (Residential Accommodation) Act 1992;
- contracts that spell out who is going to do what and on what terms are an important aspect of community care, and these should ideally be negotiated.

> For choice of residential accommodation see Chapter 23 at para. 23.5.

Priorities

After assessment it is likely that there will be a choice of care services available and resources provided to meet the needs identified. There should be a care plan for the individual and this will have many components. It is the responsibility of the social services department to design care arrangements in line with individual needs, in consultation with the consumer and other care professionals, but within available resources unless a need is identified under section 2 of the Chronically Sick and Disabled Persons Act 1970, when services must be provided to meet that need.

Priorities must be established by each local authority (i.e. eligibility criteria) and, according to the government, a clear statement thereof should be available to the public who may need support to challenge these priorities if they appear to be unlawful or unduly restrictive – see *R v North Yorkshire CC ex p Hargreaves No. 2* [1997] COD 390.

Unmet needs

There is ambiguity about the local authority's obligation to record 'unmet need'. It was suggested that it be recorded 'in aggregate' rather than in respect of individuals (Circular CI (92)34 – *'the Laming letter'*) so as to avoid a challenge in the courts by the individual:

- counsel's advice (obtained by a group of charities) was that an authority is legally obliged to inform an assessed person of any unmet needs accepted by the authority and the reasons why a service is not to be provided;
- the debate continued in the House of Commons Health Select Committee where it was suggested that the assessment of need and decisions about services are distinct processes and a distinction must be made between unmet need and unmet choice;
- authorities may be able to establish 'eligibility criteria' of need which are variable (according to resources available), then if the authority changes the criteria a service that has previously been provided on the basis of an assessed need can be withdrawn.

22.3 SERVICES FOR DISABLED PEOPLE

Specific services are available for disabled people of all ages under the statutes mentioned below and these should be considered in the context of community care. A person may have community care needs and also be a disabled person in which event these further services will be triggered – 1990 Act, s 47(2).

> See *R v Gloucestershire CC ex p Barry* (1997) 1 CCLR 19 for further definition of the effect of Chronically Sick and Disabled Persons Act 1970, s 2.

Disabled

The Chronically Sick and Disabled Persons Act 1970 ('1970 Act') definition is:

> 'substantially or permanently handicapped by illness, injury or congenital deformity or suffering from mental disorder of any description'.

The Disabled Persons (Services, Consultation and Representation) Act 1986 ('1986 Act') uses the definition found in National Assistance Act 1948, s 29:

> 'blind, deaf or dumb, and other persons who are substantially and permanently handicapped by illness, injury or congenital deformity or who are suffering from a mental disorder within the meaning of the Mental Health Act';

> 'hard of hearing or partially sighted' is included – Circular LAC (93)10.

> For definition of 'mental disorder' see Chapter 2 at para. 2.2.

Registers

Local authorities are under a duty to keep a register of disabled persons in their area – National Assistance Act 1948, s 29(4)(g); DoH Circular LAC (93)10, Appendix 4.

Individuals can register with their local authority and may become eligible for various forms of help. Provision is made by the social services department and may depend upon economic constraints and the policy of the authority.

Information

Social services departments are required to publish general information as to the services available in their area and to inform disabled persons receiving any service from them of relevant services provided by the local authority or by any other authority or organisation of which the department has particulars – 1986 Act, s 9 amending 1970 Act, s 1.

> Being on the register is optional and is not a condition precedent to receiving assistance under the legislation.

Types of services

Services for disabled persons are identified by the 1970 Act, s 2 and include:

- practical assistance in the home;
- provision of, or assistance in obtaining, wireless, television, library or similar recreational facilities;
- provision of lectures, games, outings or other recreational facilities outside the home or assistance in taking advantage of educational facilities;
- provision of facilities for, or assistance in, travelling to and from home for the purpose of participating in services;
- assistance in arranging for the carrying out of any works of adaptation in the home or the provision of any additional facilities designed to secure greater safety, comfort or convenience;
- facilitating the taking of holidays, whether at holiday homes or otherwise and whether provided under arrangements made by the authority or otherwise;
- provision of meals whether in the home or elsewhere;
- provision of, or assistance in obtaining, a telephone and any special equipment necessary for its use.

Assessment

Local authorities are under a duty to assess the needs of disabled persons for these services and must do so on the request of the disabled person or any person who provides a substantial amount of care on a regular basis – 1986 Act, s 4:

- it is not clear whether this is a separate assessment to that for community care services but a person may have more than one assessment to update provision:
    - an assessment under the 1986 Act should be specifically requested
    - many local authorities will use one assessment for this purpose and it will be multi-disciplinary
- when assessing the needs of a disabled person living at home the authority must have regard to a carer's ability to continue providing care on a regular basis (s 8):
    - carer means someone providing a substantial amount of care on a regular basis but not employed to do so by a statutory body or private agency
    - the authority should not use the presence of a carer as an excuse for not looking critically at the needs of the disabled person and for failing to provide the services that are needed (many are doing so by giving priority to those with greatest need)

- provisions to enable the disabled person or an authorised representative to make representations and, following receipt of a written statement of services, to ask for a review, have not been brought into effect (s 3).

The authority may not be obliged to release a copy of the assessment, but information can be obtained by inspecting the social services file (although this may not be possible if the person assessed is mentally incapable) – see Chapter 4 at para. 4.2. Guidance states that authorities should give a written record on request and best practice is for assessments to be agreed by the parties and signed copies retained. These will incorporate details of how the needs will be met in the form of a care package and who will provide what services when.

> Note the Carers (Recognition and Services) Act 1995.

Provision

Where a local authority is satisfied in the case of a person ordinarily resident in its area that it is necessary in order to meet the needs of that person to make arrangements to provide services under the 1970 Act, it is the duty of the authority to do so (s 2(1)):

- this does not mean that the authority must be satisfied beyond reasonable doubt, but merely that it must make up its mind in the specific case and this necessarily means making an assessment of need – *Blyth v Blyth* [1966] 1 All ER 524, HL;
- there is a requirement to provide services for carers at their request under the Carers (Recognition and Services) Act 1995:
  - a carers assessment should be made although there is an issue as to whether the duty is regardless of resource constraints
  - carers are automatically assessed in relation to those assessed: 1970 Act, s 2 and 1986 Act
- for 'ordinarily resident' see Chapter 21 at para. 21.2;
- for the specific duty to provide after-care services for those leaving hospital after being detained, see Mental Health Act 1983, s 117 and para. 22.2;
- see Age Concern Fact Sheet 32 *Disability and ageing: your right to social services*.

> It is as yet unclear how the Disability Discrimination Act 1995 will affect community care.

22.4 COMPLAINTS PROCEDURE

Authorities

- Local Authority Social Services Act 1970, s 7B [inserted by 1990 Act, s 50(1)];
- Local Authority Social Services (Complaints Procedure) Order 1990;
- Complaints Procedure Directions 1990;
- The Right to Complain: Practical Guidance on Complaints Procedures in Social Services Departments (HMSO 1991).

Requirement

Local authorities are obliged to establish a procedure for considering representations and complaints in relation to the discharge of, or failure to discharge, their social services functions in respect of persons for whom they have a power or duty to provide and whose needs (or possible needs) have come to their attention. They must:

- comply with any directions of the Secretary of State as to the procedures to be adopted in considering representations and taking consequential action;
- publicise their complaints procedure (by leaflets, notices and presentations);
- include reference to the procedure in decisions on assessment or provision;
- give support and encouragement to the complainant at all stages.

Complaints may not be anonymous or unconnected with social services functions. Other available methods of complaint are not affected, but the authority cannot insist that they be used in preference to the statutory complaints procedure. It may be necessary to adopt the complaints procedure before being able to apply for judicial review, but the procedure itself is susceptible to judicial review.

Financial assessments cannot be challenged but may be dealt with in relation to non-residential services under these complaints procedures.

Procedure

There are three co-ordinated stages in the complaints procedure:

- the *informal* stage – an attempt to resolve the problem informally;
- the *registration* stage – an explanation of the formal procedures is given and written representations invited which are then registered and responded to:
    - time-limits apply for the response which follows an investigation and must

be notified to certain persons
  - it is important to be clear that a particular complaint has been registered
- the *review* stage – if the previous stages have not resolved the complaint the complainant can ask for it to be formally considered by a panel of the authority (three people of whom at least one is independent and chairs the panel):
  - there are time-limits for this review
  - the complainant is entitled to an informal oral hearing when he may be accompanied by a representative (not normally a solicitor though this may be justified in some cases)
  - the recommendations of the panel are sent to all concerned

Outcome

The authority is not bound to accept the recommendations (but must take notice of them), although it must notify the complainant (and the person on whose behalf the representations were made) in writing within 28 days of its decision and reasons, and the action it proposes to take – see *R v Avon County Council, ex p Hazell* (QBD, 5 July 1993).

22.5 INADEQUATE PROVISION OR FAILURE TO ACT

Problems are bound to arise when the authority responsible for assessing needs and providing services is also responsible for funding such provision. As a general proposition it seems that when deciding both whether an individual has a need and whether to provide services the authority may take into account its own financial resources but not those of the individual, see:

- *R v Gloucestershire CC ex p Barry* [1997] 2 All ER 1
- *R v Sefton MBC ex p Help the Aged* (1997) 1 CCLR 57

But see also the following cases which seem to overrule the above cases:

- *R v East Sussex CC ex p Tandy* [1997] 3 WLR 884
- *R v Birmingham CC ex p Taj Mohammed* (1998) 1 CCLR 441

However, the problem may be outside the jurisdiction of the social services department (e.g. with the health or housing authority).

Identifying default

The following questions should be asked if problems are encountered in securing adequate care provision:

- has an assessment of needs been requested (or the need for this arisen)?

- if so, what has been the response?
- if not, make the request (it cannot be refused)

- has an assessment of needs been made?
  - if so, on what statutory basis and what are the assessed needs (inspect the assessment)?
  - if not, why not?
- was the assessment properly made?
  - was it under the 1970 Act or the 1990 Act, or both?
  - did those who made the assessment listen to the elderly person and carer (and any advocate)?
  - was it a fair assessment of needs?
  - if not, use the complaints procedure
- has a decision been made as to whether those needs should be provided for?
  - if so, what is that decision?
  - if not, why not?
- has a decision been made not to provide for assessed needs?
  - if so, what are the reasons for that decision?
  - does this reflect the authority's current criteria for determining when services should be provided?
- has a decision been made as to provision for assessed needs?
  - if so, what is that decision and will the provision meet those needs?
  - if not, why not?
- what provision is actually being made to meet the assessed needs?
  - does this fulfil the decision to provide for assessed needs?
  - if not, why not and what provision is available to meet these needs?
- is any restriction or condition being imposed?
  - if so, is it necessary?
  - what purpose is it intended to fulfil?
  - can this purpose be fulfilled in some other way?
- has an existing service been withdrawn or restricted?
  - if so, is this the result of a re-assessment?
  - if not, does it follow a decision or has it just happened?
  - on what basis (if at all) can this be justified?
- should the needs be re-assessed?
  - if so, start from the first question again!

- if not, the existing provision should continue
- does this assessment/re-assessment suggest that the issues are primarily health care so that the responsibility should lie with the health authority?
  - see *R v North and East Devon Health Authority ex p Coughlan* (1999) 2 CCLR 285

Remedies

In addition to the complaints procedure mentioned above, the following methods may be available of challenging the authority and enforcing its duties:

- reference to local government Ombudsman;
- judicial review;
- request to the Secretary of State to exercise default powers;
- civil action in damages for breach of statutory duty or negligence.

> See Chapter 5 at paras 5.3 and 5.4 and the books in Appendix 7; and Age Concern's *Briefing on local authority assessment procedures*.

22.6 FUNDING

Local authority resources

Local authorities receive an annual allocation from central government for all services and the money previously available to individuals through higher rates of income support for those in residential care has (apart from transitional provision) been transferred from DSS to local authorities. This is partially 'ring-fenced' for spending on community care provision by the independent sector:

- health authorities may make payments towards social services functions – DoH Circular LAC (92)17;
- the funding of community health services for those in residential care and nursing homes may also be shared – DoH Circular LAC (92)24.

Means-testing

Having made provision an authority can charge for the services provided and take civil proceedings to recover arrears, but cannot refuse or withdraw the service for non-payment – see Chapter 19 at para. 19.4 (residential care) and para. 19.3 (other services).

Insurance

Insurance packages may be one of the answers to long-term funding. There are many gaps in the insurance market and new, flexible schemes are being marketed. Advice will be needed on these, and they require similar consideration to that given to home income plans (see Chapter 29 at para. 29.6). Remember that transfers of capital made for tax purposes could have disadvantages if long-term care is then needed. Additionally the use of impaired lives policies for those entering residential care should not be overlooked.

Chapter 23
Registered Homes

23.1 LEGISLATION

The growth of the private sector in the provision of residential and nursing care resulted in legislation to introduce safeguards and rationalise earlier legislation. The current statutory framework specified below will change with the implementation of the Care Standards Bill and the new Regional Care Commissioners.

Statutes

- Registered Homes Act 1984 ('1984 Act')
  - Registered Homes (Amendment) Act 1991

Regulations

- Residential Care Homes Regulations 1984
  - (amendment Regulations 1986, 1988, 1991 and 1992)
- Nursing Homes and Mental Nursing Homes Regulations 1984
  - (amendment Regulations 1988, 1990 and 1991)
- Registered Homes Tribunals Rules 1984

Circulars and guidance

- Registration of Residential Homes and Registered Homes Tribunals
  - LAC(84)15 dated August 1984
- Health Service Management Registration and Inspection of Private Nursing Homes and Mental Nursing Homes (including Hospitals)
  - HC(81)8 dated July 1981 and HC(84)21 dated October 1984 but amended by HC(86)5
- Guidance on Implementation of [1991 Act re small residential care homes]
  - LAC(92)10 dated September 1992
- Registered Homes Tribunals – Guidance
- National Association of Health Authorities and Trusts Guidelines

23.2 TYPES OF REGISTERED HOMES

Residential care homes

Registration is required with the local social services department in respect of 'any establishment which provides or is intended to provide, whether for reward or not, residential accommodation with both board and personal care for persons in need of personal care by reason of old age, disablement, past or present dependence on alcohol or drugs, or past or present mental disorder' – 1984 Act, s 1(1).

Small homes

Registration of homes with less than four people was introduced by the 1991 Act which amended the 1984 Act. Registration authorities are concerned with fitness of the applicant rather than the premises, services and facilities, and there is no requirement for inspections so visits may only be made where concerns have arisen.

> See Residential Care Homes (Amendment) (No.2) Regulations 1992 and LAC(92)10.

Nursing homes

Nursing homes are registered with the district health authority who operate guidelines for their registration. The regulations which apply are similar to those for residential care homes but with significant variations appropriate to nursing homes.

Definition

The definition of a nursing home is lengthy but includes 'any premises used, or intended to be used, for the reception of, and the provision of nursing for, persons suffering from any sickness, injury or infirmity ' – 1984 Act, s 21.

> **Dual registration:** An establishment may need to register as both a residential care home and a nursing home.

Mental nursing homes

This is a special category of nursing home, namely 'any premises used, or intended to be used, for the reception of, and the provision of nursing or other medical treatment (including care, habilitation and rehabilitation under medical supervision) for, one or more mentally disordered patients (meaning persons suffering, or appearing to be suffering, from mental disorder), whether exclusively or in common with other persons' – 1984 Act, s 22.

23.3 REGULATION

Registration

There are detailed provisions dealing with applications for registration:

- a certificate of registration is issued and this must be displayed in a conspicuous place in the home (failure to display the certificate is an offence);
- the register kept by the registration authority is available for inspection.

Refusal

Registration may be refused on certain grounds (e.g. if the authority considers the premises to be unfit) but the burden of proof lies with the authority:

- when considering new applications the authority should ensure that the location and surrounding environment is appropriate to the stated aims and that the home will not disrupt the balance of the neighbourhood;
- see 1984 Act, s 9 (care homes), s 25 (nursing homes).

> Appeals are to the Registered Homes Tribunal.

Proprietor

The proprietor is registered rather than the home but if the manager is not in control, whether as owner or otherwise, both he and the person in control are to be treated as carrying on the home and are required to be registered – s 3:

- the authority must consider whether the person registered or to be registered in respect of a home is a fit person:
  - see DoH Circular LAC (91)4: *Disclosure of criminal background: Proprietors and managers of residential care homes and nursing homes*
- registrations cannot be transferred and re-registration is necessary if the proprietor changes:
  - provisions deal with the death of a sole registered proprietor (s 6)
- for nursing homes there is (though one person may be both):
  - a *registered person* whose name is on the certificate and who is responsible for ensuring that the requirements of the legislation are satisfied but need not be professionally qualified
  - a *person in charge* who is responsible for day-to-day management of the home and the care of patients, and must be either a registered medical practitioner or a qualified nurse

Categories

Residential homes are classified by the categories of residents that they care for. Conditions may be imposed on registration relating to the number of residents and other specified matters, and these may be varied from time to time:

- the registration authority should seek to ensure that the best possible quality of life for residents is achieved and in particular that:
  - the purposes and aims of residential establishments are clearly set out
  - the standards of care they offer match these
- for nursing homes a condition may be imposed as to the qualifications of the person in charge and the number of nurses to be on duty from time to time.

> Additional criteria apply to nursing homes to those for residential care homes.

Controls

The Residential Care Homes Regulations 1984 (as amended) include a policy statement relating to the conduct of such homes and deal with matters such as:

- the facilities and services to be provided;
- the numbers and qualifications of staff;
- the records to be kept and notices to be given in respect of residents;
- the notification of events occurring;
- the form and content of registers kept by registration authorities.

The policies adopted by a home must conform to the general principle laid down in these Regulations (see reg. 9) as well as the local social services standards set up by the Inspection or Quality Standards Department of the local authority:

- certain records must be maintained and available for inspection;
- all the standards stipulated by the fire authority and environmental health services officer of the local authority must be met.

Supervision

Local authorities are required to have Inspection Units which are independent of local authority direct provision, and an Advisory Committee to monitor and oversee their work.

Inspection and enforcement

Any authorised person may at all times enter and inspect any premises which are used, or believed to be used, for the purpose of a residential care or nursing home, and may inspect any records required to be kept under the Act (s 17):

Chapter 23 REGISTERED HOMES

- following an annual inspection a report must be submitted on the administration and state of the home, and any change of circumstances affecting the registration should be identified;
- a minimum of two inspections per year is required but more may be made;
- inspections are not obligatory for small homes.

> National Health Service and Community Care Act 1990, Inspection Units Directions 1990 and DoH Circular LAC (90)13.

Cancellation

Registration may be cancelled on any ground which would justify refusal of registration, for non-compliance with any condition or if a person has been convicted of an offence in respect of the home. There is also an urgent cancellation procedure to the local magistrates' court.

Offences

Any person who carries on a residential care home, a nursing home or a mental nursing home without being registered is guilty of an offence and further offences relate to failure to comply with conditions, breach of regulations and obstruction of inspections – see 1984 Act, s 2 (care homes), s 23(1) (nursing homes).

Appeals

There is a right to make oral representations to a committee set up by the authority which can override the registration officer. Full appeals are to the *Registered Homes Tribunal*:

- constituted under Part III of the 1984 Act and governed by the Registered Homes Tribunals Rules 1984;
- decisions of the tribunal do not create a precedent but indicate how it is likely to approach future cases and reports are available.

> The welfare of residents is a guiding principle.

23.4 CODES OF PRACTICE

The 1984 Act provides for registration and supervision of residential care homes (Part I), and registration and supervision of nursing homes (Part II). Detailed provision is found in *codes of practice* which may seek to set standards but are not legally binding as such. They are taken into account by Inspection Units and tribunals.

PART 3: SECTION C Community Care

Better Home Life - A Code of Practice for Residential Care

- published in 1996 and available from Bailey Distribution Ltd, Learoyd Road, Mountfield Road Industrial Estate, New Romney, Kent, TN28 8XU);
- comprises best practice for home owners and supplements *Home Life - A Code of Practice for Residential Care* 1984;
- sets out principles of care and the rights of residents to fulfilment, dignity, autonomy, individuality and esteem;
- self-determination and individuality are emphasised and the purpose of the home should be to enable residents to achieve their potential capacity – physical, intellectual, emotional and social.

Homes are for Living In – sets out standards laid down by the Social Services Inspectorate for care homes. The local authority will have its own additional standards.

Registration and Inspection of Nursing Homes: A Handbook for Health Authorities

- published in 1985 by the National Association of Health Authorities and supplemented by a Memorandum in 1988;
- indicates that the objective of a nursing home is to ensure that the quality of care provided to patients is of a high standard;
- patients should live in comfortable, clean and safe surroundings, and be treated with respect and sensitivity to their individual needs and abilities;
- the 1988 supplement expands this by placing emphasis on privacy, consultation with patients, and access to a relative, friend, adviser or advocate.

Also, each local authority will have some additional standards.

> There can be problem areas where there is no legal protection for residents.

Recommendations

There is set out on the following pages a summary of the guidance in *Home Life* which gives practitioners an outline of the basic standards that clients should expect from residential care homes.

23.5 CHOOSING A HOME

A residential care or nursing home may be run by:

- a company or an individual for profit;
- a charity or non-profit making organisation ('voluntary homes');

Chapter 23 REGISTERED HOMES

- the social services department of a local authority ('Part III accommodation').

Many residents rely upon public funding in respect of the fees for accommodation but within resource constraints residents should be provided with their own choice of accommodation:

- for assessment of need see Chapter 22 at para. 22.2;
- for funding and means-tests see Chapter 19 at para. 19.4.

> Age Concern Fact Sheet 29 *Finding residential and nursing home accommodation*. Some organisations provide information about homes (see Appendix 5).

HOME LIFE - GUIDANCE

- A brochure should set out:
  - the aims and objectives of the home and type of resident catered for
  - the degree of care offered and any restrictions
  - the facilities, accommodation and staffing
  - the terms on which residents are admitted
- Before taking up a long-term place there should be a full assessment of the individual and the suitability of the placement with trial periods being encouraged;
- Agreements between proprietors and residents should be in writing and cover:
  - accommodation and facilities provided, items to be provided by the resident and insurance arrangements
  - services covered and those to be charged separately
  - amount and payment period of fees, payments during temporary absences and procedure for increase of fees
  - procedure for holidays and hospital stays, serious illness or death, termination and complaints
  - terms and conditions of residence (to include any rules on matters such as keeping rooms tidy, smoking, use of drugs and medicines, visitors, pets, staying away)
- Residents should be encouraged to bring with them such personal possessions as can be accommodated; these should be treated with care and valuable items noted;
- Personal details in the records must be kept in a secure place:
  - access must be limited to those with overall authority for the day-to-day care of the resident who should be instructed in the handling of confidential information
  - disclosure of confidential information should be on a need to know basis
  - disclosure in breach of the rules should be made a matter justifying dismissal from employment
- Residents are entitled to the same health care as other members of the community:
  - they should have the right to see their own medical practitioner in private

- no drugs except simple household remedies should be given without a doctor's prescription
- any drugs should be held in a safe place and a record kept of those held and administered by the home
- Rules should be kept to a minimum and only used:
  - to fulfil statutory requirements
  - to prevent disturbance to other residents; or
  - to ensure reasonable standards of safety and hygiene
- Residents should be involved as much as possible in making decisions as to the running of the home:
  - domestic routines should take into account individual needs and preferences, and aim at achieving normal lifestyles
  - residents should have private rooms with adequate facilities in which they may keep their own possessions and spend time during the day if they wish
  - family and friends should be encouraged to visit and to maintain contact by letter and telephone and privacy should be available to residents
- Independent advice on financial matters should be available and encouraged:
  - proprietors and staff should not look after the financial affairs of residents unless it has proved impossible to find an alternative
  - separate accounts must be maintained for residents' monies
- Suitably qualified and competent staff must be employed in numbers which are adequate for the well-being of residents:
  - staff should have the right personal qualities, which include warmth and patience, and respect for and responsiveness to the needs of the individual
  - there are four main groups of staff, namely managerial and day care, night care, ancillary staff and specialist staff and the needs of residents must be considered in regard to each
  - recommended staffing ratios are laid down and there must be sufficient senior staff to provide adequate cover at all times
  - it should be made known to all staff and residents that it is the home's practice to decline personal gifts, except for small token presents; breach should be grounds for instant dismissal

SECTION D
Health Care

This Section deals with health care as distinct from community care and is divided into three distinct topics:

- an outline of the provision of health services including:
    - complaints procedures
    - hospital discharge
- medical treatment including:
    - consent to treatment
    - treatment for those who lack mental capacity
    - the powers of the court
    - the ability of the patient to anticipate incapacity ('living wills')
- mental health legislation including:
    - an outline of the provisions
    - admission to and detention in hospital
    - statutory guardianship
    - appeal procedures

Chapter 24

Provision of Health Care

24.1 THE HEALTH SERVICE

Reform

The National Health Service (NHS) was established in 1946 and reorganised in 1974. In 1989 a White Paper *Working for Patients: The Health Service - Caring for the 1990s* set out two objectives:

- to give patients better health care and greater choice of the services available;
- to provide greater satisfaction and rewards for persons working in the NHS.

The consequent changes made by the National Health Service and Community Care Act 1990 were designed to produce a more efficient service that puts the patient first, reinforcing the main aim of the NHS which is to help people live longer and enjoy a better quality of life. Provision was made for the establishment of NHS Trusts and the financing of practices of medical practitioners. NHS structures have since undergone further changes.

> National Health Service (Amendment) Act 1995; Health Authorities Act 1995.

Structure

The NHS was previously managed in each locality by the following authorities:

- *Family Health Services Authority* (FHSA) – arranged the services provided by family doctors and NHS dentists, opticians and pharmacists;
- *District Health Authority* (DHA) – responsible for purchasing hospital and community health services for many of its resident population;
- *Regional Health Authorities* (RHA) – linked local health purchasing with the requirements of the Department of Health.

The *Special Health Authorities* (SHA) managed certain specialist hospitals or had particular functions.

The *Community Health Councils* (CHC) set up by statute in each health district were not involved in management but represented the interests of patients and advised on complaints in regard to hospital and community health services.

PART 3: SECTION D   Health Care

The structure has now been changed. FHSAs and DHAs have been merged and RHAs abolished leaving in effect a single tier health authority (HA), but SHAs continue to exist. Eight *Management Executive Regional Offices* manage the development of health service purchasing and monitor Trusts.

The Secretary of State retains overall responsibility for the NHS in England and Wales. In addition to setting the strategic direction he has a number of other specific functions (e.g. under the Mental Health Act 1983) and may:

- provide any services which he considers appropriate for the purpose of discharging any of his statutory duties;
- do any other thing calculated to facilitate, or conducive or incidental to, the discharge of such duties.

> The health services are to be free of charge unless the charges are expressly provided for by statute.

Health authorities

The new health authorities (HAs) are responsible for implementing the health policy at local level for their areas and ensuring the provision of local hospital and family practitioner services. The Secretary of State may require them to exercise on his behalf such of his functions as are specified in *directions*. They:

- purchase hospital and community health services on behalf of local people;
- provide primary medical care by GPs, dental care, and pharmaceutical and optical services.

NHS Trusts

These Trusts are set up to own and manage NHS hospitals or other units previously managed by RHAs or DHAs. They:

- remain part of the NHS but are independent organisations;
- are directly accountable to the Secretary of State via the regional offices of the NHS Executive which monitor performance against financial targets;
- obtain most of their income through contracts with HAs and GP fund holders for the provision of treatment or services;
- have control over the services they provide but can be obliged to provide a service if they manage the only hospital able to do so.

> Trusts may comprise a single hospital, group of hospitals, community services provided in health centres and clinics or ambulance services.

Chapter 24 PROVISION OF HEALTH CARE

Community Health Councils (CHC)

These must be established for each area to represent the interests of the public. Specific functions are imposed by regulations and they will advise members of the public who wish to make a complaint about health services. Some provide representation for individuals on an informal basis.

Joint planning

Joint planning by local and health authorities is encouraged. This is particularly important in regard to groups such as the elderly infirm, but is made difficult by the fact that health/local authority boundaries do not coincide.

Joint Consultative Committees (JCC)

These must be established to advise the constituent bodies. *Joint care planning teams* comprise officers of both bodies but specialist sub-groups may be set up.

Financial support

Health authorities may make payments to local social services authorities, housing authorities, housing associations and certain other public bodies and voluntary organisations towards expenditure on community services. These must accord with advice from the JCC and be within directions issued by the Secretary of State, and may be made as:

- *joint finance* – usually under an arrangement to promote a new activity on the basis that the local authority will then become responsible;
- *dowry payments* – lump sum or annual payments to facilitate transfer of long-stay patients into the community;
- *other arrangements* – usually specific agreements between authorities but payments may be made to voluntary organisations.

24.2 DELIVERY OF HEALTH CARE

The Patient's Charter

This Charter applies to all parts of the NHS and sets out the rights of patients and the standards of service that they can expect to receive. The terms are not law and cannot be enforced in the courts but may form the basis of any complaint regarding inadequate services:

- *The Patient's Charter & You* is published by the DoH in a range of languages and is available from 'Patient's Charter', Freepost NEA959, Wetherby, West Yorkshire LS23 6YY (or telephone the Health Literature Line on freephone 0800 555777).

PART 3: SECTION D   Health Care

Types

There are three types of health care provided under the NHS, though health care may also be purchased privately:

- *primary health care* provided in the community by family doctors, dentists, opticians and others;
- *secondary health care* provided through hospitals and the ambulance services;
- *tertiary health care* provided through specialist hospitals, e.g. for cancer.

In the community

General practitioners

Family doctors (GPs) now provide their services in medical practices under a contract with the authority to persons who register with them. Practices may be fundholders and administer their own budget, and offer a wider range of services with more emphasis on promotion of good health and prevention of disease. Directories are produced of local GPs giving details of their practices which should produce an annual leaflet with details of the services provided:

- everyone has the right to be registered with a GP:
    - the patient may approach a GP and ask to join his list of patients (but the GP is not obliged to accept a particular patient)
    - the health authority will allocate a patient to a GP if he is unable to find one but there is then a risk of periodic transfer so the patient should seek to find his own GP
    - patients may change GP without giving reasons or getting permission
- patients have the right to see a GP (not necessarily their own) at the surgery during surgery hours which should be displayed on a notice outside:
    - an appointment system may prevail except in an emergency
    - the surgery should provide a telephone number for messages at all times
- home visits cannot be insisted upon and are in the doctor's discretion, but should be available to patients who genuinely need them;
- patients aged 75 and over must be offered an annual assessment and home visit to see how they are managing, but not necessarily at a time of year of their choice;
- patients away from home for up to three months can ask to be treated as a temporary patient by another GP and even if not accepted that GP must give any treatment immediately necessary.

See the NHS (General Medical Services) Regulations 1992, Schedule 2.

Chapter 24 PROVISION OF HEALTH CARE

Dental care

A new contract between general dental practitioners and FHSAs came into force in 1990. Patients may now be accepted onto a dentist's NHS 'continuing care' list. All necessary treatment must be offered to continuing care patients under the NHS but private treatment can be arranged in addition or as an alternative.

Hospital care

Patients generally need to be referred to a hospital by a GP, but in an emergency an *Accident and Emergency Department* will provide treatment:

- there is no absolute right to choose the hospital or consultant, but a preference may be expressed to the GP:
  - GP fundholders may refer to whichever consultant or hospital they choose
  - non-fundholders may seek permission from the DHA to do this
- there is no right to a second opinion but patients can request one if in doubt;
- for hospital discharge see para 24.5.

Private medical care

Medical care and treatment outside the NHS is provided under direct contracts between the provider and the patient. A private hospital may be set up as a commercial enterprise or a charity:

- there may be separate contracts with the private hospital, consultant, etc:
  - fees are charged which may be recovered as a civil debt
  - a matter of complaint may also be a breach of contract
- health professionals involved are governed by the same professional bodies as those working in the NHS (some also work part time for the NHS).

Private medical insurance

The potential fees for private medical care may be covered by tailor-made insurance policies or schemes, providing a level of cover for an annual premium or subscription. Refer to the conditions of the particular policy or the rules of the scheme:

- not all forms of medical treatment are eligible for a claim;
- any additional cost of the treatment must be paid by the patient but cash benefits may be available for those who receive treatment under the NHS;
- there may be age restrictions on taking out a policy or joining a scheme.

24.3 INFORMATION

There is a general duty of confidentiality imposed upon health professionals at common law, so medical information concerning an older person may only be disclosed to third parties in certain defined circumstances. Older people may themselves wish to be told what the diagnosis of an illness is or to know what is held in their medical records. The obligations of a health authority or medical practitioner in relation to the disclosure of information are dealt with in Chapter 4 and include:

- data protection legislation;
- Access to Health Records Act 1990;
- Access to Medical Reports Act 1988;
- a duty to comply with the *Code of Practice on Openness in the NHS*.

Confidentiality

A doctor is under a general duty not to disclose information which he has gained in his professional capacity but there are the following potential exceptions to this general principle, namely disclosure:

- with the patient's consent;
- in relation to the clinical management of a patient;
- to a close relative or another third party in the best interests of the patient;
- required by statute;
- in connection with judicial proceedings or in the public interest;
- for the purposes of medical audit, teaching and research.

> A doctor who discloses confidential information about a patient must be prepared to justify this under one of the above heads.

Consent to disclosure

A doctor is free to disclose medical information with the consent of the patient but the consent should cover the extent of the information disclosed and the persons to whom it is disclosed:

- if the patient is incapable of giving consent the other exceptions must be considered, e.g. is the disclosure in the best interests of the patient;
- wherever possible questions of disclosure will be discussed with the patient in advance and express consent obtained or inferred.

Chapter 24 PROVISION OF HEALTH CARE

Disclosure to other professionals

Medical information may only be disclosed to those directly involved in the care and treatment of the patient on a 'need to know' basis in relation to such care – other purposes will not suffice:

- all medically qualified staff share the duty of confidentiality;
- a doctor releasing information to non-medical professionals (e.g. social workers) must ensure that they too will treat it in confidence;
- information required for administrative purposes should be on a basis which does not identify the patient.

> If a patient is particularly vulnerable disclosure of concerns about abuse to an appropriate source may be indicated.

Disclosure to others

Doctors may need to discuss with relatives or carers the nature of an illness and any treatment, and consent may often be presumed (unless expressly refused):

- if consent cannot be given the doctor must act in the patient's best interests;
- when it is undesirable, for medical reasons, to seek a patient's express consent disclosure is essentially a matter of clinical judgment.

Public interest

It may be in the public interest for a doctor to disclose information about his patient where failure to disclose will expose the patient, or someone else, to a risk of death or serious harm, e.g:

- where a doctor considers that his patient is no longer fit to drive (though he should advise the patient first and invite surrender of the licence);
- if it is apparent that a perpetrator of abuse to the patient is also abusing other vulnerable adults.

Withholding information

It is suggested that information may only be specifically withheld from the patient if disclosure would be likely to cause serious harm to the patient's physical or mental health.

Code of Practice

In 1995 the Government published *The Code of Practice on Openness in the NHS in England* (similar Codes were published in Wales and Scotland). Each health body is required to publish locally the name of an individual responsible for the operation of the Code and how information may be requested through that individual:

- complaints about non-disclosure, delays in disclosure or charges for information should be made to the responsible individual;
- if complainants are dissatisfied with the response received they should write to the Chief Executive of the health body;
- those still dissatisfied may complain to the Health Service Commissioner (who has required a health body to establish the specific exemption relied upon in order to justify refusal to disclose information).

> The principle is that information should be made available unless it can be shown to fall into one of the exempt categories.

24.4 COMPLAINTS

A client may be dissatisfied about the delivery of health care and wish to complain. You should only pursue this on the request or with the consent of the actual patient and be careful about complaints made by other people (unless the patient lacks mental capacity and is dependent upon other people looking after his interests):

- before pursuing a formal complaint it may be appropriate for the patient or someone on his behalf to discuss the problem with the professional involved and if not satisfied that this has been done you may wish to take the step yourself (it may be more appropriate to have the discussion with that person's manager);
- the person or body to complain to depends upon the nature of the complaint and person complained about:
    - many complaints relate to service failures (e.g. waiting times, poor hygiene in hospital wards) and these should be made to the service managers
    - help and advice should be available from the local Community Health Council in regard to the different complaints procedures
- distinguish cases where there is the possibility of legal redress (e.g. damages for negligent treatment):
    - it may not be appropriate to delay matters by pursuing a complaint
    - if the complaint arises in the private sector it may amount to an actionable breach of contract
    - there is no legal justification for attempts to persuade complainants to waive legal rights before a complaint will be investigated

> The purpose of a complaint is to resolve a problem, not to increase it.

Procedures

The *Patient's Charter* reaffirms the right to have any complaint about NHS services investigated and to receive a full and prompt written reply. There used to be various procedures depending on which part of the NHS was involved, but a new NHS complaints system was introduced in April 1996:

- distinguish between oral and written complaints:
  - an oral complaint will only be considered under formal procedures if the patient remains dissatisfied or puts the complaint in writing
  - written complaints are dealt with in accordance with national and local guidance and receive a written response
- a complaint may also be made to the professional body of the particular doctor, nurse or other health professional concerned;
- it is usually necessary to exhaust all available procedures for dispute resolution before applying to the High Court for a judicial review and a similar approach is increasingly being adopted by ombudsmen.

NHS complaints procedures

There are three stages in the procedure for complaints about the NHS:

- discuss the problem with the manager or professional concerned (the local resolution stage) – this should be done within six months;
- a hearing before an independent review panel;
- reference to the Health Service Commissioner.

Hospital and Community Trust complaints

Complaints about service failures may be made to the service managers whilst a more formal complaint is made to a specially appointed officer whose name and location should be available in the hospital. A written reply will be received and if still not satisfied the patient may refer to the Health Service Commissioner.

> Hospital Complaints Procedure Act 1985 and directions made thereunder.

Family practitioner services

A complaint about family practitioner services (this includes a GP, dentist, pharmacist or optician but not complaints relating to clinical judgment or professional misconduct) should be made to the relevant health authority. The complaint should promptly be dealt with under local resolution arrangements and if it is not resolved a review panel will be convened.

Clinical complaints

For clinical judgment complaints there is a three-stage NHS procedure:

- a discussion with the consultant for an explanation and possible resolution;
- the Regional Medical Officer (RMO) considers whether:
  - it is a complaint about diagnosis or treatment by a hospital doctor
  - every effort has been made to resolve it by explanation; and
  - it is a serious matter which cannot be dealt with by a different enquiry or disciplinary action and is unlikely to go to court
- the RMO may then make a reference to two independent consultants appointed by the BMA (of whom at least one comes from a different regional health authority) who hold a review which the patient may attend with a representative. They send a report to the RMO although the complainant merely receives a letter.

Professional misconduct

Such complaints against GPs or hospital doctors are made to the General Medical Council and dealt with under established procedures. Sanctions range from a warning letter through suspension to removal from the Register. Complaints against nurses, dentists, pharmacists and other professional groups are made to the professional association concerned.

NHS discipline procedure

Discipline in respect of family health services practitioners is dealt with separately from complaints by special disciplinary committees of a different health authority. They hear evidence, make findings of fact and recommend an appropriate penalty. Appeal lies to the Family Health Service Appeal Authority (FHSAA).

Health Service Commissioner

This Ombudsman investigates certain types of complaint about the NHS. There is a time-limit of 12 months for a complaint and the matter must have been taken up with the appropriate NHS authority first.

Types of complaint

Complaints can be investigated concerning:

- failure by an NHS authority to provide a service which it has a duty to provide or in a service that is provided;
- maladministration connected with action taken by or on behalf of the authority, which includes failure to comply with a legal obligation and administra-

Chapter 24 PROVISION OF HEALTH CARE

tive action or inaction based on or influenced by improper considerations or conduct:

- e.g. unjustifiable delay, incompetence, neglect, and failing to give proper advice or follow recognised procedures or take account of representations
- complaints may relate to the attitude as well as actions of members of staff, e.g. discourtesy, harassment, bias or unfair discrimination

Complaints cannot be investigated concerning matters before the courts or:

- about the general services provided by family practitioners because these relate to their contract with the FHSA to whom complaint should be made (complaints about the FHSA itself can be investigated including how they handle complaints);
- within the clinical judgment complaints procedure (as distinct from the administration of that procedure).

Procedure

Only refer complaints which cannot be resolved with the NHS authority, and send a letter outlining the complaint and enclosing copies of all relevant documents and correspondence:

- if the complaint is accepted, a letter with a summary of what is to be investigated is sent to the complainant and the authority. An officer may visit the complainant to discuss the matter and explain what happens;
- the investigation is conducted in private and will usually be informal so legal representation is seldom necessary. A solicitor may assist in presenting the complaint and help may be given with the costs;
- a written report is sent to the complainant and the authority and this may be published. If the complaint is upheld this report will state whether the authority has agreed to remedy any injustice or hardship caused, perhaps by offering an apology or agreeing to policy changes or new procedures.

> A leaflet is available from the office of the Commissioner (addresses in Appendix 5). For ombudsmen generally see Chapter 5 at para. 5.3.

24.5 DISCHARGE FROM HOSPITAL

Patients may discharge themselves and leave hospital at any time unless detained under the Mental Health Act 1983 (see Chapter 26) or admitted under a JP's order for an infectious disease. An elderly patient whose mental capacity is impaired is likely to come under the care of a psychogeriatrician so if a report is needed as to mental capacity refer to this consultant.

Before patients are discharged from hospital, proper arrangements must be made for their return home and for any continuing care that may be necessary. All local authorities and health authorities are required to have in place discharge procedures. Problems arise when it is proposed to discharge a patient from hospital who needs continuing nursing care, because although there is no charge for services provided under the NHS the individual will be means-tested for any local authority services:

- it should be ascertained whether discharge is to the care of the health authority or social services;
- as regards discharge of hospital patients to private care, people who need continuing nursing care should not be forced to leave hospital against their wishes:
  - health authorities are not entitled to make a financial assessment of a patient
  - there is no power to compulsorily place people in residential care or nursing homes against their wishes (except National Assistance Act 1948, s 47)
- see Circular LAC(95)5 *Discharge of Patients from Hospital* and the *Hospital Discharge Workbook* (DoH);
- see Chapter 22 for community care services and Chapter 19 for funding.

The obligation to provide continuing nursing care falls on both health authorities and local authorities under National Health Service Act 1977 and National Assistance Act 1948.

Chapter 25
Medical Treatment

25.1 CONSENT TO TREATMENT

No medical treatment may be given to an adult patient without consent and treatment involving physical contact is a trespass to the person (a battery) in the absence of consent. Provision of basic nursing care may be excusable in the absence of consent (e.g. cleaning up a protesting patient) but intrusive medical treatment is not. Doctors cannot compel competent patients to accept treatment however convinced they may be that it is in the patient's best interests. Special provision is made for patients who lack competence to make a decision about medical treatment.

The nature of consent

The onus is on the patient to prove that he did not consent (*Freeman v Home Office* [1984] 2 WLR 130). Consent may be in writing (a signed form), verbal or implied by conduct (e.g. where a patient presents himself for treatment, but not where only a diagnosis is requested). The signature on a form is merely evidence which may be rebutted and the question is not whether the patient signed the consent form but whether he decided to have the treatment – see generally Chapter 3:

- consent must be specific and valid, which means that the patient consents to the treatment actually given and does so voluntarily, i.e. consent is freely given and not under threat (e.g. to discharge or use compulsory powers);

- the information the patient receives is within the doctor's discretion but any questions should be answered – see *Sidaway v Bethlem Royal Hospital Governors* [1985] 1 All ER 643. Failure to inform may nullify consent, but wrong information may give rise to an action in negligence if injury directly results, on the basis that the patient would not have consented if properly informed and damage resulted from the subsequent treatment;

- the patient must have capacity to consent (which should be continually re-assessed) and this is based on understanding in broad terms what he is consenting to, so the degree depends on the complexity of treatment. A patient's wishes in regard to treatment may be recorded in advance (e.g. in the form of a living will – see para. 25.4);

- the right of choice regarding treatment is not limited to decisions which others might regard as sensible but exists notwithstanding that the reasons for making the choice are rational, irrational, unknown or even non-existent – *Re T (An adult) (Consent to medical treatment)* [1992] 2 FLR 458, CA.

> See generally Chapter 15 of the *Code of Practice* under section 118(4) of the Mental Health Act 1983.

Refusal of consent

A patient who remains competent to make a decision about continuing treatment may refuse it and then it cannot be given even if death will result. If a refusal to consent to life-saving treatment is to be legally binding the patient must:

- have capacity to make the decision and not have had his will overborne by the influence of a third party;
- have understood in broad terms the nature and effect of the treatment; and
- have in refusing covered the actual situation in which the treatment is needed.

> *Re T (An adult) (Consent to medical treatment)* [1992] 2 FLR 458, CA.

The treating doctor determines whether the criteria are fulfilled but his view of the reasonableness or rationality of the patient's decision may influence his approach.

25.2 INCOMPETENT PATIENTS

Competence

Competence is presumed unless the contrary is proved, and means that the patient has:

- sufficient understanding and intelligence to comprehend the nature, purpose and likely consequences of undergoing or refusing treatment – *Gillick v. West Norfolk and Wisbech AHA and anor* [1986] 1 FLR 224, HL; and
- the ability to communicate his decision in relation to the particular treatment.

Key points

- The ability to communicate can be impaired by mental or physical causes but the latter may often be overcome by imaginative techniques – see Chapter 3 at para. 3.1.

Chapter 25 MEDICAL TREATMENT

- A diagnosis of mental disorder does not by itself prevent a patient from consenting: a detained mental patient may obtain an injunction to prevent physical treatment – *Re C (Adult: refusal of medical treatment)* [1994] 1 All ER 819.
- Short-term incompetence is of less significance than long-term because the minimum necessary treatment can be given until the patient can again express his wishes in regard to more drastic medical treatment.
- Whilst the decision of an incompetent person cannot validate treatment, withholding treatment from such a person may give rise to an action for breach of a duty of care.

> There is no procedure whereby the personal power to consent to or refuse medical treatment may be delegated to others, either by the patient or the state.

Treatment without consent

Emergency treatment may be given to save the life of an unconscious patient although there may be an exception where it is known that the patient would not wish to be treated because of religious or other beliefs.

Treatment without consent is also lawful in the case of an incompetent adult where it is considered by the doctor to be in the best interest of a patient:

- best interest means necessary to save life, or prevent deterioration or ensure improvement in a patient's physical or mental health, but should not be restricted to purely medical interests;
- it is necessary to consider what the patient would have chosen taking into account all the evidence including any previously expressed wishes which may include signed documents, e.g. a living will;
- a doctor must act in accordance with a practice accepted as proper by a responsible body of medical practitioners, skilled and experienced in the relevant speciality – see *Bolam v Friern Barnet Hospital Management Committee* [1957] 2 All ER 118 and *F v West Berkshire Health Authority* [1989] 2 All ER 545.

Treatment for a mental disorder (subject to safeguards) may be given to a patient detained under the treatment provisions of the Mental Health Act 1983 – see Chapter 26.

Next of kin

The next of kin (whether the lawful next of kin or those stated as such by the patient) do not have any legal right to consent or refuse consent on behalf of an adult patient:

- carers, home managers and social workers also do not have any legal status in regard to treatment decisions;
- there is no role for the 'nearest relative' similar to that for treatment under the Mental Health Act 1983.

If the treating doctor is to determine the patient's best interests he would need to consult with such persons and it may be prudent to have their approval.

Allowing the patient to die

Codes of medical ethics have never required the doctor to prolong life at any cost; caring for a patient as he dies in peace and dignity may be the last service a doctor can perform.

'Double effect'

Drugs given to relieve suffering may shorten the life of the patient – the principle of 'double effect' (the successful defence of Dr Bodkin Adams). A decision may need to be made to change from treatment for living to treatment for dying:

- administering a drug which will merely kill without first relieving suffering is murder (or attempted murder if there is no proof that it actually caused death);
- it is no defence that the patient pleaded to be put out of her misery, though juries are reluctant to convict doctors in this situation and it is also effective mitigation – *R v Cox*, 18 September 1992, unreported.

Withholding or withdrawing treatment

Doctors may withhold or withdraw treatment which is not in the best interests of their patient without being in breach of duty or in breach of the criminal law, even if death is the inevitable consequence. There is no difference between withholding and withdrawing treatment: both are omissions rather than acts – *Airedale NHS Trust v Bland* [1993] 2 WLR 316, HL.

Good medical practice

The interpretation of the law as to the extent to which the previously expressed wishes of an incompetent patient may or should be followed is difficult:

- the British Medical Association acknowledge that any patient may express views, orally or in writing, to his GP who will then be aware of them;
- open sharing of views between patient, doctors and nurses, and also relatives and other carers (with the patient's consent where this is possible) should be encouraged and any conclusions should be noted on the patient's records.

See NHS Guide to Consent and the BMA Interim Guidelines.

Chapter 25 MEDICAL TREATMENT

25.3 POWERS OF THE COURT

Where medical treatment is carried out without the consent of the patient or other justification there may be a reference to a court.

Damages

The court may award damages in various ways:

- for the tort of trespass to the person, or assault and battery, where there has been physical contact (e.g. an operation or injection). Such a claim may be brought without proof of damage;
- on a claim in negligence based upon a breach of the duty of care and damages arising from that breach. If treatment without consent goes wrong liability may be absolute as the patient does not need to prove further breach of the duty of care, though damages must still be proven;
- in the private sector, on a claim for breach of contract.

Injunctions and declarations

The High Court may also grant a declaration relating to the proposed treatment, if necessary supported by an injunction:

- the declaration procedure enables the court to declare as 'not unlawful' actions that no one (including the court) has jurisdiction to authorise:
  - *F v West Berkshire Health Authority* [1989] 2 All ER 545
  - *Airedale NHS Trust v Bland* [1993] 2 WLR 316, HL
- the court will not order a doctor to adopt a course of treatment which, in his clinical opinion, is not in the best interests of his patient but reference to another doctor may be appropriate;
- an injunction may be obtained to prevent specific treatment if a hospital refuses to give an undertaking not to carry out that treatment.

> There may be an interim injunction (made without notice if necessary – the phrase *ex parte* is no longer used), and an interim declaration is now possible under the Civil Procedure Rules 1998.

Criminal liability

A prosecution of the doctor will be appropriate in certain circumstances (e.g. for murder if he administers a fatal injection without any other medical benefits, although this may be reduced to attempted murder if there is no proof that the injection actually caused the death).

25.4 LIVING WILLS

Incurably ill and incapacitated people may be kept alive for long periods by medical treatment which, if they remained competent to make a decision, they might refuse thereby enabling death from natural causes. Can the individual anticipate this situation by expressing wishes in advance or delegating the right to make decisions to someone else?

> Terminology in this area is not yet settled and the terms 'living will' and 'advance directive' are often used in the same context.

Types

In general a living will is a document whereby a person seeks to provide for the basis on which health care decisions that affect him are made if he becomes incompetent and so unable to participate in such decisions. There are two types:

Advance directive or declaration

This is a requirement (or request) that certain treatment should, or should not, be given in certain situations if the individual is not competent to consent to or refuse treatment at the time – any presumption of consent may thus be rebutted:

- 'best interests' are no longer restricted to 'best medical interests' and it is now good medical practice to take into account the properly expressed wishes of the patient if relevant to the particular treatment decision;
- recent cases make it clear that an advance directive may be legally binding though much will depend on its terms:
  - *Airedale NHS Trust v Bland* [1993] 2 WLR 316, HL
  - *Re C (Adult: refusal of medical treatment)* [1994] 1 All ER 819
- the 'directive' is an attempt by the patient to state what must (or must not) be done whereas the 'declaration' is merely an expression of wishes.

Whilst refusal may be effective, any such document can no more require treatment to be given than the patient could have done if competent.

Durable power of attorney

This document is a delegation of the power to make decisions about treatment to another person in the event that the individual becomes unable to make those decisions (also known as a *Health Care Proxy* or *Medical Treatment Attorney*). Do not assume that relatives would necessarily wish to take the responsibility for these decisions for which they may be emotionally unprepared. There are at present no lawful procedures whereby the power to consent to or refuse treatment may be delegated and legislation would be necessary to introduce this – see Appendix 8 and the Law Commission proposals.

Implications

The concept of a living will applies to all kinds of medical treatment but it is mostly adopted for decisions relating to treatment that affects the preservation of life, invariably for refusal of treatment:

- the patients involved tend to be those who would die without treatment (e.g. on life support systems) or depend upon 24-hour care without which they would die (e.g. irreversible dementia);
- the following benefits are claimed for advance directives:
  - reassure patients as to loss of autonomy and alleviate fears as to prolonged pain or total incapacity
  - assist doctors with ethical dilemmas over treatment and create increased medical awareness
  - reduce stress and distress amongst relatives
  - reduce arbitrary medical decisions and discourage over-intrusive treatment
  - promote greater dialogue between doctors, patients and carers regarding end-of-life decisions – see BMA statement on advance directives, November 1992

Legality

A patient cannot require a doctor to take a positive step which would cause death and any document which directs this is invalid. Any person who encourages its preparation might commit an offence, but there is nothing illegal about a document relating to medical decisions within the powers of the individual. A distinction must be drawn between the following, and only the first is illegal:

- treatment intended to cause death or which will merely result in death without any beneficial effect;
- treatment to ease suffering which may accelerate an otherwise inevitable death; and
- withholding or withdrawing treatment which may prevent or delay death.

There are two main ethical views:

- the sanctity (or mere existence) of life must be preserved at all times;
- people should be allowed to die if they so choose.

> The doctrine of 'double effect' is well established; it may be necessary to change from 'treatment for living' to 'treatment for dying' and the patient should have some input in this decision.

Precedents

A simple form of living will is reproduced in Appendix 3. Remember that definitions about treatment that are too precise or too vague may give rise to later problems.

> Precedents are available from the Terence Higgins Trust and other charities.

Practical problems

There are many practical problems in the use of these documents which may need to be discussed with the client, including:

- how do you make it sufficiently specific to cover a particular situation without being so general that it is of doubtful validity? Does the client wish to address specific situations only or use a standard form?

- how do you ensure that it is drawn to the attention of a doctor when needed?
    - thought should be given as to where it is to be kept or who is to keep it
    - the aim should be to ensure that a copy is produced in the event that a serious medical treatment decision has to be made when the client is incompetent, but such documents may be overlooked or ignored in major accident treatment
    - it is no use depositing the document with the client's GP if it merely remains in the file at the surgery when the client is admitted to hospital
    - one solution is to prepare several copies (or originals) and for the doctor, next of kin (or partner) and your office all to retain one, in the hope that a copy will be produced in the event of need

- how may it be revoked or amended if wishes change, especially if several copies have been distributed:
    - express it to be of limited duration and then renew it at intervals?
    - specify the name and address of a person to be contacted about its validity?

Chapter 26
Mental Health Legislation

26.1 LEGISLATION

- Mental Health Act 1983 (as amended)
- Mental Health (Hospital, Guardianship and Consent to Treatment) Regulations 1996
- Mental Health (After-care under Supervision) Regulations 1996
- Mental Health (Patients in the Community) (Transfers from Scotland) Regulations 1996

Rules

The following rules govern the procedure to be adopted by the courts and tribunals that deal with proceedings under the mental health legislation:

- Civil Procedure Rules 1998
  - see County Court Rules, Order 49 rule 12 (reproduced in Schedule 2)
- Mental Health Review Tribunal Rules 1983
- Court of Protection Rules 1994 (see Chapter 10)

Scope

The 1983 Act applies to persons suffering from a mental disorder (called *patients*) and provides for:

- Part II: compulsory admission to and detention in hospital, etc.;
- Part IV: medical treatment in hospital without consent;
- Part V: review by a tribunal of detention and treatment;
- Part II: guardianship in the community;
- Part VII: management of property by Court of Protection (see Chapter 10);
- Part III: special treatment in criminal proceedings (see Chapter 17).

Older people may suffer from mental disorder bringing them within the scope of the legislation and allowing assessment for compulsory admission and treatment in hospital or application to the Court of Protection. These disorders include Alzheimer's disease, depression and other forms of dementia.

Guidance, circulars and practice notes

Numerous documents provide guidance on the application of the legislation including:

- the *Code of Practice* to the Mental Health Act;
- *Guidance on Supervised Discharge and Related Provisions*, HSG(96)11;
- Consent to Treatment, DHSS No: DDL (84)4;
- *The Care Programme approach*, HC(90)23/LASSL(90)11;
- *Guidance on the Introduction of Supervision Registers for Mentally Ill People from April 1994*, HSG(94)5;
- Mental Health Act Commission publications (see the Biennial Reports).
- the following topics have been covered by practice notes:
  - Administration of Clozapine
  - Administration of Medicine
  - Section 5(2) of the Mental Health Act 1983 and transfers
  - Sections 17, 18 of the Mental Health Act 1983
  - Issues relating to the Administration of the Mental Health Act in Mental Nursing Homes registered to receive Detained Patients.

The Patient's Charter

This applies to all parts of the NHS and sets out the rights of patients and the standards of service that they can expect to receive. It is not law and cannot be enforced as such in the courts but may form the basis of any complaint regarding inadequate services.

> *Mental Health Services* (DoH1997) is available free of charge in a range of languages from 'Patient's Charter', Freepost NEA959, Wetherby, West Yorkshire LS23 6YY, or telephone the Health Literature Line on freephone 0800 555777.

Definitions

Most definitions are found in Part I, section 1 of the 1983 Act:

Mental illness

This term is not defined though it is more likely to afflict older people than other forms of mental disorder. These words 'should be construed in the way that ordinary sensible people would construe them' – *W v L* [1973] 3 All ER 884.

Chapter 26 MENTAL HEALTH LEGISLATION

Mental disorder

Defined as 'mental illness, arrested or incomplete development of mind, psychopathic disorder and any other disorder or disability of mind' ('mentally disordered' is construed accordingly).

Severe mental impairment

Defined as 'a state of arrested or incomplete development of mind which includes severe impairment of intelligence and social functioning and is associated with abnormally aggressive or seriously irresponsible conduct on the part of the person concerned'. *Mental impairment* is the same as severe mental impairment but with *significant* substituted for *severe*.

Psychopathic disorder

Defined as 'a persistent disorder or disability of mind (whether or not including significant impairment of intelligence) which results in abnormally aggressive or seriously irresponsible conduct on the part of the person concerned'.

Medical treatment

Defined as including nursing and care, habilitation and rehabilitation under medical supervision – s 145(1).

Nearest relative

This person is appointed under section 26 of the 1983 Act and has the following powers and functions in respect of the patient, namely to:

- request an assessment with a view to admission to hospital, or be informed about an application for admission for assessment;
- apply, or object to an application, for admission to hospital for treatment or for guardianship;
- be informed about discharge from section and be consulted about a supervised discharge application;
- request discharge to hospital managers and apply to a Mental Health Review Tribunal.

Who is the nearest relative?

In relation to a patient the nearest relative will normally be:

- the husband or wife, son or daughter, father or mother, brother or sister, grandparent, grandchild, uncle or aunt, nephew or niece:
    - the elder of relatives in a class takes precedence

- whole blood equates to half-blood but the former take precedence
- living together as husband and wife for six months is sufficient
• a relative who ordinarily resides with or cares for the patient will take precedence, and this may apply to a non-relative after five years.

Certain persons are excluded, namely a separated spouse, a person under 18 (unless a spouse) and a person not ordinarily resident in the UK.

A nearest relative may be displaced on application to the county court if he cannot be found, is incapable of acting, or objects unreasonably to an application for treatment or guardianship. There may be human rights implications in that the patient (who may have mental capacity) cannot nominate a nearest relative and has no status in court proceedings to displace the person nominated by law.

> The nearest relative will not always be the next of kin and may be replaced.

Approved social workers (ASW)

ASWs are appointed by social services authorities pursuant to section 114 of the 1983 Act and are competent to deal with persons suffering from mental disorder. They have various statutory duties and powers over persons believed to be suffering from a mental disorder. It can be an offence to obstruct them in the performance of their duties – see section 114 and DHSS Circular LAC 86/15.

Code of Practice

A *Code of Practice* prepared by the DoH and Welsh Office pursuant to section 118(4) offers guidance on how the 1983 Act should be implemented. It:

- is primarily aimed at the needs, rights and entitlements of mentally disordered persons who are detained but may be referred to as a good practice document for the care and management of *informal* patients;
- deals with matters such as assessment prior to admission, admission to hospital or guardianship, treatment and care in hospital and leaving hospital;
- lays down the principles that patients:
  - receive respect for and consideration of individual qualities and diverse backgrounds (social, cultural, ethnic and religious)
  - have their needs taken fully into account within limits of available resources
  - receive any necessary treatment or care in the least controlled/segregated facilities practicable
  - are treated or cared for in a way that promotes self-determination and personal responsibility
  - are discharged from any order as soon as it is no longer necessary

26.2 ADMISSION TO HOSPITAL

General

- A *voluntary* admission is where the patient consents (and is capable of doing so) and admissions should be voluntary whenever possible.
- An *informal* admission arises where the patient is compliant but incapable of consenting. It relies upon the common law doctrine of necessity and is authorised under section 131(1). The safeguards under the Act are not available – see *R v Bournewood Community and Mental Health NHS Trust, ex p L* (1998) Times, 30 June, HL (law reform is contemplated).
- A *compulsory* admission is pursuant to a statutory power, often referred to as being under *section*. There are several statutory powers and various safeguards (see below).

> Admissions may be on a *voluntary, informal* or *compulsory* basis.

Statutory powers

The different statutory powers are used in the following circumstances:

Section 2: for assessment

The patient is suffering from mental disorder of a nature or degree which warrants detention in hospital for assessment and it is in the interests of the patient's health or safety or for the protection of others:

- two medical recommendations are necessary;
- detention can be for up to 28 days but cannot be renewed.

Section 3: for treatment

The patient is suffering from a specific mental disorder and it is appropriate to receive medical treatment in hospital and necessary for the health or safety of the patient or protection of others:

- two medical recommendations are required;
- detention can be for up to six months in the first instance, renewable for another six months and then one year at a time;
- there is a right to apply to a Mental Health Review Tribunal.

Section 4: for assessment in emergency

The patient is admitted on the grounds set out in section 2 but on the recommendation of one doctor in case of urgent necessity on a diagnosis of mental disorder:

- application is made by an ASW or nearest relative;
- detention can be for up to 72 hours but convertible to a section 2 on a second medical recommendation.

Section 5: short-term detention for those already in mental hospitals

A hospital in-patient may be detained by the treating doctor or by a nurse for short periods in certain circumstances.

> Powers of compulsion are rarely used in treatment and care of older people.

Medical treatment

The 1983 Act contains powers for medical treatment to be given to a detained patient without his consent in certain closely defined circumstances, but apart from this normal common law principles apply (see Chapter 25):

- treatment for 'general medical or surgical' conditions cannot be given under the provisions of the Act;
- if the patient lacks capacity treatment can be given that is in the patient's best interests.

> Detention under the Act does not mean that a patient lacks capacity to consent to general medical treatment.

Treatment for mental disorder

A patient who is detained under the treatment sections of the 1983 Act (i.e. sections 2, 3, 37, 47 and 48) can be given 'medical treatment for a mental disorder' without his consent:

- if detained under the 'short-term' sections or subject to supervised discharge or guardianship medical treatment cannot be given for a mental disorder without consent;
- there are 'safeguards' whereby particular treatments require the consent of the patient and/or a second medical opinion, with regular reviews of such treatment (see Part IV of the 1983 Act);
- there are special provisions for urgent treatment (see s 62).

Implications of detention

For the implications of admission under section refer to the books listed in Appendix 7.

There is concern about the number of older people in NHS hospitals and nursing homes who do not have capacity to consent to admission or treatment but who are not formally detained:

- these patients do not have the 'safeguards' of the mental health legislation which include application to tribunal, attention of the Mental Health Act Commission, right to a second opinion about medication and regular renewal of their stay in hospital;
- sectioning them under the Act is perceived as stigmatising and something that is best avoided.

> Reform of the Mental Health Act 1983 is seen as necessary especially now it is recognised that informal patients (of which there are many) do not have the safeguards provided under the Act to compulsory patients.

26.3 COMMUNITY POWERS

Power to inspect

An ASW may enter and inspect premises in the area of the local social services authority in which a mentally disordered person is living if he has reasonable cause to believe that the patient is not under proper care (s 115). There is no power to force entry or restrain or remove the patient.

Removal to a place of safety

A constable has power to remove to a place of safety with a view to early examination, assessment and treatment a person believed to be suffering from a mental disorder who is:

- ill-treated, neglected or out of control or unable to care for himself and living alone (s 135). This must be under a warrant issued by a magistrate and the constable must be accompanied by an ASW and a registered medical practitioner;
- in a public place in immediate need of care and control and this is necessary in the interests of the person or the protection of others (s 136).

A magistrates' court has power to authorise removal of a person in need of care and attention to suitable premises – National Assistance Act 1948, s 47 (see Chapter 22 at para. 22.2).

Statutory guardianship

A limited form of adult guardianship is available under section 8 of the 1983 Act but has been little used. It enables the establishment of an authoritative framework for working with a patient with a minimum of constraint to achieve as independent a life as possible within the community, but must be part of the patient's overall care and treatment plan – *Code of Practice*, para. 13.4.

A patient may be received into guardianship provided he suffers from one of the four specific categories of mental disorder and:

- this is of a nature or degree which warrants guardianship; and
- it is necessary for the welfare of the patient or the protection of others.

Appointment

Guardianship initially lasts for six months but may be renewed for a further six months and thereafter annually. Application is made to the social services department by an ASW or the patient's nearest relative, in each case supported by two doctors:

- the nearest relative can object or subsequently discharge the patient;
- there is a right of appeal to a Mental Health Review Tribunal.

Who is appointed?

The guardian may be either the social services department or a private individual with the approval of the local authority, but a private guardian has duties which relate to notification of the local authority and appointment of a medical practitioner.

Powers

The guardian has very limited powers in respect of the patient but may require:

- that the patient resides at a specific place (but not with a specific person);
- that the patient attends at places and times specified for the purpose of medical treatment, occupation, education or training;
- access to the patient to be given at the patient's residence to any medical practitioner, ASW or other person specified.

The guardian has no power to detain the patient and cannot restrict his movements but can only insist that the patient ordinarily resides at the place specified. He cannot authorise or require physical removal of an unwilling patient, or authorise medical treatment (the treatment provisions of the Act do not apply). He has no power over the money and property of the patient. However, the semblance of authority when everyone else is powerless can be valuable and the guardian may adopt a dominant role (which may be all that is needed).

> It is an offence to ill-treat or wilfully neglect a person subject to a guardianship order.

Aftercare

There is a specific duty on the health and social services authorities in co-operation with voluntary organisations to provide 'aftercare services' for persons who have been detained under the treatment sections of the Act – s 117:

- it arises prior to the discharge if that can only take place when the arrangements are in hand;
- it continues until the aftercare authorities are satisfied that the person is no longer in need of such services;
- the patient has a right to a community care assessment (see Chapter 22);
- services provided under this section (including residential care) may not be charged for;
- consideration may be given to guardianship or inclusion in a supervision register if there is concern about risk of harm to the person or to others.

> A 'care plan' should be established in accordance with the Code of Practice and other guidance.

Aftercare under supervision

There may be discharge from hospital *under supervision* pursuant to provisions introduced in April 1996 – ss 25A to 25J of the 1983 Act inserted by Mental Health (Patients in the Community) Act 1995.

Application

A supervision application may be made by the responsible medical officer caring for the patient in hospital:

- there are procedures that must be complied with and strict criteria as to the patients to whom this procedure may apply;
- the supervision order lasts for six months and is renewable for a period of six months and for periods of one year thereafter.

Implications

Supervision of aftercare and monitoring of the care plan will be by a named supervisor (a community nurse, a social worker or other appropriate community worker):

- there is no power to treat the patient in the community without his consent, but the supervisor can as a last resort 'take and convey' the patient to hospital using force if necessary for the purposes of receiving treatment although the consent of the patient is then required for treatment to be given;

- the responsible aftercare bodies can impose requirements to ensure that aftercare services are received by the patient, e.g. that:
  - the patient resides at a specified place
  - the patient attends at a specified place and times for medical treatment, occupation, education or training
  - access be given by the patient at any place where the patient is residing to the supervisors, the RMO, ASW or other authorised person

See *Guidance on Supervised Discharge Related Provisions*, HSG(96)11.

26.4 REVIEW AND APPEAL

Discharge

Detention or guardianship ceases if a written order for discharge is made – s 23:

- the order in respect of a hospital patient detained under section 2 or 3 may be made by the responsible medical officer (RMO), the managers or nearest relative of the patient (and in respect of guardianship also by the responsible social services authority);
- a nearest relative wishing to take the initiative must give at least 72 hours' notice in writing to the hospital managers:
  - the RMO may within that time report to the managers that in his opinion the patient, if discharged, would be likely to act in a manner dangerous to himself or to some other person
  - if such report is made the discharge by the nearest relative will be of no effect but a similar order cannot be made within the next six months

Mental health review tribunal

This is an independent tribunal comprising a lawyer, psychiatrist and lay member, governed by the Council on Tribunals and administered regionally by the Department of Health. Specific provisions and time-limits are found in section 66 of the 1983 Act.

Reference to the tribunal

Under sections 16, 20, 25, 29 and 68 cases are referred to the tribunal by:

- patients detained under sections 2 or 3 or received into guardianship;
- hospital managers where a detained patient has not applied for a tribunal hearing within six months;
- the Secretary of State for a patient liable to be detained or subject to guardianship;

- a nearest relative where:
  - he demands discharge and the responsible medical officer bars this
  - a county court order directs that the functions of the nearest relative be carried out by an acting nearest relative

The tribunal may discharge the patient, decline to do so, or may make certain other orders – s 72.

> Representation by lawyers is encouraged and legal aid is available to a panel of lawyers experienced in these cases – *contact*:
> Panel Administrator, Professional Standards and Development Directorate, The Law Society, Ipsley Court, Berrington Close, Redditch, Worcs B98 0TD.

Mental Health Act Commission

This is a Special Health Authority regulated by the Mental Health Act Commission Regulations 1983 which consists of a chairman, a vice-chairman, some 92 other members and a chief executive.

The Commission publishes biennial reports of its work and protects the interests of detained (i.e. compulsorily admitted) patients by:

- regularly visiting those hospitals and mental nursing homes with detained patients;
- reviewing their care and treatment, and investigating complaints made by them or on their behalf;
- appointing doctors to review treatment under Part IV of the 1983 Act;
- reviewing decisions to withhold postal packets.

It is of concern that the Commission has no jurisdiction over incompetent patients who are not compulsorily admitted (informal patients).

SECTION E
Employment, Money and the Home

These three practical topics are considered separately in this Section. Lawyers are called upon to advise people of all ages in regard to these aspects of their lives, but the following pages concentrate on the special circumstances of older people whilst giving an overview of the law where necessary by way of background.

Employment does not necessarily cease at normal retirement age and an overview is given of the law for those who wish to remain engaged in some form of work activity to occupy themselves or supplement their pension.

The chapter dealing with financial matters concentrates on pensions and taxation, with reference being made to other parts of the Handbook for financial advice and services.

All aspects of home ownership and occupation are considered in outline. Some difficult issues arise in regard to homes for older people and the following may prove of particular interest to practitioners:

- purchase of council houses;
- shared occupation and licences to occupy;
- gifts of the home;
- home income plans and other schemes to release capital;
- sheltered housing.

Chapter 27

Work Activity

27.1 EMPLOYMENT

Legislation

- Employment Rights Act 1996
- Employment Relations Act 1999
- Trade Union and Labour Relations (Consolidation) Act 1992
- Anti-discrimination legislation
  - Sex Discrimination Act 1975
  - Race Relations Act 1976
  - Disability Discrimination Act 1995
- Working Time Regulations 1998

General

There are no legal restrictions in relation to older people working but their employment rights are reduced and there is at present no general protection against age discrimination.

Employment or self-employment?

The common law, and most legislation, relating to employment only applies to those working under a *'contract of employment'*. This should be distinguished from self-employment or a contract to provide services, but courts and tribunals look at the reality of the situation rather than the terminology applied. The courts have devised a number of tests of employment and no single one is determinative:

- the degree of control and of integration;
- whether someone is an entrepreneur in their own right; and
- whether there is an obligation to provide work and be provided with work.

The definition is more extensive for some employment protection legislation. In particular anti-discrimination legislation extends to those who work under a contract to do personal work – Sex Discrimination Act 1975, s 82(1).

PART 3: SECTION E Employment, Money and the Home

Continuous employment

You must have worked for a minimum period to be able to claim for redundancy or unfair dismissal – see Employment Rights Act 1996, ss 155 and 135:

- there are no longer any requirements as to minimum hours of work;
- where an older worker is employed on a casual basis and does not work in a particular week, this week might still count as a 'temporary cessation of work' in which event employment rights will be preserved – s 212.

Discrimination

All employees have a right not to be discriminated against on the grounds of sex, race, disability or trade union membership or activity during their employment:

- 'sex' includes trans-sexuality but not sexual orientation;
- 'race' covers colour, race, ethnic or national origins and nationality – Race Relations Act 1976, s 3;
- 'disability' covers physical or mental impairment which is not a temporary condition – Disability Discrimination Act 1995, s 1 and Sched. 1.

An older worker deprived of opportunities for employment, transfer, training or promotion could only bring an action if the discriminatory behaviour was based on the above grounds.

> Employees are entitled to equal pay which includes all benefits and pensions.

Remuneration

No employee can have a deduction made from his wages unless this has been agreed in writing (e.g. in the contract of employment) or under some statutory provision:

- this does not apply to an overpayment of wages or expenses;
- see Employment Rights Act 1996, s 13 (formerly Wages Act 1986).

Commencement

Recruitment

An employer can freely discriminate against older people when recruiting unless this is on the grounds of sex or marital status, race, disability or trade union membership.

Chapter 27 WORK ACTIVITY

Contracts

Once appointed, or an offer is accepted, a contract comes into existence. The terms may be express (oral or in writing) or implied but cannot override certain terms implied by statute:

- there are statutory minimum provisions in regard to the notice period – Employment Rights Act 1996, s 86;
- equal pay operates as a statutory implied term – Equal Pay Act 1970;
- there are rights relating to time off and union membership or activities.

Statement of terms of employment

A written statement of particulars should be provided to most employees within two months of commencement – Employment Rights Act 1996, s 1:

- there is no financial sanction on an employer for failure but in case of dispute a tribunal may later disapprove;
- the main terms and conditions must be specified including the rate of remuneration and intervals at which it is paid, hours, holidays, sickness and sick pay;
- the period of notice and any terms relating to pensions must be included;
- the stated terms are not conclusive:
  - if the parties have behaved in a manner inconsistent with them that behaviour is likely to be the best evidence relating to the relevant term
  - the terms of the contract may be deduced from custom or implication in so far as not specified

> Terms may be implied because of long established custom and practice or simply because it is reasonable to do so.

Part-timers

The Working Time Regulations 1998 extend to part-timers and under the 1999 Act they are to be given equal rights in employment by April 2000.

Termination

Employment may be terminated by agreement, resignation of the employee, operation of law, notice from the employer, 'constructive dismissal' or expiration of a fixed term.

Notice

There are statutory minimum notice periods of one week after a month, two weeks after two years and thereafter one week per year up to a maximum of 12 weeks – Employment Rights Act 1996, s 86:

- the contract may stipulate for longer periods and there may be an implied term for reasonable notice which exceeds the statutory minimum;
- there may be instant dismissal (without notice) for gross misconduct, and the contract of employment may be frustrated, e.g. by sickness or injury.

Entitlement

Upon dismissal an employee is entitled to net salary and benefits for the entire notice period if termination is with immediate effect:

- the sum payable is subject to the duty to mitigate by finding other work which is usually more difficult for older workers;
- in some situations there may be a right to work during the period of notice.

After two years' service the employee will be entitled to a written statement of reasons for the dismissal – Employment Rights Act 1996, s 92.

Wrongful dismissal

Damages may be claimed for any dismissal in breach of contract regardless of age, but an injunction to restrain such dismissal would be unusual. Either the courts or employment tribunal have jurisdiction but the tribunal cannot award more than £25,000.

Unfair dismissal

After one year's continuous employment (reduced from two years in June 1999) an employee has a right not to be unfairly dismissed. The employer must have a valid statutory reason for dismissal and have acted reasonably in treating that reason as justifying dismissal taking into account all the circumstances, including size and administrative resources – Employment Rights Act 1996, s 94:

- there are some automatically unfair reasons but valid reasons for dismissal generally relate to the employee's conduct, capability, redundancy or breach of an enactment;
- dismissal may be fair where it relates to the capability of the employee for performing work of the kind he is employed to do assessed by reference to skill, aptitude, health or any other physical or mental quality:
  - dismissal may be fair on grounds of incapacity, e.g. due to prolonged sickness (provided this does not amount to disability discrimination) but full medical information should be obtained
  - procedures must be followed before a dismissal for incompetence or sickness (it should be ascertained if there are reasons for this, both at work or outside work and monitoring is essential)

> Dismissal may only be justified on grounds of incompetence or ill-health if proper procedures have been followed.

Remedies are provided by the employment tribunal (formerly the industrial tribunal) and an unfairly dismissed employee can request re-employment or compensation. Compensation has been limited to £11,300 for a compensatory award based on loss with a basic award (dependent on length of service up to 20 years and £210 per week as a multiplier) being payable (maximum of £6,300):

- re-employment is seldom sought, but if ordered and not complied with a further sum could be awarded of up to £5,460 (this can be doubled if the dismissal was for discriminatory reasons);
- the 1999 Act now increases the maximum compensation to £50,000;
- a person who has reached normal retiring age (see below) where this is the same for both men and women or, if none, 65 years cannot bring a claim:
    - there are exceptions e.g. where dismissal relates to health and safety reasons, refusal of a shop worker to work on a Sunday or enforcement of a relevant statutory right
    - compensation for an employee dismissed before normal retiring age may take into account that employment should have continued beyond that age

Redundancy

A redundancy occurs where there is a closure of the business or in the place where the employee works, or a cessation or diminution in the need for employees to carry out work of a particular kind. Employees who are made redundant are entitled to a redundancy payment based on the number of years' service with a maximum payment (presently £6,300) – Employment Rights Act 1996, s 135:

- employees are excluded from redundancy payments on attaining normal retiring age if there is one (see below) or 65 years (for both men and women), whichever is the earlier;
- an employer can avoid a redundancy payment if he offers suitable alternative employment to the redundant employee (i.e. employment on the same or very similar terms and conditions without any significant loss of status – the new job should not require the employee to have more than a reasonable travelling distance);
- unfair selection for redundancy may amount to unfair dismissal:
    - selection of older workers has been held to be an improper criterion and unfair
    - employers may seek to dismiss older staff on the basis that they are more expensive to employ or it is preferable to keep a younger person in a job

- care should be taken when volunteering for redundancy (e.g. for early retirement) because this could be interpreted as termination by agreement and not dismissal.

> Long years of experience is no longer a reason for retaining a job.

27.2 RETIREMENT

Normal retiring age

This may be stipulated in the contract of employment or implied, and represents the age at which this class of employee can reasonably expect to be made to retire unless there is some special reason to apply a different age. If employees retire at a variety of ages there may be no normal retiring age and the maximum age will become 65:

- the age stipulated in the contract may be varied where employees are regularly retired at some other age – the policy operated in practice or the employee's 'reasonable expectation' may apply;
- it is the employee's expectation at the date of dismissal rather than the date of recruitment which determines the retirement age.

> 'Normal retiring age' is not necessarily the same as 'pensionable age'.

Directorships

A director is not automatically disqualified by reason of age or mental incapacity, but those over 70 who wish to be appointed or continue to act as a director of a public company or its subsidiary have to be specially approved. A registered company may impose disqualification in its Articles of Association, and the terms of employment for an executive director may also provide for retirement.

Directors may be removed if they are not carrying out their duties properly:

- this can be carried out by shareholders in general meeting (whatever the Articles or any contracts say) without prejudice to the rights of the director to obtain compensation, but it is possible in a small company to make oneself irremovable by careful drafting of the Articles;
- companies may include in their Articles grounds for removal based on becoming a patient under the Mental Health Act 1983.

Pensions

For rights to pensions see Chapter 28 at para.28.2.

27.3 SELF-EMPLOYMENT

Self-employment may continue to any age and there may be tax incentives to retain a business (or a share in a business). Consider tax efficient schemes for handing on the business:

- for capital gains tax advantages on retirement see para. 28.3;
- for inheritance tax advantages in respect of business assets see para. 28.3.

Partnership

Partnership involves contracts between the partners and with persons dealing with them. In the absence of specific provision in the partnership agreement, there is no age limit to being a partner and subsequent mental incapacity does not cause immediate dissolution:

- mental incapacity is a ground for asking the court to decree a dissolution – see Partnership Act 1890, s 35;
- if a partner is mentally incapable when purportedly entering a partnership he may still be bound if the other partner did not know of this;
- a person who allows himself to be represented as partner of an incapacitated individual could be liable to third parties – see Partnership Act 1890, s 14(1).

> Partnership is the relationship which subsists between persons carrying on business with a view of profit – Partnership Act 1890, s 1.

Voluntary work

Those who engage in voluntary work must take care not to become personally involved in any contracts that are entered into. The normal law of negligence will apply as regards any injury caused to any person or damage caused to property during the course of such work.

Committee member

Before becoming a committee member of an unincorporated society, club or association it is important to consider the rules or other constitution of the organisation and its financial state. The annual accounts should be examined. Committee members are jointly and severally liable for any liabilities incurred although they may usually seek indemnity from the assets of the organisation.

It is becoming increasingly desirable to form a limited liability company, usually incorporated by guarantee without a share capital, especially where there are employees or substantial contracts or risks may be involved:

- committee members are then technically directors of the company;
- the directors can still be personally responsible if the company has traded whilst insolvent or they have acted imprudently or beyond the powers of the company;
- insurance against directors' liability should be arranged by the company.

Club trustees

Club trustees should seek to limit their liability under any contracts to the amount of the club assets from time to time under their control, or exclude the right of any creditor to claim against them personally for any shortfall:

- merely describing themselves as trustees does not limit liability;
- trustees may also wish to obtain an indemnity from the individual club members or at least the members of the club management committee.

Charity trustees

Those who are charity trustees, whether in the capacity of ordinary trustees, committee members or directors, assume further responsibilities. Full particulars are available from the Charity Commissioners.

Chapter 28

Financial

28.1 INVESTMENT ADVICE

Reference should be made to the following chapters and also the books listed in Appendix 7:

- Chapter 11 for the Practice Rules relating to investment business;
- Chapter 12 at para. 12.5 for rules relating to the giving of financial advice;
- Chapter 14 at para. 14.3 for support in relation to financial services;
- Chapters 9 and 10 where the client is incapable of dealing with financial affairs.

> *Your taxes and savings: A guide for older people* is published annually by Age Concern and could be handed to clients.

28.2 PENSIONS

Most elderly clients will be at the stage where they are drawing (or entitled to draw) such pensions as they have, but do not overlook the tax advantages of making further pension contributions when permitted and the potential growth in a pension or pension fund if the pension is deferred. There are tax incentives for individuals to provide for their own pensions:

- income tax relief is given on contributions at the individual's highest rate;
- pension funds are exempt from income tax and capital gains tax;
- part of the pension can be taken as a tax-free lump sum.

State retirement pension

It is no longer necessary to have virtually retired from work before drawing the state pension. A taxable pension is paid on attaining state pensionable age (65 for men; 60 for women) but the claimant must have an adequate NI contributions record and an inadequate record means a reduced pension or none at all:

- Category A is claimed on the claimant's own contributions;
- Category B is claimed on the spouse's (or former spouse's) record.

The state pension age is to be equalised at 65 years for both men and women,

PART 3: SECTION E Employment, Money and the Home

but this is to be phased in over 10 years from 2010 so will not affect anyone aged 50 or over in 1999.

Those living abroad should contact DSS Benefits Agency Overseas Directorate (address in Appendix 5).

> RM1 *Retirement*; NP46 *A guide to retirement pensions*; PM8 *Making the most of your personal pension.*
>
> For claims and payment relating to benefits see Chapter 18, para. 18.2.
>
> Age Concern Fact Sheet 19 *Your state pension and carrying on working* and Fact Sheet 20 *NI contributions and qualifying for a pension.*

Amount

There are three components and the amount is affected by several factors but not by earnings:

- the basic pension:
    - a weekly age addition is paid on reaching 80 years
    - if pension is deferred it increases but only to age 70 (men) and 65 (women)
    - additions may be paid for dependants (e.g. a spouse) unless they receive some other benefits or have earnings above certain limits
- additional pension based on contributions after April 1978 (SERPS);
- graduated pension based on contributions between April 1961 and 1975.

Over 80s pension

Those aged 80 or over can claim a pension even if they have not paid NI contributions, but there is a residence qualification.

> Leaflet NI184 *Over 80s pension.*

Widow's and widower's benefits

A widow aged over 60 may get basic pension based upon her late husband's contributions and also a tax-free widow's payment if he was not drawing a pension. A widow or widower may get an enhanced pension (up to the maximum pension of a single person) based upon the contributions of the couple.

> Leaflet NP45 *A guide to widow's benefits.*

Separation and divorce

It may be possible to rely upon a spouse or ex-spouse's contributions record:

- a separated wife can claim the married woman's retirement pension on the husband's record but only from the date that he draws his pension;
- following divorce either spouse may, on reaching pensionable age, use the spouse's record during the marriage (or from the start of working life to the divorce) to get a better pension than on their own record.

> Leaflet NI95 *National Insurance for divorced women.*

Occupational pensions

These are arranged by employers (e.g. company pension schemes) and may be *contributory* or *non-contributory*. A separate trust fund is set up and employees receive a booklet setting out the terms but in general:

- benefits normally include:
    - a pension at a specified age
    - a death benefit for those who die before retirement
    - a widow's (or widower's) pension
- there are Inland Revenue restrictions on:
    - the maximum pension (two-thirds of final salary)
    - the amount of the lump sum (one-and-a-half times salary)
    - the size of any continuing pension following death

Types of scheme

The available types of scheme include:

- *final salary* where pension is a proportion of salary for the last year (or average of last few years) and is based on years worked times a set fraction (e.g. 30/60ths). The pension may be contracted into or out of SERPS;
- *average earnings* where pension is based upon average earnings over the period of participation with a set calculation being applied for the pension;
- *flat rate pension* which is based on the number of years employed;
- *money purchase* pension which depends upon the size of the employee's contribution to an investment fund and the growth in that fund. Such pension may be contracted into SERPS.

Additional voluntary contributions (AVCs)

These are a way of saving for retirement through the pension scheme. Full tax relief is available on additional contributions (subject to limits) and freestanding AVCs can also be made to independent pension plans.

> There is now more flexibility including early retirement or withdrawal, pre-served rights after two years in a scheme and transfer to another company scheme or to a personal pension.

Personal pensions

Self-employed people and employees may contribute to personal pensions:

- for employees this may be instead of SERPS or an occupational scheme;
- there are revenue restrictions on contributions, retirement age and benefits;
- policies may be with-profit, unit-linked, deposit or non-profit;
- on retirement it may be worthwhile taking the maximum permitted lump sum and investing this in other ways.

Section 226 pension policies were available solely for the self-employed until July 1988 and those then in existence may continue but the revenue restrictions were slightly different from the new personal pensions.

> An employee may switch from an employer's scheme to a personal pension but many have been encouraged to do so when this was not beneficial.

28.3 TAXATION

Income tax

Allowances for elderly people

There are some allowances and reliefs in addition to those normally available:

- higher *personal allowances* are available at 65 and at 75 years;
- married couples living together used to be able to claim a *married couple's allowance* but this was restricted to the lower rate of tax from 1994/95 and has now been withdrawn entirely;
- a widow may claim the *widow's bereavement allowance* in the year of her husband's death and the following year;
- a blind person's allowance may be available and any unused part may be transferred to the spouse;
- relief becomes available on rent (subject to a limit) from rooms in the home – see IR87: *Rooms to let*.

> Note the impact of self-assessment on the elderly client.

Planning

Simple steps may reduce the annual tax bill for a married couple or assist with cash flow:

- obtain and complete a Tax Claim Form R40 if in doubt at the end of the year or when the overpayment reaches £50:
  - IR112: *How to claim a repayment of income tax*
  - IR111: *How to claim a repayment of tax on bank and building society interest*
- ensure that any Notice of Coding for PAYE on pension income is correct: *taxed income relief* should be given if appropriate to secure the lower rate of tax on investment income:
  - IR34: *Income tax – pay as you earn*
- reduce or increase income if 'caught in the margin' – higher allowances reduce proportionately if income is more than a certain sum and this means that a high effective rate of tax is paid until the allowance is lost;
- re-arrange investments so that income is received gross (without deduction of tax) where a repayment claim would otherwise be necessary – non-taxpayers can apply to receive gross interest on bank/building society accounts (form R85):
  - IR110: *Can you stop paying tax on your bank or building society interest?*
- transfer investments between spouses to equalise income so that both gain the benefit of their personal allowances and the reduced rate band, any higher rate liability is minimised and neither party is caught in the margin as regards higher allowances.

> Ensure that all eligible allowances have been claimed.

Information

Keep an updated supply of the following free Inland Revenue leaflets and offer them to clients:

IR80:   *A guide for married couples*
IR81:   *A guide for pensioners*
IR82:   *A guide for husbands on low incomes*
IR90:   *A guide to tax allowances and reliefs*
IR91:   *A guide for widows and widowers*
IR121: *Income tax and pensioners*
IR127: *Are you paying too much tax on your savings?*

> Age Concern Fact Sheet 15 *Income tax and older people.*

PART 3: SECTION E Employment, Money and the Home

Capital gains tax (CGT)

The gain in the value of an asset during the taxpayer's ownership is taxed on disposal by way of a sale or gift (transfers between spouses are not treated as a disposal):

- the expenses of acquiring, improving and disposing of the asset are deducted from the net sale proceeds or value to ascertain the gain:
  - certain assets are exempt, e.g. an owner-occupied dwelling-house
  - there is presently rebasing to March 1982 which means that only gains or losses since that date are taken into account
  - there is a taper relief (formerly indexation allowance) whereby the effect of inflation is taken into account to reduce the actual gain (this may not increase or create a loss)
- retirement relief is available on disposals of business assets for those who retire after reaching a certain age (or earlier due to ill health). This is being phased out and replaced by a taper relief on business assets;
- the net gains (after losses) of the taxpayer in the tax year are taxed at the taxpayer's highest rates of income tax for the year (top-slicing) but an annual exemption reduces or eliminates the taxable gain;
- independent taxation applies so each spouse has the benefit of the annual exemption although the losses of one spouse cannot be set against the gains of the other;
- CGT is payable on 1 December following the tax year of the disposal.

Information

The following leaflets are available from the tax office:
 CGT14: *An introduction to capital gains tax*
 CGT15: *Capital gains tax: A guide for married couples*
 CGT4: *Capital gains tax - Owner-occupied house*
 CGT6: *Capital gains tax - Retirement disposal of a business*
 CGT13: *The indexation allowance for quoted shares*
 CGT 16: *Capital gains tax - indexation allowance*

Planning

The following strategies may be adopted to reduce potential CGT bills (the first two being for married couples):

- ensure that realisations that produce gains are by the partner with the lower rate of tax;
- ensure that an asset is in joint names before disposal where one party's annual exemption or lower rates of tax would not otherwise be used up;

- dispose of assets that do not create a gain when cash is needed;
- realise losses prior to 5 April when a net taxable gain would arise;
- avoid making disposals that would produce a large gain shortly before death (all assets are re-valued on death but CGT is not then charged);
- ensure that wills and investments are neutral for CGT purposes.

> Many older people contemplate moving abroad on retirement and the implications of a change of residence or domicile upon capital taxation in this country should be first considered.

Inheritance tax (IHT)

The capital value of all net assets held at death above a threshold (£231,000 in 1999/2000) is taxed at a fixed rate (40 per cent):

- this includes lifetime gifts unless exempted – see Chapter 30 at para. 30.2;
- the capital value of trusts may be aggregated;
- certain types of asset are exempt or valued on a beneficial basis (e.g. business assets and agricultural property).

Information

The following leaflets are available from the tax office:
IHT1: *Inheritance tax*
IHT3: *An introduction to inheritance tax*

Planning

Married couples may reduce potential IHT bills by ensuring that:

- they utilise the tax-free threshold on first death by leaving up to this sum to children and the balance to the survivor (but do make sure that the survivor will be adequately provided for) or creating a nil-rate-band discretionary trust;
- a joint tenancy in the matrimonial home is severed with each spouse by will leaving his or her share as tenant in common to the children.

Other strategies include:

- making regular gifts within the annual exemptions;
- making large gifts sooner rather than later.

Trusts for disabled beneficiaries

There are special dispensations in respect of CGT and IHT for certain trusts for the benefit of disabled beneficiaries:

PART 3: SECTION E Employment, Money and the Home

- Taxation of Chargeable Gains Act 1992, s 3 and Sched. 1, para. 1;
- Inheritance Tax Act 1984, ss 3A(1) and (3) and 89.

On this topic generally refer to Chapter 32 and to the author's published material referred to therein.

Chapter 29

Housing

People do not automatically wish to move home on reaching retirement age, but it is a good time to take stock and think ahead. The starting point is whether the client is happy and comfortable in the present home and able to cope physically and financially. Then consider how long this situation is likely to continue: putting things off may reduce the options, but a move can seldom be reversed. It may be wise to anticipate future needs by applying to go on a council or housing association waiting list. When contemplating a moving ask:

- will it be possible to cope in the new home:
  - physically (access, stairs, convenience of layout, garden, security)?
  - financially (outgoings, heating, maintenance and repairs)?
  - is there room for all the personal possessions that are to be kept?
- is the location suitable:
  - are adequate facilities available (shops, transport, library, post office)?
  - are necessary services available (doctor, dentist, social services assistance)?
  - is there enough to do in the area?
  - is it a safe and congenial environment at all times of the day and night?
- is it a wise move:
  - will there be a loss of friends and acquaintances who cannot be replaced?
  - can the costs of the move be coped with (removal, estate agent, solicitor)?
  - if moving nearer to relatives, is there a risk that they will need to move?
  - is it too hasty (e.g. after a bereavement)?
  - in the case of a couple, would the survivor wish to remain in the new home?

Older clients may be 'tenants' or 'landlords' so this chapter is relevant in two respects:
1. the basis of their own accommodation;
2. the situation if they allow another person to occupy or share their home.

29.1 OWNER-OCCUPATION

Always examine the implications as regards means-tested benefits when the sale or purchase of a dwelling for personal occupation is being considered:

- the value of the owner's only or main home may not be taken into account;
- this may also be the case if the dwelling is occupied by a partner or by a relative who is incapacitated or has attained 60 years.

Sole ownership

The owner may leave the property by will or it will pass to the next of kin on an intestacy. If the owner becomes mentally incapable and it is desired to dispose of the property or an interest therein, in the absence of a registered enduring power of attorney there is no alternative but to apply to the Court of Protection for the appointment of a receiver – see generally Chapter 10.

Joint ownership

In many instances a home will be owned jointly by spouses or an unmarried couple.

Beneficial interests

Where a property is purchased or otherwise put in joint names it is important for there to be a precise statement as to how the beneficial interests are held, namely as joint tenants or tenants in common:

- under a joint tenancy the survivor will automatically inherit on death but a share as tenant in common may be left by will or pass under an intestacy;
- the statement may be in the transfer deed (a copy should be retained) or a separate deed of trust, but the statement to the Land Registry as to whether the survivor can give a valid receipt for capital money is not sufficient.

Upon a divorce (or judicial separation) the court may make a property adjustment between the spouses, but in the case of unmarried joint owners there are no similar procedures and the courts can only give effect to the intention and contribution of the parties.

> If the joint owners are *tenants in common* the precise shares should be agreed and recorded.

Equitable interests

An equitable interest in a house or flat belonging to another may arise where a person makes a financial contribution towards the cost of buying the property or pays for or contributes towards the cost of extending or improving the property.

This is likely to be of particular significance where the incentive for the financial input was the prospect of living in or sharing the home and that expectation is not fulfilled. Ideally the expectations of the parties should be clarified and confirmed in a legal document before the arrangement is entered into, though this seldom happens within families.

Contributions

An elderly client who decides to contribute a substantial sum towards the cost of purchase or improvement of a home with the intention of residing there with a member of the family will need to decide whether to do so by way of *shared ownership*, *loan* or *gift*. Factors to take into account, depending on circumstances, are:

- a gift has potential inheritance tax advantages, but the money may not be recoverable if needed (if a gift is to be made the sooner this is done the better as regards both inheritance tax and means-testing);
- a loan or joint ownership creates vulnerability to means-testing if residential care is needed at a later date;
- a loan or joint ownership protects the elderly individual in the event that the relationship breaks down but may leave the other joint owner vulnerable to having to move house;
- testamentary provision may need to be changed to compensate for a gift.

If the money is spent on building a bungalow in the grounds or providing a self-contained flat it may be best for this to be conveyed into the name of the elderly client rather than establish joint ownership in the entire property, but in that event you must ensure that the deeds are properly split and independent legal advice would be indicated.

> See the Law Society *Guidance on Gifts of Property* reproduced in Part Four.

Disputes

Disputes relating to joint ownership of property may now be resolved under the *Trusts of Land and Appointment of Trustees Act 1996*:

- this overcomes various difficulties that arose under section 30 of the Law of Property Act 1925, although previous case law may still be relevant;
- anyone who is a trustee or who has an interest in trust property may make an application to the court which is then required to have regard to the following matters in determining the application:
    - the intention of the person or persons who created the trust
    - the purpose for which the property subject to the trust is held
    - the welfare of any minor who occupies or might reasonably be expected to occupy any property subject to the trust as his home; and
    - the interests of any secured creditor of any beneficiary

Incapacity of joint owner

A trustee may not generally delegate his powers so must act personally in any sale or other transaction. There are exceptions to this:

- under section 25 of the Trustee Act 1925 a trustee can delegate his functions by a power of attorney:
  - this can only be for limited periods and is subject to specific safeguards
  - such a power cannot be an enduring power (see Enduring Powers of Attorney Act 1985, s 2(8))
  - note the amendments the Trustee Delegation Act 1999, s 5
- under section 3(3) of the Enduring Powers of Attorney Act 1985 an attorney under an enduring power could exercise all or any of the functions vested in the donor as trustee:
  - this was a last minute amendment to enable a jointly-owned matrimonial home to be dealt with but its wider implications were not then appreciated
  - it is repealed with effect from 1 March 2000 (or 2001 for subsisting enduring powers) by the Trustee Delegation Act 1999, but note the transitional provisions in s 4
- under the Trustee Delegation Act 1999 (following Law Commission recommendations to resolve the problem) an attorney can exercise a trustee function of the donor if it relates to land, or the capital proceeds or income from land, in which the donor had a beneficial interest:
  - this applies to both general and enduring powers of attorney whenever made
  - an 'appropriate statement' made by the attorney at the time of a sale or within three months thereafter confirming that the donor had a beneficial interest in the property shall be conclusive evidence (s 2) – see Land Registry practice leaflet 32
  - it will not be sufficient if the joint owner (e.g. spouse) is the sole attorney because a capital receipt by trustees needs two signatures (see s 7)
  - in all other cases the provisions of the 1925 Act, s 25 (as amended) must be complied with

Unless advantage is taken of the 1999 Act, if a joint legal owner of freehold property becomes incapable by reason of mental disorder of exercising his functions as a trustee, a new trustee may have to be appointed in his place before the legal estate can be dealt with – see Chapter 15 at para. 15.1.

Mortgages

There is no age bar to taking on a loan secured by a mortgage or charge and many lending institutions have become willing to receive applications from those at or near retirement:

- an interest-only mortgage may be available from a bank or building society under a special scheme for those who need capital – see para. 29.6 *Income from the home* for various schemes;
- mortgage interest tax relief is no longer available;
- for a cautionary tale where a mother charged her home as security for her son's borrowing and the same solicitors acted for both parties, see *Clark Boyce v Mouat* [1993] 4 All ER 268, PC.

Possession proceedings

When monthly subscriptions under a mortgage fall into arrears the lender can apply to the local county court for a possession order which may be enforced by the bailiff under a warrant for possession:

- the district judge hearing the case may suspend any possession order if the full debt or the arrears will be cleared within a reasonable time, and this may be on payment of normal monthly subscriptions plus a regular sum off the arrears (e.g. by instalments over five years) although proof will be required of capacity to pay;
- a warrant for possession may also be suspended on similar terms or for a short period to allow for rehousing;
- if the borrower is attempting to sell the property the proceedings may be adjourned for a period to see what progress can be made or an order for possession may be made but suspended for a period to give the borrower a reasonable time to effect a sale.

> The extent of any discretionary relief may be influenced by whether there is an 'equity' in the property because the lender will not be at risk if the secured debt is far less than the value of the property.

Grants

Various grants are available from local authorities – see Chapter 20.

29.2 LONG RESIDENTIAL LEASES

Types

Many older clients own their homes under a long lease, in particular owners of flats, those who have a shared ownership lease and former council tenants who have exercised the right to buy a flat.

Legislation

After examining the terms of the lease and establishing for how long it is to run and the identity of the landlord, the following legislation may need to be considered:

- *Leasehold Reform Act 1967* – gives leaseholders of houses the right to buy the freehold (and in some cases the right to extend the lease);
- *Landlord and Tenant Act 1985* – regulates such matters as service charges;
- *Landlord and Tenant Act 1987* – contains the right of first refusal, the right to apply for a manager to be appointed, the right to apply for the terms of a lease to be varied and related matters;
- *Landlord and Tenant Act 1954, Part I* (as amended by the *Local Government and Housing Act 1989*) – a long leaseholder may be entitled to a statutory tenancy at the end of the lease;
- *Leasehold Reform, Housing and Urban Development Act 1993* – a group of flat owners may be entitled to acquire the freehold, an individual flat owner may purchase a new lease, a group of flat owners can have an audit of the management of the block carried out;
- *Housing Act 1996* – introduces various safeguards including the right to appoint a surveyor to advise on service charges.

A leasehold valuation tribunal now has jurisdiction over certain matters instead of the county court.

Shared ownership

Some councils and housing associations (now known as '*registered social landlords*') operate shared ownership schemes under which homes are part purchased and part rented on a long lease. There may be an option to purchase a greater share at a later date.

These schemes enable those with limited capital to enjoy the benefits of home ownership without borrowing, and investing available capital in this way may have advantages in regard to means-tested benefits but increasing rents could become a problem.

Other arrangements for sheltered housing include:

- flexible tenure – option to buy, lease or share ownership;
- leasehold schemes for the elderly (LSE) – buy at 70 per cent of the normal price and receive 70 per cent of value when you sell;
- loan-stock schemes – 'buy' housing by making an interest-free loan to the trust or charity;

- buying at a discount – usually involves selling at a discount;
- a 'life-share' in the property (or a part thereof), usually organised through a finance company with the price depending on age, sex, marital status and the property value – there will be no return on death, but an annuity (or capital sum) may be paid to those who cease to reside in the property.

Ensure that the scheme is suitable for the client and that there are no restrictions which would inhibit resale. Most schemes are marketed for first-time buyers but some are designed for retired people.

> Housing Corporation leaflet: *Shared ownership.*
> Age Concern publication: *A buyer's guide to sheltered housing.*

Enfranchisement

Houses

Where a lease of a house (not a flat) has been granted for at least 21 years and the rateable value was below a certain level, the lessee may be able to purchase the reversion or extend the lease – see Leasehold Reform Act 1967.

Flats

Leaseholders of flats now have the opportunity to collectively purchase their freehold but must pay at least the market value thereof. To qualify at least two-thirds of the flats must be let on long leases at low rents. Advantages of enfranchisement include control of management and the power to grant new leases to overcome loss of value as the terms near expiry:

- see the Leasehold Reform, Housing and Urban Development Act 1993, Part I, Chapter I (as amended by the Housing Act 1996);
- some tenants who do not qualify are given the right to buy a 90-year lease from the end of their current lease – see the 1993 Act, Part I, Chapter II.

29.3 TENANCIES

Tenants will be concerned about security of tenure, the amount of rent payable and repairing obligations.

Legislation

- Rent Act 1977
- Housing Acts 1985, 1988, 1996
- Local Government and Housing Act 1989
- Leasehold Reform, Housing and Urban Development Act 1993

Types

The statutory rights of a tenant depend upon whether the landlord is a public sector landlord or an ordinary private landlord, and the date when the tenancy commenced. Government policy during recent years has included:

- privatising public sector housing – any tenant of a local authority whose home is transferred to the private sector ceases to be a secure tenant and becomes an assured tenant (with a preserved right to buy);
- a shift from full protection of the tenant to dependence on market forces – this is not retrospective so tenants do not lose any existing rights and should seek to retain earlier protected tenancies wherever possible.

Public sector landlords

Tenants (and some licensees) of a local authority, an urban development corporation, a housing action trust and certain other public sector landlords will usually have the status of a *secure tenancy*:

- this provides long-term security of tenure and statutory rights such as:
    - the right to take in a lodger
    - the right to exchange tenancies
    - the right to buy
- see Parts II and IV of the Housing Act 1985 (as amended).

Registered social landlords

A tenancy granted by a registered social landlord (housing association) after 14 January 1989 will usually be an *assured tenancy* (it can no longer be a secure tenancy):

- the tenants' position is also governed by the Tenant's Guarantee and other guidance produced by the Housing Corporation and Housing for Wales;
- see Part I of the Housing Act 1988.

Private sector landlords

Private sector tenancies granted before 15 January 1989 are generally *protected tenancies* governed by the Rent Act 1977:

- the tenant usually has long-term security of tenure unless:
    - the tenancy is a *protected shorthold tenancy* or excluded for one of the reasons set out in Part I of the 1977 Act
    - it is one of the cases where the landlord has a mandatory claim for possession
- the tenancy becomes a *statutory tenancy* after contractual termination;
- the tenant or landlord can refer the rent to a rent officer for a fair rent to be

registered for the dwelling;
- on the death of the tenant a surviving spouse or other family member may succeed to the tenancy.

A new tenancy granted by a private landlord after 14 January 1989 will be either an *assured tenancy* or an *assured shorthold tenancy* under Part I of the Housing Act 1988 (thus phasing out tenancies protected by the Rent Act 1977):

- it may be excluded if within one of the exceptional cases set out in Schedule 1 to the Act or the landlord is a resident landlord;
- it will be an *assured shorthold tenancy*:
  - pre 28 February 1997 if for an initial fixed term of not less than six months and the landlord serves a notice in a prescribed form before the tenancy starts
  - post 27 February 1997 unless the appropriate notice is duly served (registered social landlords are usually required to do this but there is no incentive for private landlords to do so)
- a tenant who holds an assured tenancy and agrees with the landlord to take a tenancy of a different dwelling will become an assured tenant under the new tenancy.

> You no longer need to serve a notice or create an initial fixed term for an *assured shorthold tenancy* – Housing Act 1996.

Where a long lease of a flat (or possibly a house) comes to an end by effluxion of time:

- until 14 January 1999 the tenant would be entitled to a statutory tenancy under the Rent Act 1977 – see Landlord and Tenant Act 1954, Part I;
- after 14 January 1999 the occupying tenant will be entitled to an assured tenancy – see Local Government and Housing Act 1989.

Right to buy

A tenant of a public sector landlord will usually have a statutory right to buy.

Statutory provisions

Under the Housing Act 1985, Part V (as amended) most secure tenants have the right to buy at a discount after two years and a council tenant whose dwelling is transferred to a registered social landlord or other private sector landlord has a 'preserved right to buy':

- certain types of property or tenancy may be excluded (sheltered housing and properties particularly suitable for older people and most housing provided by charitable bodies);

- the tenant may nominate certain family co-residents to jointly purchase:
  - the discount depends upon the duration of the tenancy and can be up to 60 per cent (or more for flats)
  - part is repayable upon a sale within three years of purchase but not on death

Under the Housing Act 1996 a tenant of a registered social landlord has the right to acquire the dwelling at a discount if:

- he is a tenant under an assured tenancy (other than an assured shorthold tenancy) or a secure tenancy;
- the dwelling was provided with public money, has remained in the social rented sector and was built or acquired after 1 April 1997.

> Mortgages may be obtained to cover the cost, possibly on an interest-only basis. If family members offer to underwrite the mortgage and repair costs consider whether they will be able to do so and what will happen if they do not.

Whether to buy

It is not always advantageous for an elderly tenant to purchase. When comparing outgoings take into account that:

- the owner will be responsible for additional, uncertain outgoings (property insurance and repairing obligations);
- any service charges continue even though rent ceases;
- housing benefit will no longer be available (mortgage interest is covered by income support within limits);
- MIRAS tax relief is presently available though limited.

Transitional provisions

Consider the following matters under the Housing Acts 1988 and 1996:

- a council tenant might be asked to consider a transfer to a private landlord (usually a registered social landlord) and the local authority and Department of the Environment may be considering a large-scale voluntary transfer:
  - tenants must be consulted and are entitled to be balloted and vote on the proposed transfer
  - following transfer, such a tenant ceases to be a secure tenant and becomes an assured tenant
  - if the transfer is to a registered social landlord the tenants will be granted a tenancy agreement which contains those terms recommended by the Housing Corporation in the 'Tenant's Guarantee'

- tenants in the privately rented sector may be protected tenants under the Rent Act 1977 or assured tenants under the Housing Act 1988 but some only have an assured shorthold tenancy which provides virtually no security of tenure:
  - an assured tenancy may be converted into a new assured shorthold tenancy where the tenant signs a prescribed form stating that the new tenancy is to be a shorthold but there will rarely be any advantage to the tenant in doing so
  - where a fixed term assured tenancy comes to an end the parties may negotiate a new periodic or fixed term tenancy but if they are unable to agree terms then the tenancy continues to be assured notwithstanding the switch over to assured shorthold tenancies

Allocations

From April 1997 there is a new framework for the allocation of tenancies by a local authority or registered social landlord. An authority is deemed to allocate where it grants a secure tenancy of one of its own dwellings or where a tenancy is granted by a registered social landlord under a nomination agreement with an authority. Authorities have some discretion in the manner in which they allocate but this is now subject to a greater degree of central government control:

- only a 'qualifying person' is eligible and reasonable preference must be given to a number of categories;
- authorities must have regard to guidance published by the Secretary of State and decisions on housing allocation can be challenged by judicial review;
- those on a waiting list are entitled to information on the progress of their application and there is a right to a review of a decision not to be included.

Housing Act 1996, Part VI.
Code of Guidance *Allocation of Housing Accommodation, Homelessness.*

Security of tenure

A court order is generally needed before a home is repossessed (see below for sanctions). The court can control the date for possession and when it has a discretion may make a *suspended order* which means that the landlord cannot issue a warrant of execution as long as the terms of suspension are complied with. In cases of rent arrears this may be on terms that the tenant pays the current rent and also repays the arrears by specified instalments.

Secure tenancies

A tenant (including most licensees) who has a tenancy of a separate dwelling is secure provided the landlord is a local authority or some other public sector landlord and the tenant resides in the dwelling as his only or principal home. (Problems arise where a tenant is absent from the dwelling for a significant period but absence for medical treatment should not affect rights as a secure tenant.) A landlord cannot bring a secure tenancy to an end without a court order and before starting proceedings must serve a *Notice of intended possession proceedings* in a prescribed form under section 83 of the Housing Act 1985:

- the landlord must justify a possession order on one of 16 statutory grounds (including non-payment of rent and breach of the tenancy):
    - the ground must be stated and should be examined with care
    - security may be affected by an assignment or sub-letting
- no mandatory grounds exist for secure tenancies (possession is discretionary) and for certain grounds the court must be satisfied that:
    - it is reasonable to make the order; and/or
    - suitable alternative accommodation will be available
- the court may stay or suspend any possession order made.

> Housing Act 1985, Sched. 2 sets out grounds for obtaining possession.

Protected tenancies

The tenant has a fair degree of security of tenure. If possession is sought the landlord must first serve a valid *Notice to quit* to terminate the contractual tenancy. A *statutory tenancy* then comes into existence which (if the tenant still lives there) can only be brought to an end by a court order for possession:

- a possession order may be obtained on certain grounds which are:
    - mandatory, e.g. tenancy originally created on a specific basis
    - discretionary, e.g. breach of terms of tenancy (usually rent arrears)
- a court may not make an order for possession on one of the discretionary grounds unless satisfied that:
    - suitable alternative accommodation is available (the court then has a discretion as to whether the new tenancy will be statutory or assured), or
    - it is reasonable to do so
- the court may stay or suspend a possession order based on discretionary grounds.

> See Rent Act 1977, s 98 and Sched. 15 for the grounds for obtaining possession.

Chapter 29 HOUSING

Assured tenancies

The tenant has a lesser degree of security of tenure. If possession is sought the landlord first serves a *Notice of intention to seek possession* specifying the grounds:

- a court can dispense with this where it is just and equitable to do so (unless the landlord is seeking to recover possession for defined rent arrears);
- the available grounds are similar to those for protected tenancies save that:
  - two months' rent arrears is a mandatory ground
  - rent arrears and persistent failure to pay rent are discretionary grounds
  - intention to demolish or reconstruct the property is a mandatory ground
- before ordering possession on one of the discretionary grounds the court must be satisfied that it is reasonable to make the order;
- the court may stay or suspend a possession order based on discretionary grounds

See Housing Act 1988, Scheds. 1 and 2 for grounds.

Shorthold tenancies

There are three types of shorthold tenancy and the landlord is entitled to obtain possession under each of them but still requires a court order:

- under the 'old' assured shorthold giving not less than two months notice to the tenant that possession is required is a mandatory ground for possession;
- under the 'new' (post 27 February 1997) assured shorthold giving such notice in writing remains a mandatory ground but an order for possession cannot take effect within six months of the date of the original tenancy;
- the original protected shorthold provisions were more complex.

Unlawful eviction

At least four weeks' notice is required to terminate a contractual tenancy and residential occupiers (tenants and most licensees – see para. 29.4) are protected against unlawful eviction and harassment:

- a court order is required before any eviction (except where the landlord or owner is resident in the premises and accommodation is shared);
- it is an offence for the landlord or any other person to harass a residential occupier with intent to cause that occupier to give up occupation (in whole or part) or any right or remedy:
  - the act must be likely to interfere with the peace and comfort of the occupier

329

PART 3: SECTION E Employment, Money and the Home

- but may include withholding or withdrawing services
- it is sufficient if a landlord 'knows or has reasonable cause to believe' that the conduct is likely to cause the occupier to leave
- local housing authorities must employ an officer to investigate and prosecute cases of harassment

• an action may also be brought for unlawful eviction in addition to any breach of contract or trespass – Housing Act 1988, ss 27 and 28:
  - an injunction may be granted to prevent the harassment or eviction
  - there may be general, specific, aggravated and exemplary damages
  - an award of damages may include the difference between the value of the property with and without a tenant

> Protection from Eviction Act 1977 (as amended by Housing Act 1988).

Succession

Secure tenancy

The spouse of a deceased tenant, or another member of the family (including a cohabitee of the other sex), may be entitled to succeed to a tenancy where certain conditions are met:

• this must have been that person's principal or only home at the tenant's death;
• a non-spouse must have lived there (or in other public sector accommodation) with the tenant for at least 12 months immediately prior to the death;
• there can be only one succession.

> Housing Act 1985, s 113.

Protected (or statutory) tenancy

A spouse or cohabitee, or member of the family living with the tenant for at least two years immediately prior to death, may succeed to the tenancy:

• originally two successions were permitted (spouse and member of family) but this has been restricted since 1988;
• a second succession is likely to convert the tenancy from protected to assured.

> Rent Act 1977, s 2 and Sched. 1 (amended by Housing Act 1988).

Assured tenancy

Succession rights to an assured tenancy are far more limited than those which apply to secure and protected/statutory tenancies:

- only a spouse or cohabitee may have succession rights (another family member cannot succeed to the assured tenancy);
- a second succession is not permitted (e.g. to a second spouse);
- a joint tenant will automatically succeed to the tenancy but there can then be no further transmission.

Terms of secure tenancies

The landlord must set out the terms in clear and simple language:

- there are restrictions on the manner in which the terms can be changed in the absence of agreement:
  - the landlord can serve a notice of variation and consultation is then required
  - rent/service charges are variable on one month's notice (without consultation) and depend on housing policy rather than rent control
- improvements may only be carried out with the landlord's written consent which must not be unreasonably refused;
- the landlord must keep the structure, exterior, services and installations in repair and working order (regardless of the terms of any agreement):
  - tenants who comply with certain procedural requirements may recover the cost of any qualifying repairs from their landlord
  - see Secure Tenancies (Right to Repair Scheme) Regulations 1985

Assignment and sub-letting

The tenant has no general right to assign the tenancy and if it is assigned it ceases to be secure unless:

- the assignment is made in a financial settlement following divorce;
- the assignment was to a person with rights of succession (see above) although this need not be the person next entitled (this option could be used to ensure that a child rather than a spouse succeeds);
- there has been a mutual exchange with landlord's consent (Housing Act 1985, s 92).

Sub-letting requires written agreement of the landlord and failure to obtain agreement could be a ground for possession. This does not apply to a lodger who is merely a licensee (see para. 29.4).

Rent control

Rents payable under residential tenancies are less regulated than they used to be:

- protected tenancies are being phased out;
- market rents are being introduced for assured tenancies;
- local authorities have discretion in fixing the level of rents.

Secure tenancies

Local authorities may make such reasonable charges as they determine. They are under a duty to review rents periodically and may alter rents generally in their locality or alter particular rents as circumstances allow:

- they have complete discretion as to the setting of rents but are influenced by government decisions as to the payment of subsidy to housing revenue accounts and must not act irrationally or in bad faith or take irrelevant factors into account;
- before varying the rent of a secure tenancy they must secure the agreement of the tenant or serve a notice of variation.

A secure tenant of a registered social landlord has a 'housing association tenancy in accordance with the Rent Act 1977'. Either party can refer a proposed rent increase to a rent officer using the fair rent machinery of the 1977 Act and there is a further appeal to a Rent Assessment Committee.

Protected tenancies

A system of 'fair rents' applies (notwithstanding any agreement to the contrary):

- rent officers fix the rent with an appeal to a Rent Assessment Committee;
- the rent ignores the scarcity value of accommodation so is artificially low.

Assured tenancies

There is no control over the amount of the rent which is at market levels. Rent rises can be examined by the Rent Assessment Committee if they are above market levels but not if in accordance with a rent review system in the original agreement. Any housing benefit (see Chapter 19) will be restricted to a market rent.

> Older people may be eligible for means-tested housing benefit to meet part or all of their rent.

Assured shorthold tenancies

A tenant under an assured shorthold tenancy has the right to refer the rent to a

Rent Assessment Committee:

- under an 'old' shorthold this right applied only during the first fixed term where the tenant contended that the rent was artificially high;
- under a 'new' shorthold the right applies only during the first six months.

Service charges

Tenants of flats (including those of housing associations but not local authorities) have some statutory protection in respect of service charges:

- only reasonably incurred amounts are payable for services;
- any work must be carried out to a reasonable standard;
- a written summary of relevant costs may be required and accounts inspected.

Landlord and Tenant Act 1985 (and Housing Act 1985 for houses disposed of by the public sector).

Repairs and maintenance

A landlord is usually under an obligation to repair and maintain a dwelling which is let as such.

Contract

The landlord will have a contractual liability under the terms of the actual agreement and if not there will be implied terms:

- for tenancies granted after 23 October 1961 for a term of less than seven years, the landlord is responsible for repairs to the structure and exterior of the dwelling and the installations for gas, water and electricity;
- on a tenancy of a flat granted after 14 January 1989, these repairing obligations extend to common parts of a building or other parts which are controlled by a landlord;
- the courts may imply similar obligations into older tenancy agreements in order to give business efficacy to them.

Landlord and Tenant Act 1985, ss 11–16.

A landlord is not liable to compensate the tenant for loss or injury arising from disrepair unless he had notice of the defects (including those which are latent).

Tort

Liability may also arise in tort:

- the landlord is under an obligation in tort to anyone who suffers loss as a result of his failure to carry out repairs and maintenance to the premises;
- this liability applies where the landlord knew or ought to have known of the defects;
- failure to maintain reasonable arrangements for inspection when such defects would have come to light may result in liability.

> Defective Premises Act 1972.

Remedies

A number of different remedies are available to enforce repairing obligations:

- a tenant who suffers injury or loss because of the landlord's failure to carry out repairs may seek compensation by a damages claim in the county court and/or apply for an order of specific performance;
- the tenant may request the local authority to issue a *repairs notice* whereby the owner is required to carry out works in accordance with those specified in the notice and failure to do so is an offence (a right of appeal lies to the county court):
  - local authorities are required to take certain steps where a dwelling is unfit for human habitation (as defined in the Housing Act 1985, s 604) and a request for an inspection can be made to the local Environmental Health Department (a direction can be obtained from a JP that the authority must inspect)
  - the local authority has power to carry out the works itself and charge the person responsible
  - the authority may now defer taking immediate action by serving a *deferred action notice* under the Housing Act 1996 (this avoids having to pay a repairs grant to the landlord but must be reviewed every two years)

> Housing Act 1985, Part VI.

- local authority environmental health officers have general powers in relation to a property which is a statutory nuisance (as defined in the Environmental Protection Act 1990, s 79):
  - the officer may serve a notice on the person responsible for the nuisance (e.g. the landlord or owner occupier) requiring the nuisance to be abated (appeal is to the magistrates' court within 21 days)
  - if a notice is not complied with proceedings may be taken in the magistrates' court which can order the person responsible to abate the nuisance, impose a daily fine for as long as the nuisance continues and order compensation to anyone who has suffered injury or loss (such as a tenant)

- an aggrieved person, such as a council tenant, may serve a notice on the local authority and take proceedings in the magistrates' court for a nuisance order

> Environmental Protection Act 1990.

29.4 LICENCES

Licence or tenancy?

The distinction between a licensee (e.g. a lodger) and a tenant is based upon control over the property and the degree of integration into the household (see *Street* v *Mountford* [1985] 2 All ER 289). An occupier who under the contractual arrangements has exclusive possession of a dwelling for a term and pays rent will usually be a tenant regardless of how he is described in the agreement, but there will merely be a licence where there is a genuine service occupancy or there is no intention to create a legal relationship. In many situations the individual merely has a licence to occupy which may be:

- an exclusive licence where the accommodation is self-contained;
- a licence to occupy a private room where other essential facilities are shared;
- a licence to share a room and other facilities.

> The distinction between a tenancy and a licence is important because only a tenant has security of tenure and protection as to repair and maintenance.

Informal licence

When the individual is living with relatives or friends there will usually be merely an informal (or bare) licence to occupy a room or facilities, but:

- if regular payments are made there may be a contract and reasonable notice must then be given to terminate – this could include a contribution to household expenses;
- a 'licence coupled with an interest' may arise where the occupier contributes towards the cost of buying, altering or improving the home – someone who contributes towards the costs of acquiring a property will usually acquire an equitable interest in it.

If a court is asked to exclude an informal licensee from a property it may postpone any order for a reasonable period to allow alternative arrangements to be made, but if care services are being provided as well as the accommodation it may be difficult to ensure that these continue.

Contractual licence

When money is paid for the facility there will be a contract (e.g. a lodger or a room in a hotel or care home) and the terms should be complied with:

- the terms may have been published in advance (e.g. in an advertisement, letter or brochure) and will then be incorporated into the contract but some of the terms may need to be implied;
- a contract may arise even if the resident lacks mental capacity but any agreement should then be in simple terms and carefully explained to the resident (the contract will usually be entered into by the person managing his or her financial affairs, e.g. an attorney or receiver).

Only a contractual licence provides any security of tenure but even this may be terminated on reasonable notice.

29.5 HOMELESS PERSONS

If an individual is actually and unintentionally homeless the local housing authority with whom that individual has a local connection may be obliged to provide or arrange housing or accommodation but may charge for the accommodation that is provided:

- the authority may meet its duty in many ways and need not provide a council house – lodgings or Part III accommodation may suffice (see Chapter 22 at para. 22.2);
- a person in inadequate accommodation may possibly be deemed homeless and an elderly person will be homeless if, *inter alia*, it is no longer reasonable for him to continue to occupy the existing home;
- a person who is homeless and has a priority need is entitled to permanent accommodation (this includes being vulnerable as a result of old age and an applicant who has such a person living with him, or who might reasonably be expected to live with him, will have a priority need);
- if classed as *intentionally homeless* the person may only be housed temporarily but an act or omission should not be seen as deliberate if the applicant was 'incapable of managing his or her affairs because of old age'.

> Housing Act 1985, Part III and Housing and Planning Act 1986;
> *Homelessness – Code of Guidance for Local Authorities* (Third Edition) issued jointly by DoE, DoH and Welsh Office.

29.6 SPECIAL ARRANGEMENTS

Shared occupation

Either financial circumstances or care needs may dictate that an elderly individual shares a home. This could involve:

- moving into and sharing the home of a relative or friend;
- a relative or friend moving into the elderly individual's home;
- taking a lodger;
- employing a resident housekeeper or carer;
- living in the home of a paid carer.

Family arrangements

Arrangements within the family sometimes prove unsatisfactory to one side or the other so ensure that all relevant factors are considered before it is too late. Experience shows that there may be an unacceptable loss of independence and privacy by the elderly individual or of freedom and privacy for the sharing family. The parties should consider:

- how well they get on now and are likely to get on living in close proximity (taking into account the effect upon any marriage and the existence of children in the household);
- whether the home is physically suitable and provides sufficient privacy;
- the effect on state benefits and community care provision;
- the implications of a decline in health and the need to provide care.

The arrangement should be the choice of the elderly person rather than the family (though it may be suggested by the family) and hasty decisions should not be made following bereavement or any period of ill-health. Whilst a legal document cannot provide for personal relationships, a clear enforceable agreement is desirable if either party commits capital to the arrangement (see 'Joint ownership' under para. 29.1). It may be necessary to unscramble the financial arrangements in order to separate the personal relationships and it is better to discuss this before the parties are committed than after things have gone wrong – when the parties may not be talking anyway!

> If the arrangement does not work it is seldom possible for the previous situation to be restored.

Frequently shared occupation arises without any planning where a son or (more often) a daughter remains at home with parent(s). Often the parties rely on assumptions and fail to discuss their hopes and wishes, so you can perform a valuable service by encouraging them to do so in an open way in your presence. Mother may actually desire to move into a residential care home but not wish to leave daughter alone, whilst daughter may yearn for freedom yet not wish to desert mother by putting her in a home.

Commercial arrangements

Where the arrangement is with a stranger for payment it is essential to identify the understandings and assumptions on which it is based, from both points of view, and these should be recorded in writing. A formal document is not necessary and may be off-putting, but an exchange of letters is a minimum requirement. Factors to consider include:

- taking a lodger may produce an additional income and, if the relationship works out, provide company:
    - the notice period and weekly or other payment to be made should be confirmed in advance and also what it covers (e.g. meals, laundry, telephone)
    - the effect of this income on state benefits should not be overlooked (similar principles apply if the client proposes to become a boarder)
    - there are Inland Revenue concession for income from letting one room
- if a housekeeper or carer is to live-in this will be an employment situation, but living in the home of a carer may be classed as being a boarder:
    - in either event income tax, NI contributions and the effect on state benefits should be taken into account by both parties

Gifts of the home

Advising the client

Elderly people often contemplate transferring their home to their children even though they still intend to live there, and it may be a son or daughter who puts the idea into their heads and seeks to give instructions. The following matters should be considered before acting in such a transaction:

- who is the client? If it is the elderly person you must act in that person's best interests but if it is a son or daughter then the elderly person should be advised (and expected) to take independent legal advice;
- how well do you know the client? It may be necessary to spend some time with the client and talk about wider issues before giving relevant advice;
- has another solicitor previously acted for the client? If so, should you speak to that solicitor in case there are factors to be taken into account which are not apparent (and which the son or daughter seeks to avoid)?

> Who you are acting for? Identify the client. The elderly client is entitled to independent advice before deciding to transfer the home.

- does the client have the mental capacity to make the gift? A high level of competence is required for a gift of the elderly person's main asset (see Chapter 2 for tests of competence);
- why is the gift to be made and will the purpose be achieved? Do not overlook the community care funding rules and remember that the local authority may seek to disregard or set aside the gift;
- has there been undue influence, i.e. emotional pressure to make the gift? The client should be interviewed alone so that his or her wishes may be confirmed in the absence of those who have something to gain;
- what other financial resources does the client have? There is no point in giving the home away to avoid care funding if there are other assets which would be utilised in any event;
- does the client understand the effect of the gift (that it passes ownership) and recognise and accept the vulnerability that the gift creates?
- does the client actually want and intend to make a gift or expect that some rights or benefits will be reserved?

> Ensure that the client is capable of making the decision and fully informed. Act in the best interests of the client and recognise conflicts of interest.

Reasons for making a transfer

There may be compelling reasons for the transfer by an elderly person of the home, or an interest in that home, to another member of the family or even an outsider. The legal title may not have been vested in the appropriate person in the first place, or the title may not reflect the true beneficial interests in the home. This may be the case where another person has:

- made substantial financial contributions to the home;
- provided care services over many years in reliance upon assurances that the home would become theirs after the death of the present owner.

In these (and other) situations it may be desirable to give effect to the transfer whilst the elderly owner can still make the decision so as to establish legal rights which all would wish to be acknowledged. This is of particular importance where the other person is already a joint occupier of the home.

Of most concern are gifts made to preserve the home for the next generation with vague assurances as to future occupation and provision of care if needed. Before the client decides to make the gift the factors to be taken into account should be explained on a 'for and against' (benefits versus risks) basis. Assuming that the elderly client is a widow or widower making the gift to a son or daughter these are indicated below.

Potential benefits

- assumed certainty as to the future ownership of the property;
- saving of probate fees and costs (and inheritance tax?) following death;
- avoidance of means-tested contributions towards the cost of residential or nursing home care or other services provided by the local authority;
- the release of income from maintaining the property (if the donee will meet these expenses).

Potential risks

- disputes within the family as to the validity of the gift;
- the value of the home may still be taken into account under means-testing rules (see Chapter 19 at para. 19.4):
  - the parent could be deprived of funding even though lacking personal resources and without any redress against the son or daughter
  - note that the home would not in any event be taken into account if still occupied by a partner or by a relative who is incapacitated or has attained 60 years
- effect on capital gains tax liabilities:
  - the owner-occupier exemption may be available for the gift but lost thereafter
  - there will be no revaluation of the home on the parent's death
- effect on inheritance tax liabilities:
  - there could be a liability if the son or daughter dies before the parent
  - there will be no saving whilst the parent continues to live in the home because of the 'reservation of benefit' rules (different schemes exist to mitigate this but the Revenue have challenged some of these)
- the son or daughter may:
  - fail to support the parent or seek to release the value in the home by moving the parent prematurely into residential care
  - die without making any suitable provision for the parent
  - become ill, divorced or insolvent and unable to support the parent
- the home may be put at risk or lost on:
  - the divorce of the son or daughter
  - its use by the son or daughter as security for a loan
  - the insolvency or bankruptcy of the son or daughter

> Present a 'balance sheet' to the client of the potential pitfalls and benefits, but be careful about offering a 'risk assessment'.

Some of these pitfalls could be avoided by creating a tenancy or settlement of the home to secure the parent's right to continued occupation, but this would not assist the usually desired benefit of avoiding a means-tested contribution towards the cost of care provision and may advertise the arrangement. Nevertheless the significance of proper legal documentation should not be overlooked in inter-generational arrangements.

Conclusion

Whether a gift of the home will have the desired result may be a matter for speculation rather than legal advice. Faced with limited funding, increased demands for residential care and more people who were home owners presenting themselves as having no assets, local authorities are likely to develop the expertise to challenge gifts of the home (see Chapter 19 at para. 19.4). The Government is considering giving local authorities increased powers to prevent and detect evasion of care charges whilst proposing new personal funding initiatives.

Income from the home

Your client may have considerable capital tied up in the home yet be short of income and unwilling to move. It is tempting to live off this capital especially if there is no one to inherit, and there are schemes that make this possible. Eligibility depends upon age, value and tenure of the home and whether there are other secured loans. The main providers of these schemes in the United Kingdom have launched an initiative known as SHIP (*Safe Home Income Plans*) and conform to a standard code of conduct. The basic schemes are as follows but many variations exist.

Home income plans (mortgage annuity schemes)

Capital raised by an interest-only loan secured on the property is used to buy an annuity which in turn covers the interest and leaves a surplus:

- tax relief may be available on the interest (presently up to £30,000 but being phased out so check this) and part of the annuity is tax-free;
- the size of the loan is restricted by the value of the property and the amount of the annuity depends upon age, sex and whether it is for a couple;
- a small cash sum can be taken rather than part of the annuity but the reduction in the remaining annuity should be noted.

Home reversion schemes

The home, or a share in it, is sold to a reversions company to release a capital sum which may then (if desired) be invested in an annuity:

- occupation of the house and liability for repairs is not affected but a small rent may be payable;
- much depends upon the valuation of the home, but the client only receives a proportion (according to age and life expectancy) in cash and the reversions company will enjoy the benefit of any inflationary increase.

Roll-up loans

An interest-only loan is taken and the interest is (in whole or part) added to the capital sum borrowed:

- interest on interest can escalate at an alarming rate and property values may fall (repayments may be required if the loan reaches a specified percentage of the value of the property);
- only small interest-only loans are normally acceptable, e.g. for the cost of surgery or a visit to a relative far away.

Investment bond income schemes

A secured loan is arranged and the money put into an investment bond from which regular withdrawals are made on the basis of assumed growth, thereby covering the interest on the loan and providing surplus income. Note that:

- many of these schemes have run into difficulties so FIMBRA and LAUTRO have declared them unsuitable for elderly people;
- those who have lost money on these schemes may have a claim against the firm that sold them and any advisers involved on the basis that there was inadequate warning of the risks.

General

The client should be told not to contemplate any of these schemes without taking your advice. If you act in part only of the scheme (e.g. the mortgage) you may be under a duty to enquire why the loan is required and you should not then feel inhibited about advising the client against the whole scheme. You may be liable if you do not do so and the scheme later goes wrong. Even if a scheme appears sound initially beware of a change in circumstances and take into account:

- the effect of the extra income or released capital on any means-tested benefit or contribution to the cost of community care or residential services;
- the implications of an increase in interest rates – this could reduce net in-

come from the scheme (go for a fixed-rate loan);

- the implications of inflation – the client may again run short of money and options are then reduced, and if the scheme depends on property values they may go down as well as up;
- the risk (with some schemes) that the capital may be exhausted too soon, and the considerable loss of capital if the client dies soon after taking out the scheme;
- the effect on other occupiers or dependants, and whether the scheme restricts the scope for moving in the future – the client may need to sell the home and move into sheltered housing or residential care.

> Any scheme is lucrative business for those selling it, so get several quotes and consider other options, e.g. grants, additional state benefits, reinvestment of savings, arrangements in the family.

The danger with either the investment bond income scheme or the roll-up loan scheme is that a point may be reached where the homeowners have to sell their homes during their lifetime in order to repay the mortgage.

Ask if the client really does need some available capital or extra income, and then whether it would be better to achieve this (and more) by moving to a smaller and perhaps more suitable home. Is there a member of the family who could provide assistance on more satisfactory terms? If the client does proceed, consider whether changes should be made to any existing will.

> *Using your home as capital* published by Age Concern England;
> Age Concern Fact Sheet 12: *Raising income or capital from your home.*

29.7 SPECIAL HOUSING

Sheltered housing

Housing restricted to and designed so as to be suitable for elderly people may be available and this is an option for those who want to live an independent life in their own home without all the responsibilities of home ownership. Most are apartments or bungalows, physical disabilities may be catered for and alarm systems are often installed. Schemes include:

- purpose-built or converted housing without a warden;
- warden-assisted or warden-controlled housing;
- supportive housing where residents have their own room but use communal facilities and perhaps receive a cooked daily meal (e.g. Abbeyfield homes);

- housing with care (meals and care services are usually provided).

Tenure

The basis on which the property is held may be:

- freehold or long lease at a premium with service-charge rent (enfranchisement may be possible for leasehold sheltered housing schemes);
- tenancy at a rent – those in the public sector will be secure tenancies, but private sector rent control may not apply if 'attendance' is included;
- shared ownership or shared equity arrangement;
- licensee only.

Matters to consider

It will be necessary to consider the detailed terms of the lease or other contractual arrangement in the usual way, and in particular:

- any restrictions on occupation, resale or assignment (problems have arisen over disposal of some homes following death):
  - whether younger carers are able to live in
  - the effect of the owner or spouse becoming a Court of Protection patient
  - whether the surviving spouse can remain there (especially if younger)
- what services are provided (what are the warden's duties?) and the service charge liability (is there a 'sinking fund' for property repairs?);
- the identity of the managers of the scheme:
  - are they members of the Association of Retirement Housing Managers?
  - is there a residents association and is it recognised by the managers?

Registered house builders selling sheltered housing must comply with the *NHBC Sheltered Housing Code of Practice* (1990):

- the Purchaser's Information Pack (PIP) contains useful information;
- legally binding management agreements are required to a specified standard.

A buyer's guide to sheltered housing, Age Concern.

Age Concern Fact Sheets: 2 *Sheltered housing for sale*; 8 *Rented accommodation for older people*; 9 *Rented accommodation for older people in Greater London*; 24 *Housing schemes for older people where a capital sum is involved*.

Chapter 29 HOUSING

Homes for disabled people

The Housing Act 1988 changed the role of local authorities to that of strategic planner rather than direct provider. A duty is imposed on local housing authorities to consider the housing needs of their district and they must have particular regard for the special needs of chronically sick and disabled people – see Chronically Sick and Disabled Persons Act 1970; Housing Act 1985.

Adaptations

If a local authority is satisfied that the home of a disabled person fails to meet special needs arising from the disability, it is under a statutory duty to ensure that those needs are met by arranging for any necessary adaptations to be made. This applies whether the home is owner-occupied or tenanted. The authority has power in its discretion to recover the cost, but cannot make the provision dependent upon prior payment though the disabled person will first wish to know the personal cost implications. The availability of grants (see Chapter 20) now makes it unlikely that additional help from this source will be available, though it should be considered by those who cannot cope with the means-testing implications of a grant – 1970 Act, s 2.

VAT

Building alterations are subject to value added tax, but many alterations for people with disabilities are zero-rated – see VAT leaflet 701/7/86, *Aids for handicapped persons*.

Park homes

This is a new name for mobile home parks. A fully-equipped caravan (or chalet designed so as to be classed as a caravan) may be purchased but a serviced site must be rented and security of tenure may be limited. The *Mobile Homes Act 1983* requires the park owner to enter into a legal agreement with each individual occupier dealing with rights and responsibilities regarding:

- increases in the site fees and any other charges that are made;
- the basis on which a caravan on a site may be sold or transferred (including commission charged and approval of the new occupier by the park owner);
- termination of the agreement.

Mobile homes - A guide to residents (DoE Housing Booklet No.30);
Buying a mobile home and mobile homes - An occupier's guide published by Shelter (address in Appendix 5);
The National Association of Park Home Residents (address in Appendix 5).

345

29.8 SPECIAL SITUATIONS

Consider whether you should encourage the elderly client to simplify his or her affairs rather than take on additional complications. Much will depend upon age and state of health and the involvement of other members of the family.

Second homes and timeshare

Increased leisure may make either of these options attractive for those with the energy and sufficient capital, but it is necessary to take into account:

- all the expenses involved, which will continue until disposal even if continuing use cannot be made of the property;
- the problems of management or maintenance, especially if other people must be relied upon due to a decline in mental capacity;
- the difficulty of disposing of the property (especially time-share);
- the capital tied up in the investment (which may still be included in any means-testing for benefits or services);
- the capital gains tax implications.

Foreign properties

Advise the client before moving abroad to check on:

- pension and state benefits entitlement with the DSS;
- availability of health care and reciprocal arrangements;
- the income and capital taxes situation;
- the effect of a change of residence or domicile (e.g. on testamentary provision).

When purchasing a home (or second home) abroad you must encourage the client to consult a qualified lawyer practising in the country concerned (unless you have the expertise in your own firm), because if you fail to do so you could be liable if anything goes wrong. Each country has its own conveyancing procedures and the inheritance laws of the particular country may apply with surprising consequences.

> The Law Society maintains a register of UK practitioners with recognised expertise in foreign jurisdictions.

SECTION F
Inheritance and Death

This final Section within the *Overview of the Law* considers gifts and testamentary provision that may be made in contemplation of death and the arrangements that need to be made immediately following a death.

Of particular relevance to the older client and members of the family will be:

- *gifts* – when and how these may be made, the tax implications and the incentives to make gifts to charity;
- *testamentary dispositions* – in the context of providing for cohabitees, dependants and others with whom there is a personal relationship, including statutory wills which may be made where the testator is mentally incapable;
- *inheritance provision* – the circumstances in which a will may be overridden by the court;
- *family arrangements* – the manner in which testamentary provision may be varied or overridden by the beneficiaries;
- *providing for beneficiaries who are infirm or disabled* – which may be of particular concern to an older client;
- *arrangements on death* – including registration of death, the role of the coroner, funeral arrangements and disposal of the body.

Chapter 30

Gifts

A significant lifetime gift should be considered only when the money or asset involved is surplus to the client's present or anticipated requirements. Reference should be made to:

- Chapter 19 at paras. 19.3 and 19.4 for the potential implications of means-testing for local authority services;
- Chapter 29 at para. 29.6 for gifts of the home.

Concerns may arise when a gift is proposed as to the mental capacity of the client and whether there has been undue influence, especially if the donee is pressing for the transaction to be completed. Always ensure that you see the client alone, except in the case of married couples where a joint approach to giving may be desired (though not always in the case of second marriages). If you are not satisfied that your client has capacity to make the gift or feel that undue influence has been brought to bear you should decline to act.

> Refer to Chapter 3 for further guidance on taking instructions.
> Guidance is available from the Ethics Division of the Law Society (address in Appendix 5).

30.1 VALIDITY

Capacity of donor

A gift is only valid if the donor had capacity to make the gift at the time it was made – see *Re Beaney* [1978] 2 All ER 595 and generally Chapter 2:

- for the power of an attorney to make a gift see Chapter 9 and Enduring Powers of Attorney Act 1985, ss 3(4), (5) and 8(2)(e);
- for the approach of the Court of Protection see Chapter 10.

Perfected gift

Make sure that the title to any gifted property is legally vested in the donee because a promise to make a gift is not enforceable and 'there is no equity to perfect an imperfect gift'. The donor must have done everything that he needs to do to effect the transfer but it does not matter that something remains to be done by a third party:

- chattels and cash are transferable by delivery if there is an intention to give – a signed letter is useful to confirm the intention and fix the date;
- a gift by cheque is not completed until the cheque is cleared;
- waiver of a debt must be by deed (unless there is consideration);
- a transfer of land or an interest in land must be by deed;
- in the case of securities it may be sufficient to hand over the certificates together with a signed transfer.

> For tax purposes it is wise to encourage clients to record any large gifts, especially those relying on a tax exemption.

Donationes mortis causa

This exception to the rule that a gift must be perfected applies where:

- the donor makes a gift in contemplation (not necessarily expectation) of death; and
- delivers (or causes delivery of) the subject-matter of the gift to the donee or transfers the means of getting at that subject matter; and
- the gift was only to take effect on the donor's death.

Thus if a man on his deathbed tells his housekeeper that he wishes her to have some specific shares on his death and hands her the key to a safe containing the certificates, this may constitute a valid gift of those shares (provided there is proof of this). It now seems that even freehold property is capable of being the subject matter of such a gift – *Sen* v *Headley* [1991] 2 All ER 636, CA.

30.2 TAXATION

Capital gains tax (CGT)

A gift may be a chargeable transfer for CGT – see Chapter 28 at para. 28.3 for the general rules. In regard to gifts the following should be considered:

Hold-over relief

This means that the donee takes the gifted property at the donor's acquisition value and there is no charge to tax on the transfer. Relief is not available if the transferee is not resident or ordinarily resident in UK and the relief has been abolished except:

- as between husband and wife (where there is no tax);
- on disposal of a business asset (including agricultural property);
- on transfers immediately chargeable to inheritance tax (e.g. transfers into and out of a discretionary trusts).

Timing and payment

If a client intends to make a gift of an asset with a fluctuating value it is advantageous to do so when it has a relatively low value; appreciating assets should be given sooner rather than later.

There is a right to pay by instalments over 10 years for certain types of gift.

Inheritance tax (IHT)

The value of lifetime gifts may be included in the estate of the donor – see Chapter 28 at para. 28.3 for general rules. Note that:

- a gift to a spouse is exempt from IHT (so is any inheritance by the spouse) but there are restrictions where one is not UK domiciled. Other things being equal, a gift to a spouse is useful to equalise the estates;
- there are specific exemptions:
  - small gifts (now £250 per donee) and normal, regular giving out of income
  - an annual exemption per donor (£3,000, or more on donee's marriage)
  - payments for the maintenance of certain members of the family
- certain gifts with no benefit reserved will be *potentially exempt transfers* (PETs) and become exempt if the donor survives seven years with tapering relief between three and seven years, but gifts must equal or exceed the nil-rate band at the time the gift is made. They must be made to:
  - an individual or
  - a settlement with an interest in possession or
  - an accumulation and maintenance settlement or
  - a trust for a disabled person (see para. 28.3)

The primary liability for IHT on gifts falls on the donee but there is a secondary liability on the estate of the deceased donor. Any gift which is neither exempt nor a PET is a *chargeable transfer* liable to IHT immediately at the relevant rates (these have been half normal rates) taking into account all chargeable transfers during the past seven years, but if the donor dies within seven years the full rate is charged (subject to tapering relief).

> A gift between spouses does not usually involve any capital taxes liability and may be beneficial in tax planning.

Practical points:

- do not overlook the reservation of benefit rule in regard to PETs:
  - there are several schemes for giving a share in the home
  - be alert to current Revenue practice
- consider arranging life assurance for the donee on the donor's life to cover the potential tax liability on a gift;
- take care with timing (the nil-rate band benefits earlier gifts first):
  - if the client wishes to make a PET as well as create a discretionary trust, do the latter first to ensure that the annual exemption is used (and for other technical reasons)
- establish the value of gifted property at the time (get a formal valuation).

30.3 CHARITIES

Tax incentives

Giving to charities is tax effective if made in certain ways (check these at the time because they are subject to change).

Deeds of covenant

Where these can exceed three years and there is no benefit in return:

- the charity recovers basic rate tax on the gross amount (to the extent that the donor pays such tax) and the donor gets higher rate tax relief on this amount;
- deposit covenants can be arranged for lump sums.

Gift Aid

A single outright cash gift by an individual of at least £400 free of any conditions or benefits accruing to the donor or his family is regarded as having been paid net of tax:

- the charity can recover the tax deducted whilst the donor can obtain higher rate tax relief on the grossed-up amount (see the Revenue guidance notes);
- schemes allow a single gift to be divided among a number of charities.

Reliefs from capital taxes

There is no CGT on the transfer of an asset to a charity either by way of gift or at an under-value and the charity will not pay CGT on a subsequent disposal:

- it may be better to transfer an asset and let it be sold by the charity than to sell it first and give the proceeds after paying CGT;

- check first whether it is more tax effective to sell the asset, pay the CGT and make a Gift Aid donation.

A gift or legacy to a charity is exempt from IHT and the amount is not aggregated with the donor's estate. A beneficiary under a will may (possibly) be able to get the best of all worlds by:

- entering into a deed of variation in favour of a charity thereby avoiding IHT on the amount transferred;
- also claiming income tax relief under Gift Aid on the same amount.

Gifts to charities receive extremely beneficial tax treatment.

Bargain-bounty rule

A charity is in danger of losing its charitable status (and tax relief on gifts) if it repeatedly or on a substantial scale contracts in return for gifts to provide that which it would normally provide as part of its charitable activities:

- a charity cannot legally bind itself to provide a service for a particular person in return for a gift;
- nevertheless, having received a gift, the charity may have regard to the wishes of the donor (especially if more gifts may be made).

Chapter 31

Testamentary Dispositions

31.1 SUCCESSION

An individual may state by will who is to inherit any savings or assets owned at death and appoint executors to administer the estate. The Court of Protection may make a *statutory will* for a person who lacks testamentary capacity. In the absence of a will intestacy rules specify who is entitled to inherit and the order of priority for administrators. Such outcome may be changed in three ways:

- any beneficiary may disclaim a legacy;
- beneficiaries may enter into a deed of family arrangement and in effect re-write a will or the effects of intestacy;
- the court has power to provide for dependants under the Inheritance (Provision for Family and Dependants) Act 1975.

Joint property

Any property or savings in joint names normally passes to the surviving joint owner(s) beneficially unless they are trustees, although land can be held in undivided shares (i.e. as tenants in common).

Nominations

Certain assets may be disposed of on death by a written nomination which may be statutory or non-statutory but will be of no effect if the nominee dies first:

- these may include industrial and provident society accounts;
- pension schemes may also include provision for nominations;
- those for National Savings Certificates and National Savings Bank accounts were discontinued in 1981 but any then in existence may still take effect.

Forfeiture

A person who causes the death of another is usually prevented from benefiting from the death of his victim, whether under a will, intestacy or gift:

- there is discretion in the case of manslaughter under the Forfeiture Act 1982;
- this could have implications in the case of a 'mercy killing' or suicide pact.

Chapter 31 TESTAMENTARY DISPOSITIONS

31.2 INTESTACY

Legislation

- Administration of Estates Act 1925
- Family Provision (Intestate Succession) Order 1993

Entitlement

Surviving spouse

On an intestacy a surviving spouse receives the following, but can make certain elections, including taking the matrimonial home at valuation as part of her share (or making up any shortfall):

- all personal chattels (as defined);
- a statutory legacy (with interest) which for deaths from 1 December 1993 is:
  - £125,000 when there is issue
  - £200,000 when there is no issue but there is a specified relative surviving
- when there is issue, a life interest in half the residue;
- when there is no issue but there is a specified relative surviving, half the residue absolutely;
- when there is no issue and there are no specified relatives surviving, the entire estate absolutely.

'*Specified relatives*' who may inherit apart from a spouse are a parent, brother or sister of the whole blood or the issue of such persons.

Children and grandchildren

Issue receive all that the surviving spouse does not receive, and this is on the *statutory trusts* which means equally between those who attain 18 years or marry before then, with children of a deceased child taking that child's share on the same basis.

Others

If there is no surviving spouse or issue the estate goes to a surviving parent or brothers and sisters of the whole blood on the statutory trusts, whom failing to remoter relatives (and ultimately to the Crown though *ex gratia* payments may then be made to persons whom the deceased would have been likely to benefit).

Only a spouse or blood relatives (or adopted persons) can benefit, and a co-habitee has no rights under an intestacy.

355

31.3 WILLS

Taking instructions

You should obtain all necessary information (especially if you are to be an executor) and this generally comprises:

- personal and family details including:
  - domicile
  - married status or whether any cohabitee (same or heterosexual relationship) and prospects or intentions
  - issues involving second marriages and any possible claimants on the estate
- the general nature and size of the estate including:
  - the extent of debts and liabilities (e.g. mortgages)
  - jointly owned assets
  - life assurance provision and continuing pensions (and any nominations)
  - any business interests or foreign property
- any interests in a trust or settlement (or power of appointment);
- any substantial gifts made or to be made during lifetime;
- the persons for whom the client wishes to (or should) provide;
  - any cohabitee or dependent person
  - any particular problem situations (e.g. a mentally incapacitated beneficiary)
- any relevant special wishes:
  - the importance to the client of tax planning
  - any beneficiary for whom provision is to be made in priority to all others
- any changes that may occur before death in any of the foregoing matters.

> Use a detailed in-house questionnaire or the Law Society's Instruction Sheet to cover preliminary preparation. It may be helpful to hand the client one or more of the explanatory leaflets referred to in Chapter 14 at para.14.4 and to ask the client to complete the Personal Assets Log.

Added value

Take the opportunity to consider whether the client also requires or needs:

- an enduring power of attorney – see Chapter 9;
- a living will – see Chapter 25 at para. 25.4;
- assistance with tax affairs or investment or tax planning advice.

Fees

Discuss the cost of the will and any supplemental services with the client at this stage and remember that fees may possibly be claimed under the Legal Aid 'Claim 10' scheme if the testator is:

- within the income and capital limits; and
- aged 70 or over, blind (or partially sighted), deaf (or hard of hearing), without speech, suffering from a mental disorder, or substantially and permanently handicapped by illness, injury or congenital deformity.

Testamentary capacity

When the will is made the testator must have testamentary capacity. This means that he must understand (see *Banks v Goodfellow* (1870) 5 QB 549):

- the nature of the act and its effects, i.e. that he is giving his property to persons of his choice on his death;
- the extent of that property; and
- the nature and extent of his obligations to relatives and others.

No disorder of the mind must bring about a disposal which would not otherwise have been made. Mere eccentricity or foolishness does not invalidate a will but fraud or undue influence may. See generally Chapter 2.

> There is a presumption in favour of a duly executed will if it appears rational.

Contents

A simple will may (and usually should) contain clauses dealing with:

- revocation of previous testamentary dispositions;
- appointment of executors (and guardians for any infant children);
- any specific legacies (of realty and of personalty) and pecuniary legacies;
- disposal of the residue of the estate;
- any wishes as to burial or cremation.

In less straightforward situations, especially where there are infant beneficiaries or continuing provision is intended, further clauses may need to deal with:

- the terms of any trust;
- any additional powers of the trustees;
- administrative provisions.

Precedents

Appendix 2 sets out wills dealing with two entirely different but common situations:

- a simple 'happy family' will;
- a will creating a trust to provide for an infirm sister (so far as may be required) with the estate passing to nephews and nieces after her death.

Execution

A will must be in writing and the testator must sign or make his mark:

- the testator's signature need not be at the end of the will provided it was intended to give effect to the will;
- a person may sign on behalf and by the direction of the testator in his presence (Wills Act 1837, s 9 substituted by Administration of Justice Act 1982, s 17):
- the signature (or mark) must be witnessed by, or acknowledged to, two people present at the same time who sign as witnesses:
  - an incomplete signature is only sufficient if the signatory is unable to finish for physical reasons and not because of a change of mind
- a testator who cannot read needs to have known the contents of the will before signing and the attestation clause must make this clear:
  - include 'with knowledge of the contents thereof' in the attestation clause where the testator is blind or partially sighted
  - this is also desirable where the testator's signature appears doubtful

Remember that any of these matters may need to be proved:

- witness the will when possible and keep an attendance note;
- if capacity is in doubt obtain a medical report after outlining the legal test to be applied and preferably arrange for the doctor to witness the will.

> You could be liable to disappointed beneficiaries if you accept instructions for a will but delay in its preparation or fail to ensure that the will is valid.

Revocation

A will may only be revoked by a testator, e.g. by a later will or physical destruction with intent to revoke:

- a will is revoked by subsequent marriage but not by supervening incapacity;
- the capacity required for revocation is the same as for execution of a will.

31.4 STATUTORY WILLS

The Court of Protection has jurisdiction to authorise the execution for a patient who is mentally incapable of doing so of a will making any provision which the patient could make if he were not mentally disordered – Mental Health Act 1983, s 96.

Jurisdiction

For the Court to have jurisdiction it must be satisfied that the person is:

- incapable, by reason of mental disorder, of managing and administering his property and affairs (i.e. a patient); and also
- incapable of making a valid will for himself.

Policy

'The court must seek to make the will which the actual patient, acting reasonably, would have made if notionally restored to full mental capacity, memory and foresight' (Sir Robert Megarry V-C in *Re D(J)* [1982] 2 All ER 37):

- the Court will consider the benefit of members of the patient's family and make provision for other persons or purposes for whom or which the patient might provide if he were not mentally disordered (*Re C (a patient)* [1991] 3 All ER 866);
- the Court has been prepared to exercise its powers to save tax.

Procedure

The procedure is not inexpensive so is generally only suitable for patients with significant funds or assets – see the Court of Protection Rules 1984:

- there are five categories of person entitled to apply for an order (r 17) – an attorney under a registered EPA is not included but may be authorised;
- a hearing is normally arranged with the Official Solicitor representing the patient (r 12) and certain persons being given notice (r 18);
- the test of testamentary capacity is different from that of capacity to manage or administer property and affairs so medical evidence in each respect is required;
- the formalities for signing and attesting the will are found in section 97 of the Mental Health Act 1983;
- the costs of all parties are generally ordered to be paid out of the estate.

> Form PN9, *Applications for the execution of statutory wills and codicils and for gifts settlements and other similar dealings* specifies the requirements.

PART 3: SECTION F Inheritance and Death

Practical points

The legal tests of capacity to manage and administer property and affairs, to make a will and to marry are all different. Thus:

- a person whose affairs are being dealt with by a receiver or an attorney under a registered EPA may still be able to make a will;
- a person may be able to enter into a valid marriage yet not make a will, and an application for a statutory will may then be appropriate.

31.5　INHERITANCE PROVISION

Certain persons may apply to the court for financial provision out of the estate of a deceased person:

- Inheritance (Provision for Family and Dependants) Act 1975.

Claimants

The following may apply for provision:

- a spouse of the deceased;
- a former spouse of the deceased who has not remarried, unless prevented by a court order made on the financial settlement following divorce;
- a child of the deceased, whether or not a dependant;
- any other person who:
  - was treated as a child of the family in relation to any marriage to which the deceased was a party
  - immediately before the death was being maintained by the deceased, either wholly or partly, otherwise than for full valuable consideration

Relevant matters

The application is made on the basis that the disposition of the deceased's estate effected by his will or the law relating to intestacy, or a combination of both, is not such as to make reasonable financial provision for the applicant. In deciding whether to make an order the court takes into account all the circumstances. When determining whether reasonable financial provision has been made the court must have regard to the following matters – s 3:

- the financial resources and financial needs which in the foreseeable future the applicant, any other applicant or any beneficiary of the estate has or is likely to have;
- any obligation and responsibilities which the deceased had towards any applicant or beneficiary;

- the size and nature of the net estate;
- any physical or mental disability of any applicant or beneficiary;
- any other matter, including the conduct of the applicant or any other person, which in the circumstances of the case the court may consider relevant;
- (*on an application by a spouse or former spouse*) the age of and contribution made by the applicant, and duration of the marriage – s 3(2);
- (*on an application by a child or person treated as a child of the deceased*) the manner in which the applicant was being (or might be expected to be) educated or trained and, if treated as a child, the extent to which the deceased had assumed responsibility for maintenance and whether any other person was liable;
- the standard of living enjoyed by the applicant during the lifetime of the deceased and the extent to which the deceased contributed to that standard.

> It is not clear when and to what extent the financial resources of the applicant include any means-tested state benefits or support that could be received.

Date for consideration

The facts as known to the court and the claimant's circumstances at the date of the hearing are relevant, rather than those at the date of the will or the death.

Objective test

The question is whether, in all the circumstances, the disposition of the deceased's estate makes reasonable financial provision for the applicant, not whether the deceased has acted reasonably in making no or only limited provision. Hence:

- the deceased's moral obligation, if any, may be a relevant factor, though again this must be balanced against all the other factors;
- the deceased's reasons and wishes comprise only part of the circumstances of the case and may be outweighed by other factors. A statement made by the deceased, whether or not in writing or signed, is admissible as evidence of any fact stated therein – Civil Evidence Act 1968, s 2.

Court's powers

The court may make an order in favour of the applicant for periodical payments, a lump sum, transfer of property or acquisition and transfer or settlement of property. It may also:

- treat a joint tenancy in any property as severed and the deceased's beneficial share as part of the net estate to such extent as appears just in all the circumstances;

- set aside dispositions made by the deceased within six years prior to the death with the intention of defeating an application for financial provision.

Procedure

Applications are made in the county court for the district in which the deceased resided at the date of death and there are criteria under the Courts and Legal Services Act 1990 for determining whether a case should be moved up to the High Court (Chancery Division or Family Division). Rules and Practice Directions set out the detailed procedure to be followed.

Time-limit

An application must be made within six months from the date of the Grant of Representation to the estate, unless the court in its discretion gives leave to extend time.

Tax implications

Where an order is made (including a consent order) the estate is treated for IHT purposes as if the deceased's property devolved subject to the provisions of the order – Inheritance Tax Act 1984, s 146:

- unlike variations (see below) there is no time-limit and an election is not required;
- if agreement is reached within two years this can be dealt with by a deed of variation rather than a consent order through the court.

31.6 FAMILY ARRANGEMENTS

It is not too late to change the provisions of a will or the outcome of intestacy after the death. An individual beneficiary may disclaim a benefit or the beneficiaries may agree to vary the distribution of the estate, and the testator can even provide for this by leaving the estate (or part of it) on a short discretionary trust.

Variations and disclaimers

Inheritance tax

If, within two years of death, any dispositions are varied or benefits disclaimed, such variation or disclaimer is not a transfer of value and tax is charged as if the variation had been made by the deceased or the disclaimed benefit had never been conferred – Inheritance Tax Act 1984, s 142:

- the variation or disclaimer:
  - must be in writing

- must not be made for any consideration in money or money's worth
- can be made even if the property involved has been distributed and the estate administered
- may result in a repayment of IHT or additional IHT having to be paid
- there are differences between a variation and a disclaimer:
  - with a variation the property can be given to anyone whereas a disclaimer is merely a refusal to accept the property and it passes to the next in line
  - receipt of a benefit prevents disclaimer but not a variation, and part-disclaimer may not be allowed (but one of two gifts could be disclaimed)
  - a variation will only be read back to the date of death if a written election is made within six months, whereas this is automatic for a disclaimer
  - a variation is not retrospective for income tax purposes, whereas in the case of a disclaimer the beneficiary is deemed never to have had an interest

Capital gains tax

Similar provisions exist whereby the variation or disclaimer need not be treated as a disposal for CGT – Taxation of Chargeable Gains Act 1992, s 62(6)–(10). A separate election is made for a variation, but none is needed for a disclaimer.

Practical planning

- Where a deceased spouse's estate passes entirely to the survivor a variation may enable the nil-rate band to be used, e.g. for the benefit of the children.
- The assets passing to the spouse and other beneficiaries may be redistributed so as to ensure that property with beneficial treatment (e.g. business and agricultural property) passes to the other beneficiaries.
- If a valuable property becomes worth very little within two years of death vary the will so that it passes to charity (the value at death is then exempt).

If a beneficiary dies within two years of the testator's death consider a variation (it can still be done) to achieve more advantageous overall IHT treatment – there are several possibilities.

Discretionary provision

Where flexibility is required, possibly for tax reasons, the testator may avoid the need for all beneficiaries to agree to a variation by giving a power of appointment to the executors or trustees and requiring them to exercise this within two years – see Inheritance Tax Act 1984, s 144:

- there should be a default trust at the end of the two-year period in case an appointment is not made;

- IHT is ultimately paid as if the will had provided for the outcome effected under the appointment:
  - if there is an initial discretionary trust, IHT will be charged on the basis thereof on application for a grant
  - distributions made outside the two-year period will be subject to the normal IHT exit charge
- there are no corresponding capital gains tax provisions.

Precatory gifts

Where a testator expresses a wish that property bequeathed by the will be transferred by the legatee to other persons and the wish is complied with within two years of death, that disposition takes effect for IHT as if the property had been originally bequeathed to the transferee – see Inheritance Tax Act 1984, s 143. No particular formality is required.

Chapter 32
Providing for Infirm or Disabled Beneficiaries

Introduction

An elderly testator may wish to make long-term provision for a relative who is infirm or disabled. This commonly arises in the following situations, although the principles involved may be applied by anyone wishing to make financial provision for someone suffering from a disability:

- a parent seeks to make provision for a disabled son or daughter;
- a son or daughter seeks to make provision for an infirm parent;
- one spouse seeks to provide for the other who has become frail, infirm or mentally incapacitated;
- unmarried brothers or sisters seek to provide for each other.

Key points

The beneficiary may be unable to handle his or her own financial affairs but quite apart from this there will often be:

- uncertainty as to what the needs of the beneficiary will be and the need to take into account:
  - the high cost of care and services
  - any services provided under community care policies
- uncertainty as to what provision will actually benefit the beneficiary due to:
  - loss of substantial state or local authority funding
  - means-testing in respect of the cost of services provided
- a desire to provide tax-effective support by utilising:
  - normal tax-planning principles
  - the tax concessions available in respect of disabled beneficiaries under trusts
- concern about potential inheritance claims by (or on behalf of) the disabled beneficiary – and others.

> There is no simple solution and each case must de dealt with taking into account all the likely circumstances as best as these can be ascertained, including the wishes and priorities of the testator.

32.1 CARE PROVISION

The personal circumstances of the beneficiary will depend upon:

- the resources (both personal and financial) of the individual;
- the nature and degree of the disability or infirmity;
- the availability of personal carers or care provision;
- the outside funding available, whether from a trust or from the state or a local authority.

Options

The beneficiary may, either at present or at some time in the future:

- be provided with a basic income and left to cope;
- live in his or her own home with some support;
- be cared for by another member of the family or friend;
- live in a supervised home or hostel with other disabled or infirm people;
- be looked after in a local authority care home;
- be cared for in a residential care or nursing home charging weekly fees;
- in need of full-time nursing care in hospital.

In many cases the testator is seeking to replace the care and support already being provided on a personal basis by financial support, and this will be for an uncertain period of time.

> Whatever the circumstances at the time when the provision is discussed, these are likely to change.

32.2 FUNDING

Sources

The financial resources available for the support of this beneficiary come from:

- personal income, including pensions, interests on savings and the return from any investments;
- personal capital resources, including savings and investments;
- the individual's home, if owned in full or in part;
- any trust provision available (including that now being contemplated);

Chapter 32 PROVIDING FOR INFIRM OR DISABLED BENEFICIARIES

- voluntary financial support from family and friends (or charities);
- support from society through the state or local or health authorities.

Means tests

Means tests are likely to be applied on a formal or informal basis as a prerequisite to any support provided, and these may take into account the income and capital resources of the individual. Inflexible means tests regulate:

- income support paid by the DSS to those whose income from other sources is insufficient for their needs – see Chapter 18;
- housing benefit (to cover rent) paid by the local authority – see Chapter 19;
- housing or disabled facilities grants from local authorities – see Chapter 20;
- the cost of residential, day and domicilary services provided or funded by the local authority – see Chapter 19.

> Any financial provision that is made on a legal basis could result in reduction or withdrawal of a significant source of income, or a charge for services.

32.3 FINANCIAL PROVISION

Objectives and strategy

The testator is likely to have conflicting objectives:

- provide for the disabled or infirm beneficiary to the extent necessary;
- ensure that funds that are not needed pass ultimately to other beneficiaries;
- avoid loss of other sources of funding but fill gaps in care provision.

The parents of a severely mentally disabled child may be reluctant to leave that child's future in the hands of the local authority or dependent on their trustees. But if the child is heavily reliant on state funding or support, all income or capital to which the child becomes legally entitled will be means-tested.

> Testators must decide their priorities – they cannot achieve all objectives.

Trust provision may last for many years but the means-testing rules, circumstances of the beneficiary and services needed constantly change so flexibility is desirable in the provision made. The following are key points to have in mind:

- the terms of the trust will depend upon whether the beneficiary is likely to be self-reliant or dependent upon others, though many fall between these extremes;

367

- the beneficiary's own resources and all other sources of funding, actual and potential, should be taken into account;
- do not be so concerned with tax planning and achieving the statutory concessions for disabled beneficiaries that you overlook welfare benefit planning.

Options

The testator has the following options when seeking to make provision for a disabled or infirm beneficiary, and these may apply to the entire estate, a share thereof, or a specified sum set aside for the purpose:

- leave money to:
    - the beneficiary absolutely and ignore means-testing implications
    - other relatives in the hope that they will support the disabled beneficiary on a voluntary basis (thereby avoiding means-testing)
- create a trust:
    - with the disabled beneficiary having a (protected) life interest, or
    - which is discretionary as regards income and/or capital and includes the disabled beneficiary, or
    - for charitable purposes (perhaps limited to charities with specific objectives)
- use a two-year discretionary trust to create a 'wait and see' period so that the changed needs of the beneficiary can be ascertained before the trustees choose between the above options;
- leave money to a charity on one of the special schemes available.

> If substantial funds are available a combination of these options designed to fit the particular circumstances may be best.

Challenges to the provision

An application may be made to the court under the Inheritance (Provision for Family and Dependants) Act 1975 by – or on behalf of – the dependent beneficiary on the ground that the will does not make reasonable provision:

- the court has wide powers to redistribute the estate;
- for the matters taken into account refer to Chapter 31 at para. 31.5;
- the financial resources of the potential beneficiary will be taken into account but the extent to which these include means-tested state benefits or local authority provision that would otherwise be available is not clear.

> The question is not 'did the testator act reasonably?' but rather 'has reasonable financial provision been made for this person?'

32.4 DRAFTING THE TRUST

Information required

Before advising on the terms of a will or any trust provision you need to know in respect of the incapacitated beneficiary:

- name and age;
- present capital and income and any changes that may arise;
- the nature and implications of the incapacity;
- present residence and extent of care, and any changes to be anticipated;
- present funding arrangements and any changes that may take place;
- any other financial provision that has been or may be made;
- help likely to be provided by charitable organisations.

> You must determine and take into account the potential size of the fund available for this beneficiary (is it to be a share of the estate or a fixed sum?).

Practical points

- Avoid identifying the trust fund too closely with the disabled beneficiary (to the extent that the testator will tolerate this). It may be better to:
  - have a discretionary fund identifying many potential beneficiaries including this specific beneficiary
  - adopt a trust period other than the life of this beneficiary
- Ensure that the class of potential beneficiaries includes persons who may care for or support this beneficiary (the trustees can even be given a restricted power to enlarge the class):
  - providing financial assistance to a carer often benefits the person cared for
  - if money can be paid to other people they may provide voluntary support (thereby avoiding means-testing issues)
- Take care over the inclusion of any power to advance or appoint capital to the disabled beneficiary:
  - restrict it to specific purposes
  - restrict it to specific situations
- Include adequate discretionary powers for the trustees, such as power to:
  - invest in chattels and residential accommodation
  - make loans and permit occupation and use of trust assets (a power to appoint

capital may not then be necessary)
- benefit those who may help the disabled beneficiary
- benefit or support charities (they may help the disabled beneficiary)
- pay funeral expenses for the disabled beneficiary

- Tax dispensations are available under the provisions below in respect of certain trusts for the benefit of disabled persons, but utilising these may have adverse consequences in respect of means-tested support and benefits:
    - Taxation of Chargeable Gains Act 1992, Sched. 1, para. 1
    - Inheritance Tax Act 1984, ss 3A(1)(3) and 89

> It may be a question of tax benefits or state benefits – the testator is seldom able to achieve the best of both worlds.

Side letters

Instead of revealing in the will their wishes and intentions in regard to the administration of their trust fund, testators should prepare and sign a suitable letter addressed to the trustees setting these out:

- this will reassure not only the testator but also the trustees when they consider the exercise of their powers in future years;
- for an example see Appendix 4.

Settlements

It may be advantageous to establish the desired trusts for the disabled or elderly beneficiary under a lifetime settlement:

- the settlor's will (and that of a spouse) can leave money to the trustees and thus be kept simple;
- other people (e.g. grandparents of a disabled child or children of an infirm parent) can also leave money to the trustees of the settlement and avoid having to set out their own trusts;
- life insurance and pension benefits may be held on these trusts.

The administration costs of a settlement may make it an inadvisable option if the trust fund is too small, although a nominal sum may be settled initially in anticipation of substantial sums being added under the will of the settlor or other persons.

Precedents

On this topic generally, reference should be made to the author's published

Chapter 32 PROVIDING FOR INFIRM OR DISABLED BENEFICIARIES

material in:

- Butterworths Wills Probate and Administration Service;
- Butterworths Older Client Law Service;
- Encyclopaedia of Forms and Precedents:
  - Volume 42(1) 'Wills and Administration'
  - Volume 16(2) 'Family'

and further material now available in:

- Practical Will Precedents (FT Law & Tax);
- Practical Trust Precedents (FT Law & Tax).

> Do not adopt these precedents unless you have first ascertained that they are appropriate to the particular circumstances.

Chapter 33

Death

33.1 REGISTRATION

- Births and Deaths Registration Act 1953
- Registration of Births and Deaths Regulations 1987

Obligation to register

The death of every person dying in England or Wales must be registered by the Registrar of Births and Deaths for the district in which the death occurred. The address will be found in the local telephone directory or may be obtained from the hospital, doctor, police, local council or post office.

The medical practitioner

A registered medical practitioner (RMP) who has attended a person during his last illness is required to send to the registrar a certificate stating to the best of his knowledge and belief the cause of death:

- any qualified informant who has received such a certificate from the RMP must deliver it to the registrar;
- where death was in a hospital the health authority may give the certificate to the registrar direct but a qualified informant must still register the death.

The qualified informant

The persons under a duty to register are identified as follows:

- where a person dies in a house:
  - the nearest relative of the deceased person present at the death or in attendance during his last illness or, if none
  - any other relative of the deceased residing or being in the sub-district where the death occurred or, if none
  - a person present at the death or the occupier of the house if he knew of the happening of the death or, if none
  - each inmate of the house who knew of the happening of the death or the person causing the disposal of the body
- where a person dies elsewhere or a dead body is found and no information as

Chapter 33 DEATH

to the place of death is available
- any relative of the deceased with knowledge of any of the particulars required to be registered concerning the death or, if none
- any person present at the death or
- any person finding or taking charge of the body or
- any person causing the disposal of the body

The obligation

The duty is to register within five days of the death or finding the body but if within that time written notice is given to the registrar with the doctor's certificate the registration need not be completed until 14 days after the death or finding:

- when one qualified informant gives information and signs the register the others are discharged from their duty to do so;
- these obligations do not apply where an inquest is to be held.

It is an offence wilfully to give any false information upon registration.

Particulars to be supplied

The following particulars must be registered by the qualified informant:

- date and place of death;
- name and surname, sex, maiden surname of a woman who has been married, date and place of birth, occupation and usual address of the deceased;
- name and surname, qualification and usual address of the informant;
- cause of death;
- signature of the informant and date of the registration.

Other non-obligatory questions will be asked about date of birth of any surviving spouse, the NI number and any state benefits in payment, and the deceased's medical card should be handed in if it is available.

Death certificates

The registrar issues a certificate as to registration of death (the death certificate) and duplicates may be requested for a fee. There is also issued:

- a certificate for claiming any social security benefits (with a claim form);
- a certificate for disposal by burial or cremation (the 'Green Form' which is required by the undertaker).

33.2 CORONERS AND INQUESTS

- Coroners Act 1988
- Coroners Rules 1984

Duty to report

There is a general duty to give information which may lead to the coroner having notice of circumstances requiring the holding of an inquest. In particular:

- a registrar of births and deaths must report a death to the coroner when (*inter alia*):
    - he is unable to obtain a duly complete certificate of cause of death
    - the deceased was not attended during his last illness by a RMP
    - the deceased was not seen by the certifying RMP either after death or within 14 days before death
    - the cause of death appears to be unknown
    - he has reason to believe the death to have been unnatural or caused by violence or neglect or to have been attended by suspicious circumstances
    - it appears to have occurred during an operation or before recovery from the effect of anaesthetic; or
    - it appears from the contents of any medical certificate to have been due to industrial disease or industrial poisoning
- it is normal practice for a RMP to report a death to the coroner where there is doubt or suspicion, and he may seek advice from the coroner about his certificate.

> The coroner is a judicial officer and thereby immune from legal proceedings in respect of acts done and words spoken in the exercise of his judicial duty.

Role

The coroner for the district is under a duty to inquire into a death where:

- the dead body of a person is lying within his jurisdiction; and
- he is informed and there is reasonable cause to suspect that the person has died:
    - a violent or an unnatural death; or
    - a sudden death of which the cause is unknown; or
    - in prison or in such place or in such circumstances as to require an inquest in pursuance of any Act

Chapter 33 DEATH

Post-mortem examination

The inquiry by the coroner may include the cause of death and the coroner can direct that there be a post-mortem examination and an inquest, but the inquiry may be:

- concluded without a post-mortem or inquest where a doctor has completed a certificate and the coroner concludes that there is no reason for him to intervene;
- restricted to a post-mortem where the coroner is of the opinion that this is sufficient in cases of sudden death where the cause was unknown.

Any person intending to remove a body out of the country must first give notice to the coroner within whose jurisdiction the body is and certain formalities must then be complied with – Removal of Bodies Regulations 1954.

> The coroner will take possession of the body until any inquest is concluded but may release it for burial or cremation.

Inquests

The purpose of an inquest is to decide who the deceased was and how, when and where he came by his death. It must conclude with a verdict under five heads:

1. name of deceased;
2. injury or disease causing death;
3. time, place and circumstances of injury (where appropriate);
4. conclusion as to the death (there can be an open verdict);
5. particulars required by the Registration Acts.

The coroner decides where and when an inquest is to be held, and it must normally be held in public and be formally opened and closed. A jury (of at least seven people) is only required in certain circumstances, but the coroner has a discretion to summon a jury.

Evidence

Witnesses give evidence on oath but as it is an inquisitorial process it is for the coroner to decide which witnesses to summon:

- the coroner must examine anyone with knowledge of the facts whom he thinks it expedient to examine and anyone who wishes to give evidence;
- medical witnesses may be called, including to express an opinion as to the cause of death;

- certain classes of person (see the 1984 Rules) and any person who in the opinion of the coroner has a proper interest may also examine any witness either personally or by a solicitor, but legal aid is not available.

Strict laws of evidence do not apply, but the coroner takes notes of the evidence.

Powers

The coroner has power to:

- fine a person who will not attend or give evidence after being summoned;
- issue a warrant for the arrest of a witness who fails to attend after being served with a summons;
- commit a person for contempt in the face of the court (but not otherwise).

Upon conclusion the coroner completes a certificate and the death is registered without attendance by a qualified informant. The coroner may issue an order for burial or certificate for cremation without charge.

33.3 FUNERAL ARRANGEMENTS

Authority

Upon registering the death the registrar gives the informant a disposal certificate and this must be handed to the person effecting the disposal of the body:

- the coroner authorises disposal when he is inquiring into the death;
- if after 14 days no notice as to the date, place and means of disposal of the body has reached the registrar, he must make inquiry about this.

The court is reluctant to interfere on the application of a relative with the executors' decision as to funeral arrangements:

- see *Re Grandison (deceased)* (1999) Times, 10 July;
- this may apply to those entitled to be administrators who will in any event be the next of kin.

Financial responsibility

The person who instructs the undertaker may become personally responsible for the cost but will normally be entitled to an indemnity from the estate. The deceased's bank may release funds to an undertaker direct before probate, on production of the death certificate and funeral account.

If the deceased leaves no money arrangements will be made by those prepared to pay, but assistance may be available from public funds:

Chapter 33 DEATH

- a *funeral expenses payment* may be obtained from the Social Fund – see Chapter 18:
  - there is a time-limit of three months
  - only an eligible person in receipt of means-tested benefits who takes responsibility for the costs of the funeral may claim
  - any savings of the claimant over £1,000 are taken into account and contributions from other sources will be offset
  - only essential expenses (as defined) will be covered
  - the payment is refundable out of the estate of the deceased

See leaflet SFL2 *How the Social Fund can help you.*

- the local authority (usually Environmental Health Department) must arrange and pay for a funeral where the deceased has no relatives or friends willing to do so and has not made advance arrangements:
  - the cost can be claimed from the estate, if there is one, or from any person liable to maintain the deceased
  - the health authority will make the arrangements if the death was in a hospital

Public Health (Control of Diseases) Act 1984, s 46.

Funeral directors

It is not obligatory to use a funeral director, but there are two professional bodies that regulate their activities:

- the National Association of Funeral Directors (address in Appendix 5) has a code of practice which members should follow:
  - quotes may be obtained and a basic funeral can be requested
  - the Association operates a complaints procedure
- also the Society of Allied and Independent Funeral Directors.

Age Concern Fact Sheet 27 *Arranging a funeral.*

Burial or cremation?

The decision about disposal of the body is strictly that of the executors or, in the absence of a will, the next of kin who will be the potential administrators:

- directions may be in or with the will and it is prudent to check in all cases:
  - although not legally binding these will invariably be followed where possible and will be compelling where there is disagreement between executors

377

- it is wise to consult the next of kin (and tactful to consult any cohabitee) and professional executors will usually follow their wishes unless in conflict with the will or each other.

> Always ascertain whether the deceased has already made arrangements – a grave space may have been reserved or there may be a funeral insurance.

Burial

Everyone is entitled to be buried in the churchyard of the parish in which they die – if there is one and if there is still room:

- the permission of the local clergy is required elsewhere but grave space may have been bought in advance;
- there are also cemeteries owned by local authorities or privately, and widely varying fees are charged.

Cremation

Before a cremation takes place three statutory forms must be completed, these being by:

1. the next of kin or other suitable person authorising the cremation;
2. the doctor who attended the deceased in the last illness;
3. another doctor who must also have seen the body.

Each doctor will charge a fee, but where a coroner issues the certificate there is no fee and no doctor's certificate, but the medical referee to the crematorium signs a document and a fee is charged.

Disposal of organs

The executors can decide to donate the body for medical research and would usually follow any request of this nature in the will but are not obliged to do so. Organs can be removed soon after death if the deceased has indicated in writing a wish to be a donor (e.g. by carrying a donor card) or if no objections are raised by relatives when enquiries are made – see Human Tissue Act 1961.

PART FOUR

Appendices

This final part contains additional information that may be of assistance in the running of an elderly client practice. It is divided into three sections:

1. Forms and precedents;
2. Additional information;
3. Law Society guidance.

SECTION A

Forms and Precedents

The brief selection of basic forms and precedents in this Section comprises:

Enduring power of attorney

- the prescribed form of Enduring Power of Attorney;
- further forms required if registration becomes necessary.

Wills

- a routine will appropriate to many straightforward family situations;
- a will setting up trusts for the benefit of a beneficiary who is disabled or infirm and may need to enter a residential care or nursing home or otherwise rely upon services provided by the local authority.

Living wills

- reference to forms that are available;
- a suggested precedent for a living will that can be produced within the office.

Letters and certificates

- letters to a medical practitioner who is asked to report on the mental capacity of a client;
- letter by a testator to the trustees of a will providing for a disabled or infirm beneficiary;
- certificates for use by a medical practitioner.

Appendix 1

Enduring Power of Attorney

In this Appendix are reproduced the following prescribed forms:

Enduring Power of Attorney

Enduring Powers of Attorney (Prescribed Form) Regulations 1990:

- effective from 31 July 1990.

Notice of Intention to Apply for Registration – Form EP1

Court of Protection (Enduring Powers of Attorney) Rules 1986, Schedule 1.

Application for Registration – Form EP2

Court of Protection (Enduring Powers of Attorney) Rules 1986, Schedule 1.

PART 4: SECTION A Forms and Precedents

SCHEDULE   Regulations 2 and 3

ENDURING POWER OF ATTORNEY

Part A: About using this form

1. **You may choose one attorney or more than one.** If you choose one attorney then you must delete everything between the square brackets on the first page of the form. If you choose more than one, you must decide whether they are able to act:
   - Jointly (that is, they must all act together and cannot act separately) or
   - Jointly and severally (that is, they can all act together but they can also act separately if they wish).

   On the first page of the form, show what you have decided by crossing out one of the alternatives.

2. **If you give your attorney(s) general power** in relation to all your property and affairs, it means that they will be able to deal with your money or property and may be able to sell your house.

3. **If you don't want your attorney(s) to have such wide powers,** you can include any restrictions you like. For example, you can include a restriction that your attorney(s) must not act on your behalf until they have reason to believe that you are becoming mentally incapable; or a restriction as to what your attorney(s) may do. Any restrictions you choose must be written or typed where indicated on the second page of the form.

4. **If you are a trustee** (and please remember that co-ownership of a home involves trusteeship), you should seek legal advice if you want your attorney(s) to act as a trustee on your behalf.

5. **Unless you put in a restriction preventing it** your attorney(s) will be able to use any of your money or property to make any provision which you yourself might be expected to make for their own needs or the needs of other people. Your attorney(s) will also be able to use your money to make gifts, but only for reasonable amounts in relation to the value of your money and property.

6. **Your attorney(s) can recover the out-of-pocket expenses** of acting as your attorney(s). If your attorney(s) are professional people, for example solicitors or accountants, they may be able to charge for their professional services as well. You may wish to provide expressly for remuneration of your attorney(s) (although if they are trustees they may not be allowed to accept it).

7. **If your attorney(s) have reason to believe** that you have become or are becoming mentally incapable of managing your affairs, your attorney(s) will have to apply to the Court of Protection for registration of this power.

8. **Before applying to the Court of Protection for registration** of this power, your attorney(s) must give written notice that that is what they are going to do, to you and your nearest relatives as defined in the Enduring Powers of Attorney Act 1985. You or your relatives will be able to object if you or they disagree with registration.

9. **This is a simplified explanation** of what the Enduring Powers of Attorney Act 1985 and the Rules and Regulations say. If you need more guidance, you or your advisers will need to look at the Act itself and the Rules and Regulations. The Rules are the Court of Protection (Enduring Powers of Attorney) Rules 1986 (Statutory Instrument 1986 No. 127). The Regulations are the Enduring Powers of Attorney (Prescribed Form) Regulations 1990 (Statutory Instrument 1990 No. 1376).

10. **Note to Attorney(s)**
    After the power has been registered you should notify the Court of Protection if the donor dies or recovers.

11. **Note to Donor**
    Some of these explanatory notes may not apply to the form you are using if it has already been adapted to suit your particular requirements.

YOU CAN CANCEL THIS POWER AT ANY TIME BEFORE IT HAS TO BE REGISTERED

384

Appendix 1 ENDURING POWER OF ATTORNEY

Part B: To be completed by the 'donor' (the person appointing the attorney(s))

Don't sign this form unless you understand what it means

Please read the notes in the margin which follow and which are part of the form itself.

Donor's name and address.

I _____

of _____

Donor's date of birth.

born on _____

appoint _____

See note 1 on the front of this form. If you are appointing only one attorney you should cross out everything between the square brackets. If appointing more than two attorneys please give the additional name(s) on an attached sheet.

of _____

• [and _____

of _____

Cross out the one which does not apply (see note 1 on the front of this form).

- jointly
- jointly and severally]

to be my attorney(s) for the purpose of the Enduring Powers of Attorney Act 1985

Cross out the one which does not apply (see note 2 on the front of this form). Add any additional powers.

- with general authority to act on my behalf
- with authority to do the following on my behalf:

If you don't want the attorney(s) to have general power, you must give details here of what authority you are giving the attorney(s).

in relation to

Cross out the one which does not apply.

- all my property and affairs:
- the following property and affairs:

385

PART 4: SECTION A Forms and Precedents

Part B: continued

Please read the notes in the margin which follow and which are part of the form itself.
If there are restrictions or conditions, insert them here; if not, cross out these words if you wish (see note 3 on the front of this form).

• subject to the following restrictions and conditions:

If this form is being signed at your direction:–
• the person signing must not be an attorney or any witness (to Parts B or C).
• you must add a statement that this form has been signed at your direction.
• a second witness is necessary (please see below).

Your signature (or mark).

I intend that this power shall continue even if I become mentally incapable

I have read or have had read to me the notes in Part A which are part of, and explain, this form.

Signed by me as a deed _____
and delivered

Date.
Someone must witness your signature.
Signature of witness.

Your attorney(s) cannot be your witness. It is not advisable for your husband or wife to be your witness.

on_____

in the presence of _____
Full name of witness_____
Address of witness _____
_____
_____

A second witness is only necessary if this form is not being signed by you personally but at your direction (for example, if a physical disability prevents you from signing).
Signature of second witness.

in the presence of _____
Full name of witness_____

Address of witness _____
_____
_____

Appendix 1 ENDURING POWER OF ATTORNEY

Part C: To be completed by the attorney(s)
Note: 1. This form may be adapted to provide for execution by a corporation
2. If there is more than one attorney additional sheets in the form as shown below must be added to this Part C

Please read the notes in the margin which follow and which are part of the form itself.

Don't sign this form before the donor has signed Part B or if, in your opinion, the donor was already mentally incapable at the time of signing Part B.

If this form is being signed at your direction:–
- the person signing must not be an attorney or any witness (to Parts B or C).
- you must add a statement that this form has been signed at your direction.
- a second witness is necessary (please see below).

Signature (or mark) of attorney.

Date.

Signature of witness.

The attorney must sign the form and his signature must be witnessed. The donor may not be the witness and one attorney may not witness the signature of the other.

A second witness is only necessary if this form is not being signed by you personally but at your direction (for example, if a physical disability prevents you from signing).
Signature of second witness.

I understand that I have a duty to apply to the Court for the registration of this form under the Enduring Powers of Attorney Act 1985 when the donor is becoming or has become mentally incapable.

I also understand my limited power to use the donor's property to benefit persons other than the donor.

I am not a minor

Signed by me as a deed _____
and delivered

on_____

in the presence of _____

Full name of witness_____

Address of witness _____
_____
_____

---

in the presence of _____

Full name of witness_____

Address of witness _____
_____
_____

387

PART 4: SECTION A Forms and Precedents

Court of Protection/Public Trust Office
Enduring Powers of Attorney Act 1985

Notice of intention to apply for registration

To ....

of ....

TAKE NOTICE THAT

This form may be adapted for use by three or more attorneys.

I ....

of ....

and I ....

of ....

Give the name and address of the donor.

the attorney(s) of ....

....

of ....

....

intend to apply to the Public Trustee for registration of the enduring power of attorney appointing me (us) attorney(s) and made by the donor on the .... 19 ....

1. If you wish to object to the proposed registration you have 4 weeks from the day on which this notice is given to you to do so in writing. Any objections should be sent to the Public Trustee and should contain the following details:

   It will be necessary for you to produce evidence in support of your objection. If evidence is available please send it with your objection, the attorney(s) will be given an opportunity to respond to your objection.

   - your name and address;
   - any relationship to the donor;
   - if you are not the donor, the name and address of the donor;
   - the name and address of the attorney;
   - the grounds for objecting to the registration of the enduring power.

The grounds upon which you can object are limited and are shown at 2 overleaf.

EP1

Appendix 1 ENDURING POWER OF ATTORNEY

Note. The instrument means the enduring power of attorney made by the donor which it is sought to register.

2. The grounds on which you may object are:

   - that the power purported to have been created by the instrument is not valid as an enduring power of attorney;

   - that the power created by the instrument no longer subsists;

   - that the application is premature because the donor is not yet becoming mentally incapable;

   - that fraud or undue pressure was used to induce the donor to make the power;

   - that the attorney is unsuitable to be the donor's attorney (having regard to all the circumstances and in particular the attorney's relationship to or connection with the donor).

The attorney(s) does not have to be a relative. Relatives are not entitled to know of the existence of the enduring power of attorney prior to being given this notice.

Note. This is addressed only to the donor.

3. You are informed that while the enduring power of attorney remains registered, you will not be able to revoke it until the Court of Protection confirms the revocation.

Note. This notice should be signed by every one of the attorneys who are applying to register the enduring power of attorney.

Signed .... Dated ....

Signed .... Dated ....

Court of Protection/Public Trust Office, Protection Division, Stewart House, 24 Kingsway, London WC2B 6JX

EP1

PART 4: SECTION A Forms and Precedents

No. _____

Court of Protection/Public Trust Office
Enduring Powers of Attorney Act 1985

Application for registration

Note. Give the full name and present address of the donor. If the donor's address on the enduring power of attorney is different give that one too.	The donor Name .... Address .... Address on the Enduring Power of Attorney (if different) ....
Note. Give the full name(s) and details of the attorney(s).	The attorney(s) Name .... Address .... age .... occupation .... relationship to donor (if any) ....
This form may be adapted for use by three or more attorneys.	Name .... Address .... age .... occupation .... relationship to donor (if any) ....
The date is the date upon which the donor signed the enduring power of attorney.	I (we) the attorney(s) apply to register the enduring power of attorney made by the donor under the above Act on the .... 19 .... the original of which accompanies this application.

I (we) have reason to believe that the donor is or is becoming mentally incapable.

Notice must be personally given. It should be made clear if someone other than the attorney(s) gives the notice.	I (we) have given notice in the prescribed form to the following: • the donor personally at .... on the .... 19 ....

EP2

390

Appendix 1 ENDURING POWER OF ATTORNEY

If there are no relatives entitled to notice please say so.

- The following relatives of the donor at the addresses below on the dates given:

Names	Relationship	Addresses	Date

Note. Cross out this section if it does not apply.

- The Co-Attorney(s) ....

  at ....

  on ....

A remittance for the registration fee accompanies this application.

Note. The application should be signed by all the attorneys who are making the application.

I (we) certify that the above information is correct and that to the best of my (our) knowledge and belief I (we) have complied with the provisions of the Enduring Powers of Attorney Act 1985 and of all the Rules and Regulations under it.

Signed .... Dated ....

This must not pre-date the date(s) when the notices were given.

Signed .... Dated ....

....

Address to which correspondence relating to the application is to be sent if different to that of the first-named attorney making this application ....

....

When completed this form should be sent to:—
Court of Protection/Public Trust Office, Protection Division, Stewart House, 24 Kingsway, London WC2B 6JX

EP2

391

Appendix 2
Family Wills

A 'HAPPY FAMILY' WILL

The following is a simple form of will that may be suitable for grandparents where there are no complications in the family and tax planning is not desired or necessary.

THIS IS THE LAST WILL of me [*name*] of [*address and description*]

1. **I REVOKE** all former wills and testamentary dispositions made by me

2. **I APPOINT** my *wife/husband* [*name*] to be my executor but if *she/he* dies before me or is unable or unwilling to act or such appointment does not take effect then **I APPOINT** [*name and address*] and [*name and address*] ('my Trustees' which expression includes the trustees or trustee for the time being) to be my executors and trustees

3. **IF** my *wife/husband* [*name*] survives me by one calendar month **I GIVE** all the real and personal property whatsoever and wheresoever to which I may be entitled or over which I have any disposing power at the time of my death after payment of my just debts funeral and testamentary expenses ('my Estate') to my *wife/husband* absolutely

4. **IF** my *wife/husband* [*name*] does not survive me or the gift to *her/him* fails for any reason **I GIVE** my Estate to such of my children as are living at my death and if more than one in equal shares **PROVIDED** that if any child dies before me leaving issue living at my death such issue shall take by substitution and if more than one in equal shares per stirpes the share that my deceased child would have taken had he or she survived me but so that no issue shall take whose parent is alive and capable of taking

5. **MY TRUSTEES** have the following powers in addition to their powers under the general law:

    5.1. to invest any money in or upon the acquisition or security of property of any nature and wherever situate (including a house or flat as a residence for any beneficiary) to the intent that they have the same full and unrestricted power of investment as if they were absolutely entitled thereto beneficially

    5.2. to exercise the power of appropriation conferred by the Administration of Estates Act 1925 without obtaining any of the consents required by that Act and even though one of them may be beneficially interested in the appropriation

5.3. at any time or times during the minority of any beneficiary in their discretion to raise any sum out of the capital of my Estate (not exceeding the share of that beneficiary) and to pay or apply such sum for the advancement maintenance education or benefit of such beneficiary in such manner as they think fit

6. **IT IS MY WISH** that my body may be cremated and my ashes scattered in the Garden of Remembrance – *or as appropriate*

IN WITNESS whereof I have hereunto set my hand this   day of Two thousand

SIGNED by the said [*name of testator*] as and for *his/her* last Will in the presence of us both present at the same time who in *his/her* presence and the presence of each other have subscribed our names as witnesses

WILL PROVIDING FOR A DEPENDENT SISTER

The following form may be suitable where a testator without issue wishes to provide so far as necessary for an elderly and infirm sister who has minimal assets but has shared the testator's home. Following the death she may be cared for by another member of the family or need to go into a residential care home funded by the local authority. The intention is to avoid the effects of means testing whilst supporting the sister so far as necessary and only passing the estate to the next generation following the sister's death.

THIS IS THE LAST WILL of me [*name*] of [*address and description*]

1. **I REVOKE** all former wills and testamentary dispositions made by me

2. **I DESIRE** that my body be [buried at [*place*] or cremated [and my ashes scattered at [*place*]]]

3. **I APPOINT** [*names and addresses*] ('my Trustees' which where the context permits includes the trustees or trustee for the time being) to be the executors and trustees of this will

4. **I GIVE** all my personal chattels (as defined by the Administration of Estates Act 1925 Section 55(1)(x) [but including cars]) not otherwise disposed of by this will or any codicil to my Trustees free of tax with the wish (but without creating any trust or imposing any binding obligation) that they carry out any wishes of mine which come to their attention as to the disposal of any such chattels and subject to this give or make available

to my [*description and name of relative*] any items reasonably required and that any items not so disposed of be treated as part of my estate

5. **I GIVE** free of any tax or duty arising in respect of my death:

   5.1. to [*donee*] of [*address*] the sum of £...

   5.2. to [*donee*] of [*address*] the sum of £...

6. **I GIVE** all my property both movable and immovable of whatever nature and wherever situated except property otherwise disposed of by this will or by any codicil to it to my Trustees with power for my Trustees at their discretion to sell all or any part or parts of such property when they think fit:

   6.1. upon trust to pay out of the proceeds of any such sales and my ready money (in exoneration of any property which would otherwise be liable for payment of the same) all my funeral and testamentary expenses and debts and any general legacies given by this will or any codicil to it and any tax or duty arising in respect of my death (even if not a testamentary expense) on all gifts in this will and any codicil to it given free of such tax or duty [and any tax or duty arising as a result of my death in respect of any transfers or gifts made during my lifetime (in exoneration of the recipient of any such transfer or gift and of any other person who may be liable in respect thereof)]

   6.2. upon trust if necessary to invest the remainder after such payment in or upon any investments authorised below for the investment of trust funds with power to vary and transpose the same

   6.3. upon trust to stand possessed of such investments and such of my estate as remains for the time being unsold and my ready money and all property from time to time respectively representing the same ('my Trust Fund') and the income upon the trusts declared concerning my Trust Fund below

7. **MY TRUST FUND** shall be held by my Trustees as follows:

   7.1. on trust during the lifetime of my said [*relative*] to pay or apply the income thereof to or for or towards the personal support and maintenance or otherwise for the benefit of my said [*relative*] or any of my [nephews and nieces and their issue or (*as appropriate*)] in such manner and if more than one in such shares as my Trustees being at least two in number from time to time in their absolute discretion think fit **PROVIDED** that my Trustees:

      7.1.1. have power during the period of 21 years following my death in their absolute discretion to accumulate the income or any part thereof by investing the same as an addition to the capital

7.1.2. may during that period apply the whole or any part of the accumulated income as if it were income arising in the then current year

7.1.3. in exercising their discretion shall have special regard to the needs (if any) of my said [*relative*]

7.2. on trust after the death of my said [*relative*] as to both capital and income or the remainder of the same:

7.2.1. to pay such funeral expenses (including the cost of a memorial) in respect of my said [*relative*] as they consider appropriate

7.2.2. in their discretion to waive repayment of any loan that they have made

7.2.3. as to the balance for such of [my nephews and nieces or their issue as are then living and if more than one in equal shares per stirpes so that no such issue shall take whose parent is alive and so capable of taking or (*as appropriate*)]

8. MY TRUSTEES shall exercise their discretion and powers whether express or implied so as to ensure in relation to my Trust Fund that not less than one-half of the capital that is applied during the lifetime of my said [*relative*] is applied for *his/her* benefit and that the provisions of the Inheritance Tax Act 1984 Section 89 are satisfied in relation thereto
– *this provision should be included with care as it may have an adverse effect on means testing for state and other funding*

9. MY TRUSTEES being at least two in number have the following powers in addition to those under the general law:

9.1. to invest money and change investments with as much freedom as an absolute beneficial owner and the retention or purchase of (or of an interest in) a freehold or leasehold dwelling for the occupation (or of chattels for the use) of anyone who is or could become a beneficiary shall be a proper exercise of their investment powers

9.2. to invest the whole or any part in the purchase or improvement of any dwelling house or flat and to permit the same to be used as a residence for my said [*relative*] whether alone or jointly with another person or persons without being required to insist upon the payment by any other person whether or not a joint occupier thereof of a market rent but my Trustees shall have a complete discretion as to the terms on which they permit such dwelling house or flat to be occupied

9.3. to invest in chattels notwithstanding that the value of my Trust Fund may become depleted and to permit my said [*relative*] to have the use and enjoyment of any such chattel in such manner and subject to such conditions (if any) as my Trustees consider reasonable and without

PART 4: SECTION A Forms and Precedents

being liable to account for any consequential loss

9.4. to lend capital on such terms as to interest security and repayment and otherwise as they think fit to any person to whom or any charitable or other body to which they consider that it would be in the interest of my said [*relative*] to make a loan without being liable for any consequent loss

9.5. to apply any part or parts of the capital or income in or towards meeting the cost of:

9.5.1. altering or adapting any residential accommodation in the ownership of any person or body for the more convenient occupation by my said [*relative*] as a home

9.5.2. purchasing domestic appliances or procuring domestic assistance for my said [*relative*] or the person or persons with whom *he/she* from time to time resides

9.5.3. purchasing motor vehicles appropriate to the needs of my said [*relative*] and the person or persons with whom *he/she* from time to time resides

9.5.4. holidays for my said [*relative*] and any companions or any person who bears the daily burden of caring for *him/her*

9.6. to reimburse out of income any costs and expenses incurred by them in ascertaining the circumstances and needs (if any) of my said [*relative*] and in making arrangements that they deem necessary or expedient for *his/her* care

9.7. to accept as a good discharge the receipt of any person caring or having financial responsibility for my said [*relative*] for any money intended to be paid to *him/her* or for *his/her* benefit

9.8. by deed or deeds (and so as to bind their successors) wholly or partially to release or restrict any of the powers given to them by this will or any codicil to it or the general law

10. I DECLARE that:

10.1. any of my Trustees who is engaged in a profession or business may charge for work done by him or by his firm or company in connection with the administration of my estate or the provision of this will or any codicil to it including work which is outside the ordinary course of his profession or business and work which he could or should have done personally had he not been so engaged

10.2. none of my Trustees shall be liable for any loss or damage to the capital or income of my Trust Fund which arises through the exercise in good faith of any power and none who acts gratuitously shall be liable for any such loss or damage unless it arises through an act or omission of his own which amounts to conscious wrongdoing

10.3. a trust corporation or other corporate body may be appointed as the sole trustee or as one of the trustees of this will on such terms (as to remuneration and otherwise) as may be acceptable to it

10.4. my Trustees may accept additional money investments and property which may be paid or transferred to them upon the trusts of my Trust Fund by any person either as a lifetime gift or under a testamentary disposition

10.5. the provisions of the Trusts of Land and Appointment of Trustees Act 1996 Section 11 shall not apply to any land situated in England and Wales which is subject to the trusts of this will or any codicil to it

IN WITNESS whereof I have hereunto set my hand this   day of
Two thousand

SIGNED by the said [*name of testator*] as and for *his/her* last Will in the presence of us both present at the same time who in *his/her* presence and the presence of each other have subscribed our names as witnesses

WILL PROVIDING FOR A MENTALLY DISABLED CHILD

A selection of wills by Gordon Ashton that include discretionary provision for a mentally disabled child is to be found in:

- Butterworths Wills Probate and Administration Service
- Encyclopaedia of Forms and Precedents (Butterworths)

These precedents should not be used without a full understanding of the various options available and the family circumstances.

Appendix 3
Living Wills

FORMS

Forms for completion may be obtained from:

The Voluntary Euthanasia Society

of 13 Prince of Wales Terrace, London W8 5PG

A short form entitled **Advance Directive** which, in circumstances which are defined, directs that no treatment is to be given aimed at prolonging or sustaining life and that treatment is to be given to control distressing symptoms even though it may shorten life. Medical attendants are asked to bear in mind that the signatory fears 'degeneration and indignity far more than death' when considering what his or her intentions would be.

The Terrence Higgins Trust

of 52–54 Grays Inn Road, London WC1X 8JU

An eight-page form entitled **Living Will** which provides detailed explanatory notes followed by large boxes for completion with relevant personal details and instructions. This is the most comprehensive form in:

- expressing wishes as to whether, in different specified circumstances, medical treatment should be aimed at preserving life or merely relieving suffering;
- expressing wishes about particular medical treatments or investigations;
- naming a person to be contacted when death is imminent and authorising life preserving treatment until that person is present even if to be withheld thereafter;
- appointing a person (a *Health Care Proxy*) to be consulted about and involved in decisions about medical care.

PRECEDENT

The following form is suggested for practitioners who are asked to prepare a simple living will for their clients. It merely reflects the present state of the law and does not attempt to appoint a medical treatment proxy.

Appendix 3 LIVING WILLS

It is based on a precedent by Denzil Lush first published in EAGLE in January 1994 (for subscriptions to EAGLE see Appendix 7) but has been modified to include a simple method whereby amendments to (or even revocation of) the document may be ascertained.

THIS LIVING WILL is made on [*date*]

by me [*full name*] of [*full address*] born on [*date of birth*]

I WISH these instructions to be acted upon if two registered medical practitioners are of the opinion that I am no longer capable of making and communicating a treatment decision AND that I am:

- unconscious, and it is unlikely that I shall ever regain consciousness; **or**
- suffering from an incurable or irreversible condition that will result in my death within a relatively short time; **or**
- so severely disabled, physically or mentally, that I shall be totally dependent on others for the rest of my life.

I REFUSE any medical or surgical treatment if:

- its burdens and risks outweigh its potential benefits; **or**
- it involves any research or experimentation which is likely to be of little or no therapeutic value to me; **or**
- it will prolong my life or postpone the actual moment of my death with no further benefit to me.

I CONSENT to being fed orally, and to any treatment that may:

- safeguard my dignity; **or**
- make me more comfortable; **or**
- relieve pain and suffering,

even though such treatment might unintentionally precipitate my death.

If I change the terms of this document I will notify the undermentioned person(s) so every effort should be made to contact (one of) them before relying on it:

[*name(s), address(es), telephone numbers and e-mail address(es)*]

SIGNED by me [*full name*]   Signature

in the presence of:

Name [*full name of witness*]   Signature of witness

Address [*full address of witness*]

Occupation [*occupation of witness*]

Appendix 4

Letters and Certificates

LETTERS TO A MEDICAL PRACTITIONER

These letters may be adapted and used when writing to a client's general medical practitioner for a report as to mental capacity in particular circumstances. They assume that the solicitor has already attended on the client and received preliminary instructions but that there is a doubt as to mental capacity which may need to be resolved.

Will

Dear Dr ...

Our client and your patient: *Mrs. A. B.* of [*address*]

We act for your patient and are presently advising *her* in regard to the preparation of a new will. We seek your opinion as to whether *she* is mentally capable of making a new will at this time. [We have previously made several wills for *her* the last one being some ... years ago.] *She* has [only a small estate] [a fairly substantial estate] – *amplify if there are any complications.*

The legal test of capacity in these circumstances is whether *she* understands:

1. that *she* is giving *her* property to persons of *her* choice on *her* death,
2. the extent of that property, and
3. the nature and extent of *her* obligations to relatives and others.

Your report should relate specifically to these questions and you may if you wish qualify the report by stating that you do not express any further opinion with regard to the mental capacity of your patient. Legal tests of capacity vary according to the nature of the transaction and there is no universal test. You may form your view on the balance of probabilities and do not need to be satisfied beyond reasonable doubt.

If the capacity of this patient tends to fluctuate please mention this and we may then invite you to be one of the witnesses so as to confirm your view of capacity at the time of signature. You will no doubt need to attend on *her* before preparing your report and we confirm that we will pay your reasonable fee for such attendance and the preparation of the report. *She* is presently at [*her home*] and expecting you to contact *her* there.

Yours *etc.*

Enduring power of attorney

Dear Dr ...

Our client and your patient: *Mrs. A. B.* of [*address*]

We act for your patient and are presently advising in regard to the arrangements that *she* could make for *her* financial affairs to be dealt with [in the event that *her* health deteriorates] [following *her* admission to a private nursing home].

She contemplates signing an enduring power of attorney in favour of *her two sons* which would enable them *jointly* to handle *her* financial affairs on *her* behalf even if *she* becomes mentally incapable. Subject to any limitations that *she* places on the power, they would be able to do most of the things that *she* could do with her money, and *she* would not be able to revoke this power if *she* became incapable (though *she* could do so beforehand). There are safeguards in these circumstances because the power would have to be registered with the Court of Protection after notice had been given to certain other relatives who would have an opportunity to challenge the arrangement.

We seek from you a report as to the mental capacity of your patient to sign this document. A copy of the standard form is enclosed in case you wish to read it. The legal test of capacity in these circumstances is whether *she* understands the nature and effect of the document as outlined above, is aware that *she* has financial affairs that need to be dealt with and is able to choose the person(s) who are to deal with those affairs. If she fulfils that test it does not matter that *she* is now incapable by reason of mental disorder of managing *her* property and affairs.

Your report should relate specifically to these questions and you may if you wish qualify the report by stating that you do not express any further opinion with regard to the mental capacity of your patient. Legal tests of capacity vary according to the nature of the transaction and there is no universal test of capacity. However, you may form your view on the balance of probabilities and do not need to be satisfied beyond reasonable doubt.

If the capacity of this patient tends to fluctuate please mention this and we may then invite you to be one of the witnesses so as to confirm your view of capacity at the time of signature. You will no doubt need to attend on *her* before preparing your report and we confirm that we will pay your reasonable fee for such attendance and the preparation of the report. *She* is presently at [*her home*] and expecting you to contact *her* there.

Yours *etc*.

LETTER BY A TESTATOR

The following letter, subject to any variations or additions to suit the particular circumstances, may be signed by a testator who makes limited provision for an elderly sister or brother because of mental frailty of that sister or brother and the prospect of admission to a residential care or nursing home funded by the local authority. It would accompany the will in Appendix 2.

Address

Date

To the Trustees of my Will dated ...

In my Will I have left the share of my estate that I might otherwise have left to my sister upon special discretionary trusts. This is because:

1. she may not be able to look after her own financial affairs; and
2. any money that I leave to her may be vulnerable means-testing.

I am conscious that following my death she may need to be admitted to a care home and neither she nor I have the means to finance this. Nevertheless, I am anxious to make the best long-term provision that I can for her.

It is my wish (but without imposing any binding obligation upon you) that you use your discretionary powers in regard to the Trust Fund to promote the support that my sister needs from time to time and to supplement the provision that is otherwise available to her. In so far as other persons provide personal care for my sister I would wish them to receive practical support from the Trust Fund, and in this way you may also be able to improve her environment and the standards of amenity that she enjoys.

For these reasons I have made the Trust as flexible as I can and in seeking to fulfil my objectives I encourage you to be imaginative in the use of your powers. Subject to these primary objectives you may benefit [my family who are the residuary beneficiaries]. After the death of my sister any monies remaining are to pass to my family as stipulated.

Signature of testator

Appendix 4 LETTERS AND CERTIFICATES

CERTIFICATES BY A MEDICAL PRACTITIONER

It may be of assistance to offer a medical practitioner the opportunity to make a report in the form set out below. It is assumed that a copy of the letter of instruction will be retained with the report.

Prior to signing a will

Re [*name of patient*]

of [*address of patient*]

born [*date of birth of patient*]

I [*full name, address and medical qualifications*]

HEREBY CERTIFY:

1. I have been the medical attendant of this patient for years/months and examined *him/her* on [*date(s)*] for the purpose of giving this certificate.

2. I have been asked by [*name of solicitor*] in a letter dated [*date of letter of instruction*] to express my opinion as to whether this patient is mentally capable of signing a will and the legal test of capacity that I should apply has been explained to me in that letter.

3. I have been informed in that letter or am otherwise aware of the patient's family and financial circumstances and consider that the patient **is / is not** fully aware of these circumstances.

4. In my opinion [this patient **is / is not** capable of signing a will at the present time] *or* [the capacity of this patient tends to fluctuate but at times *he/she* is capable of signing a will].

5. I base my opinion on [*set out the factors relied upon*].

6. This certificate only relates to the patient's capacity to sign a will and I express no further opinion as to *his/her* capacity.

SIGNED

Date

Prior to signing an enduring power of attorney

Re   [*name of patient*]

of   [*address of patient*]

born   [*date of birth of patient*]

I   [*full name, address and medical qualifications*]

HEREBY CERTIFY:

1. I have been the medical attendant of this patient for   years/months and examined *him/her* on [*date(s)*] for the purpose of giving this certificate.

2. I have been asked by [*name of solicitor*] in a letter dated [*date of letter of instruction*] to express my opinion as to whether this patient is mentally capable of signing an enduring power of attorney and the legal test of capacity that I should apply has been explained to me in that letter.

3. I have been informed in that letter or am otherwise aware of the patient's family and financial circumstances and consider that the patient **is / is not** fully aware of these circumstances.

4. In my opinion this patient:

    a) **is / is not** suffering from mental disorder as defined in the Mental Health Act 1983 [namely *specify the mental disorder*];

    b) **is / is not** [despite that mental disorder] capable of signing an enduring power of attorney;

    c) **is / is not** by reason of mental disorder incapable [or becoming incapable] of managing and administering *his/her* property and affairs.

5. I base my opinion on [*set out the factors relied upon*].

6. This certificate only relates to my patient's capacity to sign an enduring power of attorney and I express no further opinion as to *his/her* capacity.

SIGNED

Date

SECTION B
Additional Information

The information provided in this Section comprises:

- a list of useful addresses;
- a list of relevant websites;
- a list of books and publications for further reading.

Appendix 5

Addresses

THE LAW SOCIETY

The Law Society's Hall
113 Chancery Lane
London WC2A 1PL
Tel   020 7242 1222
Fax   020 7831 0344
DX   56 Lond/Chancery Ln

Practice Advice Service
Tel   0870 606 2522

Ipsley Court
Berrington Close
Redditch
Worcestershire B98 OTD
Tel   020 7242 1222
Local 01527 517141
Fax   01527 510213
DX   19114 Redditch

Professional Ethics enquiries
Tel   0870 606 2577

OFFICIAL ADDRESSES

Royal Courts of Justice
The Strand
London WC2R 1PL
Tel   020 7936 6000
DX   396 London/Chancery Ln

Treasury Solicitor
Queen Anne's Chambers
28 Broadway
London SW1H 9JS
Tel   020 7210 3000

Official Solicitor of the Supreme Court
81 Chancery Lane
London
WC2A 1DD
Tel   020 7911 7127

Court of Protection
Stewart House
24 Kingsway
London WC2B 6JX
Tel   020 7664 7000
Fax   020 7664 7705

Public Trust Office
Enquiries and Applications Branch
Stewart House
24 Kingsway
London WC2B 6JX
Tel   020 7664 7000
Fax   020 7664 7705

Law Commission
37–38 John Street
Theobalds Road
London WC1N 2BQ
Tel   020 7453 1220
Fax   020 7453 1297

Inland Revenue
Capital Taxes Office
Ferrers House
PO Box 38
Castle Meadow Road
Nottingham NG2 1BB
Tel   0115 974 2400
Fax   0115 974 3432

Mental Health Act Commission
Maid Marian House
56 Houndsgate
Nottingham NG1 6BG
Tel   0115 943 7100

Social Services Inspectorate
Wellington House
133–155 Waterloo Road
London SE1 8UG
Tel   020 7972 2000

OMBUDSMEN

Health Service Commissioners
Millbank Tower
Millbank
London SW1P 4QP
Tel   020 7217 4051
Fax   020 7217 4000

5th Floor, Capital Tower
Greyfriars Road
Cardiff CF10 3AG
Tel   029 2039 4621
Fax   029 2022 6909

Commissioners for Local Administration
21 Queen Anne's Gate
London SW1H 9BU
Tel   020 7915 3210
Fax   020 7233 0396

The Oaks
2 Westwood Way
Westwood Business Park
Coventry CV4 8JB
Tel   01203 695 999
Fax   01203 695 902

Beverley House
17 Shipton Road
York
YO30 5FZ
Tel   01904 663 200
Fax   01904 663 269

The Legal Services Ombudsman
22 Oxford Court
Oxford Street
Manchester
M2 3WQ
Tel   0161 236 9532
Fax   0161 236 2651
E-mail
enquiries.olso@gtnet.gov.uk

The Insurance Ombudsman Bureau
135 Park Street
London SE1 9EA
Tel   08456 006 666
Fax   020 7902 8197

The Pensions Ombudsman
11 Belgrave Road
London
SW1V 1RB
Tel   020 7834 9144
Fax   020 7821 0065

The Banking Ombudsman
70 Grays Inn Road
London
WC1X 8ND
Tel   020 7404 9944
Fax   020 7405 5052

The Building Societies Ombudsman
Millbank Tower
Millbank
London
SW1P 4XF
Tel   020 7931 0044
Fax   020 7931 8485

Appendix 5 ADDRESSES

GENERAL

Action on Elder Abuse
Astral House
1268 London Road
London SW16 4ER
Tel   020 8764 7648
E-mail   *aea@ace.org.uk*

Age Concern England
Astral House
1268 London Road
London SW16 4ER
Tel   020 8679 8000
Fax   020 8675 7211

Age Concern Wales
4th Floor
1 Cathedral Road
Cardiff
CF1 9SD
Tel   029 2037 1566
Fax   029 2039 9562

Charity Search
25 Portview Road
Avonmouth
Bristol BS11 9LD
Tel   0117 982 4060
Fax   0117 982 2846

Contact the Elderly
15 Henrietta Street
London WC2E 8QH
Tel   020 7240 0630

Counsel and Care for the Elderly
Twyman House
16 Bonny Street
London NW1 9PG
Tel   020 7485 1550
Fax   020 7267 6877
E-mail
advice@counselandcare.demon.co

Help the Aged
16–18 St James's Walk
Clerkenwell Green
London EC1R OBE
Tel   020 7253 0253
Fax   020 7251 0747

National Association of Citizens Advice Bureaux
Myddelton House
115–123 Pentonville Road
London N1 9LZ
Tel   020 7833 2181

National Council of Voluntary Organisations (NCVO)
Regent's Wharf
8 All Saints' Street
London N1 9RL
Tel   020 7713 6161

FINANCIAL

Child Poverty Action Group
94 White Lion Street
London
N1 9PF
Tel   020 7837 7979
Fax   020 7837 6414

Disability Alliance ERA
Universal House
88–94 Wentworth Street
London
E1 7SA
Tel   020 7247 8776
Fax   020 7247 8765

Disabled Living Foundation
380–384 Harrow Road
London
W9 2HU
Tel   020 7289 6111
Fax   020 7226 2922

409

PART 4: SECTION B   Additional Information

DSS Benefits Agency
Pensions and Overseas Benefits Directorate
Benton Park Road
Newcastle Upon Tyne
NE98 1YX
Tel   0191 213 5000

Financial Services Authority
25 The North Colonnade
Canary Wharf
London E14 5HS
Tel   020 7676 1000
Fax   020 7676 1099

Independent Living Fund
PO Box 183
Nottingham
NG8 3RD
Tel   0115 942 8192
Fax   0115 942 8191

Pensions Advisory Service
11 Belgrave Road
London
SW1V 1RB
Tel   020 7233 8080

Royal United Kingdom Beneficent Association (RUKBA)
6 Avonmore Road
London W14 8RL
Tel   020 7602 6274
Fax   020 7371 1807
Email *charity@rukba.org.uk*

Society of Pension Consultants
St Bartholomew House
92 Fleet Street
London EC4Y 1DG
Tel   020 7353 1688
Fax   020 7353 9296
E-mail *john.mortimer@spc.uk.com*

HOUSING AND ACCOMMODATION

The Abbeyfield Society
Abbeyfield House
53 Victoria Street
St Albans
Hertfordshire AL1 3UW
Tel   01727 857 536
Fax   01727 846 168
E-mail *abbeyf@geo2.poptel.org.uk*

Elderly Accommodation Counsel
46a Chiswick High Road
London W4 1SW
Tel   020 8995 8320
Fax   020 8995 7714

Housing Corporation
149 Tottenham Court Road
London W1P OBN
Tel   020 7393 2000
Fax   020 7393 2111

The National Association of Park Home Residents
PO Box 1067
Blandford Forum
Dorset DT11 9YA

National House Building Council
Buildmark House, Chiltern Avenue
Amersham
Buckinghamshire HP6 5AP
Tel   01494 434477
Fax   01494 735201

Sheltered Housing Advisory and Conciliation Service (SHACS)
Walkden House
3–10 Melton Street
London NW1 2EB

Appendix 5 ADDRESSES

Tel   020 7383 2006
Fax   020 7383 3614

Shelter (National Campaign for Homeless People)
88 Old Street
London EC1V 9HU
Tel   020 7505 2000
Fax   020 7505 2167
E-mail   *info@shelter.org.uk*

CARERS AND NURSING SERVICES

Association of Community Health Councils
Earlsmead House
30 Drayton Park
London N5 1PB
Tel   020 7609 8405

The Association of Crossroad Care Attendants Scheme Ltd
10 Regent Place
Rugby
Warwickshire
Tel   01788 573 653
Fax   01788 565 498

British Nursing Association
The Colonnades
Beaconsfield Close
Hatfield
Hertfordshire
AL10 5BL
Tel   01707 263 544
Fax   01707 272 250

Carers National Association
Ruth Pitter House
20–25 Glasshouse Yard
London EC1A 4JT
Tel   0808 808 7777
Fax   020 7490 8824

National Care Homes Association
45–49 Leather Lane
London EC1N 7TJ
Tel   020 7831 7090
Fax   020 7831 7040

Registered Nursing Home Association
Calthorpe House
Hagley Road
Edgbaston
Birmingham B16 8QY
Tel   0121 545 2511
Fax   0121 454 0932

The Relatives and Residents Association
5 Tavistock Place
London WC1A 9SS
Tel   020 7916 6055

HEALTH AND DISABILITY

Alzheimer's Disease Society
Gordon House
10 Greencoat Place
London SW1P 1PH
Tel   020 7306 0606
Fax   020 7306 0808

Arthritis Care
18 Stephenson Way
London NW1 2HD
Tel   020 7916 1500
Fax   020 7916 1505

The Arthritis Research Campaign
Copeman House
St Mary's Court, St Mary's Gate
Chesterfield
Derbyshire S41 7TD
Tel   01246 558 033
Fax   01246 558 007

PART 4: SECTION B   Additional Information

British Heart Foundation
17 Fitzhardinge Street
London W1H 4DH
Tel   020 7935 0185
Fax   020 7486 5820

British Red Cross Society
9 Grosvenor Crescent
London SW1X 7EJ
Tel   020 7235 5454
Fax   020 7245 6315

Disablement Information and Advice Lines (Dial UK)
Park Lodge
St Catherine's Hospital
Tickhill Road
Doncaster DN4 8QN
Tel   01302 310 123
Fax   01302 310 404
E-mail   *dialuk@aol.com*

Hospice Information Service
St Christopher's Hospice
51–59 Lawrie Park Road
Sydenham
London SE26 6DZ
Tel   020 8778 9252
Fax   020 8776 9345

Macmillan Cancer Relief
Anchor House
15–19 Britten Street
London
SW3 3TZ
Tel   020 8222 7708

MIND (National Association for Mental Health)
Granta House
15–19 Broadway
Stratford
London E15 4BQ
Tel   020 8519 2122
Fax   020 8522 1725

Mobility Advice and Vehicle Information Service (MAVIS)
Department of Transport, TRL
O Wing, Macadam Avenue
Old Wokingham Road
Crowthorne
Berkshire RG45 6XD
Tel   01344 661 000
Fax   01344 661 066
E-mail   *mavis@detr.gov.uk*

Motability
Goodman House
Station Approach
Harlow
Essex CM20 2ET
Tel   01279 635 666
Fax   01279 632 216

Multiple Sclerosis Society
25 Effie Road
London SW6 1EE
Tel   020 7610 7171

Parkinson's Disease Society
215 Vauxhall Bridge Road
London SW1V 1EJ
Tel   020 7931 8080
Fax   020 7233 9908

Patients Association
PO Box 935
Harrow
Middlesex HA1 3YJ
Tel   020 8423 9111
Fax   020 8423 9119

Royal Association for Disability and Rehabilitation (RADAR)
12 City Forum
250 City Road
London EC1V 8AF
Tel   020 7250 3222

Fax 020 7250 0212
E-mail *radar@radar.org.uk*

Royal National Institute for the Blind (RNIB)
224 Great Portland Street
London W1N 6AA
Tel 020 7388 1266
Fax 020 7388 2034
E-mail *helpline@rnib.org.uk*

Royal National Institute for Deaf People (RNID)
19–23 Featherstone Street
London EC1Y 8SL
Tel 020 7296 8000
Fax 020 7296 8199
E-mail *helpline@rnid.org.uk*

The Stroke Association
Stroke House
123–127 Whitecross Street
London EC1Y 8JJ
Tel 020 7490 7999
Fax 020 7490 2686

BEREAVEMENT AND FUNERALS

CRUSE – Bereavement Care
Cruse House, 126 Sheen Road
Richmond
Surrey TW9 1UR
Tel 020 8940 4818
Fax 020 8940 7638

National Association of Funeral Directors (NAFD)
618 Warwick Road
Solihull
West Midlands B91 1AA
Tel 0121 711 1343
Fax 0121 711 1351

National Association of Widows
54–57 Allison Street
Digbeth
Birmingham B5 5TH
Tel 0121 643 8348

Society of Allied and Independent Funeral Directors
Crowndale House
1 Ferdinand Street
Camden
London NW1 8EE
Tel 020 7267 6777
Fax 020 7267 1147
E-mail *info@saif.org.uk*

413

Appendix 6
Websites

Note: preface all (except those marked *) with '**www.**'

GOVERNMENT

Central government
parliament.uk	*Houses of Parliament*
parliament.uk/commons/hsecom.htm	*House of Commons*
parliament.the-stationery-office.co.uk/	
pa/ld/ldhome.htm	*House of Lords*
pa/ld/ldhansrd.htm	*Hansard: House of Lords*
pa/cm/cmhansrd.htm	*Hansard: House of Commons*
number-10.gov.uk	*No 10 Downing Street*
cabinetoffice.gov.uk	*Cabinet Office*
homeoffice.gov.uk	*Home Office*
dti.gov.uk	*DTI internet service*

General information
open.gov.uk	*Government Information Service*
coi.gov.uk	*Central Office of Information*
dag-business.gov.uk	*Direct Access Government*
official-documents.co.uk	*Official Documents*

Government bodies
inlandrevenue.gov.uk	*Inland Revenue*
companies-house.gov.uk	*Companies House*
landreg.gov.uk	*HM Land Registry*
eoc.org.uk	*Equal Opportunities Commission*
eocni.org.uk	*Equal Opportunities Commission Northern Ireland*

Health and Social Security
doh.gov.uk	*Department of Health*

Appendix 6 WEBSITES

dss.gov.uk	*Department of Social Security*
dss.gov.uk/ba/index.htm	*Benefits Agency*
dss.gov.uk/appeals-service	*The Appeals Service*
coi.gov.uk/coi/depts/GSS/GSS.html	*DSS (Press Releases)*
dss.gov.uk/csa	*Child Support Agency*
cas.gov.uk/nelconts.htm	*Neligan – Social security case law*
hywels.demon.co.uk/commrs/decns.htm	*Child Support Commissioners' decisions*

LEGAL

Official

hmso.gov.uk/acts.htm	*Acts of Parliament*
hmso.gov.uk/stat.htm	*Statutory Instruments*
open.gov.uk/lcd	*Lord Chancellor's Department*
courtservice.co.uk	*The Court Service*
cps.gov.uk	*Crown Prosecution Service*
open.gov.uk/civjustice/	*Civil Justice Council*
open.gov.uk/lab/legal.htm	*Legal Aid Board*
justask.org.uk	*Community Legal Service*
jsboard.co.uk	*The Judicial Studies Board*
gtnet.gov.uk/lawcomm/homepage.htm	*The Law Commission*
publictrust.gov.uk	*Public Trust Office*
offsol.demon.co.uk/index.htm	*Official Solicitor*

Civil Justice Reforms

open.gov.uk/lcd/civil/cjustfr.htm	*Civil Matters*
open.gov.uk/lcd/justice/cjdnet.htm	*Civil Justice Reform: Index*
open.gov.uk/lcd/justice/rules/rules3.htm	*Civil Proceedings Rules*
beagle.org.uk/cpr/	*CPR/PD/Schedules and Slides*

Law reports

open.gov.uk/courts/court/	
highhome.htm	*High Court*
civilhome.htm	*Court of Appeal: Civil Division*
coa_civil_judge.htm	*Court of Appeal (Civil)*
parliament.the-stationery-office.co.uk/pa/ld199697/ldjudgmt/ldjudgmt.htm	
	House of Lords – Judicial Business

lawreports.co.uk *Summaries of recent cases*

European Courts
dhcour.coe.fr *European Court of Human Rights*
europa.eu.int/cj/en/index.htm* *European Court of Justice*
beagle.org.uk/echr/ *ECHR site*

Ombudsmen
ombudsman.org.uk *Ombudsmen*
parliament-ombudsman.org.uk *Parliamentary Commissioner*
health-ombudsman.org.uk *Health Service Commissioners*
open.gov.uk/lgo *Commissioners for Local Administration*
theiob.org.uk *The Insurance Ombudsman Bureau*
www.obo.org.uk *The Banking Ombudsman*

Professional
lawsociety.org.uk *The Law Society*
barcouncil.org.uk *Bar Council*
proflist.com/ *Barristers and Solicitors in England and Wales*

lawyersonline.co.uk/ *Lawyers Online*
scl.org *Society for Computers and Law*
aaml.org *American Academy of Matrimonial Lawyers*

iaml.org *International Academy of Matrimonial Lawyers*

General legal
bailii.org *English/Irish Legal Information Institute*
austlii.edu.au *Australasian Legal Information Institute*
beagle.org.uk *Sean Overend's site (beagle)*
everyform.net *General legal forms*
makeawill.org.uk *Law Society's will site*
number7.demon.co.uk *Roger Horne's Miscellany*
justis.com *Full text legal database*
legaltheory.demon.co.uk *Deborah Charles Publications – Legal Theory*

venables.co.uk/legal *Legal Resources, Delia Venables*

online-law.co.uk	*Online Law*
lawontheweb.co.uk	*General legal site*
lmcb.com	*1 Mitre Court Buildings*
infolaw.co.uk	*Information for Lawyers Limited*
ncl.ac.uk/~nlawwww/	*Web Journal of Current Legal Issues*
west-knights.com	*L J West-Knights*
smithbernal.com	*Smith Bernal International*
casetrack.com	*Smith Bernal case reports*
harassmnt-law.co.uk	*Harassment law*
terrylynch.co.uk	*by a barrister/DDJ*

Legal publishers

hmso.gov.uk	*HM Stationery Office*
butterworths.co.uk	*Butterworths Publishers*
butterworths.co.uk/bld	*Butterworths Law Directory*
familylaw.co.uk	*Family Law*
jordans.co.uk	*Jordans*
lag.org.uk	*Legal Action Group*
smlawpub.co.uk	*Sweet & Maxwell*
butterworths.co.uk/tolley	*Tolley Publishing*
ftlawandtax.com	*FT Law & Tax*
the-lawyer.co.uk	*The Lawyer*
the-times.co.uk	*The Times*
FT.com	*Financial Times*

ORGANISATIONS

Elderly

business.virgin.net/man.web/aea/index.htm	*Action on Elder Abuse*
ace.org.uk	*Age Concern England*
accymru.org.uk	*Age Concern Wales*
alzheimers.org.uk	*Alzheimer's Disease Society*
helptheaged.org.uk	*Help the Aged*

General

amnesty.org	*Amnesty International*
adviceguide.org.uk	*NACAB information site*

PART 4: SECTION B Additional Information

nacab.org.uk	*National Association of Citizens Advice Bureaux*

Caring

carersuk.demon.co.uk	*Carers National Association*
caring-matters.org.uk	*Caring Matters*
care4free.net	*Group of charities*
kcl.ac.uk/kis/schools/kcsmd/paliative/his/htm	*Hospice Information Service*

Health and disability

arc.org.uk	*The Arthritis Research Campaign*
arthritiscare.org.uk	*Arthritis Care*
bhf.org.uk	*British Heart Foundation*
disability.gov.uk	*Disability Discrimination Act Helpline*
dlf.org.uk	*Disabled Living Foundation*
members.aol.com/dialuk	*Disablement Information & Advice Lines*
mind.org.uk	*MIND*
mobility-unit.detr.gov.uk/mavis.htm	*Mobility Advice & Vehicle Information Service (MAVIS)*
motability.co.uk	*Motability*
shef.ac.uk/misc/groups/epda/home.html	*Parkinson's Disease Society*
redcross.org.uk	*British Red Cross Society*
radar.org.uk	*Royal Association for Disability and Rehabilitation (RADAR)*
rnib.org.uk	*Royal National Institute for the Blind*
rnid.org.uk	*Royal National Institute for Deaf People*
stroke.org.uk	*The Stroke Association*

Financial

esi.co.uk	*Electronic Share Information (ESI)*
finance.yahoo.co.uk *	*Electronic Share Information*
fsa.gov.uk	*Financial Services Authority*
number7.demon.co.uk/cgt/allow.htm	*CGT Indexation Allowance*
halifax.co.uk/house/house.html	*House Price Indices (Halifax)*
savills.co.uk	*House Price Indices (FPD Savills)*
nationalsavings.co.uk	*National Savings*
napf.co.uk	*National Association of Pension Funds*
nhfa.co.uk	*Nursing Homes Fees Agency*

devon-ec.gov.uk/dris/economic/retprice.html *RPI (full table)*
ship-ltd.co.uk/index2.htm *Safe Home Income Plans (SHIP)*
spc.uk.com *Society of Pension Consultants*

Housing

vois.org.uk/abbeyfield *The Abbeyfield Society*
housingcorp.gov.uk *Housing Corporation*
nhbc.co.uk *National House Building Council*
shelter.org.uk *Shelter*

Professional

bmj.com *British Medical Journal*
bna.co.uk *British Nursing Association*
tax.org.uk *Chartered Institute of Taxation*
adss.org.uk *Association of Directors of Social Services*
saif.org.uk *Society of Allied and Independent Funeral Directors*

DIRECTORIES AND MISCELLANEOUS

eyp.co.uk *Electronic Yellow Pages*

Appendix 7
Further Reading

LAW SOCIETY PUBLICATIONS

The Guide to the Professional Conduct of Solicitors
    Eighth edition (1999)

The Office Procedures Manual
    Matthew Moore and Michael Dodd of Central Law Training (1997)

Solicitors Accounts Manual
    Seventh edition (1999)

Probate Practitioner's Handbook
    Edited by Lesley King (third edition, 1999)

The Law Society's Conveyancing Handbook
    Frances Silverman (seventh edition, 1999)

The Family Lawyer's Handbook
    Edited by Rebecca Bailey-Harris (1997)

Advising Mentally Disordered Offenders
    Carolyn Taylor and Deborah Postgate (2000)

Assessment of Mental Capacity: Guidance for doctors and lawyers
    BMA/The Law Society (1995)

AGE CONCERN PUBLICATIONS

Managing Other People's Money
    Penny Letts (second edition, 1998)

The Community Care Handbook: The reformed system explained
    Barbara Meredith (second edition, 1998)

Your Taxes and Savings 1999–2000: A guide for older people
    Edited by Sally West

Your Rights 1999–2000: A guide to money benefits for older people
    Sally West

The Retirement Handbook
    Caroline Hartnell (January 2000)

The Pensions Handbook 1999–2000
    Sue Ward

Appendix 7 FURTHER READING

Mid-Life Planning for Retirement
   Edited by Wladek Koch (2000)

Changing Direction: Employment options in mid-life
   Sue Ward (1996)

Using Your Home as Capital 2000–2001
   Cecil Hinton (2000)

Housing Options for Older People
   Louise Russell (2000)

A Buyer's Guide to Retirement Housing (1995)

Residents' Money: A guide to good practice in care homes (1996)

Health and Safety in Care Homes: A practical guide
   Sarah Tullett (1996)

Good Care Management: A guide to setting up and managing a residential care home   Jenyth Worsley (1992)

Elder Abuse: Critical issues in policy and practice
   Edited by Phil Slater and Mervyn Eastman (1999)

AGE CONCERN SERVICES

Fact sheets

Regularly updated fact sheets in a ringbinder for an annual subscription. These are referred to throughout this Handbook.

EAGLE (Exchange on Ageing, Law and Ethics)

Annual membership includes the bi-monthly journal and the fact sheet service. Telephone 020 8765 7377 for an information pack.

CHILD POVERTY ACTION GROUP PUBLICATIONS

CPAG Ltd, 94 White Lion Street, London N1 9PF

Welfare Benefits Handbook
   published annually

Council Tax Handbook
   Martin Ward (fourth edition, 2000)

Rights Guide for Home Owners
   CPAG/SHAC (twelfth edition, 2000)

Non-Means-Tested Benefits: The legislation
   Bonner et al (2000)

CPAG's Income-Related Benefits: The legislation
   Mesher and Wood (2000/2001)

CPAG's Housing Benefit and Council Tax Benefit: The legislation
   Findlay and Ward (fourteenth edition, 2000)

Distributed by CPAG Ltd:

Disability Rights Handbook
   Disability Alliance ERA (2000)

Guide to Housing Benefit and Council Tax Benefit
   Ward and Zebedee (2000)

GENERAL

Butterworths Older Client Law Service
   Various, including Ashton (looseleaf), Butterworths

Finance and Law for the Older Client
   Various (looseleaf), Tolley in association with STEP

Elderly People and the Law
   Gordon R Ashton (1995), Butterworths

The Law and Elderly People
   Griffiths and Roberts (second edition, 1995), Routledge

The Law and Elderly People
   McDonald and Taylor (1995), Sweet & Maxwell

Elderly Clients: A Precedent Manual
   Denzil Lush (1996), Jordans

Good Non-Retirement Guide
   Edited by Rosemary Brown (1999), Kogan Page

Retirement Made Easy
   Rosemary Brown (1994), Kogan Page

COMMUNITY CARE

Community Care and the Law
   Luke Clements (third edition, 2000), Legal Action

Social Services Law
   John Williams (1995), Tolley

Encyclopaedia of Social Sciences and Child Care Law
   General Editor: Richard M Jones (looseleaf – four volumes), Sweet & Maxwell

Community Care Assessments: A practical legal framework
    Richard Gordon QC and Nicola Mackintosh (1997), Sweet & Maxwell

Community Care Practice and the Law
    Michael Mandelstam (second edition, 1999), Jessica Kingsley

Community Care for Older People: Rights, remedies and finances
    Margaret Richards (1996), Jordans

Registered Homes Act Manual
    Richard M Jones (second edition, 1993), Sweet & Maxwell

Registered Homes: A Legal Handbook
    Paul Ridout (1998), Jordans

Croner's Care Home Management
    Croner Publications (looseleaf)

HEALTH

Mental health

Mental Health Law
    Brenda Hoggett (fourth edition, 1996), Sweet & Maxwell

Mental Health Services – Law and Practice
    Larry Gostin (looseleaf), Shaw & Sons

Mental Health Act Manual
    Richard M Jones (sixth edition, 1999), Sweet & Maxwell

Mental Handicap and the Law
    Gordon R Ashton and Adrian D Ward (1992), Sweet & Maxwell

Medical treatment

Medical Treatment and the Law: The protection of adults and minors in the Family Division
    Richard S Harper (1999), Family Law

Mason and McCall Smith: Law and Medical Ethics
    (fifth edition, 1999), Butterworths

Medicine, Patients and the Law
    Margaret Brazier (1992), Penguin Books

Kennedy and Grubb: Medical Law: Text with Materials
    (third edition, 1999), Butterworths

Health Care Law
    McHale and Fox (1997), Sweet & Maxwell

FINANCIAL

Management

Powers of Attorney
> Trevor Aldridge (ninth edition, 2000), Sweet & Maxwell

Enduring Powers of Attorney – A Practitioner's Guide
> Stephen Cretney and Denzil Lush (fourth edition, 1996), Family Law

Powers of Attorney – The New Law
> Phillip Kenny and Ann Kenny (2000), Northumbria Law Press

Heywood & Massey: Court Protection Practice
> Norman Whitehorn (1996), Sweet & Maxwell

State benefits

Butterworths Welfare Law
> Smith, Knipe and Tonge (two volume looseleaf), Butterworths

Inheritance

Butterworths Wills, Probate and Administration Service
> Various, including Ashton (two volume looseleaf), Butterworths

Disability Discrimination: The new law
> Brian J Doyle (1996), Jordans

Blackstones' Guide to the Disability Discrimination Act 1995
> Caroline Gooding (1996), Blackstones

Disability and the Law
> Jeremy Cooper and Stuart Vernon (1996), Jessica Kingsley

* * * * * * * *

JOURNALS

Elderly Client Adviser

A yearly subscription to this bi-monthly journal presently costs £195 and includes a news email service and access to the website: *www.ecadviser.com*.

Contact: Ark Publishing, Zeeta House, 200 Upper Richmond Road, London SW15 2SH
DX 59453
Tel: 020 8785 2700
Fax: 020 8785 9373
Email: info@ark-group.com

SECTION C
Guidance

The information provided in this Section comprises:

- a summary of current proposals for law reform in respect of decision-making for mentally incapacitated adults including:
    - the Law Commission Report No. 231 *Mental Incapacity*
    - the Government's consultation paper *Who Decides?*
    - the Government's response *Making Decisions*
- the Law Society's Guidelines for solicitors on *Enduring Powers of Attorney*;
- the Law Society's Guidelines for solicitors on *Gifts of Property: Implications for Future Liability to Pay for Long-Term Care.*

Appendix 8
Law Reform

8.1 THE LAW COMMISSION

The Law Commission was set up by Parliament to recommend ways in which the law may be improved, kept up to date and made more simple. In 1989 at the prompting of the Law Society's *Mental Health Sub-Committee* (as it then was) it included in its programme the adequacy of procedures for decision-making on behalf of mentally incapacitated adults.

Consultation

Four Consultation Papers were published:

- *Mentally Incapacitated Adults and Decision-Making: An Overview*, No. 119 (March 1991):
  - recognised that the existing law is inadequate to cope with the range of decisions that need to be made on behalf of mentally incapable people but that the issue is large and complex
- *Mentally Incapacitated Adults and Decision-Making: A New Jurisdiction*, No. 128 (December 1992):
  - dealt with private law aspects and proposed procedures whereby decisions relating to the personal care and financial affairs of incapacitated people could be made
- *Mentally Incapacitated Adults and Decision-Making: Medical Treatment and Research*, No. 129 (March 1993):
  - explored legal procedures whereby substitute decisions about treatment could be authorised at an appropriate level
- *Mentally Incapacitated and Other Vulnerable Adults: Public Law Protection*, No. 130 (April 1993):
  - considered the powers of public authorities and was expanded to cover vulnerable as well as incapacitated people

Recommendations

Following extensive consultation the final Report was published:

- *Mental Incapacity*, No. 231 (March 1995)

This Report (which includes a draft *Mental Incapacity Bill*) makes comprehensive recommendations for a statutory scheme to which recourse could be had when any decision (whether personal, medical or financial) needed to be made for a person aged 16 or over who lacked capacity. In particular the Report:

- identifies *principles* of general application;
- lays down a *test of incapacity*;
- defines a *best interests* approach to decision-making;
- proposes a *general authority* to act reasonably (thereby legalising that which happens in practice);
- proposes *continuing powers of attorney* which would extend to personal welfare, financial and health care decisions;
- supports *living wills* subject to statutory safeguards;
- provides *procedures* whereby personal welfare, financial and health care decisions may be made on behalf of an incapacitated adult, either by court orders or the appointment of a manager;
- suggests *codes of practice* to accompany the proposed legislation;
- recommends an enlarged Court of Protection with a regional presence;
- advocates regulation of non-therapeutic medical research;
- seeks enhanced powers for local authorities to provide *protection for vulnerable adults* and would impose a duty to do so.

8.2   THE GOVERNMENT RESPONSE

Who Decides?

In December 1997 the Lord Chancellor published the Green Paper *Who Decides? Making Decisions on Behalf of Mentally Incapacitated Adults* with a short period for further consultation. This was structured to follow the Law Commission's Report. The Government:

- accepted the need for law reform (whilst emphasising that there will be no move towards euthanasia);
- supported many of the recommendations; and
- expressed the wish to consult further on how they may best be implemented and those that may be controversial.

Recommendations accepted

The principles underlying the following recommendations were accepted:

- definition of incapacity;
- framework for carers;
- more extensive powers for the Court of Protection so that decisions can be made regarding a person's health care, personal welfare and finance within the same jurisdiction;
- powers of attorney for the care of the person.

Matters for consultation

The following areas were identified as raising issues of particular moral and ethical sensitivity where further consultation was needed:

- advance statements about health care (although advance refusals of treatment were accepted to be currently binding it was necessary to consider whether these should be put on a statutory footing);
- non-therapeutic medical research.

Resources

At this stage the issue of resources arose for the first time. Three questions were posed in the consultation:

1. what resource implications would arise from implementation of the proposals?
2. would the likely benefits render the costs incurred worthwhile?
3. how would these costs be met?

Making Decisions

In October 1999 the Lord Chancellor published the Government's proposals in the Report *Making Decisions*. This states that there will be:

- a new test of capacity based on a functional approach with a presumption against lack of capacity and an emphasis on assisting people to communicate their decisions;
- a best interests approach to decision-making with statutory guidance as to how this should be determined;
- a general authority for carers to act reasonably subject to restrictions but with authority for expenditure to be incurred including a 'necessaries' rule;
- continuing powers of attorney subject to safeguards;
- decision-making by the court either through one-off orders or the appointment of a manager with specified powers and subject to supervision;

PART 4: SECTION C Guidance

- a new Court of Protection with a regional presence to exercise the new jurisdiction;
- further consultation on a 'release of payments scheme'.

The future

The Lord Chancellor has announced that there will be legislation 'when Parliamentary time allows' but much of the detail has still to be worked out.

8.3 SPECIFIC PROPOSALS

Some of the recommendations of the Law Commission are already finding their way into our law through decisions of the courts. It is helpful to be aware of the proposed new principles set out below.

Definition of incapacity

A person is without capacity if, at the time a decision needs to be taken, he or she is:

- unable by reason of mental disability to make a decision on the matter in question; or
- unable to communicate a decision on that matter because he or she is unconscious or for any other reason.

The new term 'mental disability' means 'any disability or disorder of the mind or brain, whether permanent or temporary, which results in an impairment or disturbance of mental functioning'.

A person is to be regarded as unable to make a decision by reason of mental disability if the disability is such that, at the time when the decision needs to be made, the person is unable to:

- understand or retain the information relevant to the decision; or
- make a decision based on that information.

Best interests

Anything done for a person who is without capacity should be done in that person's 'best interests', and the following factors should be taken into consideration in making an assessment of the person's best interests:

- the ascertainable past and present wishes and feelings of the person concerned and the factors which the person would consider if able to do so;
- the need to permit and encourage the person to participate or improve his or

her ability to participate as fully as possible in anything done for and any decision affecting him or her;

- the views of other people whom it is appropriate and practical to consult about the person's wishes and feelings and what would be in his or her best interests;
- whether the purpose for which any action or decision is required can be as effectively achieved in a manner less restrictive of the person's freedom of action;
- whether there is a reasonable expectation of the person recovering capacity to make the decision in the reasonably foreseeable future;
- the need to be satisfied that the wishes of the person without capacity were not the result of undue influence.

Appendix 9

Law Society Guidelines: Enduring Powers of Attorney

Prepared by the Mental Health and Disability Committee
Revised September 1999

1. Introduction

1.1 The following guidelines are intended to assist solicitors in advising clients who wish to draw up an enduring power of attorney (EPA). They have been prepared by the Law Society's Mental Health and Disability Committee, after consultation with other Law Society committees and the Professional Ethics Division, in response to queries raised by practitioners.

1.2 Different considerations apply in relation to donors who make an EPA as a precautionary measure while they are still in the prime of life, and those who are of borderline mental capacity, where the EPA may need to be registered immediately. These guidelines set out general points for consideration, and their relevance will depend on the particular circumstances of individual cases.

1.3 The guidelines are based on the law in England and Wales. It should be noted that there is currently no internationally recognised form of EPA, and additional arrangements must be made for clients who have property in other jurisdictions.

2. Who is the client?

2.1 Where a solicitor is instructed to prepare an EPA, the donor is the client (The Law Society, *The Guide to the Professional Conduct of Solicitors* (8th edition, 1999) Principle 24.03 note 1).

A solicitor must not accept instructions where he or she suspects that those instructions have been given by a client under duress or undue influence *(ibid.,* Principle 12.04).

When asked to prepare an EPA on written instructions alone, a solicitor should always consider carefully whether these instructions are sufficient, or whether he or she should see the client to discuss them *(ibid.,* Principle 24.03 note 2).

2.2 Where instructions for the preparation of an EPA are received not from the client (i.e. the prospective donor), but from a third party purporting to represent that client, a solicitor should obtain written instructions from the client that he or she wishes the solicitor to act. In any case of doubt the solicitor should see the client alone or take other appropriate steps, both to confirm the instructions with the donor personally after offering appropriate advice, and also to ensure that the donor has the necessary capacity to make the power (see section 5 below). The solicitor must also advise the prospective donor without regard to the interests of the source from which he or she was introduced *(ibid.,* Principle 12.04 and Principle 24.03, note 2).

2.3 Once the EPA has been executed and comes into effect, instructions may be accepted from the attorney but the solicitor continues to owe his/her duties to the donor *(ibid.,* Principle 24.03, note 1). Before registration of the EPA, it may be advisable for the solicitor, where appropriate, to satisfy him/herself that the donor continues to have capacity and to confirm the instructions with the donor. See also the Practice Statement issued by Mrs A B Macfarlane, former Master of the Court of Protection, on 9 August 1995 *(The Law Society's Gazette,* 11 October 1995, p. 21 or The Law Society *Professional Standards Bulletin No. 15,* p. 53), which clarifies solicitors' duties in acting for patients or donors and sets out procedures for dealing with conflicts of interest.

The attorney is the statutory agent of the donor, just as in receivership proceedings the receiver is the statutory agent of the patient *(Re EG* [1914] 1 Ch 927, CA).

3. Capacity to make an EPA

3.1 The solicitor should be satisfied that, on the balance of probabilities, the donor has the mental capacity to make an EPA. Many EPAs are made when the donors are already losing capacity. Consequently they could be unaware of the implications of their actions and are more likely to be vulnerable to exploitation.

3.2 If there is any doubt about the donor's capacity, a medical opinion should be obtained. The solicitor should inform the doctor of the test of capacity laid down in *Re K, Re F* [1988] 1 All ER 358, 363 (see Appendix A attached, and *Assessment of Mental Capacity: Guidance for doctors and lawyers* issued by the Law Society and the British Medical Association (1995)). If the doctor is of the opinion that the donor has capacity, he or she should make a record to that effect and witness the donor's signature on the EPA *(Kenward v Adams* (1975) Times, 29 November).

4. Risk of abuse

4.1 The Master of the Court of Protection has estimated that financial abuse occurs in 10 to 15 per cent of cases of registered EPAs and even more

PART 4: SECTION C Guidance

often with unregistered powers (Denzil Lush, *Solicitors Journal*, 11 September 1998). When advising clients of the benefits of EPAs, the solicitor should also inform them of the risks of abuse, particularly the risk that the attorney could misuse the power. Throughout these guidelines, an attempt has been made to identify possible risk areas and to suggest ways of preventing abuse, which the solicitor should discuss with the donor. Written information for clients on both the benefits and risks of EPAs, whether in a brochure or correspondence, may also be helpful.

4.2 During the initial stages of advising a client, the solicitor should consider the following points:

i) There may be circumstances when an EPA may not be appropriate, and a later application for receivership, with oversight of the Court of Protection, may be preferable. This may be advisable, for example:

- where there are indications of persistent family conflicts suggesting that an EPA may be contested; or
- where the assets are more substantial or complex than family members are accustomed to handle; or
- in cases where litigation may lead to a substantial award of damages for personal injury.

ii) The solicitor should consider discouraging the use of an unregistered EPA as an ordinary power of attorney, particularly for vulnerable elderly clients. Instructions to this effect could be included in the instrument itself (see para. 5.3 below) or the donor could be advised to lodge the power with the solicitor, with strict instructions that it is not to be used until the donor becomes or is becoming incapable.

5. Taking instructions

The solicitor should take full and careful instructions from the donor, and ensure that the following matters, where applicable, are considered by the donor when giving instructions.

5.1 *Choice of attorney*

The choice of attorney is clearly a personal decision for the donor, but it is important for the solicitor to advise the donor of the various options available, and to stress the need for the attorney to be absolutely trustworthy, since on appointment the attorney's actions will be subject to little supervision or scrutiny (see section 4 above). The donor should be advised that the appointment of a sole attorney may provide greater opportunity for abuse and exploitation than appointing more than one attorney (see below).

The solicitor should ask questions about the donor's relationship with the proposed attorney and whether the attorney has the skills required to manage the donor's financial affairs. The donor should also consider the suitability of appointing a family member or someone independent of the family, or a combination of both.

More than one attorney

Where more than one attorney is to be appointed, they must be appointed to act either 'jointly' or 'jointly and severally' (Enduring Powers of Attorney Act 1985, s 11(1)).

One of these two alternatives must be chosen and the other crossed out. Failure to cross out one of these alternatives on the prescribed form makes the power invalid, and this is one of the commonest reasons for the Court of Protection or Public Trust Office refusing to register an EPA.

The differences between a 'joint' and 'joint and several' appointment should be explained to the donor:

- In addition to the explanatory information in the prescribed form to the effect that joint attorneys must all act together and cannot act separately, the donor should be advised that a joint appointment will terminate if any one of the attorneys disclaims, dies, or becomes bankrupt or mentally incapable. However, joint appointments may provide a safeguard against possible abuse, since each attorney will be able to oversee the actions of the other(s).

- Similarly, in addition to the explanatory information in the prescribed form to the effect that joint and several attorneys can all act together but can also act separately if they wish, the donor should be advised that, where there is a joint and several appointment, the disclaimer, death, bankruptcy and incapacity of one attorney will not automatically terminate the power.

The donor may have to make difficult choices as to which family member(s) to appoint as his or her attorney. It is possible to allow some flexibility, as in the following examples:

i) The donor may wish to appoint a family member and a professional to act jointly and severally with, for example, the family member dealing with day-to-day matters, and the professional dealing with more complex affairs.

ii) The donor may wish to appoint his or her spouse as attorney, with provision for their adult child(ren) to take over as attorney(s) should the spouse die or become incapacitated. One way to achieve this is for the donor to execute two EPAs: the first appointing the spouse as attorney, and the second appointing the child(ren) with a provision that it will only come into effect if the first power is terminated for any reason. Alternatively, the donor could appoint everyone to act jointly and severally, with an informal understanding that the children will not act while the spouse is able to do so.

iii) The donor may wish to appoint his or her three adult children as attorneys to act jointly and severally, with a proviso that anything done under the power should be done by at least two of them. This could be achieved by careful wording of the EPA document or by an accompanying statement or letter of wishes, which although not directly enforceable, would provide a clear indication as to how the donor wishes the power to be operated.

5.2 *General or limited authority*

The donor must be clear whether the EPA is to be a general power, giving the attorney authority to manage all the donor's property and affairs, or whether the authority is to extend only to part of his or her property and affairs. Any restrictions to the power should be carefully drafted and should have regard to the provisions of the Enduring Powers of Attorney Act 1985 (see also paras 5.6 and 5.11 below).

The solicitor should also discuss with the donor what arrangements should be made for the management of those affairs which are not covered by the EPA. Donors should be advised that if they leave a 'gap', so that part of their affairs are not covered by the EPA, it may be necessary for the Court of Protection to intervene and appoint a receiver.

5.3 *When the power is to come into operation*

The donor must understand when the power is to come into operation. If nothing is said in the instrument, it will take effect immediately, and can be used as an ordinary power of attorney. The donor should be advised of the risk of abuse of an unregistered power, unless s/he is in a position to supervise and authorise use of the power.

If the donor does not want the power to take effect immediately and would prefer it to be held in abeyance until the onset of his or her incapacity, he or she must expressly say so in the EPA. The donor may also wish to include a specific condition that a statement from a doctor confirming lack of capacity must accompany the application to register the EPA.

In such circumstances, it may be preferable to state that the power will not come into operation until the need arises to apply to register the EPA, rather than state that it will not come into operation until it is registered. Pending completion of the registration formalities, the attorney has limited powers, and it may be better for the attorney to have these powers, rather than none at all.

5.4 *Gifts*

Section 3(5) of the Enduring Powers of Attorney Act 1985 gives the attorney limited authority to make gifts of the donor's money or property:

- The *recipient* of the gift must be either an individual who.

- is related to or connected with the donor, or a charity to which the donor actually made gifts or might be expected to make gifts if s/he had capacity.

- The *timing* of the gift must occur within the prescribed parameters. A gift to charity can be made at any time of the year, but a gift to an individual must be of a seasonal nature, or made on the occasion of a birth or marriage, or on the anniversary of a birth or marriage.

- The *value* of the gift must be not unreasonable having regard to all the circumstances and in particular the size of the donor's estate.

The donor cannot confer wider authority on the attorney than that specified in section 3(5), but it is open to the donor to restrict or exclude the authority which would otherwise be available to the attorney under that subsection. This possibility should be specifically discussed with the donor, since improper gifting is the most widespread form of abuse in attorneyship. The donor may wish to specify in the power the circumstances in which the attorney may make gifts of money or property.

Section 3(5) applies to both registered and unregistered EPAs, but not to those which are in the course of being registered. Where an application to register the EPA has been made, the attorney cannot make *any* gifts of the donor's property until the power has been registered.

If the EPA is registered, the Court of Protection can authorise the attorney to act so as to benefit himself or others, otherwise than in accordance with section 3(5), provided that there are no restrictions in the EPA itself (Enduring Powers of Attorney Act 1985, s 8(2)(e)).

Solicitors must also take account of Principle 15.05 of the Guide to Professional Conduct (*op cit*, 1999) concerning gifts to solicitors.

5.5 *Delegation by the attorney*

It is a basic principle of the law of agency that a delegate cannot delegate his or her authority. Alternatively, this could be expressed as a duty on the part of an agent to perform his or her functions personally.

Like any other agent, an attorney acting under an EPA has an implied power to delegate any functions which are of a purely ministerial nature; which do not involve or require the exercise of any confidence or discretion; and which the donor would not expect the attorney to attend to

PART 4: SECTION C Guidance

personally.

Any wider power of delegation must be expressly provided for in the EPA itself: for example, transferring the donor's assets into a discretionary investment management scheme operated by a stockbroker or bank.

5.6 *Investment business*

Unless the power is restricted to exclude investments as defined by the Financial Services Act 1986, the attorney may need to consider the investment business implications of his/her appointment. A solicitor who is appointed attorney under an EPA is likely to be conducting investment business and if so, will need to be authorised under the Financial Services Act. In addition, the solicitor will need to consider whether the Solicitors' Investment Business Rules 1995 apply.

The Financial Services and Markets Bill due to come into effect in approximately mid-2000, is likely to change the definition of investment business and affect the need for authorisation. The detailed position, at the time of writing, is unclear and solicitors will need to keep this aspect under review.

5.7 *Trusteeships held by the donor*

The solicitor should ask whether the donor holds:

- any trusteeships; and
- any property jointly with others.

Section 3(3) of the Enduring Powers of Attorney Act 1985 has been repealed by the Trustee Delegation Act 1999 with effect from 1 January 2000. Section 4 of the 1999 Act contains detailed transitional provisions which affect existing EPAs, both registered and unregistered.

The general rule is that any trustee functions delegated to an attorney (whether under an ordinary power or an enduring power) must comply with the provisions of section 25 of the Trustee Act 1925, as amended by the 1999 Act.

However, section 1(1) of the 1999 Act provides an exception to this general rule. An attorney can exercise a trustee function of the donor if it relates to land, or the capital proceeds or income from land, in which the donor has a beneficial interest. This is, of course, subject to any provision to the contrary contained in the trust instrument or the power of attorney itself.

5.8 *Solicitor-attorneys*

Where a solicitor is appointed as attorney, or where it is intended that a particular solicitor will deal with the general management of the donor's affairs, it is recommended that the solicitor's current terms and conditions of business (including charging rates and the frequency of billing) be discussed with and approved by the donor at the time of granting the power.

Since the explanatory information on the prescribed form of EPA is ambiguous about the remuneration of professional attorneys, it is recommended that a professional charging clause be included in the power for the avoidance of doubt.

Where a solicitor is appointed sole attorney (or is reasonably likely to become the sole attorney), or where two or more solicitors in the same firm are appointed and there is no external attorney, the donor should be informed of the potential problems of accountability if he or she should become mentally incapacitated. If necessary, arrangements could be made for the solicitor's costs to be approved or audited by an independent third party in the event of the donor's incapacity.

In a number of cases solicitor-attorneys have disclaimed when it became apparent that the donor's assets were insufficient to make the attorneyship cost-effective. The Law Society's view is that, if solicitors intend to disclaim in such circumstances, they should not take on the attorneyship in the first place, or should warn the donor of this possibility at the time of making the power.

Further guidance is given in the Guide to Professional Conduct (*op. cit.,* Principle 24.03, notes 5,6,7). Solicitors are also reminded that any commission earned should be paid to the donor (see Annex 14G of the Guide to Professional Conduct).

5.9 *The donor's property and affairs*

It may be helpful for solicitors to record and retain information relating to the donor's property and affairs, even where they are not to be appointed as an attorney themselves. The Law Society's *Personal Assets Log*, which is sometimes used when taking will-drafting instructions, could be suitably adapted for this purpose. In addition, there are certain requirements under the Solicitors' Investment Business Rules where solicitors safeguard and administer documents of title to investments, e.g. share certificates.

5.10 *Notification of intention to register the EPA*

Solicitors should explain to the donor that the attorney has a duty to notify the donor in person, and at least three members of the donor's family, of his or her intention to register the EPA with the Public Trust Office if the attorney has reason to believe that the donor is, or is becoming mentally incapable.

It may be helpful to obtain a list of the names and addresses of the relatives at the time the EPA is granted. If the donor would like other members of the family, or friends or close associates to be notified in addition to those on the statutory list, details could be included in the EPA itself or in a separate letter.

In any event, solicitors should encourage donors to tell their family that they have made an EPA and perhaps explain why they have chosen the attorney(s). This may help to guard against the possibility of abuse by the attorney and may also reduce the risk of conflict between family members at a later stage.

5.11 *Disclosure of the donor's will*

Solicitors are under a duty to keep their clients' affairs confidential (The Law Society, *The Guide to the Professional Conduct of Solicitors* (8th edition, 1999) Principle 16.01). However, the attorney(s) may need to know about the contents of the donor's will in order to avoid acting contrary to the testamentary intentions of the donor (for example, by the sale of an asset specifically bequeathed, when other assets that fell into residue could be disposed of instead).

The question of disclosure of the donor's will should be discussed at the time of making the EPA, and instructions should be obtained as to whether disclosure is denied, or the circumstances in which it is permitted. For example, the donor may agree that the solicitor can disclose the contents of the will to the attorney, but only if the EPA is registered and the solicitor thinks that disclosure of the will is necessary or expedient for the proper performance of the attorney's functions.

Principle 24.03, note 4 of the Guide (*ibid.*) gives guidance where the EPA is registered and is silent on the subject of disclosure. Advice may also be sought from the Professional Ethics Division or from the Public Trust Office (see section 13 below).

The attorney also has a common law duty to keep the donor's affairs (including the contents of a will) confidential.

5.12 *Medical evidence*

It may be worth asking the donor to give advance consent in writing authorising the solicitor to contact the donor's GP or any other medical practitioner if the need for medical evidence should arise at a later date (for example, on registration of the power; or, after the power has been registered, to assess whether the donor has testamentary capacity).

5.13 *Safeguards against abuse*

Solicitors should discuss with the donor appropriate measures to safeguard against the power being misused or exploited. This could include notifying other family members of the existence of the power, and how

Appendix 9 ENDURING POWERS OF ATTORNEY – GUIDELINES

the donor intends it to be used.

The solicitor could also consider offering an auditing service, by inserting a clause into the power requiring the attorney to produce to the solicitor, on a specified date each year, an account of his/her actions as attorney during the last 12 months. If the attorney failed to render a satisfactory account, the solicitor could apply for registration of the power to be cancelled on the grounds of the attorney's unsuitability. Again a charging procedure for this service must be agreed with the donor in advance.

6. Drawing up the EPA

6.1 *The prescribed form*

An EPA must be in the form prescribed by the Enduring Powers of Attorney (Prescribed Form) Regulations in force at the time of its execution by the donor. There have been three sets of regulations and the periods during which they have been in force are:

- 1986 Regulations   10 March 1986 to 30 June 1988
- 1987 Regulations   1 November 1987 to 30 July 1991
- 1990 Regulations   31 July 1991 onwards

Solicitors should ensure that existing EPAs are in the form prescribed on the date they were executed by the donors and that the form they are currently using is the one prescribed by the Enduring Powers of Attorney (Prescribed Form) Regulations 1990 (SI 1990 No. 1376).

6.2 Provided the prescribed form is used, it does not matter whether it is a printed form from a law stationers or whether it is transcribed onto a word-processor, although a law stationer's form is more easily recognisable by third parties. What is essential, however, is that there should be no unauthorised departure from the prescribed form. So, where the donor is to be offered an EPA which is not on a law stationer's form, the solicitor should be absolutely certain that the form complies with the prescribed form regulations. Use of inaccurate or incomplete word-processed forms are common reasons for refusal to register an EPA.

Part A ('About using this form') and the marginal notes must be included in the EPA because the Enduring Powers of Attorney Act requires the prescribed explanatory information to be incorporated in the instrument at the time of execution by the donor (s 2(1) and 2(2), and reg. 2(1) of the 1990 Regulations).

6.3 *Completing the form*

Solicitors should ensure that where alternatives are provided on the form (for example for 'joint' or 'joint and several' appointments, or to specify the extent of the authority granted), the required deletions are made by

PART 4: SECTION C Guidance

crossing out the options not chosen by the donor.

There is space on the prescribed form to provide details of two attorneys. Where it is intended to appoint three attorneys, the details of the third attorney may be included in the main document, fitted in to the space after the details of the second attorney.

Where more than three attorneys are to be appointed, details of the first two attorneys should be given in the main document, followed by the words 'and (see additional names on attached sheet)' and the details given on a sheet to be attached to the main document marked clearly 'Names of additional attorneys'.

6.4 About 10 per cent of EPAs are refused registration because of a defect in the form or the wording of the instrument. In some cases, registration may be possible after the filing of further evidence to overcome the defect. Solicitors who have assisted a donor in drawing up an EPA which is subsequently refused registration because of a defect that is material may be liable for the additional costs of receivership, since at that point the donor may not have the capacity to execute a new EPA.

7. Executing the power

7.1 An EPA must be executed by both the donor and the attorney(s). The donor must execute Part B of the prescribed form. The attorney must execute Part C. Where more than one attorney is appointed, each of them must complete a *separate* Part C, the additional sheets having been added and secured to the EPA document beforehand. One Part C cannot be 'shared' by more than one attorney.

The donor must execute the EPA before the attorney(s), because the attorney(s) cannot accept a power which has not yet been conferred. However, execution by the donor and attorney(s) need not take place simultaneously. There is no reason why execution by the attorney(s) should not occur at a later date, provided it happens before the donor loses capacity. It is often advisable for the attorney(s) to sign as soon as possible after the donor.

7.2 Execution by the donor and the attorney(s) must take place in the presence of a witness, but not necessarily the same witness, who must sign Part B or Part C of the prescribed form, as the case may be, and give his or her full name and address.

There are various restrictions as to who can act as a witness, and in particular:

- the donor and attorney must not witness each other's signature;
- one attorney cannot witness the signature of another attorney;

Appendix 9 ENDURING POWERS OF ATTORNEY – GUIDELINES

- the marginal notes to Part B of the prescribed form warn that it is not advisable for the donor's spouse to witness his or her signature – this is because of the rules of evidence relating to compellability; and

- at common law, a blind person cannot witness another person's signature.

7.3 If the donor or attorney is physically disabled and unable to sign, he or she may make a mark, and the attestation clause should be adapted to explain this. Alternatively, the donor or an attorney may authorise another person to sign the EPA at his or her direction, in which case it must be signed by that person in the presence of two witnesses, as described in the marginal notes.

Although the Enduring Powers of Attorney (Prescribed Form) Regulations 1990 do not expressly state that, where someone executes the EPA at the direction of the donor or attorney, he or she must do so in the presence of the donor or attorney, it is essential that the power be executed in their presence in order to comply with section 1(3) of the Law of Property (Miscellaneous Provisions) Act 1989.

If the donor is blind, this should be stated in the attestation clause so that, if an application is made to register the EPA, the Public Trust Office can make enquiries as to how the donor was notified of the intention to register.

8. Copies of an EPA

8.1 The contents of an EPA can be proved by means of a certified copy. In order to comply with the provisions of section 3 of the Powers of Attorney Act 1971, a certificate should appear at the end of each page of the copy stating that it is a true and complete copy of the corresponding page of the original. The certificate must be signed by the donor, or a solicitor, or a notary public or a stockbroker.

9. Notification of intention to register the EPA

9.1 When it is necessary to give notice of the attorney's intention to register the power, the prescribed form of notice (Form EP1) must be used. The donor must be personally served with this notice, and the donor's relatives must be given notice by first class post.

It may be helpful, in the case of the relatives, to send the notice with an accompanying letter explaining the circumstances because, in the absence of such an explanation, there may be cause for concern. Giving an appropriate explanation and information at this stage may prevent the application from becoming contentious.

Although there is no statutory requirement to do so, a copy of the EPA could also be sent to the relatives, in view of the fact that one of the

PART 4: SECTION C Guidance

grounds on which they can object to registration is that the power purported to have been created by the instrument is not valid as an enduring power.

9.2 As stated above, the notice of intention to register (Form EP1) must be given to the donor personally. The notice need not be handed to the donor by the attorney. It can be given to the donor by an agent (perhaps a solicitor) acting on the attorney's behalf, and the name of the person who gives notice to the donor must be stated on Form EP2.

Many attorneys, both relatives and professionals, find it distressing to have to inform donors of the implications of their failing mental capacity. Schedule 1 to the Enduring Powers of Attorney Act 1985 makes provision for the attorney to apply to the Public Trustee for dispensation from the requirement to serve notice on anyone entitled to receive it, including the donor.

However, the Public Trustee is reluctant to grant such a dispensation because it is the donor's right, and the right of entitled relatives, to be informed and to have an opportunity to object to registration. A dispensation is only likely to be granted in relation to the donor where there is clear medical evidence to show that notification would be detrimental to the donor's health, and in the case of relatives, only in exceptional circumstances.

10. Statutory wills

10.1 An attorney cannot execute a will on the donor's behalf because the Wills Act 1837 requires a will to be signed by the testator personally or by someone in his or her presence and at his or her direction.

Where a person lacks testamentary capacity, the Court of Protection can order the execution of a statutory will on his or her behalf. The Court's will-making jurisdiction is conferred by the Mental Health Act 1983 – not the Enduring Powers of Attorney Act 1985 – but can be invoked where there is a registered EPA. An application for an order authorising the execution of a statutory will should be considered by solicitors where there is no will or where the existing will is no longer appropriate due to a change of circumstances. In statutory will proceedings, the Official Solicitor is usually asked to represent the testator.

10.2 The Court will require recent medical evidence showing that the donor:

- is incapable, by reason of mental disorder, of managing and administering his or her property and affairs. This evidence should be provided on Form CP3 because, in effect, the Court needs to be satisfied that the donor is a 'patient' for the purposes of the Mental Health Act; and

Appendix 9 ENDURING POWERS OF ATTORNEY – GUIDELINES

- is incapable of making a valid will for himself or herself.

The Court's procedure notes PN9 and PN9(A) explain the Court's requirements. Guidance on the relevant tests of capacity can be found in the Law Society/BMA publication *Assessment of Mental Capacity: Guidance for doctors and lawyers* (1995).

11. Support for attorneys

11.1 Section 4(5) of the Enduring Powers of Attorney Act 1985 provides that the attorney may, before making an application for the registration of the EPA, refer to the Court any question as to the validity of the power. However, such an application can only be made when the attorney has reason to believe that the donor is, or is becoming, mentally incapable. The Court will not determine any question as to the validity of an unregistered power in any other circumstances.

11.2 Under section 8 of the Act, the Court of Protection has various functions with respect to registered powers. However, the Court should not be seen as being available to 'hold the hand' of the attorney, who should in normal circumstances be able to act in the best interests of the donor, taking advice where necessary from a solicitor or other professional adviser. It should be noted that, although the Court may interpret the terms of an EPA or give directions as to its exercise, it does not have power to extend or amend the terms of the EPA as granted by the donor.

12. Where abuse is suspected

12.1 If solicitors suspect that an attorney may be misusing an EPA or acting dishonestly and the donor is unable to take action to protect him or herself, they should try to facilitate the remedies that the donor would have adopted if able to do so. In the first instance, the Public Trust Office should be notified and guidance sought from the Court of Protection as to how to proceed. This might include:

- an application to the Court of Protection under the Mental Health Act 1983 for an Order giving authority to take action to recover the donor's funds;
- an application to the Court for registration of the power to be cancelled on the grounds of the attorney's unsuitability and for receivership proceedings to be instituted;
- involvement of the police to investigate allegations of theft or fraud;
- where residential care or nursing homes are involved, using the local authority complaints procedure or involving the relevant registration authority.

13. Further advice

13.1 Solicitors may obtain confidential advice on matters relating to professional ethics from the Law Society's Professional Ethics Division (0870 606 2577) and on practice issues from the Practice Advice Service (0870 606 2522). The Mental Health and Disability Committee is also willing to consider written requests from solicitors for comments on complex cases.

Information and advice can also be obtained from the Customer Services Unit of the Public Trust Office (020 7664 7300).

APPENDIX A

Capacity to make an Enduring Power of Attorney

A power of attorney signed by a person who lacks capacity is null and void, unless it can be proved that it was signed during a lucid interval. Shortly after the Enduring Powers of Attorney Act 1985 came into force, the Court of Protection received a considerable number of applications to register enduring powers which had only just been created. This raised a doubt as to whether the donors had been mentally capable when they signed the powers. The problem was resolved in the test cases *Re K, Re F* [1988] Ch 310, in which the judge discussed the capacity to create an enduring power.

Having stated that the test of capacity to create an enduring power of attorney was that the donor understood the nature and effect of the document, the judge in the case set out four pieces of information which any person creating an EPA should understand:

1. if such be the terms of the power, that the attorney will be able to assume complete authority over the donor's affairs;
2. if such be the terms of the power, that the attorney will be able to do anything with the donor's property which the donor could have done;
3. that the authority will continue if the donor should be or should become mentally incapable; and
4. that if he or she should be or become mentally incapable, the power will be irrevocable without confirmation by the Court of Protection.

It is worth noting that the donor need not have the capacity to do all the things which the attorney will be able to do under the power. The donor need only have capacity to create the EPA.

The implications of Re K, Re F

The judge in *Re K, Re F* also commented that if the donor is capable of signing an enduring power of attorney, but incapable of managing and administering his or her property and affairs, the attorney has an obligation to register the power with the Court of Protection straightaway. Arguably, the attorney also has a moral duty in such cases to forewarn the donor that registration is not merely possible, but is intended immediately.

The decision in *Re K, Re F* has been criticised for imposing too simple a test of capacity to create an enduring power. But the simplicity or complexity of the test depends largely on the questions asked by the person assessing the donor's capacity. For example, if the four pieces of basic relevant information described by the judge in *Re K, Re F* were mentioned to the donor and he or she was asked 'Do you understand this?' in such a way as to encourage an affirmative reply, the donor would probably pass the test with flying colours and, indeed, the test would be too simple. If, on the other hand, the assessor were specifically to ask the donor 'What will your attorney be able to do?' and 'What will happen if you become mentally incapable?' the test would be substantially harder. There is no direct judicial authority on the point, but it can be inferred from the decision in *Re Beaney (deceased)* [1978] 1 WLR 770, that questions susceptible to the answers 'Yes' or 'No' may be inadequate for the purpose of assessing capacity.

[Adapted from BMA/Law Society, *Assessment of Mental Capacity: Guidance for Doctors and Lawyers* (1995) BMA]

APPENDIX B

Checklist of dos and don'ts for enduring powers of attorney

In taking instructions:

DO:

- Assess carefully the donor's capacity to make an EPA
- Advise the donor fully on both the benefits and the risks
- Discuss with the donor the suitability of the proposed attorney(s)
- Confirm instructions with the donor personally
- Clarify and specify arrangements relating to:
  - disclosure of the donor's will
  - dealing with investment business
  - making gifts
  - payment of professional charges

DON'T:

- Forget that the donor is your client

PART 4: SECTION C Guidance

- Act on the unconfirmed instructions of third parties
- Allow third parties to control your access to the donor

In preparing the EPA:

DO:

- Use the current prescribed form of EPA
- Clarify when the power is to take effect
- Ensure the power is executed by the donor while still competent
- Ensure the power is signed by the attorney(s) after the donor has signed
- Ensure the signatures of donor and attorney(s) are properly witnessed
- Ensure the power is dated

DON'T:

- Omit Part A of the form or any of the marginal notes
- Fail to make the required deletions where alternatives are offered on the form
- Include restrictions or instructions which are unclear or outside the scope of the Enduring Powers of Attorney Act 1985

In applying for registration:

DO:

- Notify the donor and the required relatives using Form EP1
- Apply for registration within 10 days of the notification of the last person required to be notified
- Enclose the original EPA with the application
- Insert on form EP2 the dates on which the people concerned were notified and the date of the application for registration
- Send the registration fee with the application
- Send medical evidence in support of any application to dispense with the requirement to serve notice on the donor

DON'T:

- Forget that Form EP1 must be given to the donor personally
- Fail to comply with specified time-limits

Appendix 10

Law Society Guidelines: Gifts of Property: Implications for Future Liability to Pay for Long-Term Care

Prepared by the Mental Health and Disability Committee
Revised March 2000

1. Elderly people or those nearing retirement may seek advice from solicitors as to the advantages and disadvantages of transferring their home or other property to relatives, even though in some cases they still intend to live in the home. The solicitor's advice will of course vary, according to the individual circumstances of the client, their motivation for making such a gift, and what they are hoping to achieve by it.

2. The following guidelines are designed to assist solicitors, both to ensure that their clients fully understand the nature, effects, benefits, risks and foreseeable consequences of making such a gift, and also to clarify the solicitor's role and duty in relation to such transactions. In particular, consideration is given to the implications of making gifts of property on possible future liability for the payment of fees for residential or nursing home care. This area of law is still under review by the Government, so solicitors should be aware that the law may change.

3. Whilst these guidelines generally refer to the making of 'gifts' they apply with equal force to situations where the disposal of property at a significant undervalue is contemplated.

THE NEED FOR LEGAL ADVICE

4. The Law Society is aware of a number of non-solicitor legal advice services which are marketing schemes for elderly people to effect a gift of property with the intention of avoiding the value of that property being taken into account to pay for residential care. Some make unjustified claims as to the effectiveness of the schemes, or fail to take into account the individual circumstances of clients. Seldom do these schemes highlight the other risks involved in making a gift of the home to members of the family.

5. These guidelines are also intended to assist solicitors to stress the need for clients to obtain proper legal advice, and to highlight the risks of using unqualified advisers.

PART 4: SECTION C   Guidance

Who is the client?

6. The solicitor must first be clear as to who s/he is acting for, especially where relatives purport to be giving instructions on behalf of an elderly person. In most cases, it will be the elderly person who owns the home or property so if the solicitor is to act in a transfer the elderly person will be the client. This will be the assumption for the purpose of these guidelines. It is important to recognise that there is an inevitable conflict of interest between the elderly person and anyone who stands to gain from the transaction, so the elderly person should receive independent advice (see also paras 30–31 below).

7. The solicitor acting for the elderly person should see the client alone, to satisfy him/herself that the client is acting freely, to confirm the client's wishes and intentions, and to gauge the extent, if any, of family or other influence (see Principle 12.05 of *The Guide to the Professional Conduct of Solicitors* (1999)). It may be necessary to spend some time with the client, talking about wider issues, in order to evaluate these aspects, clarify the family circumstances, and assess whether the client has the mental capacity to make the gift (see Appendix A for details of the relevant test of capacity).

8. If the client is not already known to the solicitor, it may also be advisable to check whether another solicitor has previously acted for the client, and if so, to seek the client's consent to contact that solicitor, in case there are factors to be taken into account which are not immediately apparent.

The client's understanding

9. It is important to ensure that the client understands the nature of a gift, that this is what is intended and the long-term implications. Before making any such gift clients should in particular understand:

    - that the money or property they intend to give away is theirs in the first place;
    - why the gift is being made;
    - whether it is a one-off, or part of a series of gifts;
    - the extent of the gift in relation to the rest of their money and property;
    - that they are making an outright gift rather than, say, a loan or acquiring a share in a business or property owned by the recipient;
    - whether they expect to receive anything in return and, if so, how much, or on what terms (e.g. someone who is giving away their house might expect to be able to carry on living there rent free for the rest of their life: but who pays for the insurance and upkeep?);

Appendix 10 GIFTS OF PROPERTY – GUIDELINES

- whether they intend the gift to take effect immediately, or at a later date – perhaps when they die, or go into residential care;
- that, if the gift is outright, they can't assume that the money or property would be returned to them on request;
- the effect that making the gift could have on their future standard of living;
- the effect that the gift could have on other members of the family who might have expected eventually to inherit a share of the money or property;
- the possibility that the recipient could die first, or become involved in divorce or bankruptcy proceedings, in which case the money or property given away could end up belonging to somebody else;
- that the donor and recipient could fall out and even become quite hostile to one another;
- whether they have already made gifts to the recipient or other people; and
- any other foreseeable consequences of making or not making the gift (some of which are considered below).

The client's objectives

10. The solicitor should establish why the gift of property is being contemplated, and whether the client's objectives will in fact be achieved by the making of the gift or could be achieved in some other way. In establishing the client's objectives, the following matters may be relevant:

    (i) If the objective is to ensure that a particular relative (e.g. a child) inherits the client's home rather than someone else, this can equally well be achieved by making a will.

    (ii) If the objective is to avoid inheritance tax on the death of the client, a rough calculation should be made of the client's likely estate to assess the amount of tax which may be payable, and whether other tax saving measures could be considered. The client might not appreciate that the value of the property, together with the remainder of the estate, may not exceed the level at which inheritance tax becomes payable.
    The client might also not be aware that if s/he intends to continue living in the home after giving it away, there may be no inheritance tax saving because of the 'reservation of benefit' rules. The consequence might also be to increase the liability to inheritance tax on the death of the relative to whom the gift has been made if s/he

451

dies before the client. Again, other schemes to mitigate these vulnerabilities should be considered.

(iii) If the objective is to relieve the elderly client of the worry and responsibility of home ownership, other ways of achieving this should be discussed, such as making an enduring power of attorney.

(iv) If the client volunteers that a significant part of his/her objective is to try to avoid the value of the home being taken into account in various forms of means-testing, the implications and possible consequences should be explained to the client. These matters are considered in the following paragraphs in relation to liability to pay for long-term care. Alternative measures should also be discussed. The solicitor may also need to consider her/his own position (see paras 28–31 below).

Other reasons for transferring the home

11. There may, of course, be good reasons for transferring the home, or a share in the home, to a relative or another person quite apart from the desire to avoid means-testing. If such reasons exist the transfer should be effected sooner rather than later and it would be worthwhile reciting the reason in the transfer deed. For example:

    (a) the home has not been vested in the appropriate names in the first place (e.g. it was funded in whole or in part by a son or daughter but vested in the name of the parent);

    (b) a daughter has given up a well-paid job to live in the home and care for an infirm parent in the expectation of inheriting the home on the death of the parent;

    (c) the parent has for some years been unable to meet the outgoings or pay for alterations or improvements to the home and these have been funded by a son in the expectation of inheriting the home on the death of the parent;

    (d) the home comprises part of a family business (e.g. a farm) which would no longer be viable if the home was 'lost'.

12. If the home is already vested in the joint names of the infirm elderly person and another occupier, or can for justifiable reasons be transferred by the elderly person into joint names, the beneficial interest of the elderly person may, on a means assessment, have little value when subject to the continued rights of occupation of the co-owner.

Severance of a joint tenancy

13. If the home is vested in the joint names of an elderly couple it may be

worth considering a severence of the joint tenancy with a view to preserving at least a one-half share for the family. Each spouse can then make a will leaving his or her one-half share to the children. This provides some protection in the event that a caring spouse dies before an infirm spouse but there may be vulnerability to a claim under the Inheritance (Provision for Family and Dependants) Act 1975. It is possible to take this step even after the infirm spouse has become mentally incapable.

IMPLICATIONS OF MAKING THE GIFT

14. A proper assessment of the implications of making a gift of the home, both for the client and for her/his relative(s) can best be achieved by listing the possible benefits and risks. These may include the following:

Possible benefits

- a saving of inheritance tax, probate fees and costs on the death of the client. Although in most cases the existence of a potential liability for inheritance tax will mean that a gift of the home by itself will not avoid vulnerability to means-testing, the high value of homes particularly in London may create this situation;
- avoiding the need to sell the home to pay for charges such as residential care or nursing home fees, thus securing the family's inheritance;
- avoiding the value of the home being taken into account in means-testing for other benefits or services.

Possible risks

- the value of the home may still be taken into account under the anti-avoidance measures in relation to means-testing (see paras 15–27);
- the capital gains tax owner-occupier exemption will apply to the gift, but may be lost thereafter and there will be no automatic uplift to the market value of the home on the client's death;
- the client may never need residential or nursing home care (it has been estimated that less than 6 per cent of people aged 75–85 need residential care), so the risks of giving away the home may outweigh any potential benefits to be achieved;
- if the client does eventually need residential or nursing home care but no longer has the resources to pay the fees him/herself because of the gift, the local authority may only pay for a basic level of care (e.g. a shared room in a home of its choice), so the client may be dependent on relatives to top up the fees if a better standard of care is desired;

PART 4: SECTION C   Guidance

- the relatives to whom the gift has been made may fail to keep their side of the understanding, whether deliberately or through no fault of their own. For example, they may:
    - fail to support the client (e.g. by not topping up residential care fees)
    - seek to move the client prematurely into residential care in order to occupy the home themselves or to sell it
    - die suddenly without making suitable provision for the client
    - run into financial difficulties because of unemployment or divorce or become bankrupt and in consequence be unable to support the client
- the home may be lost on the bankruptcy, divorce or death of the relative to whom it has been given, resulting in the client being made homeless if s/he is still living there;
- there may be no inheritance tax saving whilst the client continues to live in the home, yet there could be a liability for inheritance tax if the relative dies before the client;
- the relative to whom the home has been gifted may lose entitlement to benefits and/or services (e.g. social security benefits, legal aid) due to personal means-testing if not living in the home;
- the local authority may decide, having regard to the client's ownership of the notional capital value of the home, rather than the property itself (see paras 18–19 below), that s/he is not entitled to certain community care services, or even to be funded at all for residential care should this be needed.

Anti-avoidance measures

15. The client can be given no guarantees that there is a foolproof way of avoiding the value of the home being taken into account in means-testing, since the anti-avoidance measures in the law enable some gifts to be ignored by the authorities and even set aside by the court. Not only are these measures subject to change from time to time, but it is also unclear how far the authorities will go in order to pursue contributions they believe to be owing to them.

16. In most cases, the intention behind making the gift is the most important factor. Where the intention is clearly to create or increase entitlement to financial support from the local authority, measures can be taken to impose a charge on the asset given away in the hands of the recipients or even to recover the asset itself. However, it is necessary that the authority concerned believe that this was a 'significant' part of the client's intention in making the gift. Using one of the marketed schemes (see para. 4 above) which have been advertised specifically to help people to avoid local authority means-testing may make clear the client's intention.

Appendix 10 GIFTS OF PROPERTY – GUIDELINES

CHARGES FOR RESIDENTIAL AND NURSING HOME CARE

17. At present, a major cause for concern among many older clients is the fear of having to sell their homes in order to pay for residential or nursing home care in the future, and they may wish to take steps to protect their families' inheritance. It is important that solicitors are familiar with the eligibility criteria for NHS funded nursing home care, the charging and funding arrangements by local authorities for residential and nursing home care (when applicable), when care must be provided free of charge and, if charges may be made, the means-testing rules which are summarised in Appendix B.

Implications of the 'notional capital' rule

18. Where the local authority believes that property has been given away by the client with the intention of creating or increasing entitlement to help with residential care home fees (or nursing home fees where these are payable), then it may decide that the client has 'notional capital' equivalent in value to that of the property given away. If that notional capital value exceeds the capital cut off (currently £16,000, see Appendix B) the authority may decide that the client is not entitled to any assistance (or any continuing assistance) with the home care fees.

19. In such cases it would be the client who then had to take action if s/he wished to challenge the decision. This may involve the use of the local authority's complaints procedures, as well as the Ombudsman or a judicial review. These may all entail significant legal expense and anxiety for the client as the outcome could not be guaranteed. If a judicial review is necessary it would be the client who had to establish that the authority's decision was *Wednesbury* unreasonable (i.e. the burden of proof would be on the client).

Enforcing payment of fees (where charges may legally be made)

20. Having assessed someone as being in need of residential or nursing home care and then provided that care, the local authority cannot withdraw that provision simply because the resident does not pay assessed contributions. However, the authority can take steps to recover contributions, and in assessing ability to pay may take into account property that has been given away for the purpose of avoiding means-testing.

21. The enforcement provisions available to local authorities are as follows:

    (i) taking proceedings in the magistrates' court to recover sums due as a civil debt (National Assistance Act 1948, s 56);

    (ii) imposing a charge on any property belonging to the resident, with

PART 4: SECTION C Guidance

        interest chargeable from the day after death (HASSASSA Act 1983, ss 22 and 24);

   (iii) imposing a charge on property transferred by the resident within six months of going to residential care, or whilst in care, with the intention of avoiding contributions (HASSASSA Act 1983, s 21).

22. Once the debt for unpaid contributions reaches £750, insolvency proceedings could be taken to declare the resident bankrupt, whereupon transactions at an undervalue may be set aside within two years, or within five years if the person made bankrupt was insolvent at the time of the transaction, which is unlikely (Insolvency Act 1986, ss 339–341).

23. Under other provisions, a gift may be set aside without time limit and without bankruptcy, if the court is satisfied that the transfer was made for the purpose of putting assets beyond the reach of a potential creditor or otherwise prejudicing the creditor's interests (Insolvency Act 1986, ss 423–425). This provision is exceptionally wide, and the court has extensive powers to restore the position to that which it would have been had the gift not been made.

24. Although some local authorities have threatened to use insolvency proceedings, few have actually done so, perhaps because of lack of expertise or the prospect of bad publicity. However, with increasing pressures on local authority resources to provide community care services, there is no guarantee they will not do so in the future.

25. The burden of proof remains on the local authority to establish that the purpose behind the gift of the property was to avoid means-testing. But it may be difficult for the donor or his/her relatives to give evidence as to the donor's intentions, and if another purpose of the gift cannot be established or indicated the judge may conclude that it must have been to avoid means-testing.

26. The purpose of the gift will have been discussed in advance with the solicitor, and it would be prudent for the solicitor to retain evidence of the advice given in order to protect him/herself in the event of a subsequent family dispute or professional negligence claim. The file notes and correspondence will normally be covered by legal professional privilege or at least by the duty of confidentiality. The court will not usually order discovery of a solicitor's file unless there is *prima facie* evidence of fraud, but has done so in similar circumstances on the basis of public policy considerations (*Barclays Bank plc v Eustice* [1995] 1 WLR 1238). It is possible that a trustee in bankruptcy, or a local authority bringing proceedings under the Insolvency Act 1986, ss 423–425 may persuade the court to override privilege.

27. In *Yule v South Lanarkshire Council* (1999) 1 CCL Rep 546 Lord Philip

held that a local authority was entitled to take account of the value of an elderly woman's home transferred to her daughter over 18 months before the woman entered residential care. The court held that there was no time limit on local authorities when deciding whether a person had deprived themselves of assets for the purposes of avoiding residential care fees.

THE SOLICITOR'S DUTY

28. The solicitor's role is more than just drawing up and registering the necessary deeds and documents to effect the making of the gift. S/he has a duty to ensure that the client fully understands the nature, effect, benefits, risks and foreseeable consequences of making the gift. The solicitor has no obligation to advise the client on the wisdom or morality of the transaction, unless the client specifically requests this.

29. The Professional Ethics Division of the Law Society has advised that the solicitor should follow his/her client's instructions, provided that by doing so, the solicitor will not be involved in a breach of the law or a breach of the principles of professional conduct. Reference is made to Principle 12.02 of *The Guide to the Professional Conduct of Solicitors* (1999), which indicates when instructions must be refused. Solicitors will want to satisfy themselves in each individual case that no breach of the law is involved in the proposed transaction. Having advised the client as to the implications and possible consequences of making the gift, the decision whether or not to proceed remains with the client.

30. Solicitors must also be aware of the possible conflict of interest, or significant risk of such a conflict, between the donor and recipient of a gift. While there is no general rule of law that a solicitor should never act for both parties in a transaction where their interests might conflict, Principle 15.01 of *The Guide to the Professional Conduct of Solicitors* states: 'A solicitor or firm of solicitors should not accept instructions to act for two or more clients where there is a conflict or a significant risk of a conflict between the interests of the clients'. Given the potentially vulnerable position of an elderly client, the solicitor will have to consider carefully whether he can act for the donor and the recipient or whether there is an actual or significant risk of conflict. If the solicitor has initially advised the donor alone as to all the implications of the gift and is satisfied that there is no undue influence and that the donor has capacity, the solicitor may be able to act for both clients in the conveyancing.

31. If the solicitor is asked to act for both parties, the solicitor should make them both aware of the possibility of a conflict of interest and advise one of them to consider taking independent advice. S/he should also explain that as a result of any conflict of interest, a solicitor acting by agreement for both parties may be unable to disclose all that s/he knows to each of them or to give advice to one of them which conflicts with the interests of

PART 4: SECTION C Guidance

the other and may have to cease acting for both. Both parties must be content to proceed on this basis, be competent to do so and give their consent in writing. However, if any doubt remains, the solicitor would be advised not to act for both parties.

Further reading

[In addition to the relevant books referred to in Appendix 7].

Age Concern Fact Sheets available from Age Concern England, FREEPOST, (SWB 30375), Ashburton, Devon TQ13 7ZZ. Tel: 0800 00 99 66:

No. 10 *Local authority charging procedures for residential and nursing home care*

No. 11 *Financial support for people in residential and nursing home accommodation prior to 1 April 1993*

No. 38 *Treatment of the former home as capital for people in residential and nursing home care*

No. 39 *Paying for care in a residential or nursing home if you have a partner*

No. 40 *Transfer of assets and paying for care in a residential or nursing home*

APPENDIX A

Capacity to make a gift

The relevant test of capacity to make a gift is set out in the judgment in *Re Beaney (Deceased)* [1978] 1 WLR 770. In that case a 64-year-old widow with three grown up children owned and lived in a three-bedroom semi-detached house. Her elder daughter lived with her. In May 1973, a few days after being admitted to hospital suffering from advanced dementia, the widow signed a deed of gift transferring the house to her elder daughter. The widow died intestate the following year, and her son and younger daughter applied successfully to the court for a declaration that the transfer of the house was void and of no effect because their mother was mentally incapable of making such a gift. The judge in the case set out the following criteria for capacity to make a lifetime gift:

'The degree or extent of understanding required in respect of any instrument is relative to the particular transaction which it is to effect. ... Thus, at one extreme, if the subject matter and value of a gift are trivial in relation to the donor's other assets, a low degree of understanding will suffice. But, at the other, if its effect is to dispose of the donor's only asset of value and thus, for practical purposes, to pre-empt the devolution of his estate under [the donor's] will or ... intestacy, then the degree of understanding required is as high as that required for a will, and the donor must understand the claims of all potential donees and the extent of the property to be disposed of.'

It is arguable that, when someone makes a substantial gift, a further point should be considered, namely, the effect that disposing of the asset could have on the donor for the rest of his or her life.

[Adapted from British Medical Association/Law Society, *Assessment of Mental Capacity: Guidance for Doctors and Lawyers*, (1995) BMA.]

APPENDIX B

Paying for residential and nursing home care

Charges

Individuals who can afford to pay for a place in a residential care or nursing home may arrange this independently, though it is advisable to seek a 'needs' assessment prior to entering residential or nursing care in order to achieve continuity if local authority funding may be needed in future:

- if met with a refusal to assess in advance, point out that the assessment of need for care provision does not depend upon the need for funding;
- it may also be wise to ensure that the particular home is willing to accommodate residents on local authority funding.

Local authority

Those who enter such a home through an arrangement made by the local authority must pay or contribute to the cost, whether the authority provides or buys in the accommodation:

- each authority must fix a standard weekly charge for its own homes which should represent the true economic cost of providing the accommodation – many have a standard scale of fees geared to their eligibility criteria;
- where the authority purchases a place from an independent home the weekly charge to the resident should represent the cost of the place to the authority;
- residents must generally contribute in accordance with their resources up to the appropriate charge, but no one will be required to pay more;
- the authority either:
    - pays the full fee to the home and collects the resident's contribution, or
    - pays its share whilst the resident and any third party pay the balance
- a contract with the authority or the home should state what is included in the

PART 4: SECTION C Guidance

charge and what are extras.

Health authority

Where a health authority arranges a place in a nursing home under a contractual arrangement the individual remains an NHS patient and no charge is made but social security benefits may be withdrawn or reduced.

It is important to ascertain whether a move from hospital to a private nursing home also involves a transfer of responsibility from the health authority to social services.

Means-testing

When the resident cannot afford the full charge an assessment is made of ability to pay and this is reviewed annually but a resident should ask for re-assessment at any time if this would be beneficial:

- the assessment relates to both income and capital:
  - since April 1993 assessment has been brought largely into line with that for income support, though local authorities retain some discretion
  - the capital cut-off point is £16,000 but capital above £10,000 will result in a tariff income (an attempt to apply a lower financial threshold before acknowledging need failed in *R v Sefton Metropolitan Borough Council, ex p Help the Aged* (1997) 1 CCL Rep 57, CA
  - *notional capital* and *notional income* rules apply as for income support

- assessment relates only to the means of the resident (unlike for income support where spouses and partners are generally assessed together):
  - there is no power to oblige a spouse/partner to take part *but* spouses are liable to maintain each other (National Assistance Act 1948, s 42) and court action may be taken against a liable relative (s 43)
  - jointly owned property may be deemed to be owned in equal shares (but query whether it has a value if a home is occupied by the joint owner)
  - since 1996 one-half of occupational and private pensions of the resident are re-routed back to the non-resident spouse

- the value of the resident's home is disregarded during a temporary stay or:
  - if occupied by a spouse/partner, or a relative who is aged 60 or over or incapacitated
  - if occupied by someone else and the local authority exercises its discretion

- there is a minimum charge payable by all residents and the assessment determines what should be paid above this, but all residents retain a personal expenses allowance (revised annually):
  - to be used by the resident for expenditure of personal choice such as

460

Appendix 10 GIFTS OF PROPERTY – GUIDELINES

stationery, personal toiletries, treats (e.g. sweets, drinks, cigarettes) and presents
- the authority has a discretion to increase the amount, but it should not be used for top-up to provide more expensive accommodation
- authorities should carry out a benefits check because they have an incentive to ensure that people in homes are receiving maximum state benefits:
  - this should only be with the informed consent of the resident
  - income support will include a *residential allowance* (not for local authority homes)

Power to charge?

In two main situations no charges may be made for the care of an individual:

- where, following discharge from detention under one of the longer treatment sections of the Mental Health Act 1983 (usually s.3 or s.37), he or she requires residential or nursing home care as a result of mental disorder:
  - no charge may be made for care as this is deemed 'aftercare' service provision under Mental Health Act 1983, s.117
  - that section places a joint duty on the health and local authorities to provide the services required free of charge, unless it is decided by both that the person is no longer in need of these by virtue of their mental disorder
- (only applicable to placements in nursing homes) where his or her need is primarily a health care need:
  - the health authority must fund the entire cost of the placement and the local authority has no power to purchase such care and pass the costs to the client
  - the only exception is where the nursing care is 'merely ancillary or incidental to the provision of the accommodation' in a nursing home. This will depend on the level and type of care. Most nursing homes placements will be the responsibility of the NHS because a client will not be placed there unless their primary need is for nursing care, i.e. health care

See *R v North and East Devon Health Authority ex p Coughlan* (1999) 2 CCL Rep 285; *R v London Borough of Richmond ex p Watson* (1999) 2 CCL Rep 402.

Regulations and guidance

National Assistance (Assessment of Resources) Regulations 1992 *as amended*

Circular LAC (99)9 *'Charging for Residential Accommodation Guide' (CRAG)* (copies available from the Department of Health, PO Box 777, London SE1 6XH; Fax: 01623 724 524; e-mail: doh@prologistics).

[The above Appendix is adapted from Chapter 19 of this Handbook.]

Index

Abroad *see* Foreign countries
Abuse and violence within families 180–6, 433–4, 445
    nature of abuse 180
    remedies 181
        injunctions 181–4
        occupation of the home 185–6
    right to intervene 180
Access 140
Accountants 27–8
    information from 30
Accounts
    solicitors' practice management 109
    see also Banks; Building society accounts
Address, forms of 123–4
Addresses, list of 407–13
Adoption 178
Advance directive 398
    see also Living wills
Advertising *see* Marketing and publicity
Advisers 27–8
    information from 30
Affirmations/oaths 23
Aftercare services 294–5
Agents
    capacity and 163
    collection of welfare benefits 76, 206
Ante-nuptial agreements 171
Anti-social behaviour 184
Appeals 37
    Court of Protection 94
    mental health legislation 296–7
        discharge 296
        Mental Health Act Commission 297
        Mental Health Review Tribunal 296–7
    residential/nursing home registration 259
    welfare benefits 207–9
        courts 209
        procedures 207–8
        Social Security Commissioners 208–9
        tribunals 207
Appropriate adult 189
Approved social workers 27, 290

Attendance allowance 200, 223
Attorney *see* Enduring power of attorney (EPA)
Audit, legal 123
Authorities, challenging *see* Challenging authorities

Bail, remand on 193
Banks
    bank accounts
        capacity and 162–3
        deduction of tax 78
        exercise of financial powers 77–8
    information from 30
Bargain-bounty rule 353
Benefits *see* Welfare benefits
Best interest approach 15
Branch offices 122
Breach of contract 42
Breach of statutory duty 40–1
Brochures 143–4
Budgeting loans 203
Building society accounts
    capacity and 162–3
    exercise of financial powers 77–8
Burial 377–8

Capacity 10–15
    agents and 163
    assessment 11–14, 20–2
        appearances 12
        approaches to 11, 21
        civil proceedings 56
        criteria 12
        determining capacity 13
        evidence 13–14
        legal tests 12–13, 161
        medical practitioners and 25–7
        previous solicitor and 22
        techniques 21–2
        timing 21
    consent to medical treatment and 280–2
    contracts and
        general 162
        specific 162–3

463

INDEX

decision-making in cases of incapacity 14–15
    basis of decisions 15
    procedures 14–15
    types of decision 14
  enduring power of attorney (EPA) and 66, 84–5, 401, 404, 433, 446–7
  exercise of rights and 161–4
  freedom of information and 34
  gifts and 349, 450–1, 458–9
  insurance policies and 163
  marriage 170
  presumptions 10, 161
  wills 357
Capital gains tax 314–15, 350–1, 352–3, 363
Capital release 341–3
Carers 24–5
  caring for 25
  consultation of 24–5
  defined 24
  information from 29–30
  professional 27
  status of 24
Cautions 191
Central government
  challenging *see* Challenging authorities
  grants for community care 253
  payments from 78
Certiorari 43
Challenging authorities 35–48
  entitlement to services 35–7
  European courts 45–8
  legal remedies 39–44
    breach of contract 42
    breach of statutory duty 40–1
    complaint to minister 39–40
    judicial review 43–4
    small claims procedure 42–3
    tort 41–2
  ombudsmen 37–9
    Commissioners for Local Administration 38–9
    Health Service Commissioner 39, 276–7
    Parliamentary Commissioner for Administration 38
Charges *see* Costs and fees
Charities
  support from 229
  trustees 308
Children 175–8
  adoption 178
  intestacy and 355
  private law disputes 176–7

public law disputes 177–8
Christmas bonus 201
Civil proceedings 49–62
  costs 60–1
  Court Rules 49–50, 54–5
  damages, disposal 61–2
  discrimination 49
  evidence 51–3, 58
  injunctions 59–60
  limitation of actions 58–9
  mental disability and 54–62
    assessment of capacity 56
    costs 60–1
    disposal of damages 61–2
    general matters 58–60
    procedure 56–8
    rules 54–6
  physical disability and 51–4
    evidence 51–3
    implications and solutions 15
    representation 53–4
  reforms 50–1
  stay of execution 59
Club trustees 308
Cohabitation 171, 178–9
  intestacy and 355
Cold weather payments 204
Commission
  from third parties 107
  investment business 135–6
Commissioners for Local Administration 38–9
Committee membership 307–8
Communication
  between departments 122
  with client 19–20, 115, 126–7, 141
    forms of address 123–4
Community care 6, 27, 231–2
  assessment for 243–5
    disabled people 248–9
    duty 243–4
    form of 244–5
  community care grants 203
  complaints procedure 250–1
  funding for 214–16, 253–4
    charges 215
    enforcement 215–16
    insurance 254
    local authority resources 253
    means-testing 253
    sources of law 214
  inadequate provision or failure to act 251–3
    identifying default 251–3
    remedies 253

464

INDEX

mental health legislation 293–6
  aftercare 295–6
  power to inspect 293
  removal to place of safety 293
  statutory guardianship 243, 293–4
policies on 233–40
  directions and guidance 234–7, 239
  legislation 233–4
  local authorities and 237–9
  private sector and 240
  reports 233
private sector and 240, 245
services 214–15, 241–54
  assessment 243–5, 248–9
  for disabled people 247–9
  guardianship 243
  priorities 246
  provision 245–6, 249
  statutory basis 241–3
unmet needs 246
Community Health Councils (CHCs) 269
Complaints
  about police 189–90
  community care services 250–1
  local authorities 37
  National Health Service 37, 274–7
    procedure 275–6
  to minister 39–40
Compromise, mental disability and 57–8
Computer data protection 32
Computerised office systems 124–5, 152
Conditional fees 60
Confidentiality
  National Health Service 272–3
  solicitor/client 118–19
Conflicts of interest 106, 118
  enduring power of attorney (EPA) 67–8
Consent to medical treatment 279–80
  competence of patient and 280–2
  medical treatment without consent 281–2
    powers of court 283
  nature of 279–80
  refusal 280
Contingency fees 60
Contract
  breach of contract 42
  capacity and
    general contracts 162
    specific contracts 162–3
  employment 303
Conveyancing, costs 95
Coroner's inquests 374–6
Costs and fees
  civil proceedings 60–1

  assessment 60
  conditional fees 60
  legal aid 61
  third party costs 60–1
  wasted costs 61
community care 215
conveyancing 95
Court of Protection procedures 94–5
enduring powers of attorney 82
fee sharing 107
funeral arrangements 376–7
information on 108–9, 110–11, 117, 127–8, 152
National Health Service 225–6
private health care 271
receivership 70
Remuneration Order 128–33
residential care 216–17, 459–61
  enforcement 218–19, 455–7
  liable relatives 220–1
  means-testing 217–18, 223–4
  recovery 219–20
wills 357
Councils *see* Local authorities
County court small claims procedure 42–3
  lay representatives 53–4
Couples, information from 29
Court of Protection 86–101
  jurisdiction 86–7
  legislation 86
  officers 87–8
  orders 90–1, 99–100
  powers 89–91
    exercise of 90
    general 89
    orders 90–1
  procedure 74–5, 92–5
    complaints and appeals 94
    costs 94–5
    fees 94
    first application 92–4
    hearings 92, 94
    subsequent applications 94
  receivership and 68–9, 95–9, 100–1
  status and structure 86–9
Cremation 377–8
Crime victims 186–7
Criminal liability, medical treatment without consent 283
Criminal responsibility 188–93
  prosecution
    alternatives to prosecution 191
    decision to prosecute 190–1
    Narey scheme 192

INDEX

pleas and defences 192
remand 193
safeguards
   alternatives to prosecution 191
   complaints about police 189–90
   decision to prosecute 190–1
   police investigation 188–9
sentences 193
Crisis loans 203
Crown Prosecution Service 190–1
Custody, remand in 193

Damages
   civil proceedings, disposal 61–2
   dismissal 304
   medical treatment without consent 283
Data protection 32
Databases 125
Death
   allowing patient to die 282
     see also Living wills
   certificates 372, 373
   coroner's inquests 374–6
   forfeiture and 354
   funeral arrangements 376–8
   registration 372–3
Decision-making in cases of incapacity 14–15
   basis of decisions 15
   procedures 14–15
   types of decision 14
Declaration order 43
Declarations 23
   medical treatment without consent 283
Deeds of covenant 352
Defences 192
Delegation 120–1
Dementias 8
Demographic trends 5
Dental care 271
Depositions 52
Directorships, retirement 306
Disabilities *see* Mental disability; Physical disability
Disability living allowance 200, 225
Disability working allowance 201
Discrete investment business (DIB) 135
Discrimination 167–8
   in employment 302
   physical disability 49, 168–9
Dismissal
   unfair 304–5
   wrongful 304
Divorce 172–3
   financial provision 173–5

pensions and 175, 310–11
Doctors *see* Medical practitioners
Domestic violence *see* Abuse and violence within families
Donationes mortis causa 350
Double effect principle 282
Driving licences 164

Elderly people 5–9
   definition of 'elderly' 5
   distinguishing characteristics 6–9
   law and 9
   needs 7–8
   statistics on 5–6
   see also Individual topics
Elections, voting rights 165
Electricity bills 227
Emergencies
   assessment under mental health legislation 291–2
   exercise of Court of Protection's powers 90
   medical treatment without consent 281–2
Emigration *see* Foreign countries
Employment 301–6
   commencement 302–3
   discrimination in 302
   legislation 301
   remuneration 302, 304
   self-employment 301, 307–8
   termination 303–6
     dismissal 304–5
     notice 303–4
     redundancy 305–6
     see also Retirement
Enduring power of attorney (EPA) 66–8, 69, 75, 80–5
   advantages 72
   application 83
   capacity of donor 66, 84–5, 401, 404, 433, 446–7
   conflicts of interest 67–8
   dealing with affairs 68
   disadvantages 73
   duties of attorney 84
   Law Society Guidelines 432–48
   legislation 80–1
   living wills and 284
   medical certificate 404
   notice of 83
   objections to 83
   prescribed forms 383–91, 441–2
   as preventive measure 66
   production of powers 80

INDEX

professional attorneys 82
registration 82–4, 439–40, 443–4
requirements 81
restrictions 67, 81–2
solicitor's duty 85
who to appoint 66–7, 434–6
wills 68
Energy efficiency 227
European Convention on Human Rights 45–6
   incorporation into UK law 47–8
European Court of Human Rights (ECHR) 45–8
European Court of Justice (ECJ) 45, 209
Evidence
   of capacity/incapacity 13–14
   civil proceedings 51–3, 58
   inquests 375–6
   victims of crime 187

Families
   cohabitation 171, 178–9, 355
   domestic violence *see* Abuse and violence within families
   grandchildren 175–8
   information from 29–30
   liable for residential care charges 220–1
   marriage 170–1
      breakdown of 171–5
   nearest relative under mental health legislation 289–90
   non-consent of patient to medical treatment and 281–2
   notice of Court of Protection procedures 83
   notice of enduring power of attorney (EPA) 83
   shared occupation 337–8
   support from 228–9
   see also Inheritance
Family credit 201
Fees *see* Costs and fees
Financial institutions, information from 30
Financial powers
   bank/building society accounts 77–8
   checklists 70–5
   delegation procedures 64
      comparison of powers 72–4
   government payments 78
   hospitals 79
   income tax 78
   informal steps 65
   welfare benefits 65, 76–7, 205–6
   see also Enduring power of attorney (EPA); Receivership; Trusts

Foreign countries
   properties in 346
   social security system and living abroad 198
   tax implications of moving abroad 315
Forfeiture 354
Freedom of information 31–4
   code of practice 31
   legislation 31–3
   local authorities and 32, 33
   mentally incapacity and 34
Friends
   appropriate adult 189
   litigation friend 56
   McKenzie friend 53
   next friend 56
Funeral arrangements 376–8

Gas bills 227
Gender, numbers of elderly people and 5
Gift Aid 352
Gifts 349–53, 437
   capacity 349, 450–1, 458–9
   Court of Protection orders 91
   of the home 338–41
      advice 338–9
      benefits 340, 453
      Law Society Guidelines 449–61
      reasons for transfer 339–40
      risks 340–1, 453–4
   precatory gifts 364
   recovery to pay residential home charges 218–20
   taxation 350–2
   to charities 352–3
   validity 349–50
Grandchildren 175–8
   adoption 178
   intestacy and 355
   private law disputes 176–7
   public law disputes 177–8
Guardianship
   ad litem 56
   guardians allowance 201
   statutory 243, 293–4

Harassment 183–4
Health authorities 268, 460
Health Service Commissioner 39, 276–7
Home Energy Efficiency scheme 227
Homelessness 336
Hospitals
   admission to hospital under mental health legislation 291–3

467

INDEX

implications of detention 292–3
informal 291
medical treatment 292
statutory powers 291–2
voluntary 291
charges 225–6
complaints 275
delegation of financial powers and 79
discharge from 277–8, 296
remand in 193
sentences to detention in 192
treatment in 271
Housing 317–46
for disabled people 345
foreign properties 346
gifts of the home 338–9
advice 338–9
benefits 340, 453
Law Society Guidelines 449–61
reasons for transfer 339–40
risks 340–1, 453–4
homelessness 336
income from the home 341–3
licences 335–6
long residential leases 321–3
enfranchisement 323
legislation 322
shared ownership 322–3
owner-occupation 317–20
grants 226–7, 321
joint ownership 318–20, 354, 452–3
mortgages 320–1
sole ownership 318
park homes 345
second homes 346
shared occupation 337–8
sheltered 343–4
tenancies 323–35
allocation 327
legislation 323
rent control 332–3
repairs and maintenance 333–5
right to buy 325–6
security of tenure 327–9
succession 330–1
terms 331
transitional provisions 326
types 323–4
unlawful eviction 329–30
timeshare 346
Housing benefit 211–13
entitlement 211–13
procedure 213
purpose 211

residential care and 223
sources of law 211
Human rights
European Convention on Human Rights 45–6
incorporation into UK law 47–8
Image 146–7
Incapacity *see* Capacity
Incapacity benefit 199
Income
from employment 302, 304
from the home 341–3
see also Pensions; Welfare benefits
Income support 201–2
residential care and 222–3
Income tax 78, 167, 312–13
Independent Living Fund 229
Industrial disablement benefit 201
Information 29–34, 147–8
on community care services 247
on costs 108–9, 110–11, 117, 127–8, 152
on Court of Protection 86
financial management checklist 70–1
freedom of information 31–4
code of practice 31
legislation 31–3
local government 33
mentally incapacity and 34
from Law Society 150–5
National Health Service 226, 272–4
sources 29–31
care authorities 30–1
carers and family 29–30
client 29
financial institutions 30
partners 29
for victims of crime 186–7
on welfare benefits 198–9
Inheritance
family arrangements 362–4
discretionary provision 363–4
precatory gifts 364
variations and disclaimers 362–3
intestacy and 355
provision 360–2
claimants 360
court's powers 361–2
discretionary 363–4
infirm/disabled beneficiaries 365–71
procedure 362
relevant matters 360–1
tax implications 362
succession 354

468

INDEX

see also Wills
Inheritance tax 315–16, 351–2, 362–3
Injunctions
    abuse and violence within families and 181–4
    medical treatment without consent 283
    mental disability and 59–60
Inland Revenue, information from 30
Inquests 374–6
Insanity, not guilty by reason of 192
Instructions 19–23, 115–17, 434–41
    assessment of capacity 20–2
    confidentiality 118–19
    conflicts of interest 106, 118
    lawyer's role 22–3
    termination of retainer 23
    wills 356
    see also Communication
Insulation, Home Energy Efficiency scheme 227
Insurance
    capacity and 163
    funding for community care 254
    private health insurance 271
Internet, Law Society information on 152
Interpreters 53
Interviewing techniques 20
Intestacy 355
Introductions and referrals 106, 112–14
Invalid care allowance 201, 225
Investment bond income schemes 342
Investment management 309, 438
    receivership and 98–9
    solicitors and 108, 133–6, 138
        general advice 136
        Law Society information on 154
        regulation 133, 134–5

Jobseekers allowance 200
Joint ownership 318–20
    gifts and 452–3
    succession 354
Judicial review 43–4, 209
Judicial separation 173, 310–11
Jury service 166

Law Commission reform proposals 427–31
Law Society
    enduring power of attorney guidelines 432–48
    gifts of property guidelines 449–60
    practice management and 150–5
    promotion 150–4
    publications 154–5

solicitors financial services 154
Lay representatives 53–4
Learning disability 8–9
Leaseholds 321–2
    enfranchisement 323
    legislation 322
    shared ownership 322–3
Legal aid
    civil proceedings 61
    information on 128
    wills 357
Legal audit 123
Legal remedies 39–44
    abuse and violence within families 181
        injunctions 181–4
        occupation of the home 185–6
    breach of contract 42
    breach of statutory duty 40–1
    complaint to minister 39–40
    disability discrimination 169
    dismissal 304, 305
    inadequate provision of community care 253
    judicial review 43–4
    medical treatment without consent 283
    repair and maintenance of property 334–5
    small claims procedure 42–3
    tort 41–2
Leisure 7
Lexcel 150
Licences
    driving 164
    housing 335–6
Limitation of actions 58–9
Litigation friend 56
Living wills 284–6
    implications 285
    legality 285
    precedents 286, 398–9
    problems 286
    types 284
Loans 203, 342
Local authorities
    anti-social behaviour and 184
    care *see* Community care; Residential care
    carers and 25
    challenging *see* Challenging authorities
    Commissioners for Local Administration 38–9
    complaints procedures 37
    council tax 166–7
    council tax benefit 214
    entitlement to services 35–7

469

INDEX

freedom of information and 32, 33
funeral arrangements 377
homelessness and 336
housing 324
    allocation 327
    grants 226–7, 321
    registered social landlords 322, 324
    rent control 332
    right to buy 325–6
    security of tenure 327–8
    succession 330
    terms of tenancies 331
    transfer 326–7
information from 30–1
NHS joint planning and 269
residence requirements 239
structure 36
supervision of residential/nursing care 258–9
see also Housing benefit; Social services
Lord Chancellor's Visitors 89

McKenzie friend 53
Maladministration 38
Mandamus 40, 43
Manslaughter 354
Marketing and publicity 137–49
    areas of work 137–9
    code of practice 109–12
    Law Society and 150–4
    practice rules 106
    promotion of legal services 144–9
        contacts 145–6
        getting known 144–5
        image 146–7
        package of services 148
        provision of information 147–8
        quality of service 147
        specialisms 148–9
    targeting elderly clients 139–44
    office brochures 143–4
    relationship with clients 141–3
    user-friendly office 140–1
Marriage 170–1
    ante-nuptial agreements 171
    breakdown of 171–5
        divorce 172–3
        financial provision 173–5
        judicial separation 173, 310–11
        nullity 172
    competence 170
    formalities 170
    implications 170–1
    information from married couples 29

Means-testing
    community care 253
    provision for infirm/disabled beneficiaries 367
    residential care charges 217–18, 223–4, 460–1
    welfare benefits 201
Medical practitioners 25–7
    access to medical records 32–3, 34
    assessment of capacity 25–7
    certificates 403–4
    complaints about 275–6
    GPs 270
    letters to 400–1
    Lord Chancellor's Visitors 89
    post-mortem examination 375
    registration of death 372
    reports 26–7
Medical research, use of organs for 378
Medical treatment 279–86
    allowing patient to die 282
    consent 279–80
        competence of patient and 280–2
        nature of 279–80
        refusal 280
    defined 288
    under mental health legislation 291, 292
    without consent 281–2
        powers of court 283
Mental disability 8–9, 10
    civil proceedings and 54–62
        assessment of capacity 56
        costs 60–1
        disposal of damages 61–2
        general matters 58–60
        procedure 56–8
        rules 54–6
    criminal responsibility and *see* Criminal responsibility
    legislation on *see* Mental health legislation
    statutory community care 242–3
Mental disorder
    abuse and 182
    defined 13, 55, 288
    treatment 292
Mental Health Act Commission 297
Mental health legislation 287–97
    admission to hospital 291–3
        implications of detention 292–3
        informal 291
        medical treatment 291, 292
        statutory powers 291–2
        voluntary 291
    approved social workers 27, 290

INDEX

code of practice 290
community powers 293–6
    aftercare 295–6
    power to inspect 293
    removal to place of safety 293
    statutory guardianship 243, 293–4
definitions 288–9
guidance, circulars and practice notes 288
nearest relative 289–90
Patient's Charter 288
review and appeal 296–7
    discharge 296
    Mental Health Act Commission 297
    Mental Health Review Tribunal 296–7
rules 287
scope 287
Mental Health Review Tribunal 296–7
Mental illness, defined 288
Mental nursing homes 256
Ministers, complaint to 39–40
Mobile homes 345
Monitoring 123
Mortgages
    mortgage annuity schemes 341
    owner-occupation 320
Murder 354

Name of firms 107–8, 111
Narey scheme 192
National Health Service 225–6
    charges 225–6
    complaints 37, 274–7
        procedure 275–6
    health care delivery 269–71
        Patient's Charter 269
        types of health services 270–1
    Health Service Commissioner 39, 276–7
    hospital discharge 277–8
    information 226, 272–4
    joint planning 269
    NHS Trusts 268
    reforms 267
    residential care 217
    structure 267–9
    see also Hospitals; Medical practitioners; Medical treatment
National Insurance contributions 167, 209–10
    contribution record 210
    pension forecasts 210
    types 209–10
Necessaries, contracts for 162
Neuroses 8
Next friend 56

Nomination 354
Non-insane automatism 192
Notice
    Court of Protection procedures 92–3
    enduring power of attorney (EPA) 83
    termination of employment 303–4
Nurses 27
Nursing homes 217, 455–7
    choice of 260–1
    defined 256
    guidance for residents 262–3
    mental nursing homes 256
    registered 256
        codes of practice 259–60
        legislation 255
        proprietor 257
        refusal of registration 257
        regulation 257–9
        supervision 258–9

Oaths 23
    interpreters 53
Occupational pensions 65, 311–12
Office management *see* Practice management
Official Solicitor 88
Ombudsmen 37–9
    Commissioners for Local Administration 38–9
    Health Service Commissioner 39, 276–7
    Parliamentary Commissioner for Administration 38
Owner-occupation 317–20
    grants 226–7, 321
    joint ownership 318–20, 354, 452–3
    mortgages 320
    sole ownership 318

Park homes 345
Parking schemes 165
Parliamentary Commissioner for Administration 38
Partners, information from 29
Partnerships 307
Passports 165
Patient's Charter 269, 288
Pensions 309–12
    divorce and 175, 310–11
    marriage and 171
    occupational 65, 311–12
    personal 312
    state 78, 200, 309–11
        forecasts 210
Perfected gift 349–50
Personal contacts 145–6

INDEX

Personal pensions 312
Physical disability 8, 10
    civil proceedings and 51–4
        discrimination 49
        evidence 51–3
        implications and solutions 15
        representation 53–4
    community care services 247–9
    defined 168, 247
    discrimination 49, 168–9
    housing for disabled people 345
    register of disabled persons 247
    trust for infirm/disabled beneficiaries 365–71
Place of safety, removal to 293
Pleas 192
Police
    charging 190–1
    complaints about 189–90
    investigation by 188–9
    PACE codes of practice 188–9
Possession proceedings 321
Post-mortem examination 375
Power of attorney *see* Enduring power of attorney (EPA)
Practice management
    accounting 109
    branch offices 122
    clients
        communication with 19–20, 115, 126–7, 141
        departments dealing with older clients 121–2
        duties to 125–8
        forms of address 123–4
        guide for 144
        introductions and referrals 106, 112–14
        monitoring 123
        relationship with 115–19, 141–3
    codes of practice 109–14
    commissions from third parties 107
    conflicts of interest 106, 118
    costs
        fee sharing 107
        information 108–9, 110–11, 117, 127–8, 152
        Remuneration Order 128–33
    extra services 106
        investment business 108, 133–6, 138
    Law Society and 150–5
    name of firms 107–8, 111
    office systems 124–5
    practice rules 105–9

    professional conduct 114–19
    publicity *see* Marketing and publicity
    staff 120
        delegation to 120–1
        recruitment advice 153
Pre-nuptial agreements 171
Precatory gifts 364
Prescription charges 225
Private sector
    community care and 240, 245
    health care 271
    tenancies 324
        rent control 332–3
        security of tenure 328–9
        succession 330–1
        unlawful eviction 329–30
Probate, Law Society services 153–4
Professionals 25–8
    advisers 27–8
    attorneys 82
    carers 27
    medical practitioners 25–7
    nurses 27
    social workers 27
Prohibition 43
Promotion *see* Marketing and publicity
Prosecution
    alternatives to prosecution 191
    decision to prosecute 190–1
    Narey scheme 192
    pleas and defences 192
    remand 193
Psychopathic disorder, defined 288
Psychoses 8
Public interest disclosure 273
Public Trust Office 88
Publications, reading list 420–4
Publicity *see* Marketing and publicity

Quality of service 147
    Lexcel quality mark 150

Rail travel schemes 165, 227
Reading list 420–4
Receivership 68–70
    advantages and disadvantages 73
    application 69
    appointment of receiver 96
    costs 70
    Court of Protection and 68–9, 95–9, 100–1
    investment management 98–9
    orders 69–70
    sale of property 97–8
    status of receiver 96–7

INDEX

Recruitment 302
    advice on 153
Redundancy 305–6
Referrals and introductions 106, 112–14
Registered homes 256
    codes of practice 259–60
    legislation 255
    proprietor 257
    refusal of registration 257
    regulation 257–9
    supervision 258–9
Registered social landlords 322, 324
Registration
    death 372–3
    enduring power of attorney (EPA) 82–4
Relatives *see* Families
Remand 193
Remedies *see* Legal remedies
Rent
    help with *see* Housing benefit
    rent control 332–3
Repairs and maintenance 333–5
Representation 53–4
    lay representatives 53–4
    McKenzie friend 53
    mental disability 56–7
Reputation 144–5
Residential care 216–24
    benefits entitlements
        income support preserved rights 222–3
        other benefits 223
    charges 216–17, 455–7, 459–61
        enforcement 218–19, 455–7
        liable relatives 220–1
        means-testing 217–18, 223–4, 460–1
        recovery 219–20
    choice of home 221, 260–1
    guidance to residents 262–3
    registered homes 256
        codes of practice 259–60
        legislation 255
        proprietor 257
        refusal of registration 257
        regulation 257–9
        supervision 258–9
    small homes 256
    sources of law 216
    statutory basis 241–2
    temporary stays 221
Retainer *see* Instructions
Retirement 306–7
        directorships 306
        normal age 306

    see also Pensions
Rights and obligations
    capacity and 161–4
    civil responsibility
        council tax 166–7
        National Insurance contributions 167
        taxes 167
    civil status
        driving licences 164
        jury service 166
        passports 165
        privileges 165
        voting 165
    human *see* Human rights
    non-discrimination 167–9

Sale of property, receivership 97–8
Second homes 346
Security of tenure 327–9
Self-employment 301, 307–8
Service of proceedings, mental disability and 57
Settlements
    Court of Protection orders 91
    mental disability and 57–8
    provision for infirm/disabled beneficiaries 370
Severe disablement allowance 200, 225
Severe mental impairment, defined 288
Sheltered housing 343–4
Side letters 370
Sign language interpreters 53
Small claims procedure 42–3
    lay representatives 53–4
Social fund 203–4, 377
Social security *see* Welfare benefits
Social Security Commissioners 208–9
Social services
    community care and 237–8
        publication of information on services 247
    complaints procedures 37
    social workers, approved 27, 290
Software, computer 124–5, 152
Special verdicts 192
Staff 120
    delegation to 120–1
    recruitment advice 153
State benefits *see* Welfare benefits
State pensions 78, 200, 309–11
    forecasts 210
Statement of terms of employment 303
Statutory duty, breach 40–1
Statutory guardianship 243, 293–4

473

INDEX

Statutory wills 70, 91, 359–60, 444–5
Stay of execution 59
Stockbrokers 27–8
   information from 30
   investment management 99
Substituted judgment approach 15
Succession 354
   of tenancies 330–1
Supervision, aftercare services and 294–5

Taxation 312–16
   capital gains tax 314–15, 350–1, 352–3, 363
   charities and 352–3
   council tax 166–7
   gifts 350–2
   income tax 78, 167, 312–13
   inheritance provision and 362
   inheritance tax 315–16, 351–2, 362–3
Telephone bills 227–8
Television licences 228
Tenancies 323–35
   allocation 327
   legislation 323
   rent control 332–3
   repairs and maintenance 333–5
   right to buy 325–6
   security of tenure 329–30
   succession 330–1
   terms 331
   transitional provisions 326–7
   types 324–5
   unlawful eviction 329–30
Terence Higgins Trust 398
Termination of retainer 23
Third parties
   commissions from third parties 107
   costs in civil proceedings 60–1
Time limitation of actions 58–9
Timeshare 346
Tort liability 41–2
   repairs and maintenance of property 333–4
Transplant organs 378
Transport/travel schemes 165, 227
Tribunals
   Mental Health Review Tribunal 296–7
   welfare benefits appeals 207
Trusts 78–9
   advantages 73
   disadvantages 73–4
   employment as trustee 308
   incapacity of trustee 164
   informal 79

   information from 30
   letter by testator to trustees 402
   NHS Trusts 268
   provision for infirm/disabled beneficiaries 365–71
   Public Trust Office 88
   taxation and 315–16

Unfair dismissal 304–5
Unfitness to plead 192
Utility bills 227–8

Victims of crime 186–7
Violence *see* Abuse and violence within families
Visitors, Lord Chancellor's Visitors 89
Voluntary Euthanasia Society, advance directive 398
Voluntary sector
   community care and 240, 245
   employment in 307–8
Voting rights 165

Wasted costs 61
Water bills 228
Websites, list of 414–19
Welfare benefits
   agency 76, 206
   appeals 207–9
      courts 209
      procedures 207–8
      Social Security Commissioners 208–9
      tribunals 207
   appointee for 65, 76–7, 206
   claims 204
      backdating 204
   contributory benefits 199–200
   council tax benefit 214
   decisions on 205, 208
   during hospital stays 225–6
   housing benefit *see* Housing benefit
   income support 201–2, 222–3
   information on 198–9
   marriage and 171
   means-tested benefits 201
   non-contributory benefits 200–1
   payment 205–6
      over/underpayment 206
   procedures 204–6, 207–8
   in residential care 222–3
   social fund 203–4, 377
   social security system 197–9
      administration 197–8
      living abroad and 198

sources of law 197
Widow/widower's benefits 310
Wills 356–8
    capacity 357, 400, 403
    contents 357–8
    enduring power of attorney (EPA) and 68
    examples 392–7
    execution 358
    fees 357
    living *see* Living wills
    marriage and 171
    medical certificate 403
    promotion 151
    revocation 358
    statutory 70, 91, 359–60, 444–5
    taking instructions 356
Woolf reforms 50–1
Wrongful dismissal 304